MW01631149

BOTTICELLI TO TIEPOLO

THREE CENTURIES OF ITALIAN PAINTING

Botticelli to Tiepolo

Three Centuries of Italian Painting

from Bob Jones University

Richard P. Townsend

with an essay by Eric M. Zafran

The Philbrook Museum of Art

in association with the University of Washington Press

PUBLISHED IN CONJUNCTION WITH THE NATIONAL TOUR OF THE EXHIBITION *Botticelli to Tiepolo*

The Philbrook Museum of Art, Tulsa
11 September—6 November 1994

The Joslyn Art Museum, Omaha
18 February—16 April 1995

New Orleans Museum of Art
13 May—2 July 1995

Birmingham Museum of Art
22 July—17 September 1995

The Dayton Art Institute
30 September—3 December 1995

MADE POSSIBLE BY A GRANT FROM THE GRACE AND FRANKLIN BERNSEN FOUNDATION.

Additional funding provided by Coopers & Lybrand, Deloitte & Touche, Ernst & Young, Gable & Gotwals, Hogan & Slovacek, and the State Arts Council of Oklahoma.

Distributed in association with
The University of Washington Press
Post Office Box 50096
Seattle, Washington 98145-5096
USA

International Standard Book Number 0-295-97394-3

LIBRARY OF CONGRESS CATALOGING-IN-PUBLICATION DATA
Bob Jones University.
Botticelli to Tiepolo : three centuries of Italian painting from Bob Jones University / Richard P. Townsend ; with an essay by Eric M. Zafran.
p. cm.
Exhibition held at the Philbrook Museum of Art, 11 September-6 November 1994 and others.
Includes bibliographical references and index.
ISBN 0-295-97394-3
1. Painting, Italian—Exhibitions. 2. Painting, Baroque—Italy—Exhibitions. 3. Bob Jones University—Art collections—Exhibitions. 4. Painting—Private collections—South Carolina—Greenville—Exhibitions. I. Townsend, Richard P. II. Philbrook Museum of Art. III. Title.
ND615.B657 1994
759.945'074'73—dc20 94-20072
CIP

EDITED BY Elizabeth Allen
DESIGNED BY Carol Haralson

COVER DETAIL FROM:
Domenico Zampieri called Il Domenichino, *St. John the Evangelist* (cat. no. 17)
FRONTISPIECE DETAILS FROM:
PAGE 6, Sandro Botticelli and Studio, *Madonna and Child with an Angel* (cat. no. 1)
PAGE 8, Francesco de Rosa called Pacecco de Rosa, *The Martyrdom of St. Lawrence* (cat. no. 22)
PAGE 10, Giovanni Lanfranco, *St. Cecilia* (cat. no. 16)
PAGE 12, Pier Francesco Sacchi called Il Pavese, *The Adoration of the Shepherds* (cat. no. 4)

Printed in Canada

CONTENTS

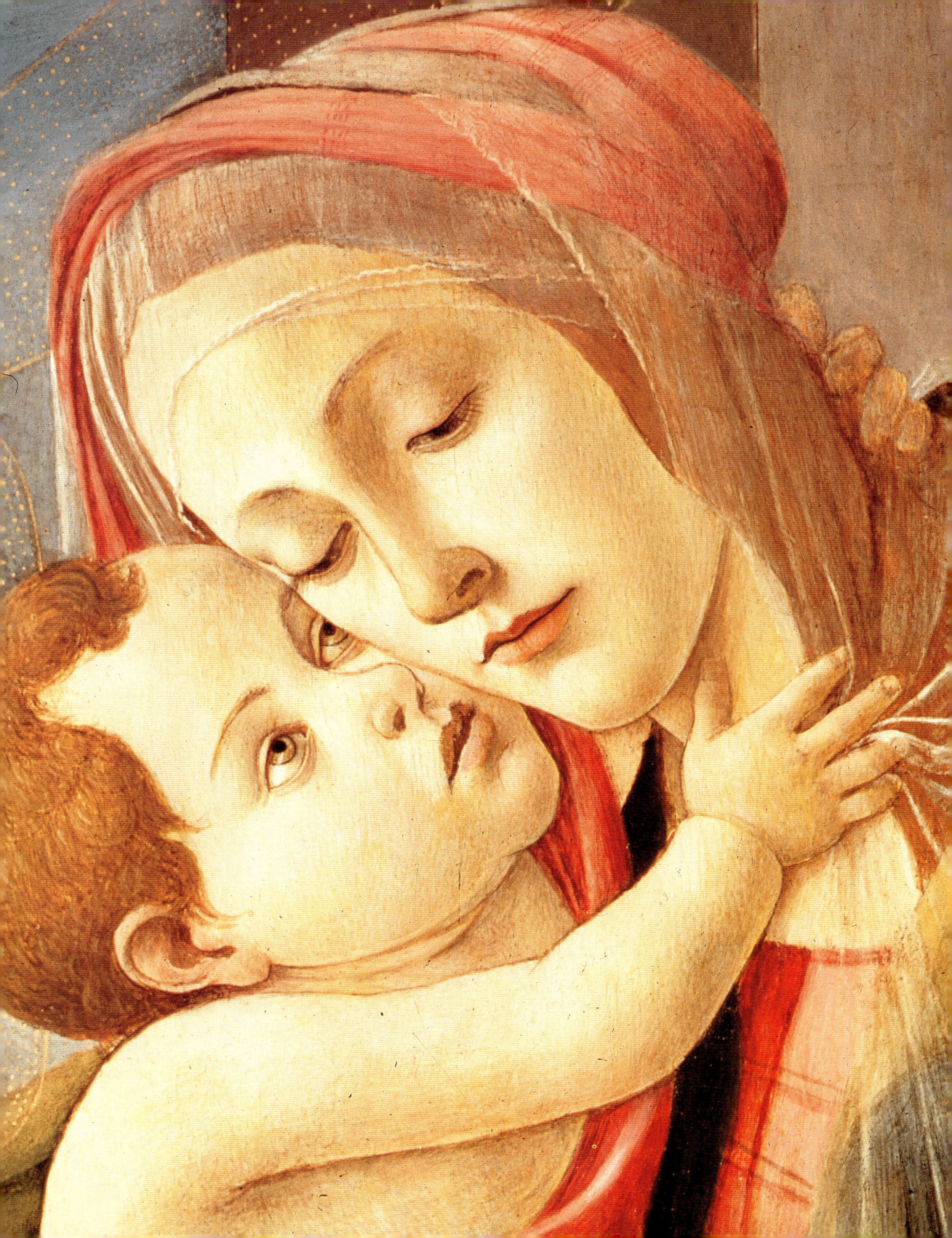

PREFACE

It is with great pride that the Philbrook Museum of Art opens this tour of Italian paintings. The Bob Jones University Collection of Religious Art is one of the finest and most comprehensive collections of old master pictures in the country. Philbrook has been given a rare opportunity to organize a national exhibition tour and to publish a new catalogue. Both will bring attention to this extraordinary but little-known collection to the public at large.

This exhibition is the most recent in a series of important projects for which our institution has become recognized, including *Gloria dell'arte: A Renaissance Perspective* (1979-80), *Caesars and Citizens: Roman Portrait Sculpture from the J. Paul Getty Museum* (1981), *What Is Native American Art* (1986), *The Eloquent Object* (1987), and *Masterworks of European Painting from the Von der Heydt Museum, Wupperthal* (1989). At Philbrook, *Botticelli to Tiepolo: Three Centuries of Italian Painting from Bob Jones University* stands out as the first significant exhibition of European paintings that the Museum has organized since 1989, and the first devoted to Italian old masters since John Spike's groundbreaking show of Italian still lifes in 1983 that we shared with the National Academy of Design, New York, and, fittingly, the Dayton Art Institute, to whom we have the pleasure of sending the present exhibition. It is appropriate that our Museum should be responsible for an exhibition of Italian painting given the depth of our own permanent collection. These pictures from Bob Jones University join, at least temporarily, works in Tulsa by Gentile da Fabriano, Bellini, Piero di Cosimo, Beccafumi, Giordano, and Tanzio da Varallo.

First and foremost, I should like to thank Dr. Bob Jones, Jr., Chancellor of Bob Jones University, Greenville, South Carolina. It is he who formed this impressive assemblage of Italian paintings and who has so generously agreed to share them with us and four other cities throughout the country. Dr. Jones has displayed enormous goodwill, patience, and enthusiasm over the course of the project. I also gratefully acknowledge the support of Dr. Bob Jones, III, President of Bob Jones University.

This glorious exhibition has been initiated and organized by Richard P. Townsend, the Ruth G. Hardman Curator of European and American Art at Philbrook. From concept to fruition of the exhibition and its accompanying catalogue, his insatiable desire as a curator to discover, to pursue, and to share is evident. His work continues our commitment to support and produce shows and publications that are based upon sound scholarship and are of the finest quality. Richard's devotion to this project is greatly appreciated and without his persistence and tireless efforts it could not have occurred. I am also grateful to Eric Zafran, curator of European paintings at the Museum of Fine Arts, Boston, for his extremely fine contribution to this catalogue.

Finally, it is my distinct pleasure to thank the tour's participating museums and their staffs: Graham W. J. Beal and Marsha Gallagher at the Joslyn Art Museum, Omaha, Nebraska; E. John Bullard at the New Orleans Museum of Art, Louisiana; John E. Schloder at the Birmingham Museum of Art, Alabama; and Alexander Lee Nyerges and Dominique Vasseur at the Dayton Art Institute, Ohio. Without them, we would not have had the great satisfaction of sharing these masterpieces with a larger audience.

MARCIA Y. MANHART
Executive Director
The Philbrook Museum of Art
Tulsa, Oklahoma

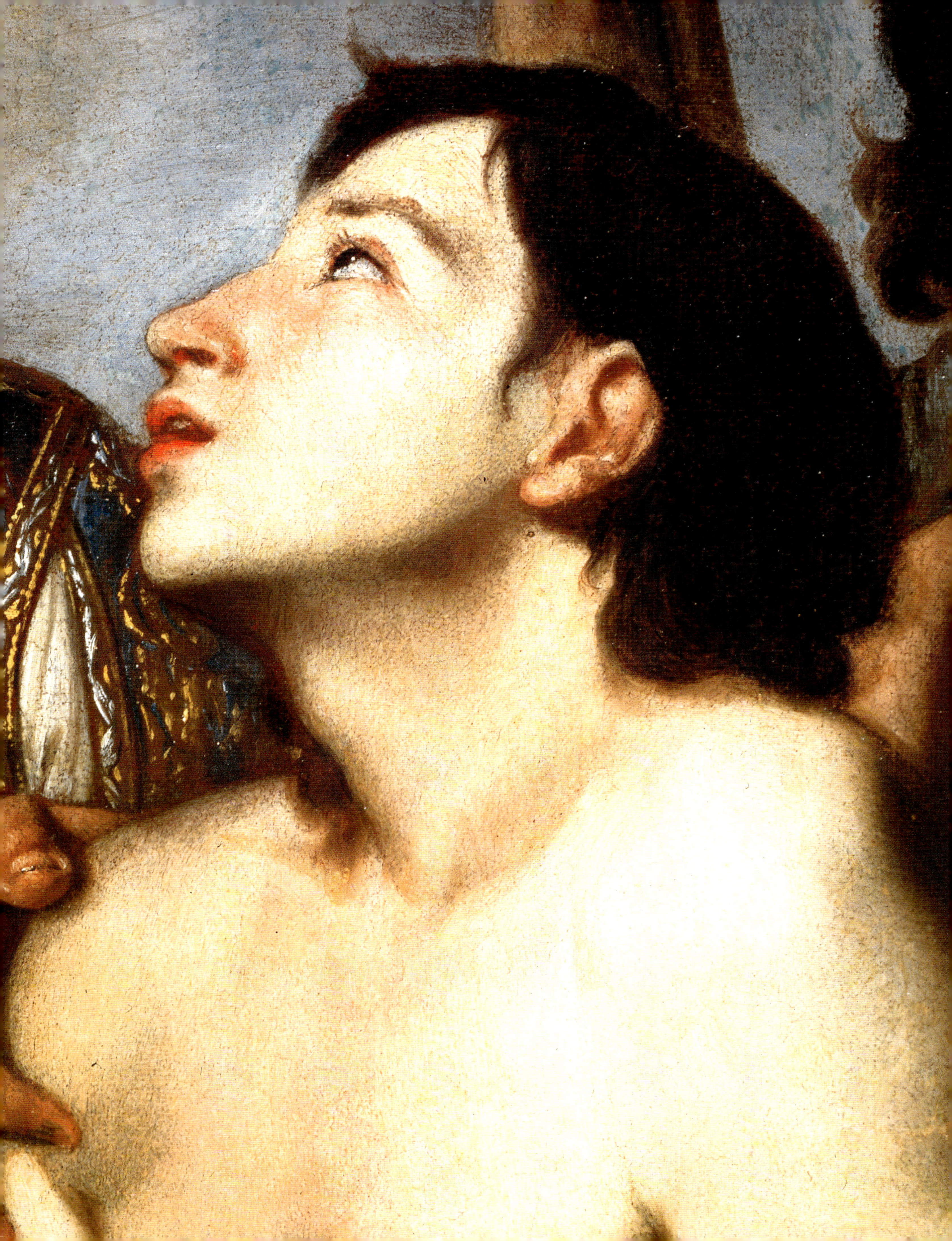

F O R E W O R D

When in 1950 the Executive Committee of the Board of Trustees authorized me to begin collecting religious paintings for a gallery to be established at Bob Jones University, I am sure it was not because of any great confidence in my expertise in the field of art or because they thought I had "a good eye." More likely, they entrusted me with this project because they knew I would stay within the budget and get good value for the money expended. I have relied heavily upon the counsel and advice of scholars and experts, and have established long-term friendships with some of the dealers who seemed genuinely glad to help a beginner build a collection that was somewhat unusual. That was half a lifetime ago.

Many kind people have expressed their appreciation for the collection and some have wondered how it could have been assembled in just over forty years. Yet I often wish that I had known then what I have come to know since, and that more funds had been on hand to tap into the opportunities offered by the art market in the 1950s. Looking back, I am amazed at the sheer number and quality of old masters then available, as well as at the prices they brought.

Some have expressed surprise that an institution strong in its emphasis on the Scriptures and Protestant in orientation would have on the walls of its museum of religious art, paintings from the Roman Catholic tradition, depicting extra-biblical scenes, saints and their legends. Yet Western Christian imagery stems from this tradition, making the inclusion of these paintings reasonable. Moreover, their place in the collection is in keeping with the philosophy of Bob Jones University as stated in its charter: *The general nature and object of the corporation shall be to conduct an institution of learning for the general education of youth in the essentials of culture and in the arts and sciences, giving special emphasis to the Christian religion and the ethics revealed in the Holy Scripture.* Accordingly, we want our students to be well-grounded in their knowledge of various beliefs and philosophies whether or not we agree with them.

In an institution that has an active fine arts program, a gallery serves somewhat the same purpose as a library, providing visual resources and an understanding of the development of the arts. And as a library accommodates the interests of a wide community, this Art Gallery benefits not only the University faculty and student body, but public school students, art history professors and their classes from nearby colleges, senior citizen groups, and even delegates who are in the area for conventions. In fact, civic leaders responsible for encourgaging foreign businesses to establish their American administrative headquarters and industrial plants in upper South Carolina have found the presence of the Gallery to be an added attraction.

The Art Gallery, therefore, serves a variety of purposes. I personally feel, however, that none is more important than giving to those who have had no previous exposure to great art the opportunity to develop an appreciation of it and to draw inspiration from it. To such a viewer, art can open up vistas new and different, and his or her life will be enriched thereby. The Bible tells us that "Every good and every perfect gift is from above, and cometh down from the Father of lights" (James 1:17), and both the neophyte and the experienced scholar may acquire spiritual truth through such visual experiences.

While I have no desire to become overly theological, my intent here has been to explain the whys and wherefores of the collection. I extend to the reader an invitation to visit the Gallery on the campus to see the collection as a whole. The paintings in this exhibition are Italian, but all of the important European schools are represented in the museum—some of them by very fine works. In addition to the paintings, the collection contains Russian and Greek icons, period furniture, sculpture, and stained glass.

It has been a pleasure to work with Richard P. Townsend, the organizer of this exhibition and the author of the catalogue. He has brought to that task not only a breadth of knowledge of art history and appreciation of art itself, but also a tremendous amount of research.

BOB JONES
Chancellor
Bob Jones University
Greenville, South Carolina

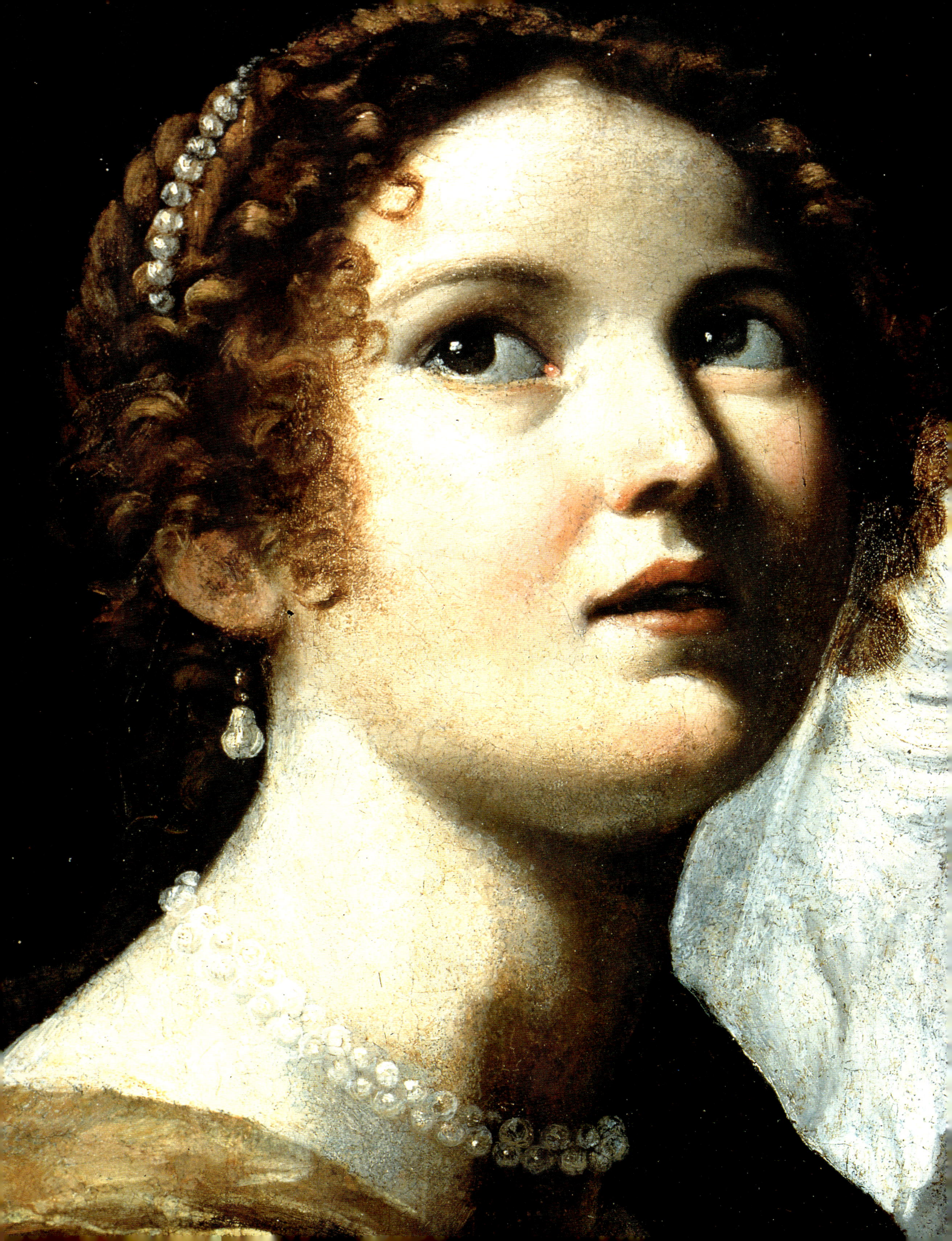

ACKNOWLEDGMENTS

I cannot adequately express my gratitude to Dr. Bob Jones, Jr. for his support and assistance during the course of this project. Without his gracious consent and enthusiasm, I could not have undertaken this effort. Dr. Jones's great wealth of knowledge and experience has been of the utmost benefit to me; moreover, his company has been a constant source of pleasure. I hope it is not presumptuous of me to say that one of the chief rewards of this endeavor has been his friendship.

This exhibition would not have been possible without the good offices of three individuals: Jonathan Bober and Mark and Kurt Haukohl. I visited Jonathan at Austin during the showing of seventeenth-century paintings from the Bob Jones University Collection that he mounted there in 1990, and it was he who first put me in contact with Dr. Jones. The credit goes to the Haukohls for my first visit to Greenville and a personal introduction to Dr. Jones.

The presence in this catalogue of Eric M. Zafran's essay on the collecting of Italian Baroque paintings in America lends it great luster. I am honored that Eric agreed to contribute what is quite evidently the definitive treatment of the subject to date, one which shall, no doubt, ensure the longevity of this publication. I am grateful to him for his support and friendship.

I have also benefited enormously from the expertise and assistance of three colleagues who kindly agreed to serve as readers for the catalogue manuscript: Everett Fahy, David Steel, and Edgar Peters Bowron. These distinguished scholars have only enhanced this effort and any errors found within these pages are solely my responsibility.

I am pleased to say that many of the pictures in the present exhibition were cleaned for the occasion; four received major conservation treatments. The able conservator was David Goist, whose familiarity with the collection, formed during his tenure as Chief Conservator at the North Carolina Museum of Art in Raleigh, was a real asset to the project. It has been a pleasure to work with him over the past several years.

At the Bob Jones University Art Gallery, Joan Davis, Jan Churdar, and Bill Reynolds have been most helpful. Bill's assistance and companionship during numerous visits to Greenville was especially welcome.

At the Philbrook Museum, I am most grateful to Marcia Y. Manhart for her enthusiastic support of this project and to Christine Kallenberger and Traci Mayes for their efforts on behalf of *Botticelli to Tiepolo.* I am thankful to Thomas Young for his long-suffering patience with my many library requests. The catalogue would have been virtually impossible to undertake without the assistance of curatorial interns Gay Clarkson, Stacey Dunn, Tina Diggs Llorente, and Jennifer Venable (who compiled the bibliography).

I am particularly grateful to the scholars, curators, and collectors who have kindly responded to my requests for information and assistance: Alessandro Bagnoli, Miles Chappell, Keith Christiansen, Diane De Grazia, Burton Fredericksen and the staff of the Getty Provenance Index, Anne Goodchild, Mina Gregori, Mary Jane Harris, Alex Kidson, George Knox, Sir Denis Mahon, Robert L. Manning and the late Bertina Suida Manning, Marcene Modeland, Emily Neff, Patty Petrochuk, Terisio Pignatti, W.R. Rearick, David Rosand, Francis Russell, David Scrase, George Shackelford, Leonard Slatkes, and Gloria Williams. I should also like to thank the staffs of the Stephen Chan Library, Institute of Fine Arts, New York University; the Frick Art Reference Library; the Watson Library, Metropolitan Museum of Art; the New York Public Library; the library of the Kimbell Art Museum; and the Oklahoma State University Library, Stillwater.

Finally, my sincere thanks for a job very well done to my editor, Elizabeth Allen, and the catalogue designer and coordinator, Carol Haralson. Elizabeth's sensitive editing makes this catalogue enjoyable to read, yet scholarly in tone; I could not have asked for anyone better. Carol's achievements are obvious—the style and beauty of the publication are due to her good taste. It has been, as always, a joy to work with them both.

RICHARD P. TOWNSEND
Ruth G. Hardman Curator of European and American Art
The Philbrook Museum of Art
Tulsa, Oklahoma

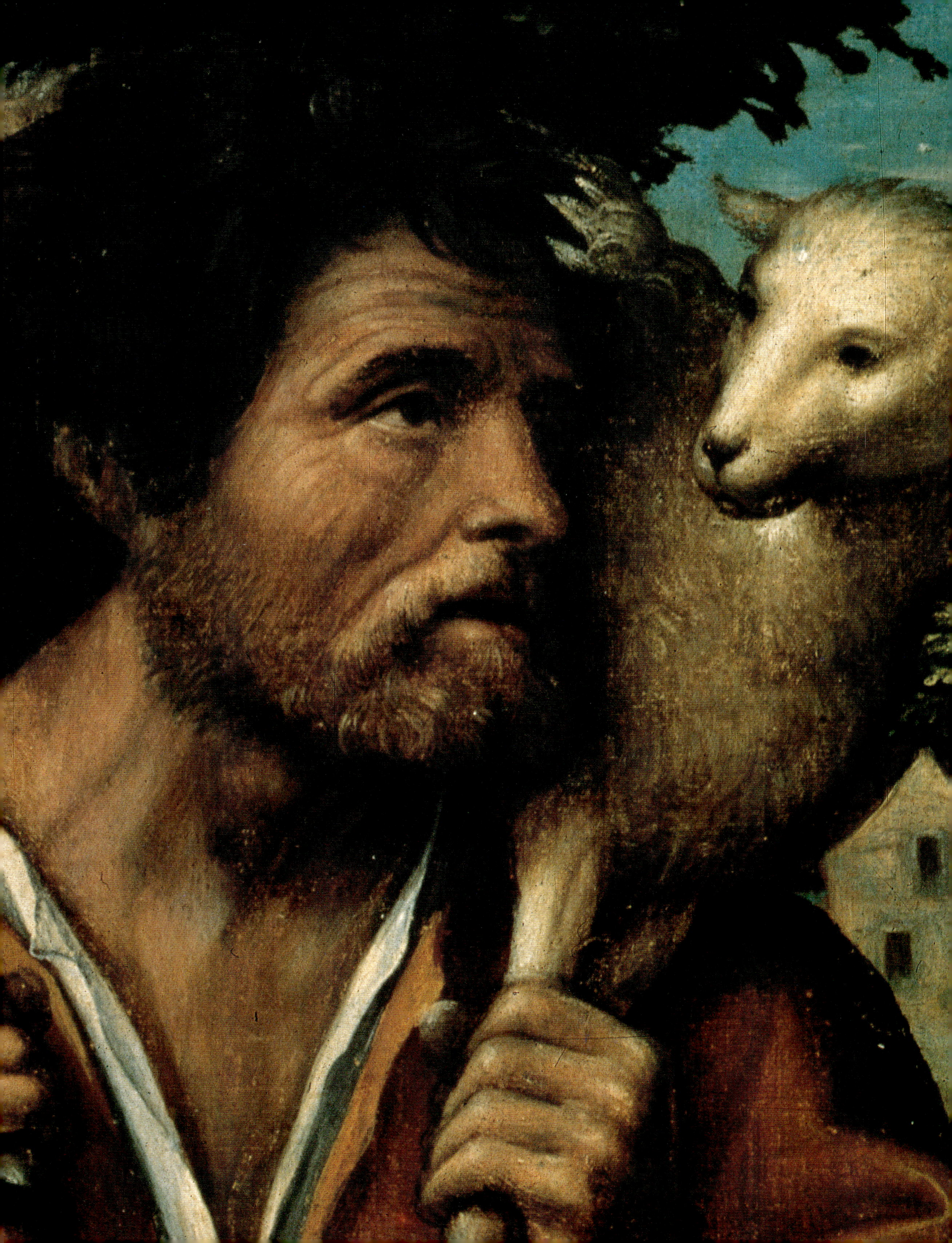

A Selection from the Bob Jones University Collection

AN INTRODUCTION TO PAINTING IN ITALY, 1500-1750

RICHARD P. TOWNSEND

THE FORTY PAINTINGS IN THIS EXHIBITION drawn from the holdings of Bob Jones University constitute less than a quarter of the 186 Italian pictures in the University's Art Gallery. While the entire collection of over 400 paintings contains fine examples from every important European school, including those by such figures as Cranach, Honthorst, Rubens, Van Dyck, Vouet, Champaigne, Zurbarán and studio, and West, its greatest strength lies in its Italian art.

The Bob Jones Collection of Italian old masters is remarkable for its comprehensive coverage of religious painting in Italy from around 1350 to 1750, and comprises not only intimate cabinet pictures, small devotional works, and more typical easel productions, but important large-scale altarpieces, a number of which are signed and dated (for example, cat. nos. 11, 15). As in the great European picture galleries, the visitor to Greenville can study the major and the minor masters side by side. Walking through the Italian galleries, one comes upon the room filled with fifteenth- and sixteenth-century *tondi* (round paintings) by Sandro Botticelli (cat. no. 1), Girolamo della Pacchia, and the Master of the Greenville Tondo; shortly thereafter is the large gallery given over to altarpieces of the same period, including works by Francesco Menzocchi (cat. no. 7) and the Master of the Fiesole Epiphany. A subsequent room contains the overpowering altarpiece by Sodoma of *Christ Carrying the Cross to Calvary,* one of the finest works by the master in this country (too fragile for inclusion in the present exhibition). The following gallery is devoted to pictures by sixteenth-century Venetians: Catena (cat. no. 8), Palma Giovane, Tintoretto (cat. no. 10), the Bassano family, Bonifazio de'Pitati and so on, as one proceeds through the rooms to the later Italian pictures. Despite the riches to be seen there, comparatively few museum-goers have visited the Greenville campus, and even the most dedicated who have enjoyed the University's frequent loans to national and international exhibitions cannot appreciate the range and extent of its holdings. Thus, the quality of the collection, which offers perhaps the most extensive overview of Italian painting in America, and its relative obscurity have prompted this first-ever national tour of Italian works from Bob Jones University.

The pictures selected for display here enable the visitor to survey Italy's artistic achievements from the later Renaissance of Botticelli and Granacci, to the close of Italian dominance of the art world in the eighteenth century, as represented by Batoni and Tiepolo. Over these three hundred years, Italy saw great changes which are reflected in her art. The present works were chosen not only because they are among the finest examples in the collection, but because they display some of these changes, representing the major schools of Italian painting and their phases of development during this period. (The catalogue entries on the paintings are arranged accordingly.) With the exception of Rome, the most important artistic centers of the Cinquecento (sixteenth century) are represented: Florence, Siena, Milan, and Venice. In the Seicento (seventeenth century), the crucial roles played by Bologna and Rome are underscored by the inclusion of ten paintings, with the vital center of Naples represented by five. Even the relatively neglected schools of Florence and Genoa are accorded three or more paintings each, by some of the major artists in those cities. Finally, the two dominant centers of the Settecento (eighteenth century)—Venice and Rome—are highlighted, and three paintings from this period reflect the waning glories of the Neapolitan school.

Typically, any account of art in Renaissance Italy dwells at length on Florence and the artists the city produced in the fifteenth and sixteenth centuries. After the innovations brought about by the sculptures of Ghiberti and Donatello, Brunelleschi's architectural projects, and the paintings of Masaccio, Fra Angelico, Domenico Veneziano, and others in the first half of the fifteenth century, the stage was set for the crowning achievements of Leonardo, Raphael, and Michelangelo. Leonardo left Florence for Milan by 1484, Raphael for Rome in 1508, and Michelangelo moved first to Bologna in 1506 and to Rome in 1508, leaving the field open to other artists. Sandro Botticelli stands on the cusp of this new age of the High Renaissance. His paintings combine the subject matter and studio practices of the Quattrocento (fifteenth century), while foreshadowing the stylized aesthetic of the later Renaissance. The *Madonna and Child with an Angel* (cat. no. 1) is a typical example of the many images of the Virgin and Child produced in his large workshop to meet the high demand for private devotional pictures. While the drapery and the background of the *tondo* were executed by studio assistants, the crucial areas, such as the faces and hands of the Virgin and Christ Child, were reserved for the master. In Francesco Granacci's *Rest on the Flight into Egypt* (cat. no. 2), the High Renaissance ideals of symmetry, grace, and harmony are fully realized. Granacci's composition displays a balance in the arrangement of the figures and in the use of color. Granacci was a lifelong friend of Michelangelo and so, not surprisingly, the viewer can see in this panel echoes of the work of the great painter-sculptor.

Leonardo da Vinci's sporadic presence in Milan, the capital of Lombardy, from the 1480s through the early years of the sixteenth century, exerted great influence on North Italian painting. Leonardo was especially interested in natural phenomena and recorded his observations in numerous codices or notebooks. In his paintings, these concerns are reflected in the use of *sfumatura,* or the subtle play of light and shadow. Leonardo's work was much admired by the Milanese painters, Andrea Solario and Bernardino Luini, and by lesser-known masters such as Marco d'Oggiono (cat. no. 5) and Pier Francesco Sacchi (cat. no. 4). D'Oggiono—probably the Marco mentioned in Leonardo's studio in 1490—not only worked in Leonardo's style but also borrowed the master's designs, making close copies of Leonardo's renowned paintings, as well as adapting their separate elements to suit his own purposes. Sacchi, a Lombard artist whose paintings exhibit Leonardesque influences, moved by 1501 to Genoa and painted there until his death from the plague in 1528. His presence there exemplifies the trend in Genoese painting of absorbing the art of Lombardy, which continued well into the next century.

Although scholars have debated the view that the Sack of Rome by Charles V in 1527 influenced the development of the style commonly called Mannerism, the seizure of the seat of the papacy was a watershed event with great political and cultural repercussions. *Maniera,* or Mannerism, however, was not so much a break from the ideals of the High Renaissance, but rather a variation or extension of them. While the new style—with its esoteric mythological and literary subject matter, strident colors, and crowded compositions—addressed a smaller, more erudite audience, painters and sculptors still relied on the artistic models of Raphael and Michelangelo. Florence remained a major center during this period, with the generation succeeding Leonardo and Michelangelo (the latter still very much alive in Rome and an exponent of the new *maniera* himself), such as Pontormo, Rosso Fiorentino, and slightly later, Bronzino, working at the Medici court. The versatile Giorgio Vasari, in addition to being a great architect, prolific painter, and a keen collector of drawings, wrote at this time his *Lives of the Most Excellent Painters, Sculptors, and Architects* (1550). Vasari's love of his native city and his friendship with and admiration for his compatriot Michelangelo informed much of his writing. As a theorist and as a painter, Vasari's influence in Florence at mid-century was enormous. One of his disciples was Francesco Morandini, called Il Poppi, whose *Meeting of Abraham and Melchizedek* (cat. no. 3) has long been attributed to Vasari himself because of its dependence on compositions by the master. Just as Vasari's idol, the "divine Michelangelo," supplied designs to his close followers to produce paintings from, Vasari most probably furnished Poppi with this composition.

Poppi's *Abraham and Melchizedek* displays the hallmarks of the Mannerist style: a crowded composition filled with elaborate, highly stylized figures painted in contrasting, jewel-like colors. Northeast of Florence, toward Venice, the city of Forlì produced a little-known but talented painter, Francesco Menzocchi, whose frescoed decorative projects ranged from those for Forlì's town hall to the Duke of Urbino's Villa Imperiale, near Pesaro. He was particularly influenced by the major Mannerist artist, Parmigianino. Like the panel by the Florentine Poppi, Menzocchi's altarpiece of the *Holy Family with St. John the Baptist and Putti* (cat. no. 7) features a shallow picture plane, with the figures painted in brilliant colors.

It was with the Bellini artistic dynasty—father Jacopo and brothers Giovanni and Gentile—that the Renaissance truly got underway in Venice. Giovanni Bellini, in his role of *caposcuola,* or head, of the Venetian school, was the teacher of Giorgione and Titian. A work in the Greenville collection by another of Bellini's pupils, Vincenzo Catena, depicts a favorite subject of Bellini and his followers, the *Holy Family with St. John the Baptist* (cat. no. 8), a devotional picture of the Madonna and Child shown seated in a landscape. Bellini himself perfected this pictorial type, which provided the ideal vehicle for the Venetian interest in both figure and landscape painting. His two most famous pupils were also to profoundly influence the course of painting in Venice. During his brief life Giorgione continued to develop the recently adopted technique of oil painting, producing a soft-edged, luminous style, where the forms seem to be suffused with light and air; while Titian, during his long and productive career, expanded upon these concerns. In the several phases of Titian's style, the artist journeyed from the literalism of Bellini through the lyricism of Giorgione to develop his own visual language in which linear form is subservient to color, light, and emotion, although never completely subsumed by them. Titian was the most sought-after painter of his day, patronized by the likes of Pope Paul III, Emperor Charles V, and King Philip II of Spain.

In the *Christ the Redeemer* (cat. no. 9) by Paris Bordon, we see the impress of Titian. Bordon, who was born in Treviso and worked in and around Venice, was both an exponent of Mannerism and of Titian's mature style, which was characterized by the scumbling of paint and the layering of colored glazes—a painterly yet acutely descriptive technique that Titian exploited most in his late, great poetic works. Toward mid-century, there appeared in Venice an artist more fully steeped in the Mannerist style, Jacopo Robusti, called Tintoretto, after his father's occupation as a cloth dyer (*tintore*). He carried out numerous projects in the city, painting altarpieces and decorations for churches and the various *scuole* (meeting halls) of the religious confraternities, such as the Scuola di S. Rocco. Tintoretto and his slightly younger contemporary, Paolo Caliari, called Veronese, were to dominate the field for the rest of the century.

Tintoretto's *Visit of the Queen of Sheba to Solomon* (cat. no. 10) was painted around 1545, the same year that a momentous undertaking—the Council of Trent—was begun just north and west of Venice. This convocation, which lasted close to twenty years (it concluded in 1563), was concerned with the reform of Church doctrine and practice in light of the recent Protestant challenge led by Martin Luther in Germany and John Calvin in France. The bishops who met in Trent sought to explicate the sacraments of the Church (for example, the Eucharist, marriage, and penance), as these had come under Protestant attack. Since the spirit of the convocation was one of consolidation and consistency, the visible manifestations of Church doctrine called for reform as well. Sacred images and the intercession of the saints were integral to Roman Catholicism, and these elements of the faith were addressed along these lines:

> In the invocation of the saints, the veneration of relics, and the sacred use of images, all superstition shall be removed . . . so that images shall not be painted and adorned with seductive charm, or the celebration of saints and the visitation of relics be perverted by the people into boisterous festivities. . . . Finally, such zeal and care should be exhibited by the bishops with regard to these things that nothing may appear that is disorderly or unbecoming and confusedly arranged, nothing that is profane, nothing disrespectful, since holiness becometh the house of God. That these things may be the more faithfully observed, the holy council decrees that no one is permitted to erect or cause to be erected in any place or church, howsoever exempt, any unusual image unless it has been approved by the bishop . . . (25th Session, 4 December 1563; quoted from H.J. Schroeder, *The Canons and Decrees of the Council of Trent,* Rockford, Illinois, 1978, pp. 216-17).

Two prelates charged with the reformation of the Church and particularly concerned with guiding artists in the proper interpretation of these new dictates were the Archbishops Gabriele Paleotti of Bologna and Federico Borromeo of Milan. Paleotti—who knew the Carracci, the Bolognese family of artists—wrote the *Discourse on Sacred and Profane Images,* which appeared in 1582. In it he discussed the origins of Christian and pagan imagery, the early artists who made them, and the importance of the "pittore cristiano" (Christian painter), who was to produce pictures that were legible, educational, and emotive. Borromeo, who succeeded his cousin Carlo Borromeo (later canonized as a saint) as Archbishop of Milan, issued his treatise *Of Sacred Pictures* in 1624, which set forth guidelines for artists to follow in the production of devotional imagery. The goal of the Roman Church after Trent was to ensure a certain consistency of depiction that would result in clearly understandable religious messages. A more secular effort, Cesare Ripa's *Iconology* (first published in Rome in 1593, with subsequent illustrated editions), which was a compendium of allegorical emblems for use by artists, among others (see, for example, cat. nos. 17, 37, 38), also contributed to the recognition of ideas (usually moralizing) through images.

Finally, prints were an important vehicle for the transmission of religious imagery; these early reproductions provided readily available models on which artists could base their particular concepts, and, in turn, enabled viewers to identify the painted subject from its prototype in print form. Therefore, much of the imagery of the saints in the Seicento is very close to early examples found in devotional prints of the fifteenth century. Thus—from the treatises that were directed toward a relatively small audience to the more accessible prints—were ideas codified and transmitted, from artist to artist and subsequently to the general populace.

Following hard on the heels of the Council of Trent and the ripple effect it had on prelates and artists who began to rethink the representation of the sacred and the secular were the great "reformers" of Italian painting, Caravaggio and Annibale Carracci, along with his brother Agostino and his cousin Ludovico. While Caravaggio and Annibale would appear to be diametrically opposed in terms of style, they drew inspiration from the same sources and were concerned with very much the same things. Namely, both were interested in the actual appearances of things, and the way in which the artist's observation of natural phenomena could be recorded. One has only to recall at this time Galileo's investigations into the universe or the exploration and mapping out of the New World to realize how pervasive was the spirit of inquiry—both artistic and scientific. This preoccupation with naturalism allied painting with the physical sciences, and was embodied in men of culture such as Ulisse Aldrovandi of Bologna and Cassiano dal Pozzo of Rome. Aldrovandi, who taught botany and the natural sciences at the University of Bologna, formed a collection of specimens and their artistic renderings that was consulted by leading artists of the day. He was active in artistic circles and knew Archbishop Paleotti and Agostino Carracci. Similarly, Dal Pozzo simultaneously patronized contemporary artists (Pietro da Cortona and Nicolas Poussin, among others) and collected insect specimens, flora and fauna, as well as classical antiquities, which he then commissioned young artists to record. (These drawings formed his Museo Cartaceo, or "Paper Museum.") It should come as no surprise, then, to find new types of painting—still life, genre scenes (depictions of everyday activities), and proper landscapes—emerging in this period. Caravaggio and Annibale, both of whom were integral in the development of some of these new genres, arrived in Rome at about the same time. Their presence contributed to the preeminence of the Eternal City as the center of the art world, dominating Europe until well into the eighteenth century, a trend initiated a century earlier by Raphael and Michelangelo before it was interrupted by the consequences of the Sack of Rome.

Caravaggio, born in the town of the same name in Lombardy, reached Rome in 1592. Already proficient in still lifes and genre scenes, Caravaggio first fully revealed his genius in the paintings completed in 1600 for the Contarelli chapel in S. Luigi dei Francesi, which depict scenes from the life of St. Matthew. The figures in these works are dressed as contemporary Romans, arranged in dramatic poses, and illuminated by a strong source of light. His tenebrism (the use of dark passages to make the lighted forms appear in high relief) made a tremendous impact on his compatriots in Rome, for while this device had its origin in sixteenth-century North Italian art, Caravaggio was the first to combine it with a powerful realism.

Only a few American collections own paintings by

Caravaggio; indeed, the artist is a relatively recent "discovery," having only come back into art-historical discourse in the early part of this century. (His first monographic exhibition was held as late as 1951 in Milan.) Bob Jones University owns several fine works by his followers, the Caravaggisti. Giovanni Baglione, whose *Entombment of Christ* (cat. no. 11) is included here, while essentially remaining a late Mannerist painter, nevertheless responded to the first impulses of Caravaggism. As his commissions declined, Baglione turned critic and biographer, publishing in 1642 an important account of the artists he knew, including Caravaggio.

Two other paintings at Bob Jones University—the *St. Jerome* (cat. no. 12), here attributed to Pietro Paolini, and the *Christ Disputing with the Elders* (cat. no. 13), here given to Rutilio Manetti—represent the next generation of artists after Caravaggio. Indeed, the very difficulty of attributing these works is testament to Caravaggio's pervasive influence through the 1620s—an influence that attracted to Rome painters from the Netherlands, particularly the city of Utrecht, who carried back North their brand of Caravaggism. In turn, these artists—notably Gerrit van Honthorst (represented in the Bob Jones Collection by the superb *Holy Family in the Carpenter's Shop,* c. 1617), Hendrik Terbrugghen, and Dirck van Baburen—inspired Italian painters in the third decade of the seventeenth century, among them Paolini and Manetti. Pietro Paolini, a native of Lucca, near Florence, worked in Rome in the 1620s. He was particularly taken with the internal light sources and the figural types employed by the Northern Caravaggisti. Another painter from Tuscany (from the city of Siena), was Rutilio Manetti, who was additionally influenced by Bartolomeo Manfredi and also may have come to Rome, possibly around 1625. Manfredi, along with Baglione, was among the earliest of the Roman artists to experiment with Caravaggio's style, but, unlike Baglione, he continued to work in that vein and, in fact, is credited with his own compositional innovation, the "Manfredi method," in which half-length genre figures, usually seated at a table, are arranged horizontally across a shallow space. The Sienese Manetti employed this formula on many occasions; in his *Christ Disputing with the Elders* exhibited here, the artist adapted it to a religious subject.

The influence of the other major figure of the Seicento, Annibale Carracci, is well represented by some of his most important pupils: Domenichino, Guido Reni, and Giovanni Lanfranco. Annibale went to Rome in 1595, having worked for the first part of his career in Bologna, where he established an art academy with his brother Agostino and his cousin Ludovico. In this academy, the Carracci and their students were engaged in the pursuit of naturalism and consequently emphasized drawing from life (many extant studies of nude models and everyday scenes by the Carracci and their circle attest to this fact). By this method, the Carracci hoped to turn Bolognese art away from the highly artificial Mannerism of the preceding generation of artists, such as Denys Calvaert (cat. no. 15), the erstwhile teacher of Domenichino, Reni, and Francesco Albani. After his arrival in Rome, Annibale was commissioned by Cardinal Odoardo Farnese to fresco the ceiling of the gallery in the Palazzo Farnese from 1597 to 1600, the same moment of Caravaggio's landmark paintings in the Contarelli chapel. The resulting masterpiece, illustrating Ovid's tales of the Loves of the Gods and featuring at its center the *Triumph of Bacchus and Ariadne,* set the pace for the revival of classicizing art.

Annibale Carracci's admixture of Antique and Michelangelesque models, filtered through his own interest in nature, became the basis for the painting of Domenichino, Reni, and to a lesser extent, Lanfranco—all of whom followed their master to Rome. Closest in spirit to Annibale was Domenichino; his *St. John the Evangelist* (cat. no. 17) evokes his teacher's idealism, which is grounded in the art of the High Renaissance, especially that of Raphael and Michelangelo. Domenichino excelled at large fresco programs, such as that dedicated to the life of St. Cecilia in S. Luigi dei Francesi. The work of Lanfranco, who initially collaborated with Domenichino, contrasts markedly with Annibale's Roman style and that of the others; his spirited, "baroque" compositions and dramatic light effects were derived first from Ludovico Carracci and later, Caravaggio. The Greenville *St. Cecilia* (cat. no. 16) combines these aspects of Lanfranco's work (the painting was once given to both Domenichino and Caravaggio). Of the three Carracci students, Guido Reni attained the greatest reputation both during his lifetime and thereafter until the middle of the nineteenth century. His early masterpiece, the ceiling fresco of the *Aurora* in the Casino Rospigliosi-Pallavicini of 1614, marks the high point of his work in Rome; soon after he returned to his native city of Bologna, where he remained mostly for the rest of his life, producing works ranging from important large-scale altarpieces to modest-sized easel paintings and devotional pictures, such as the series of Evangelists (cat. nos. 18, 19). Giovanni Francesco Barbieri, called Guercino ("the squinter"), rounds out our discussion of the great Bolognese painters. Lacking formal training of any kind, he claimed to have learned all he knew from Ludovico Carracci's magnificent altarpiece in Guercino's hometown of Cento, outside Bologna. When his Bolognese patron Alessandro Ludovisi became Pope Gregory XV in 1621, Guercino went to Rome, where he painted his monumental altarpiece *The Burial of St. Petronilla* for St. Peter's (now in the Capitoline Museum). Guercino returned to Bologna after the pope's death in 1623, gradually transforming his style from that of a synthesis of Ludovico and Caravaggio to an idealized one closer to Reni's later, silvery style, with a cooler palette and more restrained compositions. The painter's *St. Anthony of Padua* of 1658/63 (cat. no. 20) is an example of this late manner. Guercino assumed the role of leading artist in Bologna after Guido's death in 1642.

After Caravaggio's hasty departure from Rome in 1606 (due to his having killed a man over a gambling dispute), he journeyed to Naples. There he seized the artistic imagination of the city, which remained a stronghold for Caravaggio's tenebrism well past mid-century, due in large part to the efforts of Jusepe de Ribera. Caravaggio's influence in Rome died out after two decades, while the revival of Renaissance idealism sparked by Annibale and his followers became increasingly dominant in that city. After a tour of the art centers of Italy, including Rome, the Spaniard Ribera settled in Naples, which was a Spanish possession at the time and one of the largest cities and most active ports in Europe. His paintings reflect the rich culture and the coexisting currents of deep religious piety and extreme cruelty to be found in Neapolitan society. Ribera painted in two different manners according to subject matter: a refined, classicizing style for religious and mythological pictures, and a rougher, realistic mode for others, especially genre pieces. These styles are marked by a knowledge of Bolognese art (in addition to what the Spaniard had seen on his art tour, both Domenichino and Lanfranco worked in Naples), as well as by the widespread influence of Caravaggio. Ribera's *Ecce Homo* (cat. no. 21) is an excellent example of Neapolitan pietistic art; the face of Christ is marked by a refinement of form and touch, heightened by a Caravaggesque emotional drama.

Ribera supervised a large studio, and one of his pupils, Luca Giordano, continued in his teacher's vein, as can be seen in the impressive *Christ Driving the Merchants from the Temple* (cat. no. 23). But this painting also reveals other tendencies that made up his eclectic style, such as Bolognese and Venetian influences. Indeed, Giordano enjoyed a truly cosmopolitan career, for he not only journeyed twice to Venice, but also painted for the Medici in Florence in the 1680s, and, at the end his life, for the king of Spain at the Escorial near Madrid. Giordano was very prolific owing to his speed with the brush; he was nicknamed "Luca fa presto," or "Luca does it fast." Neapolitan biographer Bernardo De Dominici reported in his account of the artist (included in his *Lives of the Neapolitan Painters, Sculptors . . .*, published in the 1740s) that Giordano painted with three "brushes" — one of gold, one of silver, and the last of copper — presumably according to the fee earned. In light of this anecdote, the artist would have painted the Bob Jones picture with the first of these; it is "golden" in its Venetian-derived palette and in its superior quality. Mattia Preti, a contemporary of Giordano's, was also peripatetic, working in Rome, Naples, and Malta. A painting such as Preti's *Christ Seating the Child in the Midst of the Disciples* (cat. no. 25) combines the tenebrism and realism of Caravaggio and Ribera, as mediated by Lanfranco's art. Another accomplished Neapolitan, Giovanni Battista Beinaschi, worked in Rome as well and was a follower of Lanfranco, whose influence is evident in Beinaschi's *St. Cecilia* (cat. no. 24).

Two of the most important schools of painting outside the major centers of Rome, Bologna, and Naples, are also included in this survey of Italian painting. Relatively neglected until recently, Seicento painting in Florence and Genoa has an appeal all its own, and these schools are represented here by some of their finest practitioners.

Concurrent with the reform of Italian painting by the Carracci and Caravaggio during the late sixteenth century, artists in Florence were transforming the Mannerist legacy of Giorgio Vasari into acceptable Counter-Reformation imagery. Earlier figures such as Ludovico Cardi, called Il Cigoli, and Jacopo di

Chimenti da Empoli passed on to their younger contemporaries and followers an interest in pietistic imagery tempered with naturalistic detail, which can be seen here in the *Head of the Young Christ* from Matteo Rosselli's circle (cat. no. 28). Rosselli's pupil, Jacopo Vignali, is represented by the large *Triumph of David* (cat. no. 29), once ascribed to his teacher; despite its empathetically portrayed characters and acutely observed details, the painting reveals Vignali's love of the bizarre, which derives from his not-too-far-distant Mannerist heritage. In the work of Vignali's student, Carlo Dolci, this taste for the bizarre manifested itself in the obsessively meticulous and highly finished surfaces of his paintings, which were mostly religious in content. Florentine artists from Pontormo and Vasari onward were primarily in the service of the Medici grand dukes of Tuscany. Dolci was no exception, and for Grand Duchess Vittoria and her son Grand Duke Cosimo III, the painter turned out the type of exquisite devotional image exemplified by the Bob Jones *Madonna and Child* (cat. no. 30).

Genoa, like Naples, was a thriving port, and like Milan and Naples, under Spanish influence. As mentioned above, from the late fifteenth century the impact of Milan on Genoese painting was great. That this was the case through the Seicento is demonstrated in the art of the dean of Genoese painters, Bernardo Strozzi. In addition, the visits of the Flemish artists, Peter Paul Rubens in 1606 and Anthony van Dyck on and off from 1621 to 1625, contributed to the eclecticism of Genoese art. Because of Genoa's relationship with Milan, the leading painters of this hotbed of the Counter-Reformation—Cerano (painter to Cardinal Federico Borromeo), Giulio Cesare Procaccini, and Morazzone—left their mark on Strozzi's work, as is evident in paintings such as the *Christ and the Woman of Samaria* (cat. no. 32), executed before the painter's departure for Venice in 1631. The impression that contemporary Roman painting made on Genoese art, as exemplified by the Bolognese émigrés and Caravaggio, can be seen in an earlier painting, the *Flight into Egypt* (cat. no. 31) by Domenico Fiasella, who worked in Rome during the second decade of the seventeenth century.

It was later in the seventeenth century in Rome, when Caravaggio's influence had waned and Annibale's classicizing legacy had triumphed, that the Roman High Baroque came into full flower. Among its most brilliant artists were sculptor-architect-designer Gianlorenzo Bernini and painters Andrea Sacchi and Pietro da Cortona. Sacchi's most famous student, Carlo Maratta, is represented in the Greenville collection. In his *Martyrdom of St. Andrew* (cat. no. 26), Maratta borrowed elements from a composition by Sacchi, taking care to vary the overall effect. This sort of skillful reworking of earlier art was one of the lessons over his long career that Maratta codified and then passed on to his large following, which included Benedetto Luti and Giuseppe Chiari (cat. no. 35). By this time in Italy, the art academy had risen to great prominence from its sixteenth-century origins in Florence under Vasari's direction and in Bologna with the life drawing classes of the Carracci. The already venerable Accademia di San Luca of Rome taught young artists the basics of drawing from the model, compositional principles, and art theory; in 1701 Maratta was made the Accademia's *Principe,* or president, for life. The seventeenth and eighteenth centuries saw the proliferation of such academies outside Italy: in the cities of Paris, London, Madrid, Berlin, and Vienna. With them came the institutionalization of art training by the state, whose patronage of artists eventually replaced that of the Church during the increasing secularization of Europe.

In the middle of the eighteenth century, one of the leading painters of the day was Pompeo Batoni, his art being a product of the classicizing tradition of Renaissance and Baroque Rome. His *St. James the Major* (cat. no. 39) displays a lucid and intellectual employment of design and color that heralds Neo-Classicism. Batoni's international clientele—his portraits were especially popular with British patrons—reflected the growing pan-Europeanism of the art world. The Neapolitans Sebastiano Conca (cat. nos. 37, 38) and Francesco de Mura (cat. no. 36) were also products of stringent academic training, having been taught by Francesco Solimena, who became the preeminent artist after the deaths of his teacher, Luca Giordano, and Maratta. Conca, in fact, became president of the Roman academy, a post previously held by Maratta, Chiari, and Luti. Classicism—with its references to Antiquity and the Renaissance and its emphasis on academic training as practiced by Maratta, his circle, the prominent Neapolitans Solimena and Conca, and Batoni—set the stage for Neo-Classicism, which continued into the nineteenth century.

The art-historical trends discussed so far point

toward Neo-Classicism and the end of the eighteenth century, thus suggesting Pompeo Batoni's *St. James* as the last painting to be included in our survey. However, this would leave out a significant excursus in the development of eighteenth-century Italian art; therefore our coda is a Venetian one. While the sixteenth century saw the "Golden Age" of painting in Venice—with such luminaries as Titian, Bellini, Giorgione, Tintoretto, and Veronese—by the seventeenth century, this golden age had all but run its course. However, the early eighteenth century witnessed something of a revival, due to the efforts of the painters Sebastiano Ricci, Giovanni Antonio Pellegrini, Canaletto, and Giovanni Battista Piazzetta. Out of this milieu came Giovanni Battista Tiepolo (who had studied with Piazzetta) and his talented sons Domenico and Lorenzo. Tiepolo's international renown was second to none. The Tiepolo family and their assistants frescoed palaces, villas, and churches from the Veneto to Germany to Spain, where Giambattista died in Madrid in 1770. His art, which was dictated in part by the architectural spaces he was commissioned to paint, is a perfect summation of mid-eighteenth-century Rococo style: colorful, light in tone, airy, and highly illusionistic. The easel painting of a *Philosopher Holding a Book* (cat. no. 40)—once attributed to Domenico but now rightly recognized as belonging to an important series of works by Giambattista—represents, on a small scale, one of the greatest history painters of all time. With Tiepolo, we conclude our consideration of one of America's finest collections of Italian paintings, which in its scope and quality amply reveals the glories of Italian art.

Notes on the Use of the Catalogue

As previously noted, the paintings entries are arranged in approximate chronological order according to school. For literature published prior to 1984 and biographical entries on the artists represented in the exhibition, the reader is referred to Stephen Pepper's catalogue of the Bob Jones University Italian painting collection (Pepper 1984a) and the exhibition catalogue *Baroque Paintings from the Bob Jones University Collection* (Raleigh 1984). Sources not cited in either location are included in the present catalogue entries, and information on the artists' lives has been updated where appropriate.

A History of ITALIAN BAROQUE PAINTING IN AMERICA

ERIC M. ZAFRAN

This exhibition and tour of a selection of Italian paintings from the Bob Jones University Collection of Religious Art—at the heart of which is a remarkable group of Baroque works—takes place in the last decade of the twentieth century, serving as yet another reminder of the fluctuating fortunes of this school of painting. Dr. Jones is one of a small number of American collectors who are credited with reviving a taste for Italian Baroque art in the 1950s. This is certainly true, but, as we shall see, while the Baroque fell from its former high regard in America during the late nineteenth century, it never went totally out of fashion; throughout the early decades of this century, individual collectors and institutions stalwartly pursued seventeenth-century pictures, especially those by a few favorite artists, until the great efflorescence of collecting, beginning in the 1950s, which has continued to the present day.

EARLIEST INTEREST

In the early eighteenth century, knowledge of European art in colonial America was slight. According to William Dunlap, the first writer on the arts and collecting in this country, the English painter John Smibert, who settled in Boston in 1729, brought with him a group of copies after famous paintings he had made during his stay in Italy in 1717-20.[1] These included not only examples after Raphael and Titian, but also a copy of an Alessandro Magnasco depicting a landscape with monks at prayer.[2] For one young Bostonian, John Singleton Copley, these copies provided a first taste of European art.[3]

During this period, only a few educated individuals who were able to travel to Europe were cognizant of the then acknowledged great masters of Western art. One such person was the distinguished Philadelphia doctor John Morgan who went abroad in the 1760s and returned with copies of works by, among others, Domenichino, Francesco Albani, and the Carracci.[4] Another well-known citizen of Philadelphia, Benjamin Franklin, owned a series of engraved reproductions of famous paintings, including Domenichino's *St. Agnes* and Guido Reni's *Venus and the Graces*.[5]

Somewhat later, in 1786, when the painter Rembrandt Peale was a boy of eight, 130 Italian paintings, the first significant group of reputed old masters to come to America, arrived in Philadelphia (to be sold by the merchant John Swanwick) and were exhibited at the museum created that very year in his house by Charles Willson Peale.[6] The sale of European works of art must already have been an established practice by this time, since in the same year in New York City there was advertised a sale of "a capital and well chosen collection of French, Italian, and Dutch paintings, mostly in good preservation." Among the "esteemed masters" were "several good paintings," including "The Adoration of the Eastern Sages and Our Saviour by Guido."[7]

Another of the founding fathers who developed a taste for European art was Thomas Jefferson. Even before journeying to Europe, he had made lists, based upon his reading of Horace Walpole, of paintings he desired to have copied for his home at Monticello; among these were Salvator Rosa's *Belisarius* and *Prodigal Son,* as well as works by Pietro da Cortona and Pier Francesco Mola.[8] Once he arrived in Paris in 1784, Jefferson bought a supposed Carlo Maratta. In 1785, at the Saint-Séverin sale, he purchased a *St. Peter Weeping* by Reni, a *Penitent Magdalen* by Jusepe de Ribera, and a *Herodias Bearing the Head of St. John the Baptist* that was called Vouet but is actually after Guido Reni.[9] Jefferson traveled to Italy in April of 1787, but he only had time to visit the cities of Turin, Milan, and Genoa. Nevertheless, his attraction to Italian art grew, and he wrote home that Carlo Dolci had become a "violent favorite."[10] Other pictures acquired by him in France that hung in the entrance hall of his home at Monticello included copies after Reni's *David with the Head of Goliath* and an *Ecce Homo.*[11]

Also active as a purchaser of paintings in Paris in the late eighteenth century was the Boston merchant Richard Codman. In 1794 he reported buying eighty-odd pictures "done by the finest masters," and in 1796 he acquired another twenty from the dealer Lebrun, among which was Agostino Carracci's *Virgin and Child* from the Marquis de Sabrand and a *Marriage of St. Catherine* by Federico Barocci. A further ten paintings came from the dealer Brunot in 1797 and all were sent to Codman's older brother John in Boston. The latter's son Charles R. Codman wrote a descriptive catalogue of the collection, which, in addition to those works already mentioned, lists a Sassoferrato *Madonna* and a painting of two boys thought to be by either Guercino or Annibale Carracci.[12]

AMERICAN PAINTERS AND THE BAROQUE

The leading American painters of the late eighteenth century were also drawn to Europe to further their artistic education. Both Benjamin West and John Singleton Copley, who visited Italy and particularly admired the seventeenth-century Bolognese school, settled in England and never returned. West had learned his craft, in part, by making paintings after prints, including Strange's engraving of Rosa's *Belisarius.* Once in Italy, West continued his practice of copying, and in Bologna was so taken with Reni's *St. Peter and St. Paul* in the Zampieri palace that he created a copy from memory. Later in Rome, he copied Guido's *Herodias with the Head of St. John* in the Corsini palace.[13] Copley reacted similarly to the work of Reni and wrote from Bologna in June of 1775 to his wife, "Guido shines with a lustre equal to any artist; the pictures in Rome by him give no idea of his genius. I saw one that astonished me, it is so fine; the subject, St. Peter, seated, leaning on his hand, and St. Paul standing by him. The famous picture of the martyrdom of St. Agnes, by Domenichino, is also at Bologna, and merits all the praises that have been bestowed upon it."[14]

One painter who did return to the new United States was John Trumbull, and he brought with him a small group of supposed old masters that he had purchased on speculation in Paris in 1795. These included a "Guido, *Patron Saints of Bologna,* Luca 'Jordano' *The Earth,* and a Domenichino *Madonna.*"[15] According to Dunlap, Trumbull exhibited his paintings at the Park Theatre when he returned to New York in 1804. Apparently they did not sell,[16] and "the collection of old pictures was returned to Europe," whereupon a sale of eight paintings belonging to Trumbull was held in London in 1812. One of these was identified as "The Madonna with the Infant Saviour surrounded by Angels in celestial glory appearing to Saint Mary Magdalen and Santa Lucia," by Guido Reni.[17]

EARLY COLLECTORS

By the early nineteenth century, more Americans were traveling to Europe. Among their pantheon of great artists whom they could have read about in various English texts such as that by C. A. du Fresnoy or Matthew Pilkington's *General Dictionary of Painters* were the Italian Baroque masters Reni, Domenichino,

Rosa, the Carracci, Luca Giordano, the Gentileschi, and even Giovanni Lanfranco, Domenico Fetti, and Caravaggio.[18]

Emulating their English compatriots making the Grand Tour of Europe, Americans found that it was almost mandatory to acquire some examples, either originals or copies, of Italian masterpieces. One of the first to make this excursion and to seriously pursue the collecting of paintings was Robert Gilmor, Jr. (1774-1848), a merchant of Baltimore. He went to Europe twice, with one trip lasting from 1799 to 1801, and after his return continued buying from the few American dealers such as Michael Paff. After his father's death in 1822, Gilmor devoted himself to his collection, which he created as much to educate others as for his own pleasure. He had, in fact, hoped to found a public museum, but financial reversals made this impossible and the collection had to be sold. Fortunately, from his own records and correspondence with Dunlap, it is possible to obtain some idea of its contents. The Italian Baroque works consisted of an *Adoration of St. Francis* by Antonio Balestra, *The Augurs* by Rosa (of which the collector wrote had been bought in New York seventy or eighty years earlier), a *Magdalen* by Michelangelo da Caravaggio, a *Repose in Egypt* by Francesco Albani, a *St. Francis* by Ludovico Cigoli, a *Stoning of St. Stephen* by Luca Cambiaso, and a *Holy Family* by Simone Cantarini; other works that appear in his lists were by Reni, the two Carracci, Sassoferrato, and Mola.[19]

Several collectors from New England were in Europe during the early nineteenth century. One of the best known was James Bowdoin III, who served in diplomatic positions in Spain and France in 1809. His father, a former governor of Massachusetts, had already acquired some of those Italian copies brought to Boston by Smibert, and the younger Bowdoin continued the collecting habit during his travels. Upon his death in 1811, he bequeathed to the college in Maine named after his father, his library and seventy paintings, including one believed to be by Rosa, one now attributed to Balestra, and a copy after Reni's *Salome with the Head of St. John the Baptist*.[20]

Another New Englander, William Henry Vernon of Newport, Rhode Island, went to France after graduating from Princeton University in 1778. When he returned nineteen years later, he brought with him a collection of fifty-two paintings, which was eventually sold in 1835. This contained not only a version of the *Mona Lisa*,[21] but also two works ascribed to Salvator Rosa.

American diplomats of various rank were able to obtain, through a variety of surprising ways, works of art to bring home. One of the most notable was Colonel Richard Meade, America's fiscal agent in Calais at the time of the Peninsular War. In 1812 he received as a guarantee for some bad debts a group of paintings and returned with them to America in 1820. Placed on view in what was known as the Meade Gallery at the Pennsylvania Academy of Fine Arts were Giordano's *Faith and Charity Surrounded by Flowers* and by the same artist a large *Calling of St. Matthew;* by Ribera there was a "St. Onope [Onofrio] in Penance," and by Rosa, two small landscapes and a battle scene. Colonel Meade was never able to regain the money from his loan, and in 1860, upon his wife's death, the paintings were sold by his daughter. The Ribera was supposedly purchased by the Spanish government; other pictures were reported to have been bought by a Roman Catholic institution. The great Giordano *Calling of St. Matthew* was, in fact, acquired by America's first Catholic college, Georgetown University in Washington, D.C.[22]

Yet another diplomat obtained a painting in a rather unusual manner. This was Bernhard Henry, the United States Consul to Gibraltar from 1812 to 1836. Supposedly, he harbored Joachim Murat, the deposed King of Naples, in disguise, and on learning his identity helped him escape quietly. In appreciation, the Bonapartes presented Mrs. Henry with a pearl necklace and a copy after Caravaggio's famous painting *The Cardsharps*. This was given by their great grandson Barklie McKee Henry and his wife to the Art Institute of Chicago in 1961.[23]

A great many other works from the Bonaparte collection were brought to the United States when Joseph Bonaparte, the former King of Spain, fled from France and established himself by 1817 at the estate called Point Breeze in Bordentown, New Jersey. His well-known collection was visited by many artists, and when sold there in 1845, included works identified as Guercino's *Herodias Receiving the Head of St. John,* Annibale Carracci's *Christ and his Disciples at Sea,* and by Luca Giordano, a pair of shell and fish still lifes, as well as a *Hercules and Omphale, Rape of Deianeira, Rinaldo in the Garden of Armida,* and *Burning of*

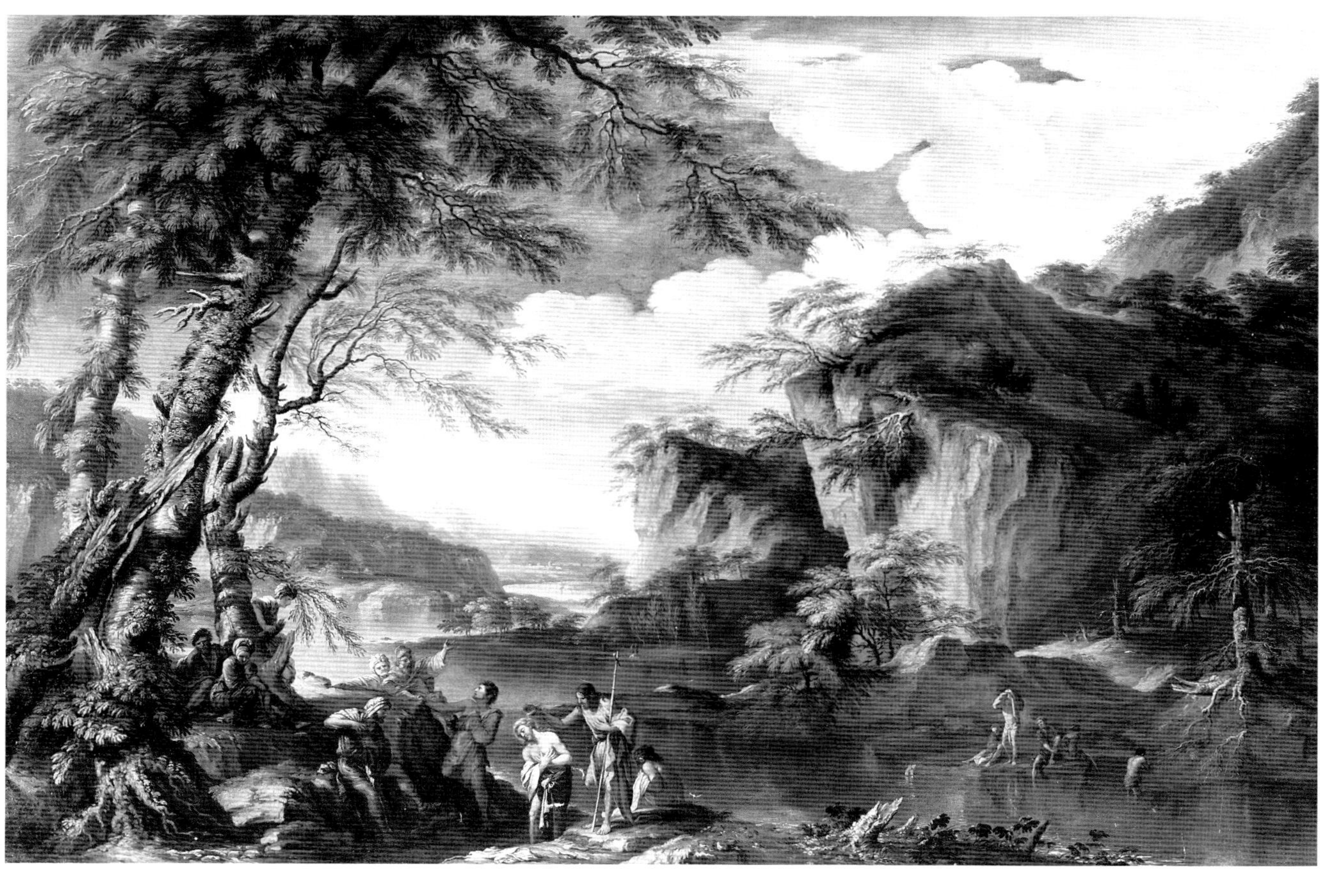

FIGURE 1

SALVATOR ROSA, *Landscape with the Baptism of Christ,* Bob Jones University Collection, Greenville. Photograph courtesy of Bob Jones University.

Olindo and Sophronia. Other of the Bonaparte works were described as of the school of the Carracci and Guido Reni.[24] Not only Bonapartes traveled with their art, but also members of the *ancien régime,* for when Louis Philippe was exiled to America, he purportedly brought with him to New Orleans in 1796 a painting then believed to be by Caravaggio (now given to Mattia Preti).[25]

Americans continued to return from Europe with paintings bearing impressive attributions or copies of the acknowledged masterpieces. For example, a Giordano *Apollo in his Chariot* along with Maratta's *Sacra Conversazione* and Albani's *Rest on the Flight* were acquired from the Rinuccini gallery of Florence by Francis George Shaw in 1852 for Francis Cabot Lowell of Boston. The Giordano remained in the Lowell family until 1933, when it was inherited by Mrs. Harriet Roper Cabot, who gave it as a Reni to the Boston Museum of Fine Arts in 1947.[26] An earlier Cabot, Samuel, who was in Rome in 1832, commissioned a copy of Caravaggio's *Cardsharps,* then in the Sciarra collection, from the painter Galliadi, and this in turn was donated to the Fogg Art Museum at Harvard University by his descendant Dr. Lloyd Cabot Briggs in 1957.[27]

In 1836 two other Americans visiting Florence, Henry Wilde of Georgia and Colonel James Thomson of New York, acquired several paintings from the Ricciardi family. These included a pair of landscapes by Rosa, one of which was the *Landscape with the Baptism of Christ* (Fig. 1) now in the Bob Jones University Collection, and a supposed *Self-Portrait* (Fig. 2) by the same artist. The pictures were shipped to New York, but Wilde died in New Orleans before he could receive them. After storing them for a time, Thomson sold them in New York in 1848 along with works by Francesco Solimena, Guercino, and Albani. The landscape was acquired by a Mr. Arnold and the Rosa *Self-Portrait* by Aaron Livingston. Upon the latter's death in 1873, the portrait passed to Mary Livingston Harrison, who in 1921 bequeathed it to the Metropolitan Museum of Art in New York.[28] While in

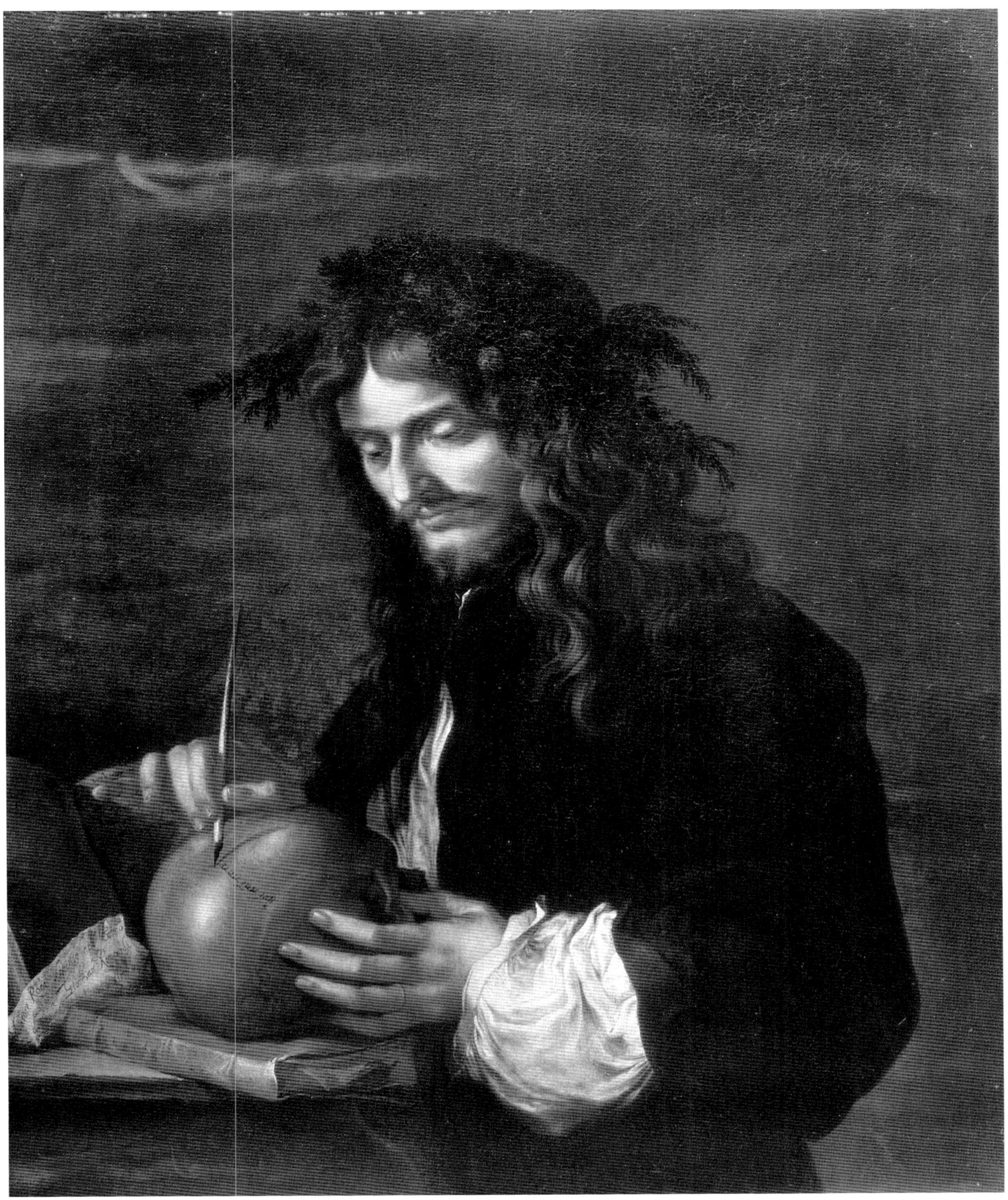

FIGURE 2

SALVATOR ROSA, *Self-Portrait (?),* The Metropolitan Museum of Art, New York, Bequest of Mary L. Harrison, 1921, (21.105). Photograph courtesy of The Metropolitan Museum of Art.

Italy, Thomson is also recorded in July of 1837 to have sent from Rome to a friend, E. Jackson of Middletown, Connecticut, copies of Alessandro Allori's *Judith,* Sassoferrato's *Madonna,* and Dolci's *Magdalen,* as well as a small Fra Bartolommeo and a *Madonna and Child* by Allori.[29]

NEW YORK COLLECTORS AND DEALERS

New York typically produced individuals who were extraordinary or compulsive in their collecting taste. One of the first of these was the former Betsy Bowen of Rhode Island, who married the coffee planter Stephen Jumel from Santo Domingo, Haiti, and went with him to Paris in 1815. So profligate was her behavior that he sent her home the following year; now known as Madame Jumel, she returned to New York with a collection of 105 supposed old master paintings. These were exhibited in 1817 but, due to financial woes, she had to sell her entire holdings of 243 works in 1821. Madame Jumel's collection included several Rosas, a Guercino *Doubting Thomas,* and a *Cleopatra* by Reni.[30] More serious in their pursuit of art were Dr. David Hosack, who owned a Carracci, and Philip Hone, who among his many works had two copies after Rosa.[31]

The most significant New York connoisseur of this era, however, was Luman Reed (1785-1836). Reed became interested in art about 1830, at first purchasing old masters from dealers such as Paff, but soon shifting his emphasis to contemporary American artists, notably Thomas Cole, whose great canvases were the highlight of an exhibition of Reed's collection the year before his death. Purchased by his friends, Reed's works were given to the New York Gallery of Fine Arts and housed in 1849 in the National Academy of Design; later, in 1857, the collection was incorporated into the New York Historical Society. Reed had prints after Guido and Rosa, and of his eighteen European paintings, one was an *Assumption of the Virgin,* then believed to be by Carracci but now given to Albani.[32]

While most Americans were content with a few representative examples, the New York dealer Michael Paff, one of America's first collector-dealers, exhibited the recurrent tendency found in this country to obsessively amass works of art. His home, because it contained such a great variety of "original" works, was a popular meeting place of artists and art lovers. After thirty-five years of his collecting activity, there were in the sale of 1838 following his death, over one thousand paintings. According to Dunlap, Paff had "long possessed a valuable collection, which varies with the sales and purchases he makes; but he retains many that he justly values beyond the price which every day purchasers can give. Among these I may specify his 'Magdalen,' by Carlo Dolci, but so much superior to any Carlo Dolci within my limited knowledge, that I would fain attribute it to a higher source."[33] What was remarkable about the Paff collection was not only the sheer number of works, but also the variety of schools and artists to whom the paintings were attributed by the owner. Famous and lesser-known Italian Baroque masters are named in the sale catalogue and distinctions made between presumed school works and copies. By Guido there were a *Cupid Sleeping,* a sketch of the *Aurora,* a *Cleopatra, St. Sebastian,* and *Repentant Magdalen.* Of the many Guercinos listed, the most intriguing are a *Mercury and Bacchus, King Ahasuerus in Council,* and *Solomon with his Concubines.* Other artists represented included, besides Dolci, all three of the Carracci, Rosa, Cortona, Giordano, Giovanni Benedetto Castiglione, Maratta, Valerio Castello, Andrea Sacchi, Pietro Testa, Sebastiano Ricci, Bartolomeo Schedoni, Carlo Cignani, Guido Cagnacci, Albani, Balestra, Domenichino, Benedetto Gennari, Mola, and Paolo de Matteis.[34] Whether or not they were authentic, it is still amazing that so many Italian seventeenth-century masters should be known in America in the late 1830s.

OFFICIAL INSTITUTIONS

As befit a growing country, eager to express its cultural aspirations and provide education to its citizens, several major cities in the early nineteenth century inaugurated institutions where art of the present and past could be viewed. Naturally, the Baroque masters were to be well represented.

As Lillian B. Miller points out in her pioneering study of American art institutions, the Society of Fine Arts in New York City organized in 1802 was "the first art academy of importance founded in the country as a result of community effort."[35] It was this group that sent the young artist John Vanderlyn abroad in 1803 to copy such old masters as Domenichino and Caravaggio.[36] In 1808 the organization became the American Academy of the Arts, and from 1816 held large exhibitions. (It was renamed again in 1817 the American Academy of the Fine Arts.) In 1828 these included the two Rosas from Joseph Bonaparte's collection in New Jersey and from Signor Antonio Sarti of Florence a large group of paintings, including examples by Reni, Schedoni, and Rosa.[37] An exhibition in 1830 of European paintings brought by Richard Abraham of New Bond Street, London, presented a wide variety of alleged Baroque masters, and in 1835 John Watkins Brett showed a group of paintings that he claimed had formerly been in the Colonna palace, Rome, and in the collection of Sir Joshua Reynolds.[38]

As mentioned earlier, the New York Gallery of Fine Arts was founded in 1844 as a permanent gallery of art around the Luman Reed collection and housed in the National Academy of Design. In addition to the Reed gifts, its inaugural exhibition included a prize-winning copy of Dolci's *St. Cecilia* by Koffman. By the exhibition of 1850, the Gallery's collection also boasted a landscape by Domenichino, a Dolci *Madonna,* Reni *Ecce Homo,* Guercino *Virgin with the Infant Christ,* Cignani *The Miraculous Impression,* and by Annibale Carracci, a *Martyrdom of St. Sebastian,* as well as a loan from Lewis Cruger of a *Portrait of an Austrian Princess* by Reni.[39]

The Pennsylvania Academy of the Fine Arts in Philadelphia, founded even earlier in 1805, is, as its publicity claims, "the oldest [surviving] institution dedicated to the fine arts in the United States."[40] From the start, the Academy presented annual exhibitions with both loans and gifts. Shown there in 1811 from the John Hare Powell collection were a supposed Caravaggio still life of fruit, as well as works by the Carracci, Domenichino, a *St. Cecilia* by Reni, and a Sassoferrato *Madonna.*[41]

One of the earliest donors to the Pennsylvania Academy was Joseph Allen Smith of South Carolina, who first presented a group of European works in 1807. In 1812 he sent another twenty-one paintings from Italy on an American ship that was forced by a British cruiser to Halifax; the Academy had to sue for their return. Among these works were a presumed Reni of *Ganymede, Jove's Cup Bearer,* Schedoni's *Cupid with a Vase* and *Cupid Musing,* and three landscapes by Rosa of which the largest was *Mercury Deceiving Argus.*[42] The Academy purchased in 1813 from Robert Fulton a pair of paintings, *Adam and Eve* and *The Death of Abel,* that were believed to be by Carlo Loti (Johann Carl Loth).[43] The Rosa *Mercury Deceiving Argus* was sold off in 1989,[44] as were the two supposed Loths, now attributed to Antonio Molinari and Antonio Balestra.[45]

The Pennsylvania Academy also had on loan the previously mentioned group of Italian paintings brought to this country by Colonel Richard Meade. In addition to repeated showings of these works, it also presented traveling exhibitions. That in 1833 was of a celebrated "Gallery of Paintings" brought from England by Mr. Brett, which included Guido's *Judith* and a Domenichino supposedly from the Colonna palace, a Carlo Dolci purchased in Italy by Sir John Sitting, and, also by Reni, a *Flight into Egypt* and an *Ascension,* Caravaggio's *Christ and Martha,* a Sassoferrato *Madonna,* a *Martyrdom of St. Sebastian* by Carracci, as well as other works by Dolci and Reni.[46] The 1830s and 1840s saw additional loans, such as a Domenichino *St. Cecilia* and a Guido *Holy Family* in 1843.[47]

The Athenaeum of Boston was incorporated in 1807; in 1823 money was raised for its gallery of art, which opened its doors in 1827.[48] The first public loan exhibition of paintings was held that year. Old masters were lent from Boston collections, and the Italian Baroque works included an Elisabetta Sirani *Magdalen* and a Domenichino *St. John* (from a Mr. Sears). Other paintings on view were a Carracci *St. Francis,* Dolci *Virgin and Child,* Ludovico Carracci *Virgin and Child,* Domenichino *Cruelties of Nero* and *St. Peter,* and Cagnacci *Magdalen.*[49] The exhibition was such a success that the Athenaeum had the funds to make its first purchase, a painting believed to be a *Self-Portrait* by Annibale Carracci, bought for $100 from Mr. William Harris Jones, who in 1827 had been the first to rent the Athenaeum's exhibition space.[50] Since 1865, however, the portrait has been attributed to an unknown artist.[51]

In 1828 the Athenaeum bought for $250 Guercino's *Christ Healing the Blind.* That same year, the collection of Thomas Jefferson was exhibited with its copies of Baroque paintings. Signor Sarti of Florence rented the gallery in the following year and showed a collection of "rare and valuable paintings," including works purportedly by Annibale Carracci and Guercino. In exchange for his rent, he gave the Athenaeum two Guercinos entitled *Animals Feeding* and *Moses.* In 1830 a *Madonna* by Dolci was purchased for $120, and the gallery was rented to Charles Beaumont, who showed a painting by Pietro da Cortona "from the Milan Gallery." Loans from farther afield continued with the Meade collection of Philadelphia and the Vernon collection of Newport, both of which contained works by Rosa.[52]

Then in 1833 the Athenaeum showed the same group of works from Mr. John Watkins Brett of England that was exhibited in New York, Philadelphia, and Washington.[53] One of the Dolcis, a copy of his *Salome,* found a buyer in Boston and passed by descent to Mrs. Otis Kimball of Boston, who gave it to the Museum of Fine Arts in 1915.[54] In 1837 the Athenaeum made an unwise exchange with Brett, trading two very grand paintings by Giovanni Paolo Pannini for a copy after Reni's *Judith with the Head of Holofernes,* supposedly from the Colonna palace collection, and the *Angel Gabriel Warning Joseph to Flee into Egypt* by Ludovico Carracci (now attributed to a follower of Lanfranco).[55] Nathaniel Hawthorne, after he had seen the original Reni in Rome, remembered how the copy "used to weary me to death, year after year, in the Boston Athenaeum."[56]

Henry Pickering, a merchant of Salem (b. 1781) who made his first gifts to the Athenaeum in 1824, was a refined man who wrote poetry and traveled to Italy, where he perhaps acquired some of the works of art he was to sell and give the Athenaeum when he suffered business reversals in 1837. Of the three paintings he sold to the Athenaeum, two were Italian—Maratta's *Christ and the Woman of Samaria* for $400 and Giordano's *Flaying of Marsyas* for $100 (Fig. 3). To these he added as a gift a *Hagar and Ishmael* by Cignani (Fig. 4).[57] Unlike so many other "Baroque" paintings brought to America during the nineteenth century,

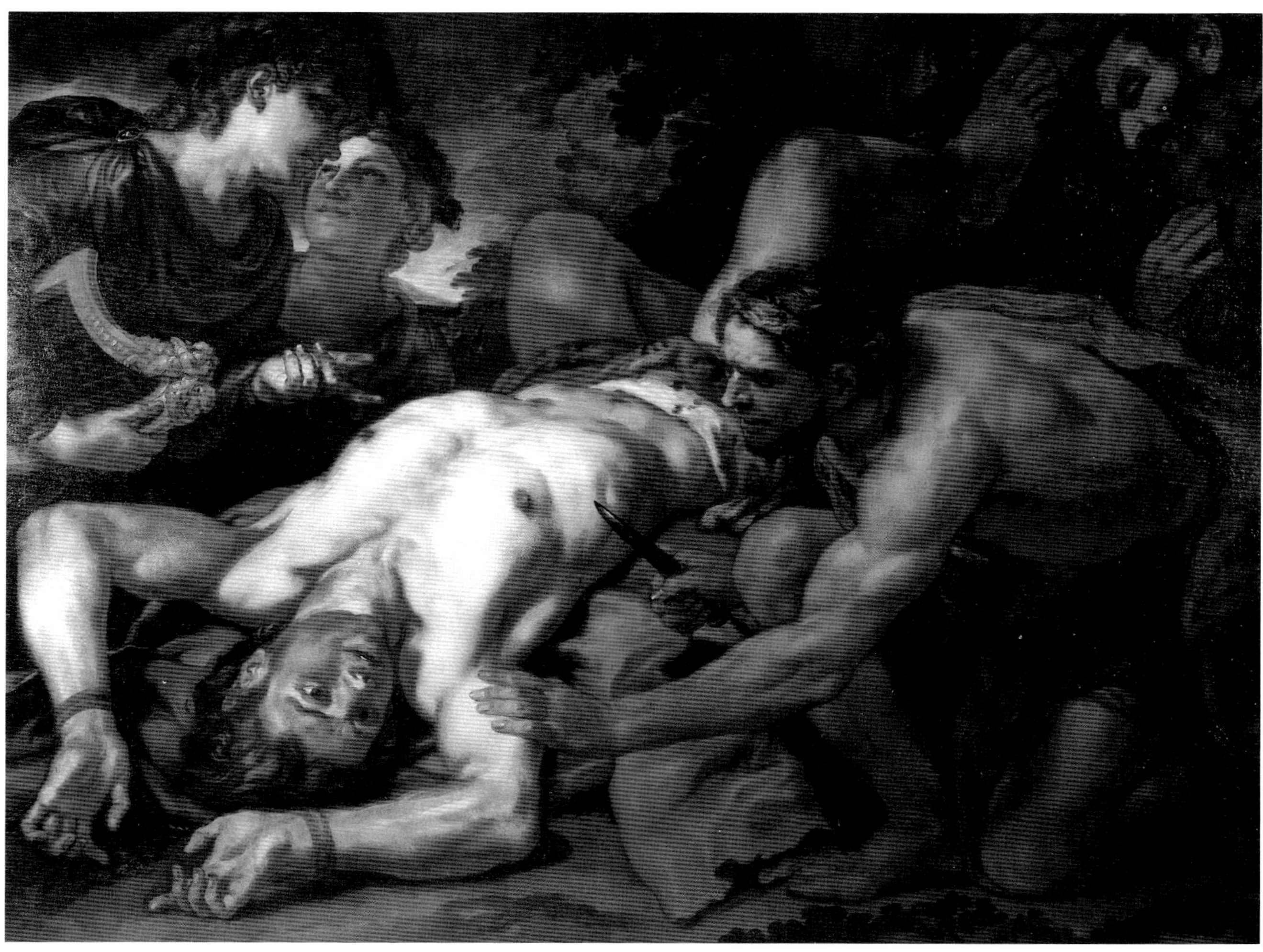

FIGURE 3

LUCA GIORDANO, *Flaying of Marsyas,* Boston Athenaeum. Photograph courtesy of the Boston Athenaeum.

these were authentic, if not by the masters claimed. Both the Cignani and Maratta were on view for many years at the Museum of Fine Arts until sold by the Athenaeum in the late 1970s. The supposed Maratta, already identified by Fredericksen and Zeri as by Giuseppe Chiari, was recognized as such by Robert Manning who purchased it (Fig. 5). The Giordano fortunately was maintained by the Athenaeum, and a recent cleaning has revealed it to be an autograph work of high quality.[58]

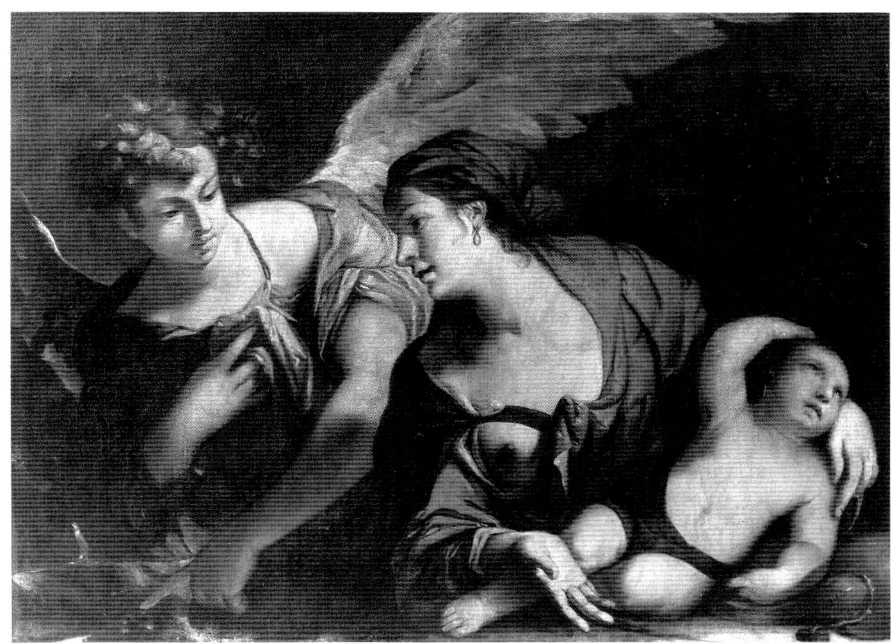

FIGURE 4

SCHOOL OF CARLO CIGNANI, *Hagar and Ishmael,* Present location unknown (formerly in the Boston Athenaeum). Photograph courtesy of the Museum of Fine Arts, Boston.

The next purchase by the Athenaeum occurred in 1838 when nine paintings were acquired from the Florentine dealer Count F. Celestine for $4,000, including *Judith with the Head of Holofernes* by Allori and *Christ Shown to the People* by Marinari.[59] In April of that year, the Bostonian George W. Brimmer wrote to the Athenaeum from Rome, saying that he was shipping "an old and I may say perfect copy of Guido's celebrated picture of *The Martyrdom of St. Sebastian* in [the] papal collection of [the] Capitol." In addition, he sent a "Head of Young Guido by himself."[60]

Appearing among the loans to the Athenaeum's annual exhibition were many Baroque pictures that eventually found a permanent home in Boston, even if the attributions changed. In 1840 J.S. Amory lent a Guercino *Flora.* This was given to the Museum of Fine Arts in 1920 by his descendants, the Gardners, and is now identified as by Bartolomeo Gennari (Fig. 6) .[61] In 1849-50 the Athenaeum moved to its new building on Beacon Street, where it had more gallery space.[62] In 1853 H.J. Bigelow sent to Boston for exhibition a painting identified as Caravaggio's *Herodias with the Head of St. John the Baptist* from the collection of Louis Philippe; this was donated in 1926 to the museum by his descendant William Sturgis Bigelow, and is one of the major works in this country by Francesco del Cairo.[63] George M. Wales gave in 1861 a work thought to be by Luca Giordano, *The Golden Age,* and it was exhibited as such in the later part of the nineteenth century at the Museum of Fine Arts. It has most recently been attributed to Gregorio Lazzarini.[64] In 1863 a Domenichino *Repose in Egypt* was lent from the R.C. Winthrop collection, a painting later given to the Museum of Fine Arts by Miss Clara Bowdoin Winthrop in 1926, and now attributed to Giovanni Francesco Grimaldi.[65] In this same year, a special loan exhibition featured works by Rosa, Maratta, and Cignani; another in 1864 boasted a painting by Sassoferrato, a *Fortune Teller* by Caravaggio, as well as works by Cagnacci and Reni.[66]

Another atheneum that was to be of major importance in the history of Baroque collecting in the United States was that founded in Hartford, Connecticut, by David Wadsworth in 1842. The Wadsworth Atheneum, which opened officially in 1844, can claim to be the oldest public art museum in the country still in operation today.[67] Like its fellow organizations, it hosted changing loan exhibitions. Those of the 1860s included Baroque paintings, particularly from the collection of a rich local collector James G. Betterson. In 1864 Betterson lent a Guercino, a Caravaggio *Fortune Teller,* and a Sassoferrato; in 1868, works by Annibale Carracci and Reni.[68] Despite its early foundation and its ability to

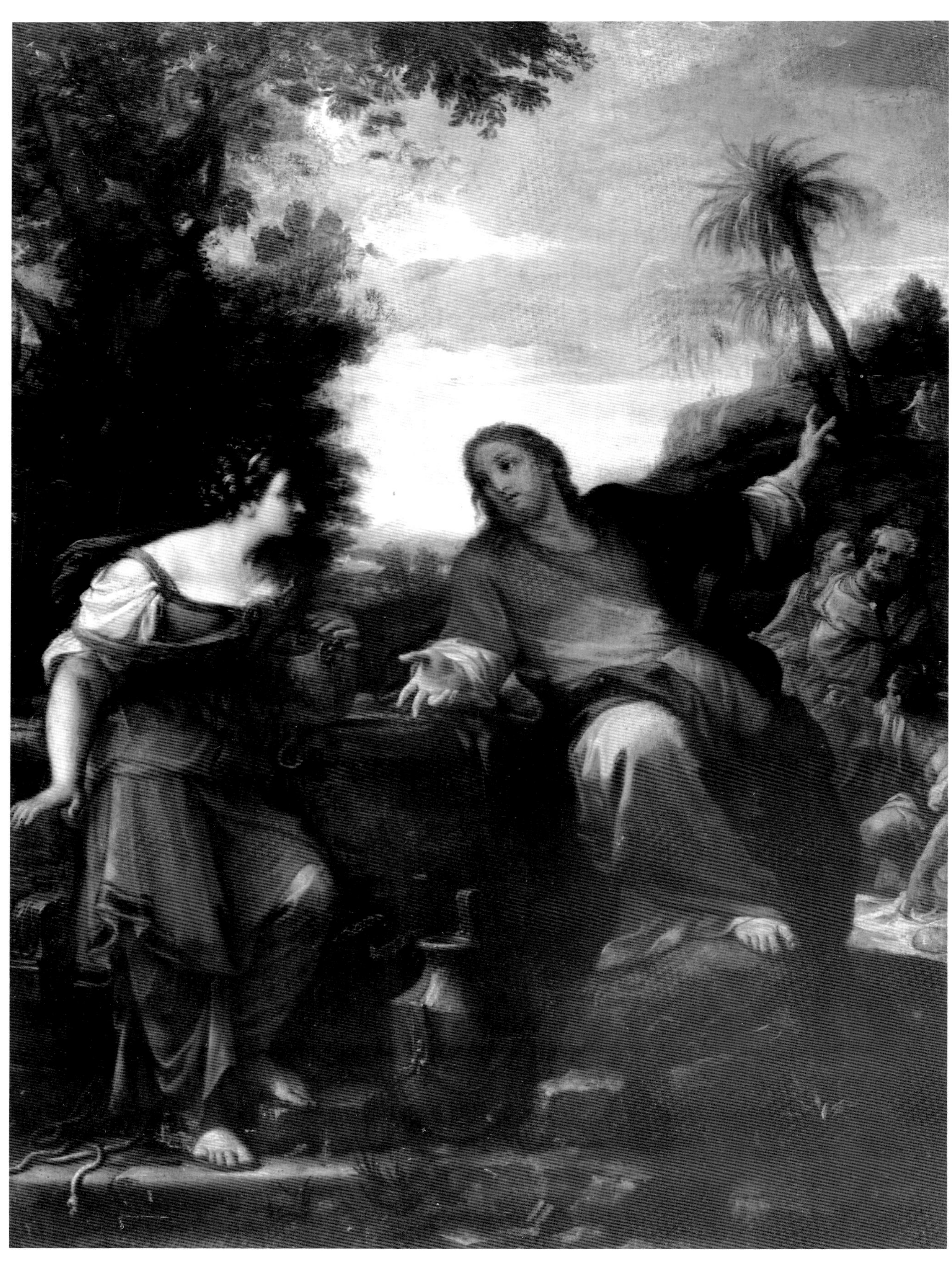

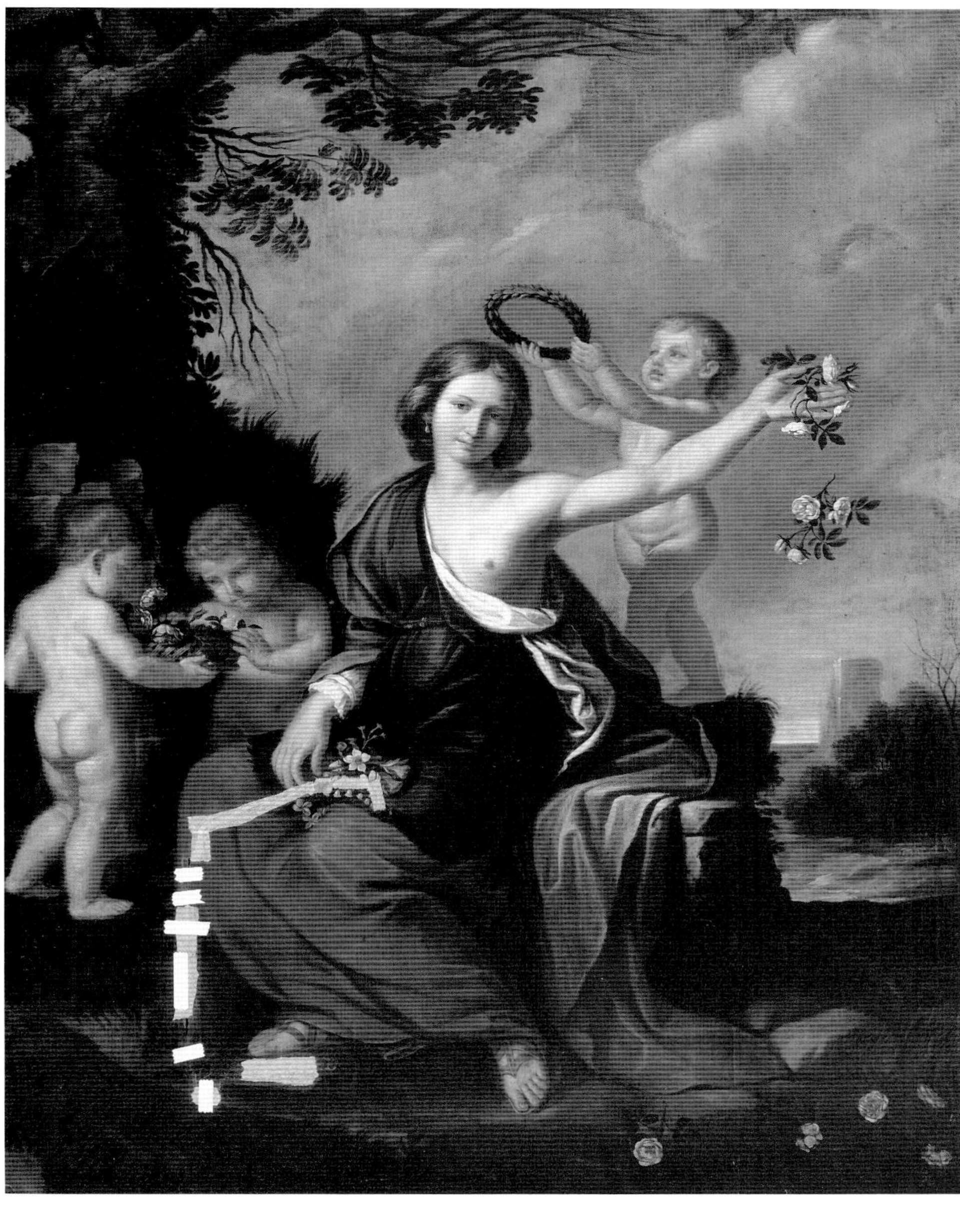

F I G U R E 5

GIUSEPPE CHIARI, *Christ and the Woman of Samaria,* Suida Manning Collection, New York. Photograph courtesy of Robert L. Manning.

F I G U R E 6

BARTOLOMEO GENNARI, *Flora,* Museum of Fine Arts, Boston. Photograph courtesy of the Museum of Fine Arts, Boston.

attract important loans, however, the Wadsworth Atheneum's own collection did not become significant until later.

Still other organizations and institutions were formed to present art to the public. Baltimore's Peale Museum, founded by Rembrandt Peale in 1814, began in 1822 to sponsor annual exhibitions of the fine arts and showed examples of Baroque painting, including in 1823 loans from the Gilmor collection. Later, beginning in the 1840s, the Maryland Historical Society and the Maryland Institute in the 1850s also provided venues for seeing such works.[69] In Philadelphia the Pennsylvania Academy was later joined by the Union League Club as a location hosting occasional exhibitions.

The public exhibition of art during the nineteenth century was not confined to the major eastern cities; organizations all over the country were established to encourage education and culture, and special expositions served to celebrate regional pride. These displays often included paintings by the well-known Italian Baroque masters. Thus, for example, the Carolina Art Association in Charleston, South Carolina, was particularly active in the 1850s and early 1860s, presenting works from local collections believed to be by Annibale Carracci, Solimena, Rosa, Giordano, Dolci, and Domenichino. The American National Gallery of New Orleans presented in 1847 an "extensive and valuable collection from the galleries of several Italian Noblemen" that included many of the same names. Other shows around the country were those sponsored by: the Mechanical Association of Portland, Maine, in 1859 with a Caravaggio *St. Dominic;* the Buffalo Fine Arts Academy in 1863 with loans of Caravaggio and Maratta; the Michigan State Fair in Detroit in the 1860s and 1870s; the Mississippi Valley Sanitary Fair in St. Louis in 1864 with a Sassoferrato and a Guercino; the Industrial Exposition at Louisville in 1873 with a work by Bernardo Strozzi; the Cincinnati Industrial Exposition in 1873 and 1874 with a variety of Baroque paintings; and finally, the San Francisco Art Association in 1872 (its inaugural exhibition) with a painting by Guido Reni.[70]

COMMERCIAL EXHIBITIONS

It is evident from the very first showing of paintings in 1786 at the Peale Museum in Philadelphia and the subsequent rentals of public gallery spaces in Boston, Philadelphia, and New York that exhibitions were often organized primarily for commercial purposes and only secondarily for enlightenment. There were, in fact, a number of less permanent spaces that served as locations for resident dealers or traveling salesmen to set up shop temporarily.

Shown in New York City in 1835 at the City Dispensary was a collection belonging to Joseph Capece Latro, "the Archbishop of Taranto in the Kingdom of Naples." This exhibition featured works by Castiglione, Domenico Antonio Vaccaro, Rosa, Guercino, Dolci, and Caravaggio.[71] Three years later, the New York Academy of Fine Arts presented the Sanguinetti collection from Florence. Also at the Academy in 1839, organized by John Clark, was what may have been the largest collection of old master paintings ever shown in the country to date, and at its sale at Lyman & Co. on 4 November there were works attributed to all the major Italian Baroque masters as well as such lesser figures as Testa and Spadarino. Other commercial galleries active in showing Italian Baroque works from the 1840s to 1860s were the Lyceum Gallery, Roman Gallery, Napoleon Gallery, Henderson Gallery, Düsseldorf Gallery, and Derby Gallery.[72] At the Leeds Art Gallery in 1870 was auctioned a collection of over 1,500 paintings begun in the 1830s by Mr. Thomas Thompson, who originally intended to give the works to the city of Boston, but after a falling out, moved to New York. In addition to the usual names of Guercino, Domenichino, and Giordano, were those of Ludovico Carracci, Schedoni, Pietro da Cortona, Giovanni Francesco Romanelli, and Jacopo da Empoli.[73]

A number of independent commercial galleries operated in the first half of the nineteenth century in Boston as well. As early as 1817, a Signor Ferin of Naples showed a collection of paintings with a Domenichino, Annibale Carracci, and Rosa.[74] In the 1820s Doggett's Repository of Art had several sale exhibitions; that of 1821 claimed to be "a truly splendid and valuable Collection of one hundred and sixty-four Cabinet Paintings in elegant frames...warranted to comprise the works of the Great Masters from the 13th Century to the Present Time." This was succeeded by showings at Corinthian Hall (a Dolci in 1831), the American Gallery of Fine Arts (a Rosa in 1835), Hayward's Gallery (a Domenichino *St. Cecilia* in 1840), Harding's Gallery (a Giordano in 1841), the Boston Museum and Gallery (a Reni *Head of Archimedes* in 1841),[75] and at Howe, Leonard & Co. auctions of collections in 1843 and 1846 with most of the major names, including a pair of Caravaggios called *The Bagpipers* and *The Fiddlers.*[76]

RELIGIOUS INSTITUTIONS

In addition to exhibitions at public institutions and commercial establishments, Italian Baroque paintings could also be seen in the nineteenth and early twentieth centuries in Catholic churches and schools, where they were sent and acquired for purposes of religious education and inspiration. The earliest such works to come to America were probably the five Italian paintings obtained about 1827 by Father Bertrand Martial for the cathedral of St. Joseph in Bardstown, Kentucky: three of the Bolognese school, one by Preti and his workshop, and one of the Neapolitan school.[77]

Founded in 1782, Georgetown University was the first Roman Catholic institution of higher learning in the United States. Administered by the Society of Jesus, the school seems to have acquired its first Italian Baroque painting, the large Luca Giordano *Calling of St. Matthew,* from Miss Martha Meade in 1860.[78] Later in the nineteenth century, another lesser-known group of Italian Baroque pictures was assembled by the Jesuits of Boston College. The specific provenance of these works is not known, but the finest, as revealed by a recent cleaning, is the Sassoferrato *Virgin in Glory*

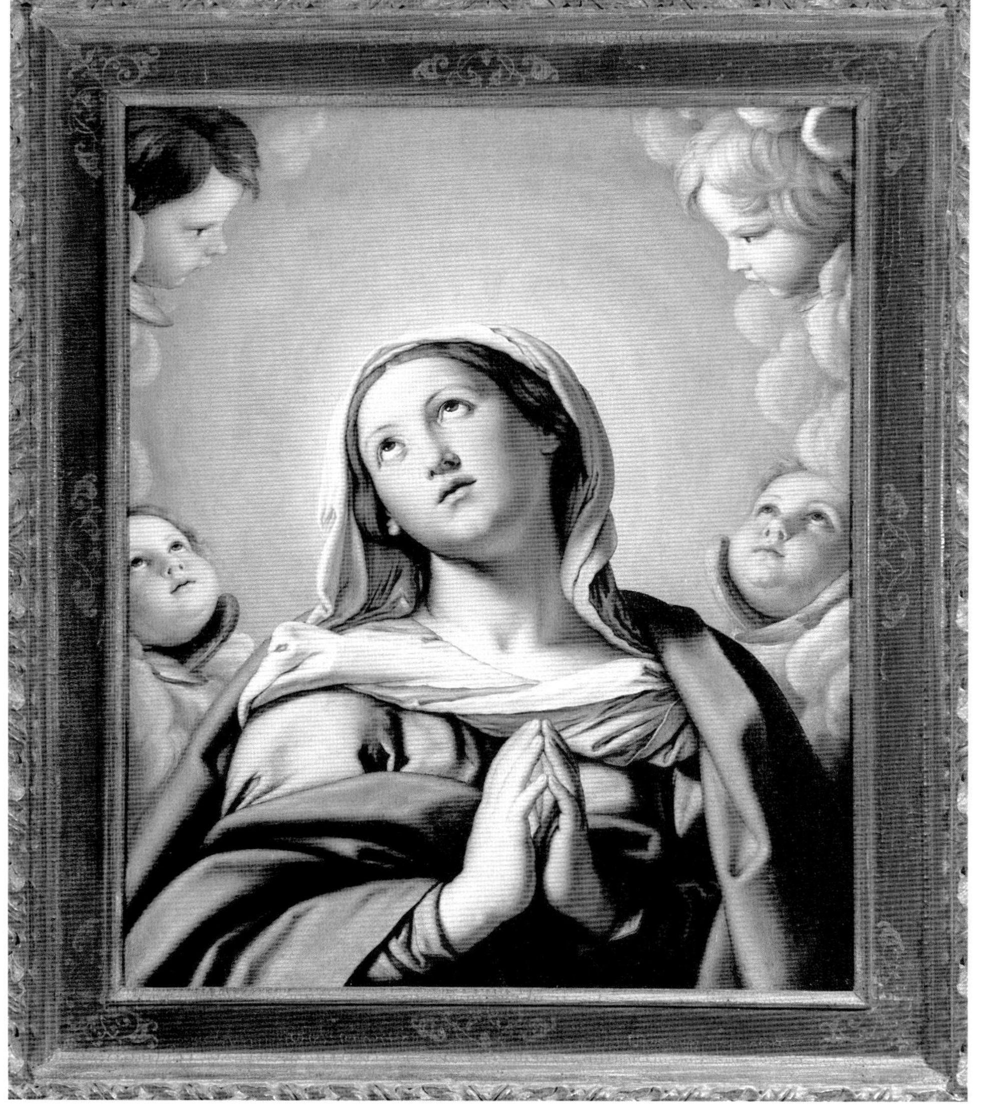

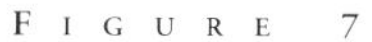
FIGURE 7

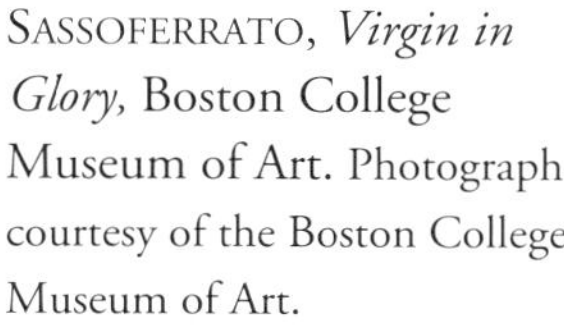
SASSOFERRATO, *Virgin in Glory,* Boston College Museum of Art. Photograph courtesy of the Boston College Museum of Art.

(Fig. 7). Also in this group is a *Christ and the Adulteress* attributed to Orazio de Ferrari, as well as copies of Dolci's *Madonna and Child,* Annibale Carracci's *Holy Family* and Reni's *Judith with the Head of Holofernes.*[79]

Smaller monastery schools throughout the country have also come into possession of Italian Baroque paintings. The Archabbey of St. Meinrad in Indiana was settled in 1857 by Benedictine monks from Switzerland and rebuilt after a fire in 1887. Some paintings seem to have been given already in the nineteenth century and others were added later, but with the exceptions of copies after Dolci and Reni, the majority are of the Neapolitan school with attributions to Giuseppe Mazzuoli, Sisto Badalocchio, Bastarolo, and Giovanni Do.[80] St. Anselm College in Manchester, New Hampshire, also houses several paintings, most notably, a *Martyrdom of St. Sebastian,* probably of North Italian origin.[81]

A much larger collection is at St. Gregory's Abbey in Shawnee, Oklahoma. Established in 1875 by the Benedictine order, it sent one of its members, Fr. Gregory Gerrer O.S.B., who was also an artist, to Rome in 1900 to further his study of art. Fr. Gerrer remained there until 1904, both painting and acquiring works of art to bring back to Shawnee, where he became founder and curator of an art gallery. Later he was also director of the Art Museum at the University of Notre Dame. Fr. Gerrer died in 1946, and since records were not carefully maintained, it is difficult to trace the provenance of the paintings he acquired. According to the oral legends recorded by the registrar of St. Gregory's Abbey Museum, now called the Mabee-Gerrer Museum, Fr. Gerrer received one group of works, including a version of Guercino's *Esther before Ahasuerus,* from the Barberini collection of Rome—either from a papal major-domo or a countess living in the Barberini palace. Other paintings came from the collection of the Countess Braschi, which were also distributed to Notre Dame and a monastery in Toronto. The works now in the Mabee-Gerrer Museum are a *Penitent St. Peter* and a *Magdalen in Ecstasy* after Reni, an *Annunciation* by Francesco de

Mura, a *Madonna* attributed to Maratta, a *Pietà* by Massimo Stanzione, a *Jacob Wrestling with the Angel* by Solimena, and two supposed paintings by Ribera, *Archimedes* and *Diogenes.*[82]

PAINTINGS REAL AND FAKE

Clearly all the Italian Baroque paintings that came into the United States in the nineteenth century could not have been authentic, and already in 1827, in a speech at Columbia College, the painter Samuel F.B. Morse, who was himself on occasion inspired by Italian Baroque models, warned against "the propensity for collecting Old Pictures," since most Americans could not distinguish between forgeries and real masterpieces.[83] This situation was addressed later in an editorial of 1855 in the American art journal *The Crayon,* which lamented:

> There is probably no country in the world where the want of critical taste in pictures is accompanied to such an extent by credulity as to their worth and disposition to buy them. A gentleman who could not be taken in by a horse-jockey, and who would not even buy a pig in a poke, will yet suffer himself to be cheated by a picture-vendor, and, what is more, will exhibit the fraud with complacency as an evidence of his singular good fortune. Probably there are in the country...ten thousand works of the old masters, Raphaels, Murillos, Claudes, Salvators, Titians, Correggios, or what not, every one of whose possessors procured that wonderful picture, by a lucky chance, from somebody who had bought it without its origin being known, and had been compelled to smuggle it out of Italy or Spain in order to get off with his prize. In this way it is safe to affirm that there is not another land under the sun which contains so many worthless, smoky, and dirty old daubs as this, nor another that offers so good a market to the busy manufacturers of such impostures. The supplying of the United States with pictures by the old masters is accordingly, an important branch of European industry.[84]

An even more damning indictment of American credulity, with special regard to a favorite Baroque master, is given in the same magazine by the painter Rembrandt Peale. One of a group of paintings that a collector gave him to clean was

> so much cracked, the paint falling off in scales, that I retained it to experiment with, and succeeded in reattaching the scales, but had to *repaint* the entire neck and other parts. It was a Madonna, and was stolen from me. A New York collector of Oil Paintings visited me, some time after, with three pictures which he found in our neighborhood. I instantly recognized one of them as my Madonna, and told him its history, of which he took no heed. Some years after, he surprised me by showing me the same picture, further repaired, elegantly framed, with a plate glass over it, to protect from injury, "the only authentic and uninjured Guido in the country." I did not care to mortify him by renewing my claims, at least to the neck, which he pronounced the most beautiful of Guido's work. Such things are well known to artists, who now rejoice that a better taste prevails, not only in England but America, in the encouragement of living talent, and more authentic Guido.[85]

THE INFLUENCE OF ITALIAN BAROQUE ART ON AMERICAN PAINTING AND LITERATURE

That Rembrandt Peale should have been able to simulate a Guido Reni is not surprising, for he had copied Italian works and even established a short-lived Italian gallery of copies in 1831.[86] During his trip to Italy in 1829-30, he had been especially impressed by the Baroque masters, recording that in the Vatican the "best known" works were the *Transfiguration* by Raphael and the *Communion of St. Jerome* by Domenichino, "but the most excellent is the *St. Petronilla* by Guercino."[87] He also paid special attention to the famous works of Guido Reni in Rome, noting of his *Aurora* and then his *St. Michael Subduing Satan:*

> Morghen's [*sic*] excellent engraving gives almost a perfect idea of it; for though the color of many parts is good, yet the effect of the whole, from injudicious repairs, is harsh and dissonant. The limbs are heavy, and the hands lifeless—but the left hand figure possesses a beauty of face that is not rendered in the engraving.
>
> In the Church of the Capuchins is the celebrated picture by Guido, representing *St. Michael subduing Satan,* which was uncovered for my inspection by

an obliging monk of the barefoot fraternity....The coloring of the head and shadowy neck, and the celestial tranquillity of the face, simply regarded as beautiful objects, are worthy of much praise; but I cannot agree with those enthusiastic admirers who commend it for wanting an expression suitable to the action, and applaud that action, because it is deficient in the energy of a mortal form, since the painter chose to represent nothing but a mortal form. Neither is it an excellence in the *Demon* that he makes no signs of resistance. Energy of expression was not the talent of Guido. Still, however, we must return to the head and neck, and admire the softness of its coloring and the mild but steady look of the angel.[88]

Washington Allston was another American painter smitten with the Italian Baroque, especially, according to Dunlap, a painting by Ludovico Carracci.[89] He was also much impressed by the "awe inspiring" landscapes of Salvator Rosa.[90] The typical nineteenth-century approach to Rosa was that of the German writer Dr. Waagen, whose views were actually published in *The Crayon:* "Although compared with Claude and Gaspard Poussin, he [Rosa] takes but a third place, still his originality is decided, and in some respects great. Himself of a passionate and wild temperament, his Art partakes of the same character. He delights in all that is lonely and fearful in nature. . . . "[91] It is no wonder that the early collector Robert Gilmor, Jr. encouraged Thomas Cole to study Rosa.[92]

Just as the picturesque and romantic nature of Rosa's landscapes struck a responsive chord with American painters and collectors, so too did they appeal to leading American writers of this period who visited Italy. James Fenimore Cooper described American scenery that "Rosa would have delighted to draw."[93] However, it was the sentimental and even pietistic quality of Baroque pictures as well as their high finish that most American writers admired. In this they followed the taste of the English colony of writers and poets in Italy, typical of whom were "Robert Browning and his illustrious wife," who, according to Henry James, "burnt incense to Domenichino."[94] Browning also wrote a poem in praise of a painting by Guercino, and Shelley composed the verse drama that immortalized the legend of Guido Reni's supposed Beatrice Cenci.[95] Even Lord Byron could write in a letter, "of painting I know nothing, but I like a Guercino."[96]

No American was more enthralled with Italian Baroque art than Nathaniel Hawthorne, who when in Rome noted in his journal of 1858 the powerful impact of Domenichino's *St. Sebastian* and Reni's *Beatrice Cenci.* Of the latter he observed:

> I might as well not try to say anything; for its spell is indefinable, and the painter has wrought it in a way more like magic than anything else....It is the most profoundly wrought picture in the world; no artist did it, nor could do it again. Guido may have held the brush, but he painted better than he knew.[97]

He then proceeded to the Rospigliosi palace and saw Guido's *Aurora,* of which he wrote, "The picture is as fresh and brilliant as if he had painted it with the morning sunshine which it represents. It could not be more lustrous in its hues, if he had given it the last touch an hour ago." The same painter's *St. Michael* in St. Peter's he found "surely one of the most beautiful things in the world, one of the human conceptions that are imbued most deeply with the celestial."[98]

The strong impression of the *St. Michael* on Hawthorne was transformed by his creative genius into an appropriate leitmotif for his novel *The Marble Faun* of 1859, but it was actually Guercino's *St. Petronilla* altarpiece that precipitated one of the book's most profound moments.[99]

THE TASTE FOR BAROQUE AT MID-CENTURY

The 1840s and 1850s may have been the apogee of the American taste for the grandiose and sentimental Baroque, and this fashion lingered on in conservative upper-class circles for quite some time. For those later writers who recreated the period, this taste played a notable role. Henry James, for example, has one of his most fatuous female characters say "We have a Sassoferrato, you know, from which we're inseparable—we travel with our picture and our poodle."[100] It was this very taste that in part formed the crux of Edith Wharton's *False Dawn,* her novella of Old New York set in the 1840s, in which the hero Lewis Raycie is requested to go to Europe by his father to form a proper collection: "Yes, my dear Lewis, I

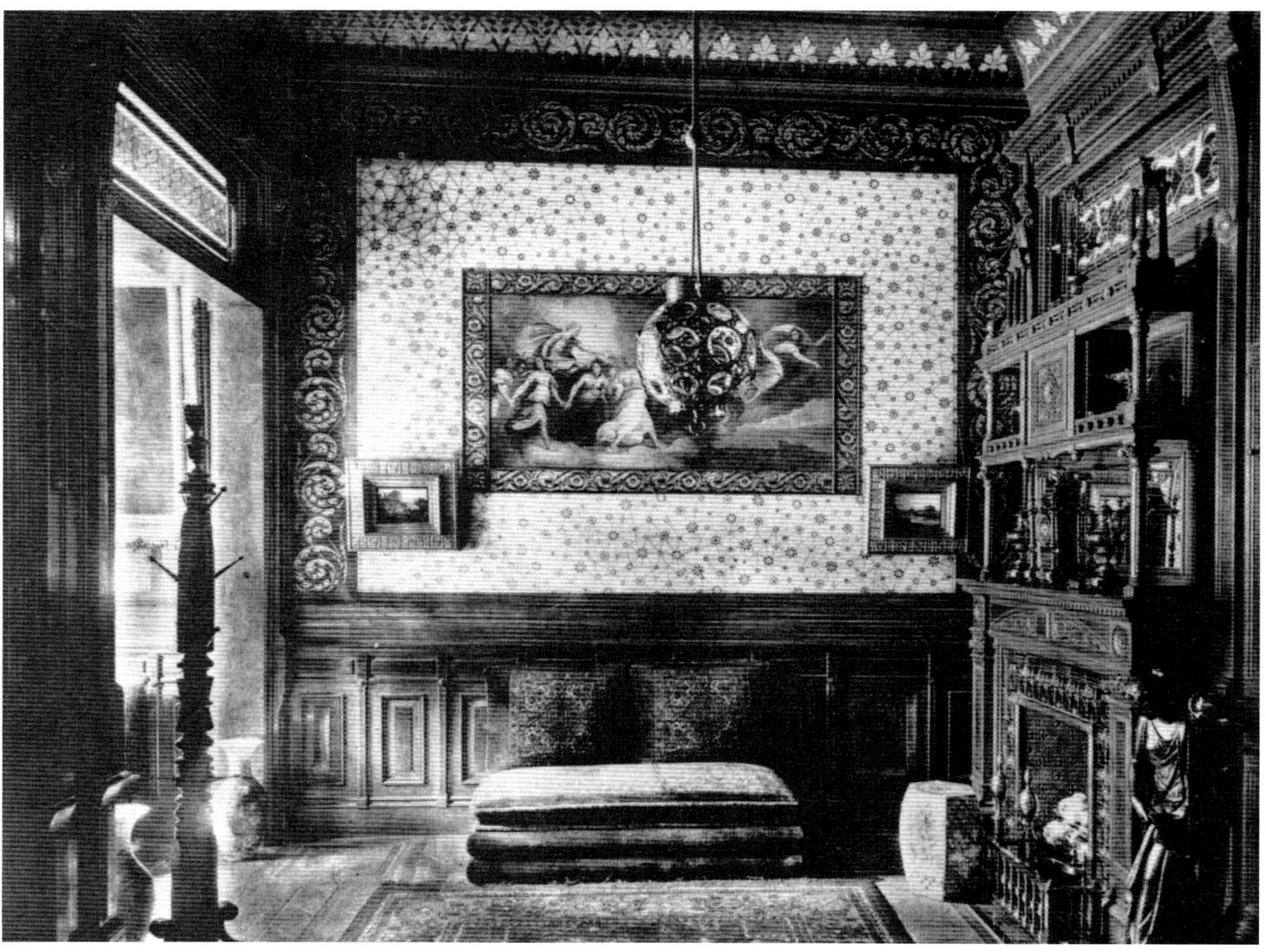

FIGURE 8

The J.H. Schoenberger Home at 43 West 57th Street, New York City, c. 1883. Reproduced from *Artistic Houses,* New York, 1883.

wish to create a gallery, a gallery of Heirlooms. Your mother participates in this ambition—she desires to see on our wall a few original specimens of the Italian genius. Raphael, I fear, we can hardly aspire to; but a Domenichino, an Albano, a Carlo Dolci, a Guercino, a Carlo Maratta—one or two of Salvator Rosa's noble landscapes...." The young man, however, modeled upon the eccentric and innovative American collectors James Jackson Jarves and Thomas Jefferson Bryan, becomes a disciple of Ruskin, buying early Italian gold ground paintings, so that he "forgot Sassoferrato, Guido Reni, Carlo Dolci, Lo Spagnoletto, the Carracci, and even the Transfiguration of Raphael. . . . He could remember quite distinctly the day when he had given up even Beatrice Cenci."[101]

This anti-Baroque sentiment was ahead of its time, for Reni's *Cenci,* as Bernard Berenson was to observe, had in the nineteenth century its own "cult."[102] Even the crusty Herman Melville during his trip to Italy in 1857 had been impressed by it, writing in his terse *Journal,* "Expression of suffering about the mouth—(appealing look of innocence) not caught in any copy or engraving."[103] Washington Irving also "shared the fashionable taste" for the Bolognese painters Carracci, Domenichino, and especially for Guido Reni's *Aurora.*[104]

The significance for the age of this last work is captured in the writings of the New York traveler W.M. Gillespie, for whom Guido's *Aurora* is "the masterpiece of its painter." He wrote of this and the "rival Aurora" of Guercino in the Villa Ludovisi: "whether Guercino's or Guido's Aurora is to be preferred, has been much debated, and will depend on individual taste. Guido's is the sweeter, and Guercino's the stronger; the former has more beauty and the latter more spirit."[105]

Reni's *Aurora* and others of this master's output kept what Hawthorne had tellingly designated "the Guido machine"[106] producing copies for many years. The writer and collector James Jackson Jarves observed this "rage for copies" in Florence in the 1850s and noted that popular taste centered on a comparatively few works, including "Sassoferrato's blue-mantle Madonna and Carlo Dolci's poetry and devotion."[107] Grand Victorian parlors or libraries typically had to have such a work, so that copies of Reni's *Aurora* can still be seen today in the Gibson House of Boston; the Athenaeum in St. Johnsbury, Vermont; the gallery of the collector Matthias Arnot in Elmira, New York;[108] at Amherst College in a gift of about 1890;[109] and recorded in a wonderful period photograph of Mr. J.H. Schoenberger's home in New York at 43 West 57th Street (Fig. 8) .[110] In print form, Reni's pious but sexy *Magdalen* would make her way across the American heartland (Fig. 9) .[111]

MID-NINETEENTH-CENTURY COLLECTORS

The American passion for acquiring works of art abroad at this time was documented by the well-known writer William Cullen Bryant, who wrote from Rome:

> Men who would never have thought of buying a picture or statue at home are infected by the contagion of the place the moment they arrive. No talk of money market here; no discussion of any public measure; no conversation respecting new enterprises, and the ebb and flow of trade; no price current except of marble and canvas; all the talk is of art and artists. The rich man who, at home, is contented with mirrors and rosewood, is here initiated into a new set of ideas, gets a taste, and orders a bust, a little statue of Eve, a Ruth, or a Rebecca, and half a dozen pictures for his luxurious rooms in the United States.[112]

Some Americans bought more than just a few paintings. Large-scale collections of European paintings continued to be formed around the country, and the Italian Baroque masters figured prominently among them. One of the earliest galleries that had many Italian paintings was that of Thomas Jefferson Bryan (1800-1870). He had been born in Philadelphia

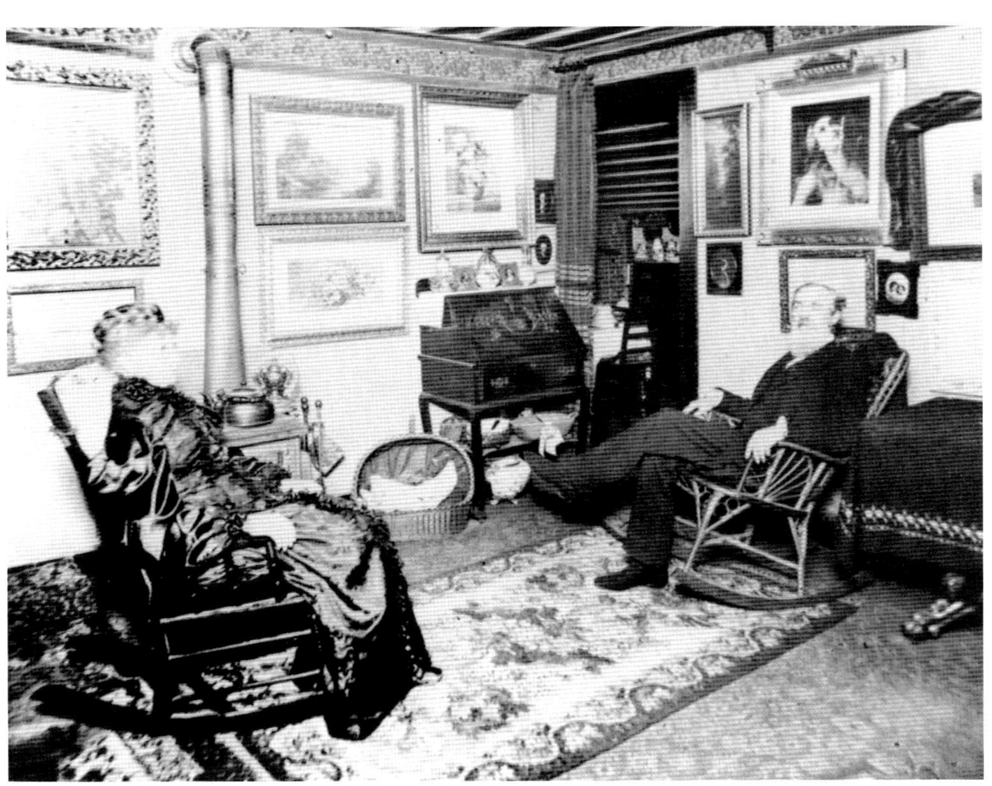

FIGURE 9

The Foote Family Home in Boise, Idaho Territory, 1880-90. A print of Guido Reni's *Magdalen* is seen on the right wall. Reproduced from W. Seale, *The Tasteful Interlude: American Interiors through the Camera's Eye, 1860-1917,* New York, 1975.

and studied briefly at Harvard before going to Paris where he began acquiring paintings, spending $100,000 by his return twenty years later in 1853. After his collection was rejected by his native city, he moved to New York, and the following year opened the "Bryan Gallery of Christian Art" in a house on the corner of Broadway and 13th Street. In April of 1864 he offered the collection to the New York Historical Society; his 381 paintings were installed there shortly thereafter and presented to the Society in 1867. He continued adding to these until his death in 1870 when he was returning from Europe with sixty more works.[113] In the collection's first catalogue Richard Grant White described Bryan's goal as "to collect a gallery which should not only give pleasure to casual visitants but afford efficient aid to the student of the history of Art."[114] Although primarily paintings of the Dutch school were included, there were several of the Italian Baroque. These included two so-called Annibale Carraccis, a Domenichino *St. Paul Borne to Heaven,* a Reni *Christ Crowned with Thorns* ("if not the original, it is the best copy ever seen by the donor"), a school of Reni *Magdalen in a Trance,* four by the school of Carlo Dolci, an Artemisia Gentileschi *Christ Disputing with the Doctors,* Sassoferrato *Virgin and Child,* Rosa *Landscape,* and three Rosa school works.[115] Sadly, in more recent times, most of these have been sold by the New York Historical Society.[116]

In Philadelphia Dr. Isaac Lea (1792-1886), who in 1829 had acquired some European paintings locally, had shipped from Europe 192 pictures in 1852, purchased mainly in Italy on the advice of the painter Gagliardi. These were later distributed among his descendants in Philadelphia. Among those that have been located are a *Triumph of David* (once given to Matteo Rosselli but now identified as Jacopo Vignali, which is in the Bob Jones University Collection; cat. no. 29), an Allori *Head of a Youth,* and a large school of Rosa *Harbor Scene.* Other works from the Lea collection given to the Philadelphia Museum of Art by his descendants are a Giovanni Biliverti *St. Catherine of Alexandria,* a Strozzi *Female Saint,* and several anonymous seventeenth-century Italian pictures.[117]

A Mr. Isaac Fenno of Boston, in Rome in 1869, purchased from Leopoldo Fabri a pair of paintings attributed to Pietro Paolo Bonzi and a supposed Lanfranco. These works were donated to the Worcester Art Museum by his descendants in 1935.[118]

THE ANTI-BAROQUE SENTIMENT

At the very time that Reni, Rosa, Guercino, and their contemporaries were being enthroned as the exemplars of taste and quality, a contrary movement that would have enormous ramifications was slowly growing first in England and then in America. As W.G. Constable succinctly put it, "John Ruskin and Charles Eliot Norton had decided that all Italian art after Michelangelo was decadent."[119]

Ruskin, a brilliant writer and critic who championed J.M.W. Turner, was part of the English Pre-Raphaelite movement that regarded the early Italian painters as the greatest masters both for their style and their religious humility. Ruskin actually devoted very little of his writing to the artists he disliked, but his taste was already formed on a visit to Italy in 1845 when he wrote to his parents: "I have pretty well now arranged my scale of painters," and the lowest group that he labeled "the School of Errors and Vices" included the Carracci, Guido, Dolci, Caravaggio and "my usual group of landscapists," by which he meant Rosa, among others.[120] In America, where Ruskin's stance reinforced a widespread native prejudice against Catholic subjects, one was able to read telling portions of his *Stones of Venice* in the art journal sympathetic to the Pre-Raphaelite movement, *The Crayon.* A section printed in 1855 stated:

> I believe that the four painters who have had, and still have, the most influence, such as it is, on the ordinary Protestant Christian mind, are Carlo Dolci, Guercino, Benjamin West, and John Martin. Raphael, much as he is talked about, is, I believe, in very fact, rarely looked at by religious people; much less his master, or any of the truly great religious men of old. But a smooth Magdalen of Carlo Dolci, with a tear on each cheek, or a Guercino Christ or St. John rarely fails of being verily, often deeply, felt for the time.[121]

The leading American collector and writer inspired by Ruskin's taste was James Jackson Jarves (1818-1888) of Boston. In 1856, following his first extended stay in Italy, he judged the deficiencies of various artists: "we all wish that Guido had found smaller heads and less expansive throats for his models—that Carlo Dolci had put less jewelry and finish upon his holy women."[122] Of Guido he relates the incredible story that "the fierce painter in completing his 'Crucifixion' eager to catch and transfer to his canvas the expression of a dying agony, snatched a knife and stabbed in the side his helpless model bound to a cross to represent the dying saviour. The poor wretch was murdered, but Guido caught the parting breath, completed his picture that night and fled."[123] In his more serious study *Art Hints,* Jarves concentrated on interpretation and described "the School of the Carracci as more remarkable for technical excellence than for originality"; Rosa he thought "in a half-robber, half-artist like manner, vigorously gave vent to his new passion in a medley of coarseness and refinement, truth and falsity, that alternately perplexes and pleases"; and Caravaggio was "perhaps a solitary instance among Italian artists of repute who has condescended to recognize the vagrant humors and families of everyday humanity; but with so much coarseness that we can well forgive the rarity of his pictures."[124] Writing in his later *Art-Idea* of 1864, Jarves calls Domenichino's *St. Jerome* in the Vatican "a violation of artistic rule, instigated by the ascetic side of religion...his choice of subject is as faulty in regard to the canon of high art as his treatment of it is irreconcilable to aesthetic taste and a proper understanding of Christian art."[125] Nevertheless, in order to make his extensive collection of early Italian pictures palatable to American taste, Jarves was willing to add works said to be by Domenichino and Reni;[126] still no institution or individual in New York or Boston would make an effort to acquire it, and the paintings finally went to Yale University to pay off a loan Jarves had received from that school.[127]

Most significant for the course of American taste for the Italian Baroque was Jarves's chance meeting with Charles Eliot Norton on shipboard. It was he who provided the young scholar of Italian literature from Boston with an introduction to Ruskin. Norton became the leading American disciple of Ruskin; his appointment in 1874 to Lecturer on the History of Fine Arts as Connected with Literature at Harvard University, a position he held until his retirement in 1897, enabled him to influence several generations of scholars and collectors, including Bernard Berenson and Isabella Stewart Gardner.[128] Already in 1860, he wrote in his travel notes a critique of the, until then, highly regarded book on Italy by John Bell.[129] Whereas that author interpreted Domenichino's *Martyrdom of St. Agnes* in Bologna as "irradiated by an expression of rapt holiness and heavenly resignation infinitely touching," Norton found instead that the expression was one of "coarse materialism, disgusting exaggeration, and the utter want of elevation or truth of expression," and that "this picture is one of the worst of the Bolognese School." For him, "no works of Art were ever created with a purer spirit, with a sweeter piety than those of Fra Angelico."[130]

The impact of Norton and his Ruskinian approach began gradually to affect attitudes toward seventeenth-century art. Already in the 1870s, the former Baroque favorites began to be displaced. The Boston writer Thomas G. Appleton, in a guide to the Museum of Fine Arts, spoke of the "fading academic school of Bologna,"[131] and Henry James now found that, despite his talent, Domenichino's "imagination was cold."[132]

COLLECTING AGAINST FASHION ACROSS AMERICA

It naturally took some time for Ruskin's and Norton's academic notions to filter down to the general public, and Baroque paintings still continued to be sold in good numbers at auction.[133] Indeed, not all art lovers agreed with the judgments of the new critics. A charming small volume on Reni by M.F. Sweetser published in Boston in 1878 noted in its preface that, "at the present day Guido is out of fashion and men decry his works as sentimental and insipid. . . . A century ago the Bolognese artists were held in the foremost rank, and the Pre-Raphaelites were almost unheard of; and a century hence a new school of criticism may elevate new idols. In view of the instability of the criterions of excellence, I have felt at liberty to follow the hearty admiration of Malvasia [the seventeenth-century biographer of Reni and other artists] rather than the present vogue and the opinions of the London critics."[134]

Like-minded independent collectors across America were not bound by Ruskin's prejudices and continued to pursue Baroque works during the late nineteenth and early twentieth centuries. In Boston itself, Mrs. D.N. Spooner is recorded to have had in her dining room "an original Domenichino."[135] The distinguished Bostonian collector Quincy Adams Shaw, best known for his Millets and Renaissance sculpture, also possessed two purported Salvator Rosa paintings that were lent to the Museum of Fine Arts in 1889.[136]

In the New York area a collector who had begun acquiring the now desirable Italian primitive paintings as early as 1881 was Samuel Longstreth Parrish. Following his trip to Italy in 1896, he determined to build a museum for his collection in Southampton, New York. To this he added one sentimental Baroque painting purchased at the Barlow sale of 1890, a *Virgin Holding a Crucifix* by Carlo Dolci, which is still in the museum that bears his name.[137]

In Detroit the journalist James E. Scripps, a founder of the Detroit Institute of Arts, purchased between 1887 and 1888 seventy-two diverse paintings, many with alleged noble provenances, for the "elevated amusement of the people and as a means for an education in art." He gave them to the Institute in 1889, and his wife added fifteen more in 1909 after his death. Among these works were a Sassoferrato *Madonna and Child* (from the Gillott collection that had sold in London in 1872), a Reni *Head of Christ,* and others attributed to Albani, Annibale Carracci, Dolci, Giordano, Guercino, Maratta, and Sacchi.[138]

The painting collection formed by Mr. and Mrs. W.P. Wilstach of Philadelphia was first shown in Memorial Hall during the Centennial Exposition of 1876. It was willed to the city in 1890 along with an endowment fund to be managed by Samuel Thompson until 1909, and then by another distinguished Philadelphia collector, John G. Johnson.[139] The first catalogue of the collection published in 1893 consisted mainly of nineteenth-century works, but by 1922 a number of Baroque paintings had been added. These included a Giacinto Brandi *St. Cecilia* (now in the Bob Jones University Collection as by Giovanni Battista Beinaschi; cat. no. 24), Ribera *St. Sebastian* (now given to Giordano), Giordano *Archimedes,* and Rosa *Battle Scene,* as well as several works attributed to Reni, Maratta, Dolci, Cagnacci, and Ludovico Carracci.[140] With the exception of the two Giordanos, a Magnasco, and the Rosa, all were sold in 1954.[141]

Farther afield, an active collector in the city of Duluth, Minnesota, was George P. Tweed (1871-1946). Not bound to any one school of art, he purchased several Italian Baroque works over the course of his life. In 1918 he acquired, probably from a New York dealer, a *Scourging of St. Blaise* by a follower of Caravaggio. Other works added were a Sebastiano Ricci *Ecstasy of St. Francis,* a Solimena *Death of St. Joseph,* and in the style of Rosa, a work entitled *Travelers Ambushed.* All of these were given by Tweed's widow Alice to the University of Minnesota in the 1950s and 1960s.[142]

Another collection formed in the early part of the century was that of Thomas B. Walker (1840-1928) of Minneapolis, who established a public gallery there that bore his name. This too consisted of paintings from a variety of schools, including, of the Baroque, two by Carlo Dolci, a *Christ Driving out the Moneychangers* and a *Madonna,* in addition to Reni's *Last Hours of Cleopatra* (formerly in the collection of the Miles Family at Leigh Court), a Domenichino *St. Cecilia,* and a Schedoni *Bacchus and Ariadne.* As the Walker was gradually transformed later into a museum of contemporary art, all these works were sold.[143]

On the West Coast the lawyer E.B. Crocker (1818-1875), born in the state of New York and trained in Indiana, arrived in Sacramento in 1852. He became both a founder of the Republican party and a successful railroad man. He first decorated his home with works by California artists, but in 1870, with a new art gallery to fill, he went to Europe, and in Dresden purchased a private collection of "Old Masters." He eventually assembled seven hundred paintings, which became the core of the Crocker Art Museum, the first of its kind in the West, founded by his widow in 1885.[144] As W.G. Constable kindly put it, "though a monument to enlightened public spirit, this collection scarcely measured up to its maker's intentions. Many of the paintings bear great names...but very few of the attributions would survive modern critical examination."[145] There are still to be seen there, however, works by Barocci, the Strozzi school (bought as Murillo), school of Cagnacci, Solimena, Luca Giordano school, Paolo de Matteis, and Ludovico Mazzanti.[146]

MUSEUM ACTIVITY IN BOSTON, NEW YORK, BALTIMORE, AND ELSEWHERE

Two of America's most important art museums—the Museum of Fine Arts in Boston and the Metropolitan Museum of Art in New York—were both founded in 1870. Naturally, among the first works of art they received and acquired were examples of the then still popular Italian Baroque school.

In Boston the paintings accumulated by the Athenaeum—two Luca Giordanos, *The Golden Age* and

Marsyas (Fig. 3), Guercino's *Moses,* Cignani's *Hagar and Ishmael* (Fig. 4), and the Maratta (now Chiari) *Christ and the Woman of Samaria* (Fig. 5)—were all deposited for a time at the new Museum of Fine Arts.[147] Like the Athenaeum, the museum continued during its first years to host loan and traveling exhibitions. The first of these drew from the collection of the Duke de Montpensier, which, reflecting the taste of his father Louis Philippe, was primarily Spanish, but did, however, include two landscapes by Rosa. Among other loans to this exhibition was an Annibale Carracci *Holy Family* from Mr. George Walker of Springfield.[148] In subsequent loan shows, there were in 1877 so-called Renis lent by Miss Greenough, Miss J.M. Warren, and Edward T. Potter of Newport; paintings attributed to Guercino and Sassoferrato lent by Francis Brooks of West Medford in 1878; and in 1890 a *Madonna and Child* by Sassoferrato, a *St. Barbara* and an *Ecce Homo* by Guercino, and a *Landscape with Fishermen* by Rosa, also from Mr. Brooks.[149]

The first major bequest to the institution was the rather miscellaneous collection of Senator Charles Sumner in 1874. It included ninety-three paintings of which there were a so-called Caravaggio *Itinerant Musicians* (later identified as by a follower of Bernard Keil) and a Guercino *Magdalen* (subsequently called simply Bolognese), both now deaccessioned.[150] One of the first donated paintings came from the Boston museum's president Martin Brimmer in 1883, an *Entombment* by a rare Bolognese master, Lucio Massari, which had just been sold in the auction of the Toscanelli collection in Florence.[151] A large and important picture by Luca Giordano, *The Institution of the Eucharist* (Fig. 10) was presented to the museum in 1882 by Mrs. Louis Thies, widow of a Harvard professor, who had obtained the work from a Bohemian baron in the late 1840s.[152] In 1890 a school of Sassoferrato *Madonna and Child* came as the bequest of Mrs. Henry Edwards, and in 1894 the Turner-Sargent bequest brought the museum an *Adoration of the Shepherds* then given to Ludovico Carracci but now identified as by Benedetto II Gennari, a supposed Ribera *Judith with the Head of Holofernes* now rightly attributed to Stanzione, and a *Head of a Sibyl* by Elisabetta Sirani.

FIGURE 10

LUCA GIORDANO, *The Institution of the Eucharist,* Museum of Fine Arts, Boston. Photograph courtesy of the Museum of Fine Arts, Boston.

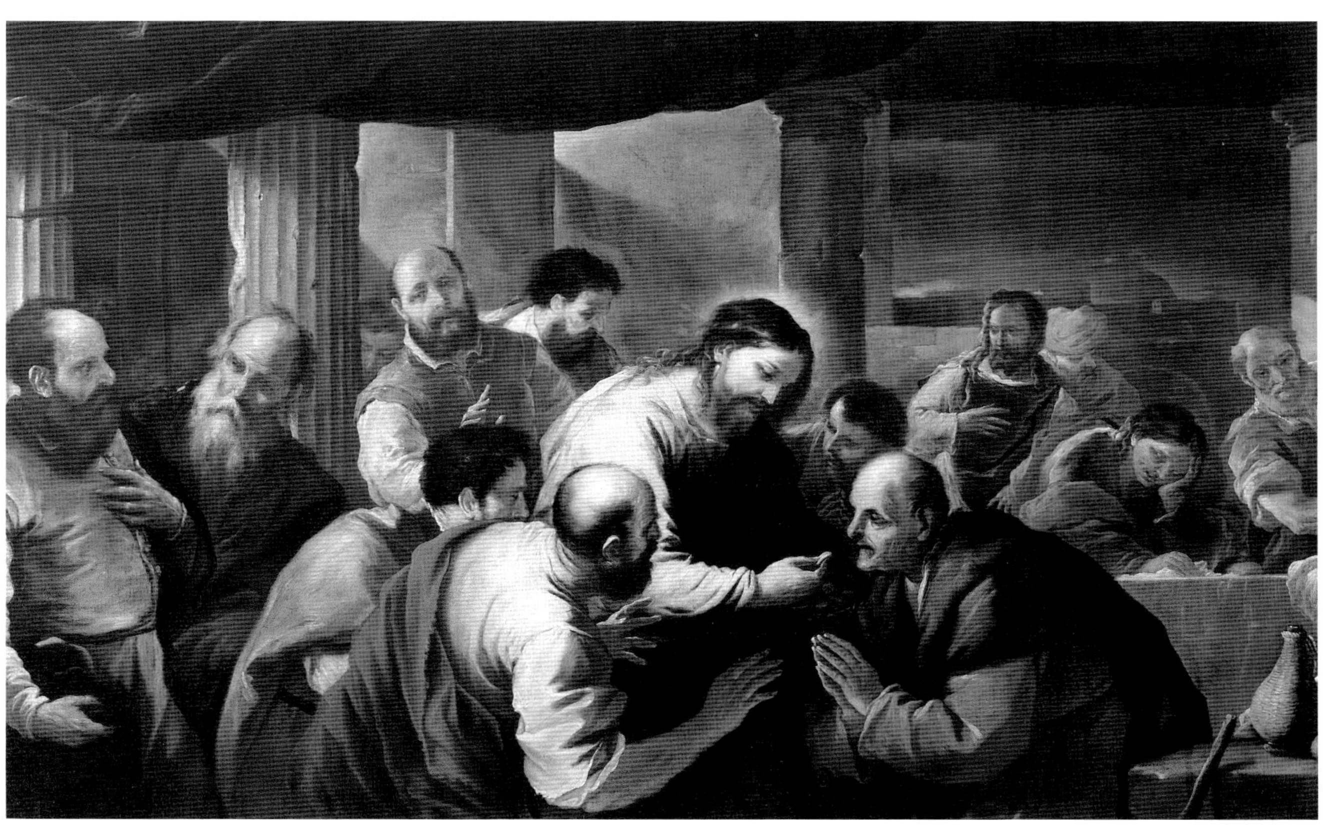

FIGURE 11

FRANCESCO SOLIMENA, *Birth of the Virgin,* The Metropolitan Museum of Art, New York, Rogers Fund, 1906, (07.66). Photograph courtesy of The Metropolitan Museum of Art.

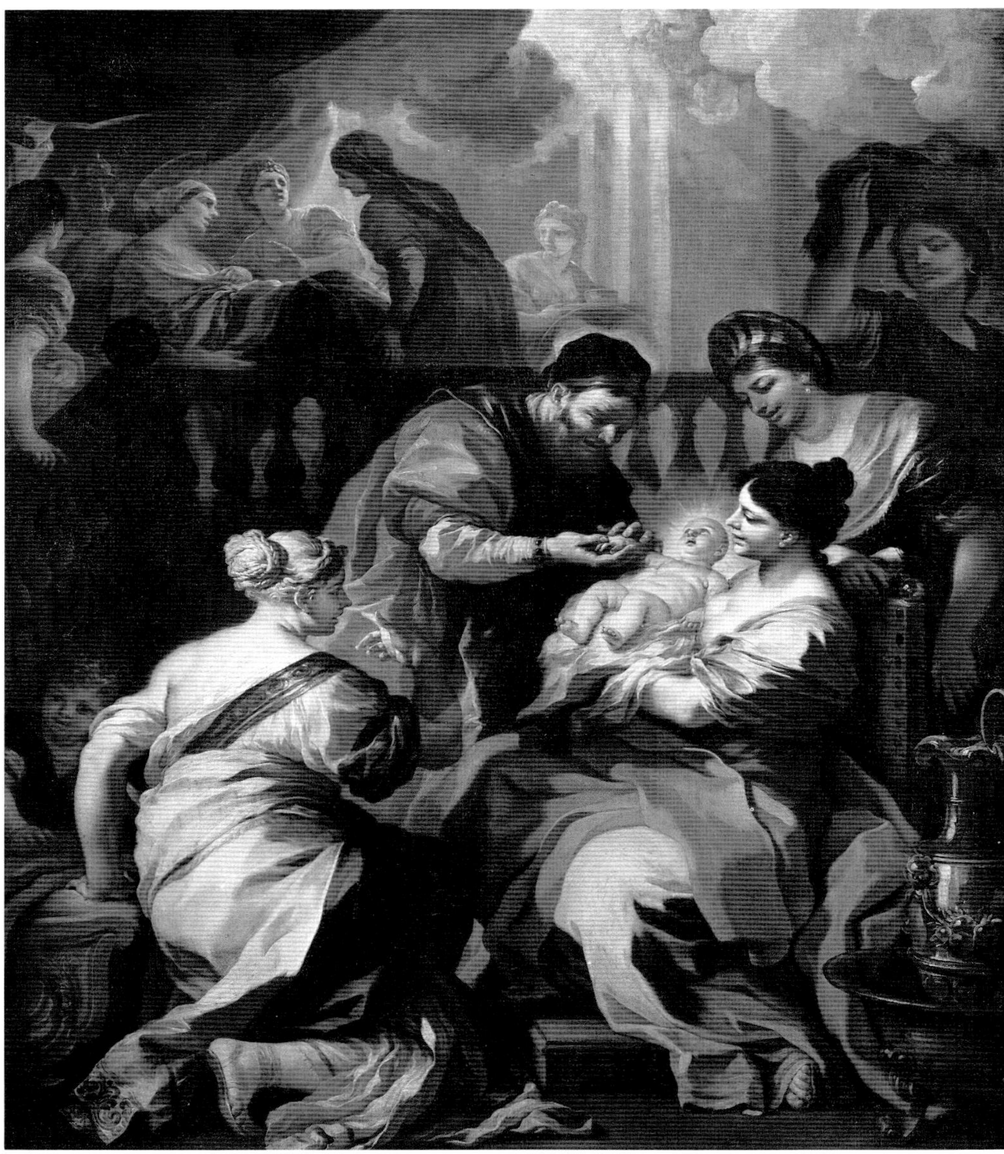

Another bequest in 1910 added a purported Albani *Europa and the Bull,* which was recently sold.[153] One of the museum's greatest benefactors was the Harvard professor, artist, and writer, Denman Ross, who in 1917 presented a supposed Tiberio Tinelli *Portrait of Lorenzo Ghiradello, Chancellor of Bergamo,* which is now attributed to Carlo Ceresa. Later he gave as a Poussin a lovely Andrea de Leone, as well as a pair of paintings depicting *Hunters* and *Wrestlers* that he believed to be Fragonards—these were subsequently attributed to Mola, and are now called Italian seventeenth century.[154]

At the Metropolitan Museum of Art in New York, the first group of paintings were purchased in Europe during the summer of 1870 and became the property of the museum in March 1871. According to the catalogue published the next year, one hundred were bought in Brussels and among these were four attributed to Francesco Albani and two still lifes later attributed to Giovan Battista Ruoppolo and an unidentified Neapolitan artist. Another nearly sixty were acquired in Paris and included a Sassoferrato *Holy Virgin* "from the famous Barca collection and one of the most perfect of the master" and, by the Neapolitan painter Giuseppe Recco, *A Thief.* Of supplemental gifts received by the museum, there was a Francesco Furini *Birth of Cyrus* presented by J.J.A. Bristed.[155] Later gifts in the nineteenth century were a Volterrano *Angel and Child* from Cornelius Vanderbilt in 1880, a Maratta *Portrait of Pope Clement IX* from Archer M. Huntington in 1891, and a Ricci *Esther Before Ahasuerus* from Henry G. Marquand in 1894. More serious acquisitions undertaken in 1906 with the Rogers Fund brought a Barocci *Holy Family,* a

Giordano *Birth of the Virgin* (later attributed to Solimena; Fig. 11) in 1906, and in 1908 a Castiglione *Prodigal Son* (sold 1956; now in the collection of David Rust, Washington, D.C.). A supposed Ribera *Lucretia* was purchased in 1912.[156] The Metropolitan Museum of Art also held annual exhibitions of works lent by private collectors in the 1870s; the most intriguing Baroque examples are those by Rosa from the painter Frederick Edwin Church.[157]

The Art Institute of Chicago was incorporated in 1879, and when its first paintings catalogue was published in 1914, it included only two Italian pictures, of which one was a Sassoferrato *Virgin* given in 1910.[158]

Already opened in the 1880s on a limited basis to the public was the Walters Art Gallery in Baltimore. It was the creation of the railroad man William T. Walters, whose taste was primarily for the traditional nineteenth-century French school. His son Henry, however, greatly expanded the collection, especially in the area of Italian paintings. He had acquired a few individual works from unknown sources such as a Cignani (now Crespi), an Alessandro Turchi, and a Giordano (then thought to be by Goltzius), but then in 1902 Mr. Walters made one of the most significant single purchases in American collecting history when he obtained in Rome the entire contents of the palace belonging to the papal official Don Marcello Massarenti. This included over one thousand paintings.[159] The catalogue of the Walters collection published in 1919 listed works from the Massarenti palace attributed to Scarsellino, Guercino, Reni, as well as a supposed Caravaggio of the *Magdalen*.[160] All of these turned out to be erroneous attributions or copies, but, as the distinguished 1976 catalogue by Federico Zeri recognized, lurking under other names were a remarkable number of lesser-known masters, especially of the later seventeenth and early eighteenth centuries. In addition to two paintings by Fetti, a pair of Sassoferratos, two by Giacomo Recco, and a pair of Nicola Malinconico still lifes, there were works by Angelo Caroselli, Agostino Tassi, Chiari, Furini, Viviano Codazzi, Gennari, a large Strozzi portrait, and perhaps most beautiful of all, a Strozzi *Adoration of the Shepherds*, originally thought to be by Murillo. The "Caravaggio" was now identified as by Spadarino.[161]

In the nation's capital, the Corcoran Gallery of Art had by 1889 acquired only two Baroque works, a *Madonna* by Carlo Dolci, supposedly brought by Napoleon to France from the Pitti palace, and a *Portrait of Anne of Austria* "said to be by Guido."[162] Also in Washington in the early part of this century, as part of the Smithsonian Institution, was the small National Gallery of Art. To it in 1919 a local collector, Ralph Cross Johnson, gave a group of twenty-four paintings. Among these was one formerly in the Earl of Dudley's collection that Johnson had purchased from Agnew's of London in 1908 as a Titian *Portrait of a Cardinal*. So it remained identified for many years,[163] until Denis Mahon recognized it as Guercino's lost *Portrait of Pope Gregory XV*. The museum, whose name had been changed in 1937 to the National Collection of Fine Arts and was now specializing in American art, sold the Guercino to the J. Paul Getty Museum in 1987.[164]

Other American museums and institutions also began to add Baroque paintings in the first two decades of the twentieth century. In Pittsfield, Massachusetts, the Berkshire Museum was founded by Zenas Crane as an educational institution of natural history and art in 1903. To it he donated his own collection in 1914. This included a *St. Francis in Ecstasy* purchased from the Ehrich Gallery in New York as a Murillo but later correctly identified by Longhi as by Strozzi.[165] In 1904 the Philadelphia Museum of Art obtained both a Solimena and a work by Giambattista Langetti, and in 1917 the Saint Louis Art Museum received a Reni *Magdalen*. There was also activity at several colleges and universities. Oberlin College in Ohio, for example, was given a Langetti in 1904 and Vassar College in Poughkeepsie a Neapolitan school work of *Erminia and the Shepherds* from Charles Pratt in 1917. In Madison, Wisconsin, a group of paintings was purchased in Germany between 1911 and 1912 by a professor of political science, Paul Reinsch, but when he was appointed Ambassador to China by President Wilson, he sold these to a local business man, Charles Crane, who in turn gave them in 1913 to the University of Wisconsin. These paintings included a Carlo Bononi, Domenico Gargiulo, and school of Maratta.[166] Notre Dame University, it will be recalled, through the intermediary of its first museum director, Fr. Gerrer, acquired paintings from the Braschi collection of Rome, and those still there are Allegrini's *Judith*, Vignali's *The Fallen Tancred*, and Andrea de Leone's *Saint with a Possessed Man*.[167]

It is perhaps indicative of the still suspect quality of many of the old masters coming to America that the country's first great compilation of international painters' biographies, the *Cyclopedia of Painters and Paintings* by Champlin and Perkins of 1885-86, while including all the major Baroque masters, noted as examples to be found in America only three Rosas, all in the New York Historical Society.[168]

THE GREAT COLLECTORS DON'T GO BAROQUE

At the end of the nineteenth century and into the first two decades of the twentieth century, huge new fortunes were made in America, and many of the millionaires turned their wealth into art. As René Brimo's excellent survey of this subject has shown, these members of the industrial bourgeoisie, whom the author dubs "the Great Collectors," were imbued with a nostalgia for the grandeur of Europe and bought, on the one hand, the contemporary anecdotal genre, orientalist, and Barbizon school works, or on the other, the sanctified "Grand Masters" of the Dutch, Flemish, and English schools.[169] The collectors in the first category were well documented in the profusely illustrated large volumes by Edward Strahan (the pseudonym of Earl Shinn) and very few owned works of the Italian Baroque school. The only exceptions were Mrs. Marshall O. Roberts of New York, who is listed as having a Guido *Cleopatra,* and in Louisville, Kentucky, Mr. Jouett Menifee. A grandson of one of Gilbert Stuart's best pupils, his collection was said to consist of a Dolci *Ecce Homo,* Guercino *St. Sebastian,* and Solimena *St. Michael.*[170]

For the most part, however, when it came to collecting Italian art in this period the influence of Charles Eliot Norton as transmitted by Berenson and others of the international circle of scholarly advisors—among them Lionello Venturi, Langton Douglas, Wilhelm von Bode, Otto Siren, and Roger Fry, and key dealers like Joseph Duveen, Colnaghi, Knoedler, and Kleinberger—assured the deification of Renaissance artists such as Bellini and Raphael, along with the gold ground painters. These earlier masters totally unseated the Baroque ones, although the eighteenth-century Venetians—Guardi, Canaletto, and Tiepolo—remained popular for their decorative qualities. Berenson's prejudice toward the Baroque was made explicit when he wrote "our grandfathers were thrilled by Guido Reni's ecstatic visages, whose silly emptiness now rouses our laughter."[171] Then, in the face of the Baroque revival of the 1950s, Berenson published a book on Caravaggio, acknowledging that he was "a great artist," but nevertheless felt compelled to observe that this painter inspired "some aspects of the Baroque" that he still found "offensive," such as "the over big heads [and] the dubious expressions" that "may have encouraged the gigantism and bestiality which characterize no little of Italian Seicento painting." While observing that both Guercino and Reni were at first influenced by Caravaggio, Berenson added that "no direct immediate follower like Saraceni and the far from negligible Gentileschi, nor any other of his Italian imitators, not even the Neapolitans Battistello Caracciolo, Massimo Stanzione, Bernardo Cavallini [*sic*], Mattia Preti, have remained in the memory of men interested in the art of the past."[172]

Given this hostile attitude, it is not surprising that the collectors who relied on Berenson—Mrs. Gardner, Johnson, Widener, and others of their generation and the next, such as both the Tafts and Mary Emery in Cincinnati, J.P. Morgan, Yerkes, Elkins, Frick, Lehman, Bache, Blumenthal, and Mellon—should have had hardly any Baroque paintings. The same was true at the museum collection formed in Williamstown, Massachusetts, by Sterling Clark. The occasional exceptions are therefore almost shocking. In one case John G. Johnson acquired a Giordano unwittingly under the guise of Mazzolino, since it was deceptively painted in an older style.[173] The Ryerson collection in Chicago had a Magnasco, and a notable Sassoferrato *Madonna* belonged to John Hay.[174] In Tulsa, Mrs. Waite Phillips, whose estate Philbrook was to become the Philbrook Museum of Art, bought a Furini *Judith and Holofernes* in 1926 from a Florentine dealer,[175] and the collection of W. A. Clark that was given to the Corcoran in Washington and is known for its French and Dutch paintings had one supposed Annibale Carracci of a *Madonna and Child with St. John.*[176] Two great exceptions to this prejudiced taste among wealthy American private collectors were John P. Ringling and Samuel H. Kress, and there were also museum curators and directors throughout the country who continued acquiring and exhibiting Baroque paintings.

FOREIGN EXHIBITIONS AND

PUBLICATIONS

As with so much in American taste, the impetus to reverse the anti-Baroque sentiment came from abroad. Of far reaching significance was the great exhibition *Pittura italiana del Seicento e del Settecento* of 1922.[177] William Milliken, director of the Cleveland Museum of Art, wrote in 1929 that "the remarkable exhibition held in the Palazzo Pitti under the auspices of the Comune of Florence, between the months of April and October 1922, will always be a renewed starting point for a study of these centuries. In that exhibition thirteen hundred pictures were brought together, scattered canvases from churches and from public and private collections. Personalities imperfectly known before, were revealed clearly, and many almost forgotten figures emerged in full light."[178] Thirty years later, Wolfgang Stechow could still recall that it was this exhibition that "opened the eyes of scholars and the general public to the astonishing wealth, the unexpected artistic scope, and the captivating splendor of Italian baroque paintings" and that it inspired the visitor with a "sense of sweeping surprise and pleasure."[179]

Shortly afterward in England, Sacheverell Sitwell published in 1924 his brilliant book *Southern Baroque Art* with a chapter devoted to recreating the Naples of Solimena, and he could boldly declare, "Baroque art needs no defense now; the victory has been won a long time."[180] Perhaps as if to prove his point, the Burlington Fine Arts Club in London organized the very next year the *Exhibition of Italian Arts of the Seventeenth Century* with many distinguished lenders, including the king himself. What Osbert Sitwell's "Introduction to the Pictures" says of England and the impact of the Ruskinian revisionism of taste was equally true for America: "Guido Reni and Carlo Dolci, Caravaggio and Luca Giordano, and a whole host of brightly plumaged underlings were hurled from those pedestals which for over a century they had shared with Phidias and Praxiteles into the outer darkness of stables, cellars, and London mews. Extravagant abuse was, as ever to exceed extravagant admiration."[181] A small sign of the changing taste in America was a re-creation at the Philadelphia Museum of Art of the nineteenth-century collection of Dr. Isaac Lea. The museum's director Fiske Kimball wrote, in a vein that would become common whenever seventeenth-century Italian works were being shown, that the collection "represented a period which has recently been emerging from a cloud of disapproval, the Baroque."[182]

Another factor in this international movement to rehabilitate the Baroque was the new scholarship of the German school of art history. Most significant was the publication in 1915 of Heinrich Wölfflin's major study that was translated into English in 1932 as *Principles of Art History.* Wölfflin's great contribution was to provide a framework for looking at the history of art in which judgments on the relative merits, such as the supposed decadent nature of the Baroque, were no longer relevant. In his interpretation, the split between the Renaissance and subsequent eras was seen as a turn to a more painterly and less balanced style, but one still worthy of scholarly pursuit.[183] That is, in fact, what Italian seventeenth-century art got, first in 1924 with a study of the Roman Baroque by Hermann Voss and then in 1928 with the publication of the most detailed and insightful book on the subject yet written, Pevsner and Grautoff's *Barockmalerei in der romanischen Ländern,*[184] in which not only Caravaggio, the Carracci, Lanfranco, Strozzi, and Giordano were discussed and illustrated, but also, by city and region, such lesser-known figures as Gioacchino Assereto, Francesco del Cairo, Cantarini, Caracciolo, Cavallino, Giacomo Cavedone, Cigoli, Empoli, Domenico Fiasella, Francesco Maffei, Rutilio Manetti, Francesco Rustici, and Schedoni.

THE ECCENTRIC COLLECTORS

The impact of these foreign exhibitions and publications was to be an increase in scholarship, acquisitions, and exhibitions by American museums, but it seems unlikely that they had a direct influence on the one truly remarkable collector to appear at this time. Probably no single American collector before the 1950s accomplished more in the field of Italian Baroque paintings than John W. Ringling (1866-1936). The circus impresario's parents were from Bavaria, and it has been suggested that even though he was born in America, Ringling, who often traveled to Germany, had a desire to create a grandiose home like that of a Bavarian aristocrat.[185] It was, however, only in 1925 while in Naples with the sagacious German dealer Julius Böhler (whom he had met in New York through a business partner and art collector Albert Keller) on a trip to acquire furnishings for a hotel he was planning to build in Sarasota that Ringling first proposed the idea of forming an art collection. Since he went annually to Europe to audition new circus acts, Ringling had the opportunity to travel to Genoa and other Italian cities, where he probably became acquainted with Baroque paintings. In any case, as a man with theatrical flair who loved gaudy shows and elephants, he was not afraid to purchase large, bold, and very Catholic paintings, like the gigantic set of tapestry cartoons by Rubens and his studio that were acquired from the Duke of Westminster in 1925. With Böhler acting as Ringling's agent, other major paintings, primarily from noble English families, were purchased in rapid order over the next few years and many of these were of the Italian Baroque school. There were, for example, the Rosa *Allegory of Study* and the Sassoferrato *Virgin and Child* also from the Duke of Westminster that were acquired in 1926. Within six years, Ringling had assembled an extensive collection. Some of his other major Italian Baroque purchases were two paintings by Fiasella and the *Susannah and the Elders* by Agostino Carracci (now Sisto Badalocchio) from the Holford collection; Guercino's two-part *Annunciation* and Sirani's *Salome* from the Earl of Yarborough; an *Annunciation* by Gennari; two works by Pietro da Cortona, *Hagar and the Angel* and the *Emperor Augustus and the Sibyl;* Sassoferrato's remarkable *Portrait of Cardinal Rondini;* Vaccaro's *St. John the Baptist;* and several examples by Giordano and Rosa. The John and Mable Ringling Museum of Art in Sarasota was built in 1928 and opened in 1929, but the onset of the Great Depression caused a slowdown in acquisitions by Ringling, and the last painting he purchased was Lazzarini's *Berenice Cutting off her Hair* at a Christie's sale in 1931.[186] The museum remained open until Ringling's death in 1936, at which time it closed for a decade until the state of Florida acquired it in 1946.[187] After it reopened in 1951, W.G. Constable could rightly observe that the "quality is very uneven...but the collection has been saved by Ringling's very positive liking for large pictures, especially when they were striking in design...and with the seventeenth- and eighteenth-century Italian masters, whose recent vogue had not begun, the group of Bolognese, Neapolitan, Roman and Venetian painters of that period is perhaps the most important in the United States."[188]

Also active in the 1920s was William Randolph Hearst, but of him Mr. Constable was not so flattering: "he bought wholesale on a scale that must have completely outrivalled Morgan . . . whether he knew all that he possessed and whether he ever saw it is very doubtful. Cases are known of things Hearst purchased never having been unpacked, until they were sold after his death. . . . Hearst must go down in history not as a collector but as a gigantic and voracious magpie."[189] This judgment is perhaps too harsh, for Hearst was buying with the idea of decorating on a large scale. He had inherited art works from his mother, including an anonymous seventeenth-century Florentine *Marriage of St. Catherine;* among the many things he bought himself were a few Baroque paintings. As early as 1920 from the Anderson Galleries he obtained an unusual set of four large frescoes by Francesco Maffei. These, a Sassoferrato *Madonna and Sleeping Christ Child* purchased in 1926, and a Francesco de Mura *Madonna and Child with St. John* are installed at his palatial California home, San Simeon.[190] As we shall see, a number of the better Baroque works from his vast holdings were given by Hearst in the 1940s to the Los Angeles County Museum of Art.

MUSEUM COLLECTING IN THE 1920S

The changing attitude of the 1920s toward Italian Baroque art, at least in museum circles, is nicely summarized by the Metropolitan Museum of Art's curator of European painting Harry Wehle in a *Bulletin* article of 1929:

> During the past generation or two the entire body of baroque art, except the paintings of Rubens and Van Dyck, may be said to have been generally out of favor, but the last few years have shown signs of their gradual reinstatement to the public's good estimation. Among the Italian baroque paintings owned by the Metropolitan Museum are the Lucretia considered to be by Massimo Stanzione, a portrait of Pope Clement IX by Carlo Maratta, a self-portrait by Salvator Rosa, the Birth of the Virgin by Luca Giordano [now attributed to Francesco Solimena; Fig. 11] and The Passing of Joseph by Guido Reni. Recently, three additional paintings have been purchased, namely, a Landscape by Alessandro Magnasco, David with the Head of Goliath by Bernardo Strozzi and Joseph Sold by His Brethren by Giovanni Battista Piazzetta.[191]

In addition, the Metropolitan also received as a gift from Eustace Conway in 1928 Cavaliere d'Arpino's *Perseus and Andromeda* and, in 1927, Pacecco de Rosa's *Christ Blessing the Children* (sold in 1979).

The Metropolitan Museum's major new acquisitions were all by artists who had been featured in the Florentine exhibition of 1922. Other American museums also responded to it by adding their first Baroque works. This was the case in Cleveland when the museum in 1929 acquired as a Gift of the Friends, Strozzi's *Minerva.* Of this painting, the director William Milliken wrote that it was "an acquisition of primary importance in a field hitherto entirely unrepresented" and that it had "as a whole been surprisingly undervalued." He observed further that "a time of reappraisal has come" and that the *Minerva* is "unquestionably one of Strozzi's masterpieces."[192]

Of the other big city museums, Detroit acquired a Guercino studio work in 1926 from Baron von Hadeln of Florence and a Sebastiano Ricci *Camillus and Brennus* was given in 1927; Worcester added a Magnasco in 1929. In Boston, the Guercino (now Gennari) *Flora* (Fig. 6), which had been in the city since 1840, was donated by the Gardner family in 1920. Zoe Oliver Sherman presented the Museum of Fine Arts with a *Head of a Young Girl* by Furini in 1922; the next year brought a Pignoni from another donor, the Francesco del Cairo *Herodias,* and Giordano's *Isaac Blessing Jacob* from Helen O. Bigelow. By bequest also came, from Ernest Wadsworth Longfellow in 1923, another Giordano, the *Entombment of Christ,* which had been in Boston since 1849, and a *Hercules and Omphale* (later sold). At the Minneapolis Institute of Arts, director Russell Plimpton showed great taste in acquiring, first from the New York dealer Julius Weitzner in 1928 Reni's *St. John the Baptist,* and the following year, Guercino's *Toilet of Venus,* described as "an excellent example of his best manner."[193] Sadly, both were sold off in the 1950s;[194] the former went to a private Italian collection and the latter has recently reappeared on the New York art market.

What was then considered "an important and highly typical work" of Domenico Fetti was his *St. Stephen,* a gift of Mr. and Mrs. George Clark of Rochester to that city's Memorial Art Gallery in 1929.[195] The painting was featured in nearly every Baroque exhibition in America for the next fifty years, but it has more recently been downgraded.[196]

The Fogg Art Museum of Harvard University, reflecting the interest of its faculty, received a Vaccaro in 1922; a school of Caravaggio *Martyrdom of St. Sebastian,* later identified as by Caracciolo, was a gift of Herbert Pope, Arthur Pope, E.W. Forbes, and Paul J. Sachs in 1924; Magnascos came in 1920 and 1930; a Rosa *Landscape* (now Domenico Brandi) and a copy after Domenichino, *Putto with Book,* were gifts of Denman Ross in 1922 and 1929. Another putative Caravaggio of the *Cardsharps* was purchased from Wildenstein in 1929 and described as "an authentic masterpiece by one of the greatest seicento artists, which must rank among the most important acquisitions in the museum's history."[197]

Other college museums were also beginning to grow in this area. The University of Notre Dame was given a Stanzione *Holy Family* in 1924 by Charles A. Wrightsman, and Princeton received a *Landscape with Bandits* by Rosa in 1926 from Professor Frank Jewett Mather and a work by a Caravaggio follower in 1928 (deaccessioned 1989).

Private individuals, perhaps also inspired by the change in taste, continued to collect the most popular of Baroque painters—Magnasco. In Chicago at the Art Institute, four of the Genoese master's works, three from Charles Worcester and one from Martin Ryerson, were lent for exhibition and prompted the observation that "interest in Italian painting, at one time limited to the primitives and Renaissance periods, has lately been widening to include some of the best baroque masters, long regarded as decadent examples of a great style."[198] Another collector who responded to the seemingly modern quality of Magnasco was Duncan Phillips, who acquired a picture called *The Shipwreck* from the Ehrich Gallery in 1920 and another, *The Singing Birds,* in 1943.

THE FIRST AMERICAN EXHIBITION

It is ironic that the first American exhibition of Italian Baroque paintings took place in the very backyard of Charles Eliot Norton, the implacable foe of this "decadent" art. But indeed presented at the Fogg Art Museum in January and February of 1929 was an *Exhibition of Italian XVII and XVIII Century Paintings and Drawings.* This, as the typed information sheet stated, was "in connection with a course of lectures recently given at the museum by Mr. Arthur

McComb covering the period in question, but will also be of interest to the general public. It is apparently the first exhibition of its kind to be held in the United States, where this epoch in the history of art has suffered an astonishing neglect. The organizers have confined themselves to obtaining loans from institutions and the individuals in Boston and the vicinity." Describing the contents of the exhibition, it continues:

> The early 17th century is represented by a fine St. Sebastian of the School of Caravaggio, but otherwise the exhibition leans heavily to the 18th century. The outstanding painting is, without any doubt, ex-Governor Fuller's Piazzetta, a large Madonna and Saints, remarkable for its sweep and breadth of handling and easily ranking among the masterpieces of this artist. Mr. Pope's "Caritas" ascribed to the almost unknown Domenico Napoletano, is also a revelation in the richness of its impasto, while the beautiful Deposition from the [Denman] Ross collection illustrates perfectly the typical baroque diagonal composition with the main action going on in the second plane. The name of Magnasco is attached to no less than five paintings, four of which are decorative landscapes from the Ross collection, but these, as well as the large "Monks in Prayer," owned by the Fogg Museum, seem to lack the nervous touch, the characteristic spotty brushwork of the great Genoese. Moreover, the orange tones in the last-mentioned painting are, to say the least, unusual for this master.[199]

The exhibition, which, as the first of its kind, received mentions in both *Art News* and *Parnassus,*[200] also included Giuseppe Maria Crespi's *Vision of a Monk* given to the Fogg by Denman Ross and a group of drawings lent by John Nicholas Brown of Providence by Rosa, Guercino, Annibale Carracci, and Gianlorenzo Bernini.

Summing up the activity of the decade in the English *Burlington Magazine* Ella Siple wrote:

> The current bulletins of at least six American museums bear on their covers illustrations of recently acquired seventeenth-century paintings. These and the *Exhibition of Italian Seventeenth- and Eighteenth-Century Art* held recently at the Fogg Museum in Cambridge—the first exhibition of its kind in America—are evidence of a growing interest in the period and a revaluation of the [Baroque] painters. . . . The revival of interest is by no means new, by no means confined to America. It had been gathering strength even before *La Mostra* . . . held at the Pitti Palace in 1922 and, after that great exhibition, took definite form and centred about Caravaggio and those later men, Fetti, Strozzi, Lyss, and others who carried on the tradition to Piazzetta, Tiepolo, and Guardi. Out of the "dark ages" between Michelangelo and eighteenth-century Venice—that decadence usually summed up in one paragraph in our text books of Italian art—certain personalities began to emerge. But they were not the personalities which had been known to the Victorian era; they were not painters who, like Guido Reni, coated Renaissance forms with a hard, sweet glaze. . . . The exhibition in Florence and the publications which appeared in connection with it, many books on the Baroque and the introduction of college courses covering the period, have created in America a demand for Italian painting of the seventeenth and eighteenth centuries. Museums are meeting that demand. . . .
>
> Now the works of such men as Strozzi and Fetti are coming to be known here. But American museums are still in need of fine figure paintings by Rubens and Caravaggio. In the seventeenth and the early eighteenth centuries the Baroque and Counter-Reformation did not, for obvious reasons, take root in the United States and Canada as it did in Mexico. To-day, however, the art of that period interests us. Now, as then, we are swinging away from the restraint of classicism, away from the repose of formally balanced design towards a more dynamic feeling.[201]

HARTFORD TO THE FORE

Out of the same Harvard milieu that produced the groundbreaking exhibition of 1929 came an extraordinary individual. A. Everett Austin, Jr., known as Chick, was born in Brookline, Massachusetts, in 1900. His father was a distinguished doctor and his mother an inveterate collector. He graduated from Harvard in 1922 and joined an archaeological expedition to Egypt. Austin returned for graduate studies at Harvard in architecture, but, having become interested in artists' methods, next went to Italy to study with the famed restorer and forger Ioni. He then spent three years at Harvard assisting the museum's director Edward Forbes in teaching techniques of painting; in connection with this he was sent to help restore the frescoes at Chichen Itza.

When Forbes was asked in 1927 to suggest a new director for the Wadsworth Atheneum in Hartford, he heartily recommended Austin. Combined with his interest in art was a love for theater, dance, and music that helped Austin make the city a national center of the arts, with a strong regard for both the Baroque and contemporary fields.[202] Inspired by the 1922 Florentine exhibition, the writing of the Sitwells, and the Fogg's modest exhibition, he organized in 1930 his own grander version entitled *Exhibition of Italian Art of the Sei- and Settecento.* In the Atheneum's *Bulletin* his Harvard mentor Arthur McComb wrote, "In the last three or four years only have American collectors turned at all to that demoded field, Italian painting of the seventeenth and eighteenth centuries. What has already been accomplished, what unsuspected beauty has come to light, how rewarding the effort, the visitors to the Wadsworth Atheneum will be able to judge."[203] Although Austin had written to Mr. Ringling in the fall of 1929, "I am a great admirer of seventeenth- and eighteenth-century painting and want to do all I can to change the underestimation in which it has been held for so many years,"[204] there were no loans from Ringling in the exhibition. But it could boast Caravaggio's supposed *Cardsharps* from the Fogg and also attributed to this artist a *Portrait of a Young Boy* from Wildenstein and a *David* from the Ehrich Gallery, as well as the school of Caravaggio *St. Sebastian* (now Caracciolo) also from the Fogg. Fetti was represented by the *St. Stephen* from Rochester, Balestra by the *Nativity* from Detroit, Guercino by the *Toilet of Venus* from Minneapolis, and Preti by the *Erminia and the Shepherds* from Vassar. From dealers and private collectors came works by Strozzi, Ludovico Carracci, Dolci, Furini, Reni, Solimena, and Stanzione. The best represented artist, as had been the case in the Fogg exhibition, was Magnasco with, as McComb noted "no less than eleven," leading him to speculate that "the popularity of this Genoese master who was so intensely personal, with his exciting and vivacious use of paint, with the indefinable macabre air which hangs over all his creations, indicates that many collectors may have come to appreciate the Italian Baroque by way of El Greco with whom Magnasco has a certain affinity of temperament."[205]

Through good fortune, the very year that Austin became director of the Wadsworth Atheneum the institution received a major purchase fund from the bequest of the Sumner family. With this he was able to acquire a number of outstanding Baroque works. His friend, the dealer Kirk Askew, wrote after Austin's death, in 1958, "much as he loved the baroque, his interests were never limited to the seventeenth century. However, he did realize that in the late nineteen-twenties and the nineteen-thirties one could find really great Italian baroque paintings at a much more reasonable price than in other fields. Consequently we find at Hartford one of the finest collections of Italian paintings of the sei- and settecento outside of Italy."[206]

Some of Austin's first additions to the collection were included in the 1930 exhibition. There were two large Giordanos, *The Rape of Helen* and *The Rape of Europa.* Apropos of these, the Atheneum's *Bulletin* observed, "Giordano has as a painter little to say, but he says it with a wealth of eloquence, a vivacity and a versatility which is disarming."[207] Also displayed was a new *Night Scene* by Rosa (now called after the master) of whom Henry Russell Hitchcock, Jr. wrote, "among seventeenth-century Italian painters, Salvator Rosa stands somewhat apart. He was in the midst of the Baroque a Romantic."[208] Later, in 1930 Austin acquired from the Venetian dealer Italico Brass the beautiful *St. Catherine* by Strozzi, which had been shown in the 1922 Pitti Palace exhibition. As Askew later wrote, "Ecstasy did not embarrass him as it does so many Americans. He reveled in it and reacted to it. He bought certainly one of the most ecstatic paintings [of] the baroque 'St. Catherine of Alexandria' by Bernardo Strozzi. Not only in her eyes, her gestures, but in the nervosity of every brush stroke and of the color, ecstasy, just short of hysteria, reigns."[209]

Austin's other purchases of Italian Baroque paintings throughout the 1930s and early 1940s included Guercino's *St. Sebastian* (now called workshop), Rosa's *Tobias and the Angel,* Cavallino's *Flight into Egypt,* Caracciolo's *Annunciation,* Crespi's *Artist in his Studio,* three Magnascos, and notable works by Dolci, Solimena, and Tiberio Tinelli. A *Daedalus and Icarus* bought as a Cavallino in 1944 has now been attributed to Orazio Riminaldi. There is a fine group of still lifes with examples from the circle of Evaristo Baschenis and Recco, and an important one of flowers and fruits by a follower of Caravaggio. Austin's purchases may be said to have culminated in the Caravaggio *Ecstasy of St. Francis* bought in 1943 from Arnold Seligman. The only authentic example by the master in America at that time, it became the centerpiece of his final Hartford exhibition, *Caravaggio and the Seventeenth Century,* held from June 1943 to January 1944, for he resigned on 1 January 1945. Appropriately enough, however, he was hired the following year, again on the recommendation of Forbes, as the first director of the reopened Ringling Museum in Sarasota.[210]

AMERICA'S FIRST BAROQUE BOOK AND ITS INFLUENCE

The impetus for the Fogg's 1929 exhibition and a guiding light for Austin had been Harvard professor Arthur K. McComb. The author of a pioneering study on Bronzino, he published in 1934, *The Baroque Painters of Italy: An Introductory Historical Survey,* the first such work in English, and one destined to be greatly influential in the formation of American taste. It was remarkably wide-ranging in the number of artists mentioned and extremely sensitive in its interpretation of both individual works and artistic personalities. Following the time-honored precedent in art-historical surveys, it combined the seventeenth- and eighteenth-century Italian schools into one continuous flow, so that Piazzetta, Tiepolo, Guardi, and others were included under the rubric "Baroque."

Reminiscent of the writings of Norton, McComb often made harsh moral judgments on the once-revered artists. Thus for him Reni was "a figure of greater brilliance but of less integrity" than Domenichino, and he characterized Reni as "this famed, not to say spoiled and over-satisfied child of fortune." After establishing the development of the painter's golden first manner and the silvery tone of his mid and later period, he described "the sentimental cloying piety which worries us in almost all the works of Guido," which "came to a head in the half-length Lucretias, Cleopatras and Sibyls, etc., which were exported in bulk. They largely account for his popular reputation at one time, and equally for the neglect into which he has fallen." McComb recognized the quality of Guercino, "the last and in a way the most talented of all the Bolognese," and noted that "his draperies have the color and texture of Victorian velvets," but that his later work "becomes entirely oleographic, commercial, and negligible."[211]

One of the ways in which McComb pressed the case for the acceptance of his favored artists was to compare them to better-known Northern painters or to show their relevance to modern taste. Thus, for example, he compared Caravaggio to Manet, called Cavallino the "Vermeer of Naples," and found that Fetti's scenes of daily life attained an almost Protestant, Rembrandtesque air. Even Sassoferrato in "his rather sentimental half-length Madonna-figures sometimes achieves a clear, unshadowed color in a rather 'modern' acute manner." Nevertheless, it is clear that his sympathy lay with the more painterly artists, with the technical brilliance of Strozzi, with Crespi by whom some paintings reminded him "subtly of Fragonard and the best French work of the century," and, most especially, with the Rococo Magnasco, who "gives us an intensification of that pantheistic attitude we find appearing in the seventeenth century for the first time in European art, in the drawings of Poussin and Claude, and in some paintings of Rosa and Tempesta." According to McComb, Magnasco seemed to speak to the anxieties of the twentieth century, as he "depicts men as taken up in the rhythm of nature, victims struggling in vain in a storm-tossed world."[212]

McComb's fondness for the later Venetian artists was echoed in another classic of American art-historical scholarship, Frank Jewett Mather's *Venetian Painters,* published in 1936. Here, in the section following upon that devoted to the city's great Renaissance masters, he noted the innovations of Fetti, the spontaneity of Johann Liss, Strozzi's "elevated genre," Antonio Zanchi's powerful and picturesque art, and the bizarre appeal of Maffei.[213]

Despite the novel brilliance of his book, McComb's ideas were slow to be accepted by the mainstream authorities on art in the thirties and forties, who gave only grudging acknowledgement to a few select Baroque artists. Not surprisingly, a book published in 1929 titled *Old World Masters in New World Collections* contained not a single Italian Baroque painting.[214] By 1933, however, Lionello Venturi, in his series of large format volumes, *Italian Paintings in America,* did include a small number of seventeenth-century examples—the Fogg's "Caravaggio" *Cardsharps,* the Cleveland and Hartford Strozzis, and the Magnascos in Cleveland and a New York private collection.[215] That same year the Art Institute of Chicago presented an exhibition celebrating "A Century of Progress," not only in art but in American collecting. But while the eighteenth-century masters Tiepolo, Guardi, and Longhi were shown in great profusion, only the Art Institute's Magnasco *Arcadian Landscape* and Mola *Homer Dictating,* and a Solimena *Erminia and the Shepherds* from the Chicago collector August Bontoux represented the seventeenth century.[216] Similarly, Hans Tietze's selection of Baroque works in *Masterpieces of European Painting in America* of 1939 also included only Cleveland's Magnasco of the *Synagogue,* the Fogg's "Caravaggio," and Hartford's Strozzi.[217] Exhibitions of ostensible masterpieces that also took place in that year included some Italian Baroque examples. *The Golden Gate Exposition: Masterworks of Five Centuries in San Francisco* organized by Walter Heil featured, among other paintings, Caravaggio's *Boy Bitten by a Lizard* (on loan from an Italian collection) and works by Cavallino and Orazio Gentileschi. American collections were represented by a Crespi from Samuel Kress and a Guercino from the Detroit Institute of Art. At the 1939 World's Fair exposition of *Masterpieces of Art* with a catalogue by McCall and Valentiner that same year, out of over four hundred paintings there were only a handful of Baroque works—two supposed Caravaggios, the *Cardsharps* from the Fogg and a "Table of Fruits" from the Kress collection (later identified as by the Pensionante del Saraceni), the Crespi *Self-Portrait at an Easel* from Hartford, and the Magnasco *Synagogue* from Cleveland again.[218] The next year a different selection of masterpieces was presented. While more works of seventeenth-century origin were now shown, a number from dealers had dubious attributions: two Crespis, and works by Strozzi, Fetti, Magnasco, and Giordano, plus a supposed Guercino *Portrait of a Man* and an even more suspect Caravaggio *Portrait of a Woman.*[219] Even as late as 1948 among the one hundred and one "Great Paintings in America" selected by Fiske Kimball and Venturi, there were no Italian Baroque works.[220]

Some sense of how gradually McComb's book changed the tide of taste can be gleaned by a look at one of the first standard American introductory art-historical textbooks, Helen Gardner's *Art Through the Ages.* The preface of the revised edition of 1936 states that one of the improvements over the first edition of 1926 is "a brief chapter now devoted to the Baroque." This short chapter, however, deals almost entirely with architecture and sculpture. The single paragraph devoted to painting began, "Baroque painting involves carrying to a climax, at times to an extravagant climax under the stimulation of melodramatic ideals, many of the tendencies of the sixteenth century." A rather hazy notion of the period is conveyed as it is stated, "Correggio is as truly, though less extravagantly baroque...as are the frescoes of Il Gesù....Caravaggio's realism and violently contrasted light and dark and the Mannerists' types become more sweetly sentimental. Tintoretto's conquest of space design set the three-dimensional organization as the normal type. . . . Veronese's use of a cooler, more silvery light and largeness of decorative quality reappear in Giovanni Battista Tiepolo with whom we are still in the baroque yet largely in the eighteenth century when dramatic intensity eases into flowing grace."[221] No paintings were reproduced to convey a visual sense of this seemingly elastic period. However, by the fourth edition of 1959 "Italian Baroque Painting" had its own subheading and Caravaggio as well as Annibale Carracci are credited with creating a distinctive style and are allotted illustrations—Caravaggio an early work, the *Youthful Bacchus* in the Uffizi, and Carracci a detail from the Farnese palace. Also illustrated are two examples of ceiling design—Giovanni Battista Gaulli's ceiling in the Gesù and a Tiepolo from Strà.[222] The recent edition of 1991 has an expanded section devoted to "Italian Baroque Painting"—ten pages now with illustrations not only of Carracci's Farnese palace decorations, but also of both the Reni and Guercino *Aurora,* and by Caravaggio, examples of his more serious pictures, the *Conversion of St. Paul* and *Death of the Virgin.* Totally new is a section on Domenichino and Artemisia Gentileschi; the former's *Last Communion of St. Jerome* is illustrated, and the latter, described as "one of the best" of Caravaggio's followers "whose work is increasingly appreciated by many modern critics," is represented by her *Judith* in Detroit. Another section deals with landscape and illustrates Annibale's *Flight into Egypt* and Salvator Rosa's *St. John in the Wilderness;* the chapter concludes with a section on illusionistic ceilings.[223] Undoubtedly, this now politically correct appraisal of Baroque painting would bring a smile to McComb's lips.

GALLERIES AND EXHIBITIONS IN THE 1930S

To find a more immediate impact of McComb's approach on contemporary taste, one has to look, in addition to Austin's activity at the Wadsworth Atheneum, to the commercial galleries of old masters in New York City and to a number of smaller, regional museums. There is no doubt that, in terms of exhibitions and the promotion of Italian Baroque art very much in the McComb taste, the most important art gallery was Durlacher Brothers in New York. Kirk Askew, its socially well-connected director, had studied art history at Harvard, became friendly with Austin, and even married McComb's former wife; the couple made their home at 166 East 61st Street a lively salon for the most exciting people in the arts.[224] Askew was a pioneer in presenting serious one-man and period exhibitions within the commercial gallery walls.

From January to February of 1932, Durlacher's gallery at 670 Fifth Avenue launched their Baroque attack with an *Exhibition of Italian Paintings and Drawings of the Seventeenth Century.* Eighteen paintings were shown, including the Fogg's "Caravaggio" *Cardsharps,* Mola's *Homer Dictating* from the Art Institute of Chicago, the "Fetti" *St. Stephen* from Rochester, the Strozzi *St. Catherine* from Hartford, a Massimo Stanzione from Mrs. Eugene Atwood, and a Reni from August Bontoux. Other artists represented, much in the McComb taste, were Caracciolo, Fiasella, Maratta, Castiglione, Magnasco, Crespi, and Giordano.

Two years later Durlacher's presented the exhibition *Venetian Painting 1600-1800.* Of Baroque paintings, there were three Fettis, the Worcester *Parable of the Sowing of Tares,* a *Tobias and the Angel* from the Drey Gallery, and a *David with the Head of Goliath;* a Liss *Vision of St. John* from the Fogg; the Hartford Strozzi and another for sale of a *Concert;* a Girolamo Forabosco *Portrait of a Girl* from Detroit; a Zanchi *St. Elizabeth;* and a Sebastiano Ricci *St. Francis* from Julius Weitzner.

This last mentioned dealer was to be over the course of his career and until his death in 1986 the most prominent supplier of Baroque paintings to American collectors and museums (see Fig. 18 below). Born into a musical family in New York in 1895, he first made his living by fiddling in restaurants, but subsequently earned a master's degree in chemical engineering at New York University in 1917. From this he went into the profitable business of importing paint pigments. Following his marriage in 1924, he took his wife Ruth for a honeymoon to Paris. It was there, at the Hôtel Drouot, that he began buying paintings. Returning to America, Weitzner discovered that his savings invested with a bankrupt firm were gone, and he started art dealing in earnest. Weitzner's catholic taste, eye for good pictures and his ability to clean them himself, and talent for salesmanship soon established his gallery at 36 East 57th Street as a key locale in the New York art market.[225] He claimed that his first museum client was the Art Institute of Chicago,[226] but his first major transaction may have been the sale of Reni's *St. John the Baptist in the Wilderness,* which he had acquired for only $600 from the Ehrich Gallery, to the Minneapolis Institute of Arts. He was later able to buy it back from them and sell it to a private collector for $35,000. Unlike Durlacher's, Weitzner did not embark on scholarly exhibitions and seems to have published in 1936 only one small catalogue, *A Selection of Paintings,* consisting of thirty-two works ranging over five centuries from Giovanni del Biondo to Fantin Latour, and including, of the Baroque, a Barocci, a Ribera, and a fine Cavallino *St. Cecilia.*

Another important commercial gallery already established on the New York scene by this time was F. Kleinberger & Co., and in 1932 it, with the assistance of Chick Austin, Venturi, and Hermann Voss, assembled for the College Art Association an exhibition of *Italian Baroque Paintings and Drawings, XVI, XVII, XVIII Centuries.* The foreword of the catalogue by Venturi stated that the exhibition "should be very useful to American scholars and collectors. It may destroy several prejudices which exist both for and against Italian painting of the seventeenth and eighteenth centuries." Many of the loans came from European dealers, but among those from American sources were a "Caravaggio" (now French school) *Head of a Youth* from Hartford, a Dolci *Flight into Egypt* from New York's Ehrich Gallery, and from Weitzner, an Annibale Carracci *Pietà* and a Guercino *St. Peter.*

The next recorded showing of Baroque paintings took place in a museum setting at Oregon's Portland

Art Museum in December 1936. This was a collection of Italian paintings from the late Renaissance and Baroque periods belonging to the dealer Siegfried Aram of New York and Los Angeles. Baroque art, the catalogue contended, had not been well understood and had "been unjustly condemned," but "the freedom and movement and vital coloring of the best Baroque painting makes it a most vital and estimable style."[227] The truly Baroque works on view were Barocci's *Holy Family,* Solimena's *Armida,* and others by Annibale Carracci, Domenichino, Fetti, and Maratta.

The following year in January and February, Durlacher's presented the *Exhibition of Paintings by Giuseppe Maria Crespi,* consisting of ten works. On the single printed sheet an introduction by Askew's friend, Agnes Rindge, professor of art history at Vassar College and director of its museum, stated: "Crespi belongs to the great company of such eighteenth-century painters as Hogarth, Chardin, and Goya," but "he was a greatly gifted late Baroque Italian painter." Two works were lent by Kress, others came from Cleveland and Hartford. Later that year, the Nelson-Atkins Museum of Art in Kansas City organized a loan exhibition of *Venetian Paintings, Drawings, and Prints of the Eighteenth Century.* This included two Fettis, those from the Metropolitan and Rochester; the Liss from the Fogg; Magnascos from Kansas City, Chicago, Jacques Seligman, and Lilienfeld Galleries; Sebastiano Riccis from Detroit, Arnold Seligman, and Paul Drey; and the Strozzi from Hartford.

In 1938 at Vassar, Agnes Rindge organized an *Exhibition of Old Masters of the XVII and XVIII Centuries* with works from the museum's collection and loans by a variety of New York dealers. Included were Vassar's own school of Caravaggio *Cardsharps* and a seventeenth-century Roman *Romantic Landscape.* That same year the Springfield Museum of Art in Massachusetts presented a Magnasco show with thirty-one examples of the painter's work. In the catalogue essay, Winifred Muller described how Magnasco's "evolution of the *al tocco* style gave breath to the spirit of the Baroque."[228] Works were lent from the museums of Boston, Cleveland, Detroit, Hartford, Kansas City, Philadelphia, Springfield, and Worcester; from Dumbarton Oaks, the Fogg, the Metropolitan, Rhode Island School of Design; and from the dealers Drey, Durlacher, Lilienfeld, Arnold Seligman, and Weitzner, as well as several private collectors.

Durlacher's held their own Magnasco show in early 1940 with twenty paintings, most of which had been exhibited in Springfield, with the notable exception of an *Artist in his Studio.*[229]

MUSEUM ACQUISITIONS IN THE 1930S

As the major American exhibitor and purveyor of Italian Baroque paintings in the 1930s, it was only just that Kirk Askew's efforts should result in many sales to a variety of museums. In 1930 the Metropolitan Museum of Art purchased from Durlacher's the Fetti *Good Samaritan.* It was described by Ella Siple as "one of the most thoroughly delightful, though not the most important of the pictures acquired recently by the museum,"[230] and it was subsequently included in many exhibitions, even though later it would be downgraded. In 1934 Kirk Askew acquired from the Earl of Jersey at Osterley Park, Salvator Rosa's *Landscape with Tobias and the Angel,* and he wrote immediately offering this, as well as a pair of Rosas representing *Soldiers on a Rocky Coast* and a *Landscape with a Herdsman,* to Harry Wehle, curator of paintings at the Metropolitan. The *Tobias and the Angel* was priced at $3,200 and was finally acquired by Hartford for $3,100. The Metropolitan purchased the *Soldiers on a Rocky Coast* for the more modest sum of $1,400, and Mrs. William Levitt bought the companion piece for Vassar College in 1935. Reflecting the still prevalent attitude, the Metropolitan's acquisition was announced in the *Art Digest* with the headline "Appreciation for Salvator Rosa, Decadent."[231]

Also purchased by the Metropolitan in 1936 from a private collector was a painting presumed to be by Caracciolo representing *Christ and the Woman of Samaria* (Fig. 12) ; its changing fortunes reflect the fluctuation of taste and scholarship concerning Italian Baroque paintings. This work had first been lent to the museum, as a Preti, eight years earlier by the Wildhagen family of Hollywood, California. According to them, it was purchased in Italy "in an auction sale of the personal effects of a cardinal who must have died approximately in 1886." The attribution to Caracciolo (also known as Battistello) was made by the Metropolitan's first curator of paintings, Bryson Burroughs, and the picture was included as such by McComb in his book. At the opportunity to acquire the painting, the next curator, Harry Wehle, wrote to his superiors, "Caracciolo is one

FIGURE 12

SEVENTEENTH-CENTURY NEAPOLITAN SCHOOL, *Christ and the Woman of Samaria,* Private collection, Rome (formerly in The Metropolitan Museum of Art, New York). Photograph courtesy of The Metropolitan Museum of Art.

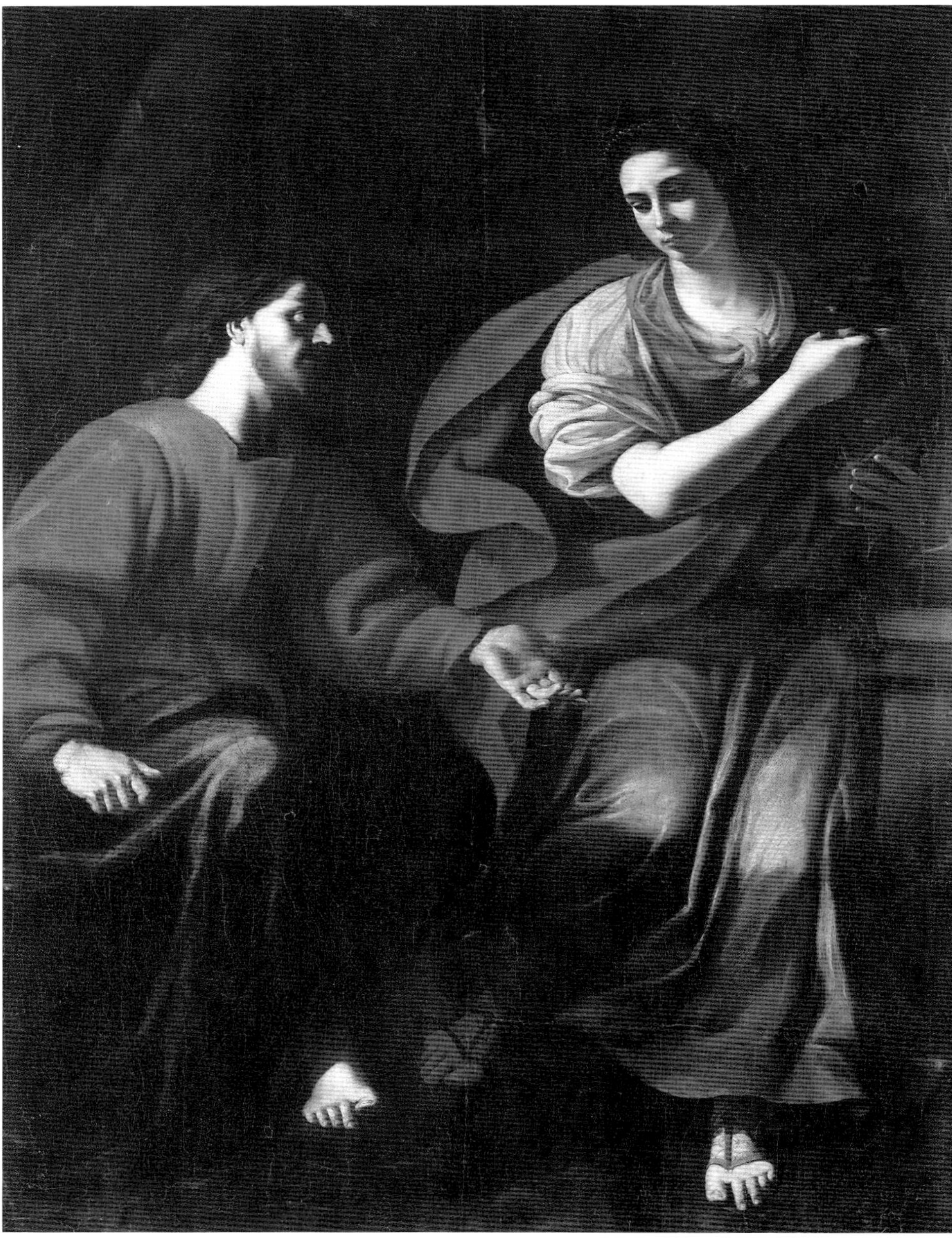

of the most independent and dignified of Caravaggio's contemporaries....It may be a long time before we can get a picture by Caravaggio himself, if we ever do get one, and even if we had one I should think it could house no better supplement than such a Caracciolo as this."[232] The painting was purchased and published in the museum's *Bulletin* by Margaretta M. Salinger, who observed that the influence of Caravaggio "tempered later by contact with the Roman School and still further modified by a basic personal feeling for balance, dignity, and poise, formed Caracciolo into an artist who in Longhi's words makes Manfredi seem a mere varnisher of pictures, Saraceni an invertebrate, Valentin a French classic, and Gentileschi a tailor de luxe."[233] Nevertheless, the attribution was later doubted; it was assigned to an anonymous Neapolitan artist identified as the Master of the Sarasota *Emmaus,* and finally, in 1980 the once-prized painting was deaccessioned.[234]

Dealer activity remained brisk throughout the 1930s, especially in the Midwest, where museums had a penchant for Baroque paintings. In his hometown of Kansas City, Askew failed to establish a hoped-for monopoly as the Nelson-Atkins Museum's agent for old master paintings, but did succeed in selling them a Rosa in 1932 and a Magnasco in 1933.[235] Acting at this time as a chief advisor to both Kansas City and Cleveland was Harold W. Parsons, and he assisted the former in acquiring from Duveen a Cecco del Caravaggio in 1930 (sold in 1988; now in the Prado, Madrid) and a Cavallino *Rape of Europa* in 1931.

Other midwestern museums followed suit. The

Cincinnati Art Museum acquired in 1938 Strozzi's *David with the Head of Goliath,* which evoked the observation that until recently, "the work of the seventeenth-century Italians had been obscured by the cult of the primitive....Fortunately, today the reorientation of ideas regarding the art of the seventeenth century has brought about a clearer understanding of its importance, and the period takes its rightful place as a vital connecting link between the High Renaissance of the sixteenth century and the Rococo of the eighteenth century." The writer continued with praise for the Strozzi, which he characterized as displaying "rich, glowing color, dramatic light, vigorous brushwork, free but careful modeling of the flesh and features—a modeling that in some areas approaches Impressionism."[236] Cleveland received a Crespi by gift in 1936 and Magnasco's famous *Synagogue* in 1930. A Sassoferrato went to the Indianapolis Museum of Art in 1938. Chicago enriched its holdings through the generosity of its major collectors: the Mola *Homer Dictating,* the vast *Resurrection* by Cecco del Caravaggio, and a *Judith* now attributed to Felice Ficherelli were all gifts from the Worcester collection in 1930, 1934, and 1939, respectively, and Magnasco's *Monks at Supper* came from the Rysersons in 1933. Detroit added three Magnascos; a putative Caravaggio *Fruit Vendor* (now identified as by the Pensionante del Saraceni) as the gift of Edsel Ford in 1936; a Crespi in 1936 as the gift of Jacob Heimann; a Niccolò Renieri in 1938; and Fetti's *Dream of Jacob* in 1939. The Saint Louis Art Museum obtained a Strozzi in 1937, and in 1939, G.A. de'Ferrari's *Abraham and the Angels* (as a Murillo) from Arnold Seligman. Minneapolis acquired a Fiasella *Flight into Egypt* in 1934, but it was later deaccessioned and went to Weitzner, who sold it to Bob Jones, Jr. (cat. no. 31).

To Harold Edgell, director of the Museum of Fine Arts in Boston, Kirk Askew in 1935 offered a Magnasco, Fetti's *David with the Head of Goliath* (which he claimed was the only large figure piece by the artist in the country and one admired by McComb), and the *Musicians* by Strozzi from Casa Maggioni, Legnano, that had been published by Fiocco.[237] The museum did indeed purchase from him the next year Magnasco's *Soldiers at Play,* and in the *Annual Report* it was noted that "The Museum is very weak in baroque painting, and was fortunate in acquiring a really important example of the work of probably the best known Italian baroque painter."[238] That same year the Museum of Fine Arts also obtained from Julius Weitzner his Cavallino *St. Cecilia.* According to correspondence from the dealer, this painting had been in a private collection in New York since about 1916 as a Caravaggio, but in 1926-27 Hermann Voss identified it as a Cavallino and made an offer on it for the Berlin museum. The owner, however, held out for a Caravaggio price and did not sell. Weitzner was able to finally get it in 1935, published it in his exhibition catalogue, and then offered it to Boston. The museum's assistant curator Charles Cunningham wrote that he was "extremely anxious to have the Cavallino stay here in Boston. It is a fine example of the Tenebrosi school and would make a very distinguished addition to our collection." In order to get it, the museum had to trade seven paintings, including a Willem Kalf, Pieter Claesz. Molenaer, Jan van Goyen, and Francesco Guardi. Weitzner, who later regarded this exchange as a major coup, wrote to Cunningham at the time, "I was a little disappointed in not getting the better items like the Corots etc., but I am satisfied with my share."[239]

The Worcester Art Museum purchased their Fetti *Parable of the Sowing of Tares* in 1934, and on this occasion, the museum's *Bulletin* noted that, until then "of the later phases of the seventeenth century" there had been "virtually nothing except two fine canvases by Alessandro Magnasco."[240] Of other museums, San Francisco obtained a Gaulli in 1935; Springfield, a Magnasco and Solimena in 1936; and Philadelphia, a Strozzi, Simone Pignoni, and Caravaggio copy in 1938.

University museums also continued to collect actively in this field. Vassar with its Durlacher connection acquired a Caravaggio school work (possibly Bartolomeo Manfredi) of the *Cardsharps* in 1934, a Rosa in 1935, and Giordano's *St. Theresa of Lima* (now identified as St. Rose) and Lorenzo Lippi's *Finding of Moses* (later attributed to Jacopo Vignali) both in 1937. Princeton in 1930 added an Annibale Carracci *Rest on the Flight* (now Francesco Albani) and a follower of Caravaggio *St. Matthew and the Angel* (now called French) in 1931, as well as a Sebastiano Ricci in 1937, and, as gifts in 1939, two Hercules subjects by a follower of Domenichino. The Rhode Island School of Design got a Guercino copy and a

Fetti in 1936; Wellesley, a Rosa in 1934, and in 1938 as a gift from Durlacher's, a Furini; and the Fogg, works by Rosa in 1932 and 1937. Notre Dame received as a gift in 1934 a Pacecco de Rosa *St. Cecilia in Heavenly Concert* (later attributed to Andrea Suppa). To Amherst were given in 1939 an *Angelica and Medoro* after Matteo Rosselli and a school of Rosa *Conversion of St. Paul* by Mrs. George Pearsons in memory of her husband.

AMERICA'S GREATEST COLLECTION

Samuel H. Kress (1863-1955), who had made his fortune from a chain of five-and-ten-cent stores, began buying paintings in 1927 during a trip to Italy, when he purchased from the collector-dealer Count Alessandro Contini-Bonacossi, Sebastiano Ricci's *St. Francis.* For the most part Kress preferred early gold-ground and Renaissance pictures, but occasionally in the 1930s a remarkable seventeenth-century work might catch his fancy. Thus in 1932 he acquired a Fetti *Parable of Lazarus and Dives,* and an exhibition of Italian paintings lent by Mr. Kress to the Los Angeles County Museum of Art in 1934 included a Giuseppe Ghislandi *Portrait of a Young Man* and a pair of religious subjects by Ricci, as well as a scene of *Ruins and Figures,* a collaboration of Sebastiano and Marco Ricci.[241] More major works came in 1935 with both Tanzio da Varallo's *St. Sebastian* and a *Still Life* attributed to Caravaggio (but now given to the Pensionante del Saraceni). In 1939 a second Tanzio, the great *St. John the Baptist,* was purchased, and shortly thereafter placed on loan to the Philbrook Museum of Art in Tulsa where it was eventually donated in 1944.[242] Most of the collection, however, was given in 1939 by Mr. Kress to the new National Gallery of Art in Washington, but he continued adding to it. Among the additional Baroque works were several by Donato Creti, Magnasco, and one by Carlo Francesco Nuvolone. In the 1940s came works by the Carracci, Cavallino, Dolci, Pietro Novelli, Sirani, Strozzi, and Antonio Maria Vassallo.[243]

In 1945 the National Gallery published *Paintings and Sculpture from the Kress Collection,* in which the chief curator John Walker could declare, "Mr. Kress has assembled the most complete and systematic collection of Italian paintings and sculpture ever brought together by one person...every significant change in Italian style is shown and most of the great masters and their followers are represented." Walker, however, had trained with Bernard Berenson, and for him the leading Baroque artists were not among these great masters.[244] The Gallery's survey of Italian art was still far from complete, and the artists displayed at this time and highlighted with illustrations in the book presented a skewed view of artistic activity in seventeenth-century Italy. The works included two big Crespis, *Tarquin and Lucretia* and *Cupids with Sleeping Nymphs;* Fetti's *Veil of St. Veronica;* a Francesco Furini *Angelica and Ruggero* (now Cecco Bravo at the Smart Gallery of the University of Chicago); Rosa's *Warrior;* Magnasco's *Christ Calling St. Peter;* Ricci's *Last Supper;* and the Tanzio *St. Sebastian.* The situation would change dramatically after 1946 when Kress became incapacitated and his brother Rush took over. Advised by William Suida, who had joined the Kress foundation in 1941, Rush Kress would expand the scope of the collection to include, in particular, paintings of the Italian Baroque period.

EXHIBITIONS IN THE 1940S

The new decade began with the Vassar College Art Gallery in Poughkeepsie presenting in 1940 an *Exhibition of Italian Baroque Paintings of the Seventeenth and Eighteenth Centuries.* It consisted of thirty-four paintings and drawings of which twelve were from the college's own collection, and twenty-two from the Jacob Heimann Gallery of New York. A brief essay noted that "Italian painting did not disappear with the close of the Renaissance, but continued to be a great generative center," and that this exhibition represented "all the important regional centers of Italy and many of the foremost painters." Among Vassar's works were the school of Caravaggio *Cardsharps,* Giordano's *St. Rose,* Lippi's *Finding of Moses,* Rosa's *Landscape,* and the Neapolitan school *Erminia and the Shepherds.* From Heimann came a Caracciolo, Fetti, Forabosco, Magnasco, and Strozzi.

That same year another exhibition attesting to the popularity of Venetian art was presented by the Toledo Museum of Art. *Four Centuries of Venetian Painting* was organized by Hans Tietze, and in its later section included the Fettis from the Rhode Island School of Design and Rochester, Strozzis from Hartford and Cleveland, and the same *Portrait of a Lady* by Forabosco from Heimann shown at Vassar, as well as a Ricci from the same source.

In 1941 the California Palace of the Legion of Honor in San Francisco presented one of the largest specialized shows up to that time. It was organized by the museum's director, Thomas Carr Howe, Jr., who wrote in the catalogue foreword that the exhibition afforded "an opportunity to study the accomplishment of a period, which until comparatively recent years in this country, has been neglected in favor of the art of other epochs. . . . Representative works by many of the leading artists of the various important regional schools—Bolognese, Roman, Neapolitan, Genovese, and Venetian are included."[245] The museum, according to a reviewer, was "confined to American-owned examples," but that "despite this restriction, the exhibition gives a good idea of the wide scope of artistic activity which made Italy of the Baroque the cradle of modern European painting."[246] All told, 115 paintings were on view, of which those of the eighteenth century and those by artists such as Valentin are outside the boundaries of our concerns. The Legion of Honor presented its own Bettera *Still Life.* Displayed as a Caravaggio and accepted by Voss as such was the great *Chastisement of Love* from the Worcester collection of Chicago (now in the Art Institute properly identified as a Manfredi), which also lent the Crespi *Woman Looking for Fleas.* Also gracing the walls were the Caracciolo from Hartford, Cavallino from Kansas City, Crespi and Strozzi from Samuel Kress, Fettis from the Metropolitan and Detroit, Pietro da Cortona from Sarasota, Sassoferrato from Indianapolis, and Rosa's *Self-Portrait* (Fig. 2) from the Metropolitan. Loans from dealers abounded, such as a Dolci *St. Cecilia* from Mortimer Brandt, Crespi's *Portrait of Chancellor Florius Senesius* from Heimann, and Annibale Carracci's *Self-Portrait* from Weitzner.

In January and February of 1942 the Schaeffer Galleries of New York City held an exhibition entitled *Gems of Baroque Painting.* A small catalogue with a preface by William Suida noted previous exhibitions, but called the Baroque "a field just being discovered. . . we enjoy the manifold artistic charms which this epoch spreads before us in so lavish a display." The works, all from a collection formed nearly forty years earlier, included a Castiglione, Cavallino's *St. Agatha,* and examples by Crespi, Fetti, Orazio Gentileschi, Magnasco (two), and Stanzione. Reviewing the exhibition in *Art News,* Alfred Frankfurter stated that there was "no need to talk any more about rediscovery of the Baroque or its curious adaptability to the modern way of seeing. From being a decade and a half ago the rarefied darling of the cognoscenti. . . the painting and the decoration of *seicento* and *settecento* Italy have progressed to set the pace for department store stylists and furniture and costume jewelry," and he found that the exhibition "clears the atmosphere by its explorations of the lesser known currents of these schools of Italian painting."[247]

The Baltimore Museum of Art, seeking ways to broaden the appeal of the Baroque, presented in 1942 a surprising grouping of artists in *Contrasts in Impressionism: Alessandro Magnasco, Claude Monet, and John Marin.* Two years later it mounted an exhibition of three rather more companionable artists from the seventeenth and eighteenth centuries: Strozzi, Crespi, and Piazzetta. According to the museum's director Adelyn Breeskin, these painters "represent a period in Italian art which has not been generally recognized or given due attention in our midst, coming as they do between the Venetian school of Titian and that of Tiepolo."[248] The show's organizer, Hans Tietze, wrote of the Baroque: "Let us not deceive ourselves. There is hardly any period within the art of the past to which we find the approach more difficult than to the Italian Baroque and its counterparts elsewhere. . . . It is not my intention to offer an apology of Baroque art, but my task is to explain our opposition to it." He then went on to note that "the painters represented as a group for the first time in the exhibition of the Baltimore Museum are in the process of emancipating themselves from the Baroque."[249] Regarding the two seventeenth-century masters, the Strozzis included those from Cincinnati, Hartford, the Metropolitan, St. Louis, the Walters, and Worcester, as well as loans from the dealers Heimann, Adolph Loewi, and Knoedler; the Crespis came from Detroit, Hartford, St. Louis, and the Kress Foundation, with the *Portrait of Chancellor Florius Senesius* lent by Heimann, and from the dealers and collectors Arnold Seligman, A.F. Mondschein, Schaeffer Galleries, Victor Spark, Suida, and Kirk Askew.

Magnasco continued to exert a powerful appeal and received yet another exhibition, this time at the Phillips Memorial Gallery in Washington in early 1943. For the collector Duncan Phillips, Magnasco "was one of the precursors of 19th-century romanticism in painting but, more specifically, of its

20th-century development known to us as Expressionism."[250] The paintings for this show came from many private dealers and collectors, including Mr. Phillips himself, the museum men G.H. Edgell and John Walker, and from museums in Boston, Cambridge, and Springfield.

In 1946 Durlacher Brothers presented at its East 57th Street gallery another Baroque exhibition, this one devoted to *Caravaggio and the Caravaggisti.* The Hartford *St. Francis* was the only authentic painting by the master, as the Fogg's *Cardsharps* was now called "follower." In addition to the Caracciolo from Hartford, Italian paintings included the Cavallino from Kansas City and a Ribera *Geographer* from Boston (now simply Neapolitan school). For sale were works by Orazio Gentileschi, Manfredi, and Stanzione. Two years later Durlacher's organized *A Loan Exhibition of Paintings by Salvator Rosa,* with nineteen works, almost all from museums: two were from the Art Institute of Chicago, and others came from Boston, Detroit, Hartford, Kansas City, the Metropolitan, Princeton, the Ringling, Vassar, and from the private collectors Mr. and Mrs. Lynes and Paul W. Cooley.

A significant museum exhibition was that shown at Smith College, Northampton, in February of 1947 entitled *Italian Baroque Paintings, 17th and 18th Centuries.* Its catalogue described the organizer's "attempt to exemplify from American collections a few episodes in the rich history of Italian seicento and settecento painting. Many great artists could not be represented at all. Some minor masters appear out of proportion to their real importance. Yet it has been possible to illustrate unusually well the works of one or two painters." These well-represented artists were Magnasco, Fetti, and Crespi. From the Boston Museum of Fine Arts came landscapes by Annibale Carracci and Domenichino; from the Fogg, its popular *Cardsharps* by a follower of Caravaggio; Hartford sent its Cavallino, Crespi, Guercino, and Rosa; the Metropolitan, a Castiglione; and Oberlin, Bazzani's *Death of Saphira.* The remaining works were primarily from New York dealers, including a *Four Seasons* attributed to Caravaggio from Piero Tozzi.

Down south, the Norton Gallery and School of Art in West Palm Beach, Florida, organized in 1949 the exhibition *Baroque Paintings of the Sixteenth to Eighteenth Centuries.* All the paintings were from the stock of E. and A. Silberman Galleries of New York, and these included a so-called Guercino *Judith with the Head of Holofernes* (now Bob Jones University Collection as Flaminio Torre), as well as works by Giovanni Battista Carlone, Fetti, Lippi, Solimena, and Stanzione.

MUSEUM ACQUISITIONS OF THE 1940S

The decade from 1940 to 1950—despite, or perhaps because of the Second World War—witnessed a tremendous upsurge in the number of Italian Baroque gifts to and acquisitions by American museums. The exhibition of 1941 in San Francisco may have stimulated greater activity among West Coast institutions. The De Young Memorial Museum received that year as a loan from the Hispanic Society of New York, founded by Archer M. Huntington, a Stanzione *Neapolitan Woman Holding a Chicken,* and in 1949 purchased a Magnasco *Woman and Soldier Resting.* There was also growth at the Los Angeles County Museum of Art where the acting director William Valentiner wrote in the museum's *Bulletin* in 1947:

> Until not long ago art historians were of the opinion that the seventeenth century did not produce artists of an importance and influence equal to those of other epochs. . . . They are of special interest to us today as their ideas and not those of the Renaissance became the starting-point for some of the most modern art movements, such as surrealism. . . . It is not accidental, therefore, if American museums have become greatly interested in recent years in Italian Baroque painting at a moment when the influence of Baroque ideas becomes evident in modern art. We can trace the beginning of this movement to the middle of the 'twenties—about fifteen years after it appears in Europe.[251]

Through the friendship Valentiner had established with the now ailing William Randolph Hearst, he was able to obtain for the museum a Strozzi *Berenice,* a Filippo Tarchiani *Supper at Emmaus,* and Rosa's *Ulysses and Nausicaa.*[252] Other gifts that came to the museum in the forties included Fetti's *Tobias and the Angel,* Castiglione's *Shepherd Scene,* Andrea de Leone's *Laban,* as well as works by Sacchi, Andrea Boscoli, Alessandro Gherardini, and Empoli (later identified as a Rosselli but sold). The dealer Jacob Heimann gave in 1946 the Caracciolo *Madonna* he had lent to the San Francisco exhibition.

During the early 1940s the Fine Arts Gallery of San Diego received several Baroque paintings. An anonymous gift of 1942 was the supposed Caravaggio *Portrait of a Woman* discovered by Voss and previously in the collection of Dr. Hans Schaeffer, Berlin, which had been shown at the New York World's Fair in 1940. The Gallery's 1947 catalogue noted apropos of this painting that "twentieth-century realism and the modern cinema are a projection of Caravaggio's thought." Also in 1942 it received as another anonymous gift a Magnasco *Fisherman,* and this elicited in the same catalogue the comment that "the painter's thick impasto and emotional vigor of his landscape have their counterpart in contemporary painting."[253] The next year saw the anonymous gift of a *Good Samaritan* by Fetti, which was recently sold. This was followed by a Mola in 1946, a Strozzi *David* in 1947, and a Maffei in 1949. The Putnam family also placed on loan a fine still life attributed to Caravaggio, which, now assigned to Cagnacci, is in the Timken Gallery later founded in San Diego by the Putnam sisters. The Seattle Art Museum was given a school of Reni *Magdalen* in 1943 and a Crespi *Adoration of the Shepherds* in 1949.

On the East Coast, the 1944 exhibition of *Three Baroque Masters* seemed to crystalize the particular Baroque taste already espoused by McComb and Askew of Durlacher Brothers. The Baltimore Museum of Art acquired its only Magnasco the following year, and the Boston Museum of Fine Arts in 1942 added a second Magnasco of *A Shipwreck,* as well as a supposed Annibale Carracci *Landscape* through another swap with Weitzner. This time in order to receive the two Baroque landscapes, Boston traded a Romney, Pissarro, Ruisdael, two Daubignys, a Leutze, and a Brouwer.[254] The Museum of Fine Arts also turned to a variety of other sources for some choice works. An unfinished painting by Pietro da Cortona was a gift from the dealer A.F. Mondschein of New York City in 1942, since it had been correctly identified by the museum's curator of paintings, W.G. Constable.[255] Then in 1945 the Crespi *Portrait of Chancellor Senesius,* which had been exhibited at San Francisco in 1941, was purchased from Heimann. On 7 October 1946 Constable wrote to the New York dealer Hans Schaeffer, "Do you think it would be worth your while to send Domenico Fetti's *The Good Samaritan* here? I personally am deeply interested in it. Whether I can sell it to the Committee is another matter."[256] On November 15th he would write with the good news that he had succeeded. Another Luca Giordano, *Apollo in his Chariot,* was given in 1947, but by far the most important Baroque painting acquired by the Boston museum in this decade was the great Guercino *Semiramis,* which the *Annual Report* of 1948 described as "a fine characteristic work by a master, paintings by whom are rare in the United States."[257] The painting had passed from the dealer Roderick Thesiger to the London firm of Colnaghi, and after its sale he joined that gallery in 1949. Thesiger's enthusiasm for the Baroque and his friendships with American curators and directors, such as Anthony Clark, facilitated the placement of many pictures in the museums of this country during the following decade.[258] The news of the Boston museum's purchase also elicited a letter to Constable from the young English scholar and student of Pevsner, Denis Mahon, who provided the information that the Guercino had formerly been in the collection of King Charles II and that he had recently published a study of Seicento art theory with particular emphasis on the change in Guercino's style, that was so evident in this painting.[259]

Following the resignation of Chick Austin at Hartford, the next director was W.G. Constable's assistant, Charles Cunningham, and he almost always reviewed his proposed acquisitions with his former boss. In 1949 they had a potentially sticky situation. The New York dealer David Koetser had a splendid Orazio Gentileschi *Judith and her Maidservant,* which had been identified by Voss as an important lost work and called by Frankfurter "the finest Baroque painting to come on the market for several years." This he offered to both Hartford and Boston. The price of $14,000 Constable thought was "on the high side but not unreasonable," and he proposed trading a Monet in partial payment. He was on the point of proposing this to his museum's purchase committee when he learned by telephone from Cunningham that Hartford was definitely interested in the painting. Boston politely withdrew from the competition, and the Wadsworth Atheneum was thus able to gain another Baroque gem and for only $12,500.[260]

The collecting of Baroque pictures continued

unabated in the Midwest: in Chicago, the Art Institute received as gifts its Cambiaso *Venus and Cupid* from the A. A. Munger collection in 1942, and in 1947 from the Worcester collection the Crespi *Woman Looking for Fleas,* Manfredi *Chastisement of Love,* and Magnasco school *The Witch.* A version of Magnasco's frequent subject of the *Synagogue* was also given from the Coburn collection in 1949. St. Louis acquired its Magnasco from Durlacher's in 1940 and by Strozzi a *St. Lawrence* from Heimann in 1944. Kansas City added the trio of Strozzi, Crespi, and Fetti. The Crespi *Young Man in a Helmet* was a gift in 1944 of Mr. and Mrs. Fred C. Vincent, who had bought it that year from Durlacher's. The Strozzi *St. Cecilia* was the mate to the painting in Hartford and had been placed on loan to the museum by the Italian dealer Italico Brass in 1940, but when he died in 1943 the work was sequestered by the U.S. Office of Alien Property and then offered for sale by sealed bid in July 1949 at which time it was purchased by the Nelson-Atkins Museum of Art.[261] The Fetti *Pearl of Great Price* was bought from the Schaeffer Galleries in 1948. Detroit was also particularly acquisitive with, in 1942 Cortona's *St. Jerome in the Desert* and Saraceni's *Susannah* (later discovered to be signed by Ottavio Leoni), a Giordano *Adoration of the Shepherds* purchased from Schaeffer Galleries in 1944, a Cavallino *St. Agatha* given in 1945, an Annibale Carracci in 1946, and a Barocci in 1949. The Institute of Arts was fortunate in that Edgar Whitcomb and his wife Anne Scripps Whitcomb followed in the tradition of her father by donating art works that were selected by the museum staff. In 1947 they gave in this way an important Rosa, *The Finding of Moses,* formerly in the Colonna collection and later with the Duke of Buckingham before being bought by F.E. Goodheart of Chicago, where it remained until acquired by Durlacher's.[262]

At other museums around the country, the following additions of Baroque paintings could be reported. The National Gallery received a Tiberio Tinelli portrait from Samuel Fuller in 1946, and to the Phillips Collection, joining its Magnascos, went a Salvator Rosa. Smaller museums also made notable gains, such as Springfield with a Sebastiano Ricci *Assumption of the Virgin* in 1945. Ralph Norton in 1948 acquired from Silberman a large and important Valerio Castello of *Diana and her Nymphs,* formerly in the Herbert Sears collection, which he gave the next year to the museum he founded in West Palm Beach. In Bennington, Vermont, a collection formed by Joseph Henry Colyer, Jr. was bequeathed to the local museum in 1948 and contained a supposed Caravaggio *Christ Crowned with Thorns,* a Rosa *Battle Scene,* and a Dolci *Self-Portrait,* among its several Baroque works,[263] which were, however, deaccessioned in 1978.

The university museums continued to build their collections, with a Ruoppolo going to Vassar in 1944, and to Harvard a Rosa in 1941 and a Vaccaro in 1945. Columbia received a Preti in 1943, and Brown University, a Solimena in 1942, while Oberlin got a Magnasco in 1943. At Wellesley College, John McAndrew, who taught Baroque architecture, became director of the museum in 1947; for the next ten years he successfully cultivated collectors and made wise purchases to build a small but representative group of Baroque works.[264] From the Worcester Art Museum he purchased in 1949 a little Magnasco of a *Saint in Meditation,* and a Crespi study for his large *Sacrament of Ordination* came from Weitzner in 1948. At Yale, the pendant to the St. Louis Magnasco was obtained in 1945, and Notre Dame was given a work of the studio of Luca Giordano in 1942. The University of California Art Museum at Berkeley was enhanced in 1943 by a *Judith with the Head of Holofernes* attributed to Cavaliere d'Arpino.

EXHIBITIONS IN THE 1950S

The 1950s was to be the decade of the great new collectors and it was also highlighted by several memorable exhibitions. In late February of 1950 Durlacher's mounted *A Loan Exhibition of Paintings by Domenico Fetti 1589-1624.* It consisted of twelve paintings and one drawing and had a catalogue introduced by Bernice Davidson, who wrote of the painter's "poetic romanticism which appears to anticipate the art of the eighteenth century." Included were the well-known paintings from the museums in Rochester and Detroit. Of special interest was the showing of three versions of *The Good Samaritan,* those from Boston, the Metropolitan Museum, and San Diego. Works were also lent from the museums of Worcester, Kansas City, and Cleveland, and from the collection of Henry P. McIlhenny. Fetti's *David with the Head of Goliath* was for sale.

In 1951 the first large exhibition of works by

Caravaggio was held in Italy.[265] Then the following year, one of the first signs of the burgeoning American interest in the Baroque was the *Exhibition of Italian Paintings of the Seventeenth Century,* presented by the Allen Memorial Art Museum at Oberlin College in Ohio. It was organized by the museum's director Charles Parkhurst and had a catalogue essay by the school's distinguished art history professor Wolfgang Stechow. The latter noted that this exhibition limited to eighteen paintings "deliberately omits not only the Settecento (including even such transitional figures as Magnasco), but also the immediate circle of Caravaggio," as well as Annibale and Ludovico Carracci, Domenichino, Pietro da Cortona, Bernardo Cavallino, "yet, there certainly remains enough spontaneous creativity."[266]

The paintings shown at Oberlin included some that were already well known. On view were Allori's *Madonna on Clouds* (University of Kansas, Lawrence); Bamboccio's *Carnival* (Hartford); Bartolomeo Cavarozzi's *Holy Family* (Piero Tozzi, New York); Fetti's *Parable of the Pearl* (Kansas City), *Parable of the Mote and Beam* (Princeton), and *St. Stephen* (Rochester); Giordano's *Christ Driving out the Money Changers* (Weitzner); Guercino's *Semiramis* (Boston) and *Portrait of a Man* (Gabarty, New York); Preti's *Christ Seating the Child in the Midst of the Disciples* (Weitzner, and then acquired the next year by Bob Jones, Jr.; cat. no. 25); Reni's *Head of a Saint* (Gabarty); Rosa's *Landscape with the Finding of Moses* (Detroit), *Landscape with Tobias and the Angel* (Hartford), and *Mercury and Argus* (Oberlin); and Strozzi's *Adoration of the Shepherds* (Walters Art Gallery), *St. Lawrence* (St. Louis), and *Calling of St. Matthew* (Worcester).

The wider appeal of the Baroque was evident in 1955 when that bastion of conservative taste, the gallery of Wildenstein & Co. joined the parade and presented in London the exhibition, *Artists in 17th-Century Rome,* a collaboration of Denys Sutton and Denis Mahon, who lent his own Annibale Carracci *Coronation of the Virgin* (now in the Metropolitan Museum of Art) and Domenichino *St. Jerome and the Angel.* Later, in 1958, the New York branch of the firm featured a selection of paintings with a slim catalogue entitled *Italian Baroque.* A brief introduction noted, "The history of taste is not simply a chronicle of affirmations but also one of neglects. It is only fairly recently that values inherent in the Baroque vision as a whole have again been widely recognized." The anonymous writer suggested that this may be due to the influence of contemporary art:

> Perhaps the present widespread awareness of the Baroque contribution may be related, through cause or effort, to a renewed appreciation of sweeping rhythms—dramatized by enlargement of norms just past—that is characteristic of some painting today. Also the contemporary outlook appears to have been affected by an emotional import that could be closer to the Baroque than the classical forms. Cant of the day aside, the spiritual aim behind the wry manipulation of orthodoxies which appealed to the surrealists may be compared with the grave ecstasies sought in the dark glass of mannerism or by artists of the seventeenth century. Whatever the reasons, now there is something in the air which seems to make the Baroque breath congenial. This small selection is an attempt to catch the atmosphere.

The works presented were a Strozzi *Portrait of a Bishop,* a *Lute Player* from the Barberini collection attributed to Saraceni (recently upgraded to Caravaggio himself),[267] a Rosa *Glaucus and Scylla,* and by Giordano a pair representing *Judith and Holofernes,* a Fetti *The Grief of Artemisia,* a Guercino school *Marriage of the Virgin,* a Chiari *Allegorical Incident,* a Domenichino *Portrait of a Cardinal,* a Fabrizio Santafede *Marriage of St. Catherine,* and a signed and dated Elisabetta Sirani of 1664 of *Portia Wounding her Thigh.*

THE NEW YORK MILIEU

What made the flourishing of Baroque taste possible in the 1950s was a fortuitous combination of circumstances, the first of which was a new generation of collectors imbued with a modern sensibility of taste that made them receptive to expressionism whether in abstract or baroque form. Second, there was a group of dealers with the contacts to supply the offbeat works that appealed to the collectors, and third, a cadre of scholars to provide the intellectual underpinnings for this taste.

Although some of the buying was done at the auction houses and some abroad at Colnaghi's and Agnew's in London, at Heim in Paris, or at Sestieri in Rome, the great bulk of it took place in New York

City. There, Julius Weitzner, as we have seen, was already long established and even after he moved to London in 1959 was to be the single most significant supplier of Baroque paintings to both collectors and museums. But he was by no means the only one. Durlacher's, of course, continued in the trade, as did Silberman, Heinemann, Newhouse, and Schaeffer.

There were, however, several significant new players who now became active. The London firm of Koetser, founded by a Dutch couple and continued by their three sons, was one of these. David Koetser first came to New York in 1939, and became an independent dealer on 57th Street in 1948.[268] A reserved, even secretive man, he nevertheless had a sharp eye for good pictures, wide-ranging knowledge, and a keen judgment of potential clients. He bought in Europe and also from his fellow dealers such as Weitzner. His stock, as one of his few published exhibition catalogues *From Van Cleve to Tiepolo* of 1941 makes clear, covered all areas. In this instance, the only Italian Baroque works were six biblical scenes on copper by Luca Giordano. As is clear, however, from the paintings he sold to American collectors and also from those he set aside for his personal collection (which was willed to the Kunsthaus in Zurich, where Koetser settled in 1966), he had a particular fondness for the Baroque.

Another gallery that was to be, like its name, central to the enormous upsurge of interest in the Baroque throughout the 1950s, was the Central Picture Galleries. It was founded by Oscar Klein, fondly remembered as a delightfully owlish man, who had been both an artist and a successful art dealer in his native Prague. When the Germans invaded, he was able to flee on an artist's visa first to Oslo and then to New York. There, a chance meeting on the street with a former client, a cinema owner from Prague, Oswald Kosek, led to the opening of the new art gallery in New York at 624 Madison Avenue on the corner of 59th Street. The gallery was later moved to 57th Street. Klein's son Jan had gone to England during the war as a member of a Zionist youth group and then returned to Prague as a soldier in the independent Czech army. There he entered the university but had to escape to Germany in 1948 when the Communist government came to power. Receiving a displaced persons visa from the United States, he was able to rejoin his father in New York to assist in running the gallery (Fig. 13).[269]

It was Oscar Klein whom Jan credits with the taste for the large Baroque pictures of both the Northern and Italian schools, which, since they were still relatively unfashionable, were reasonably priced and allowed the new gallery to prosper. There was a great deal of trading and selling between the various other dealers who had similar taste, and Koetser was especially kind in giving the Kleins credit. Walter Chrysler, Jr., introduced to them by Robert L.

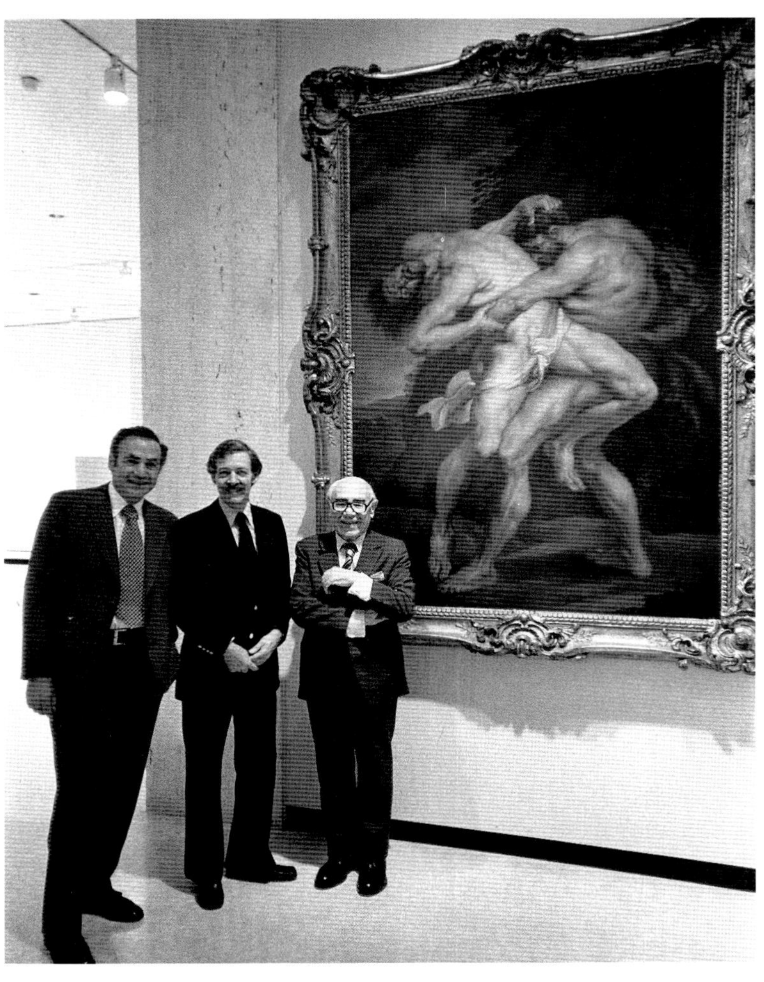

FIGURE 13

From left to right are Jan Klein, the Baroque scholar John Rupert Martin, and Oscar Klein. Photograph courtesy of Jan Klein.

Manning, became their first major private client in the early 1950s, and despite his difficult personality remained supportive of them over the years, even serving as a witness at the ceremony in which Jan Klein became an American citizen. Another of the fifties generation of collectors, Paul Ganz, who told the Kleins he was proud of never having had to work in his life, both bought from and sold works to them as did all the other notable collectors of the era: Robert and Bertina Suida Manning, Bob Jones, Jr., and Luis Ferré. The last, who was first brought to the Kleins by the art historian Julius S. Held, became a regular visitor and close friend.

Another dealer active in New York at this time—one who had actually begun his career there in 1921 and remained in business until the late 1970s—was Nicholas M. Acquavella.[270] His gallery at 38 East 57th Street carried art of all periods, but often provided large Italian Baroque works to the leading collectors. To Mr. Chrysler he sold a great Crespi spotted by Mr. Manning in a hotel in San Remo, Italy, and also a Gregorio de'Ferrari; to Paul Ganz, a Valerio Castello; and to Mr. and Mrs. Jack Linsky, a Magnasco of *Nuns Making Lace.* His friendship with Theodore Rousseau, curator of paintings at the Metropolitan Museum of Art, resulted in the museum's acquiring an Artemisia Gentileschi from Mr. Ingersoll, and also a large Guido Reni of *The Immaculate Conception* from the Ellsmere collection. This came to the English dealer Leger, who stored it a garage from where it was bought sight unseen by Oscar Klein and sent rolled up to America. The restorer Mario Modestini and Robert Manning looked at it for the Kress Foundation, but Acquavella traded Klein a painting by Kalf and cash for it and then sold the painting to the Metropolitan.

Frederick Mont was yet another dealer in New York with exceptional taste who sold many works through the Newhouse Gallery. He had connections in Vienna and imported, for example in 1962, from the famed Czernin collection, an Andrea de Leone *Tobit Burying the Dead* that Paul Ganz bought in 1965 and lent to the Metropolitan, which later acquired it.

The two major universities of New York City provided the intellectual support for the triumph of Baroque art during this decade. To New York University's Institute of Fine Arts in 1935 at the age of sixty had come the indefatigable Dr. Walter Friedländer.[271] An expert on Poussin, he now turned his attention to Caravaggio and produced his groundbreaking book *Caravaggio Studies* in 1955. Among those who came to study with him and who would later help spread the gospel of the Baroque were Donald Posner, Guy Walton, Jane Costello, Kenneth Donahue, Frances Huemer, and M.G. Zucconi.

Columbia University invited another European scholar, Rudolf Wittkower from the Warburg Institute in London, to join the faculty of the art history department in 1949. He became chairman in 1956 and retired in 1969. The foreword of his monumental *Art and Architecture in Italy 1600 to 1750,* published in 1958, contained the dismissive warning:

> Excepting the beginning and the end of the period under review, i.e. Caravaggio, the Carracci, and Tiepolo, the history of painting would seem less important than that of the other arts and often indeed has no more than strictly limited interest—an ideal hunting-ground for specialists and "attributionists." This fact has been somewhat obscured by the great mass of valuable research made during the last forty years in the field of Italian Baroque painting at the expense of studies in the history of architecture and sculpture. Roughly from the second quarter of the seventeenth century on, the most signal developments in easel-painting lay outside Italy.

Nevertheless, in his text Wittkower did cover a remarkable number of painters, from the major figures of Annibale, Caravaggio, and Reni to such lesser-known names as Caracciolo, Furini, Langetti, Mastalletta, Giovanni Serodine, and Alessandro Tiarini, and on into the eighteenth century with Crespi and Ricci. Wittkower attracted many junior faculty members and students who were to become distinguished in the Baroque field as writers, teachers, collectors, and dealers, including Milton Lewine, Howard Hibbard, D. Stephen Pepper, and Joan Nissman. At Columbia's affiliate college of Barnard was to be found a famous expert on Northern Baroque art, Professor Julius Held, who also advised collectors interested in Italian painting (see Fig. 20 below).

Even before the new generation of collectors was launched, there was already one other very notable operation dealing in Baroque art active in New York City. This was the Kress Foundation. As we have noted, its direction changed significantly in 1946 when

Rush Kress became director. He had as his chief advisor Professor William Suida (1877-1959), who had studied in Heidelberg and taught at the University of Graz and the German Institute in Florence. Early in the century he had gone to Genoa, become immersed in its art, and published a remarkable history of its achievements.[272] Then in 1937, for the Galerie Sanct Lucas in Vienna, Suida with Hermann Voss and others had prepared a major exhibition of Italian Baroque art.[273] He came to America in 1939 to write the first catalogue of Ringling's paintings,[274] and must at that time have also seen the fledgling Kress collection, for he published a German article on the latter in 1940.[275] In this he noted that there were only two seventeenth-century paintings—the supposed Caravaggio *Still Life* and Fetti *Parable of Lazarus and the Rich Man.* Suida was teaching at Queens College when in October 1947 Rush Kress appointed him librarian and research curator for the foundation. With his wide-ranging interests and sheer love of collecting, he was an excellent choice to join forces with the Kress's restorer, Mario Modestini, to proselytize for the Italian Baroque. The story of how they built up this collection has been told in detail quite recently,[276] but for our purposes, it is worth noting that the 1950s, the last active decade of Kress collecting, was its most adventurous, with purchases of works by such lesser-known masters as Cagnacci, Caroselli, Ludovico Carracci, Ciro Ferri, Lorenzo Lippi, Mastaletta, Sebastiano Mazzoni, Mola, and Stanzione, as well as filling in the gaps of some of the most famous names, with a Reni, Guercino, two Orazio Gentileschis, two Castigliones, several Rosas and Strozzis, and more Magnascos.[277]

The collection of Italian paintings formed by the two Kress brothers, Samuel and Rush, thus stands as the most monumental achievement in art collecting of the twentieth century both for its span and the sheer number of distinguished works. Today its breadth can only be experienced in book form, as the paintings—especially those of the Baroque—were dispersed to museums around the country in 1961, after the National Gallery of Art, under the directorship of John Walker, had chosen what it considered suitable for its needs. The result is, as Edgar Peters Bowron has observed, that there are an "extraordinary number of fine paintings in relatively provincial cities across the nation."[278] The fortunate cities that had been home to the Kress department stores and that benefited from the dismantling of the Kress collection, include Tulsa, Seattle, Tucson, Memphis, Miami, and Atlanta, to name just a few.

THE SUIDA MANNING COLLECTION

It is fitting that the first of the five major Italian Baroque collections of the 1950s to be addressed here grew out of a mixture of the very New York sources just discussed. Attracted to study at the Institute of Fine Arts with Friedländer in 1946 were two young art historians, Robert Manning from Texas and Bertina Suida, daughter of the Kress advisor. William Suida had been collecting assiduously from his own student days, and his taste, especially his love of Genoese and all Baroque art, was inherited by Bertina, who became one of the world's leading experts on Cambiaso and the Genoese school. With her thorough knowledge and Manning's brilliant eye, the couple made a formidable team when they married shortly after meeting (Fig. 14).[279] Through Suida, Manning became assistant curator of the Kress collection from 1950 to 1961 and was introduced to the heady world of art dealing in New York, for at that time the Kress Foundation was given first option on many major works, especially of the Baroque school.

The Suida Mannings were to have a significant role over the next few decades as organizers of exhibitions and as advisors to other collectors, most especially Walter Chrysler, Jr., for whom Mrs. Manning served as curator for a time beginning in 1950. Most importantly, building on Suida's collection, they lovingly assembled a remarkable hoard of Italian paintings and drawings by both famous and lesser-known artists to which they continued adding until Bertina Suida Manning's untimely death in 1992.

Regrettably, there has never been an exhibition of their entire collection, and only a small one of eighteenth-century material was held in 1969 at Duke University in North Carolina, which did, however, include works by artists born in the seventeenth century, including Crespi, Creti, Ghislandi, Giordano, Magnasco (two), and Solimena (two).[280] Nevertheless, from visits to their delightful home in Queens, the catalogues of various exhibitions to which they have generously lent, and other publications, particularly catalogues raisonné, it is possible to obtain some rough idea of its scope. To highlight but a few of the

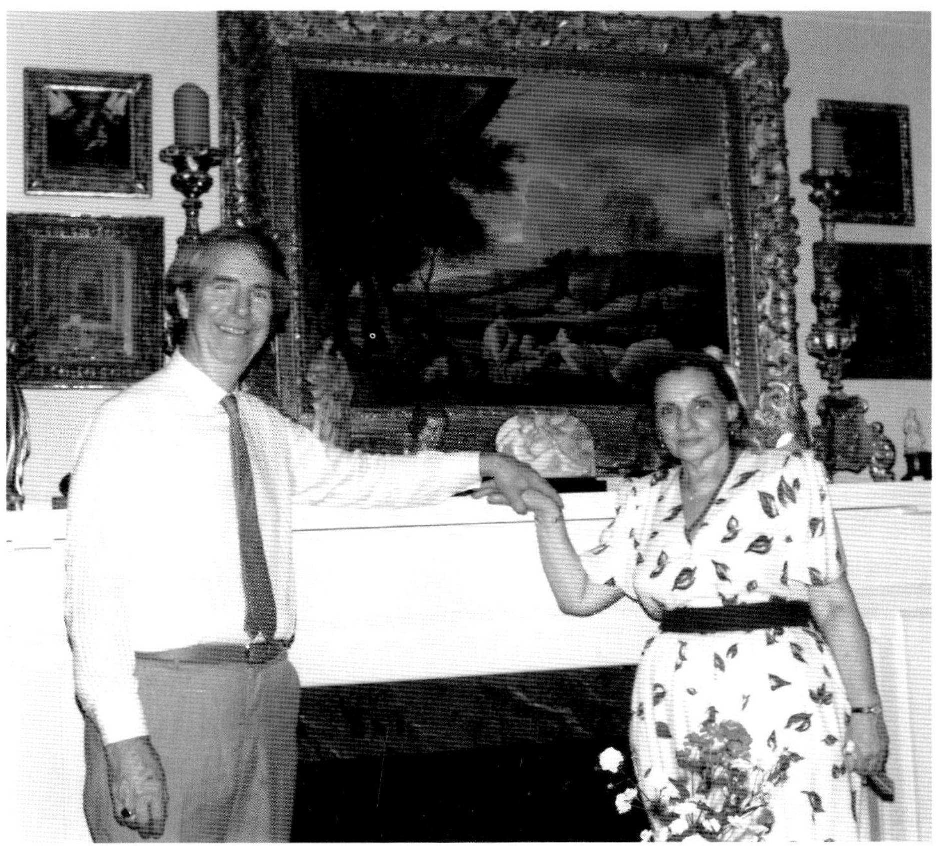

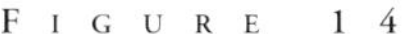

FIGURE 14

Robert L. Manning and the late Bertina Suida Manning in their living room. Photograph courtesy of Mary Jane Harris.

outstanding Italian Baroque works in the Suida Manning collection, there are Passeri's *Musical Party in the Garden,* a *Flora* by Ricci, Saraceni's *Martyrdom of St. Cecilia,* Domenico Piola's *Adoration of the Shepherds,* Guercino's *Penitent Magdalen,* Daniele Crespi's *Conversion of St. Paul,* Fetti's *Artemisia,* Ponzone's *Cleopatra,* and Lanfranco's *Sleeping Venus.* In addition, there are paintings by Giulio Carpioni, Sirani, Strozzi, Reni, Cavallino, Francesco Guarino, Preti, and of course, a large number of Cambiasos.

THE CHRYSLER COLLECTION

The next link in this thoroughly intertwined chain of personalities in the Baroque art world of the 1950s was also forged by Robert Manning. Through Thomas C. Colt, Jr., who had gone from the directorship of the museum in Richmond, Virginia, to that in Portland, Oregon, and then Dayton. Manning was introduced in the early fifties to Walter P. Chrysler, Jr., and with his combination of good taste and business acumen was able to convince the collector to turn his attention from the Dutch and Flemish art that was then occupying him to the Italian Baroque.

Son of the car manufacturer, Chrysler was—despite the mean-spirited obituaries that appeared after his death in 1988 prompted by the memory of his 1962 exhibition *The Controversial Century* shown in Provincetown and Ottawa, which included a number of fakes,[281] and by his less than scrupulous business dealings over the years—one of the most important American collectors of the twentieth century (Fig. 15). Perhaps acquisitor is a better word, for Mr. Chrysler never displayed much love for his individual works of art and was not reluctant to sell them off or trade them away when it suited him or when he sought to build up other aspects of his collection. To acquire what he wanted he would use any means, sweet promises or threats, cajoling or intimidation, and, since he hated to pay cash, he would often give promissory notes or more usually trade other works of art, jewels, or even on one occasion, a unique custom-made Chrysler car. Like another American collector, Henry McIlhenny, whom he knew slightly, Mr. Chrysler made his first precocious art purchases while still in school. Realizing that his talents did not lie in business, his goal gradually seems to have become the building of an overall collection of world art to be housed in a museum bearing his name. More than likely, his intention was to outdo the memory and fame of his father, for he was heard to say more than once that in the future the name Chrysler would be better known for the museum than for the automobile company. To this end in 1958 he opened his first museum, the Chrysler Art Museum of Provincetown, in that Cape Cod resort town with an inaugural exhibition of seventy-four paintings.[282] While resident in Provincetown, Mr. Chrysler befriended and supported many of the contemporary artists who summered there, such as Franz Kline and Hans Hoffmann. In 1970, after disagreements with the town fathers over parking rights, he closed his museum in Provincetown and moved it to Norfolk, Virginia, home of his wife, Jean Outland Chrysler. The city government obligingly changed the name of the already extant Norfolk Museum of Arts and Sciences to the Chrysler Museum, and provided funds to maintain and greatly expand the facility.[283]

As a young man, Chrysler had visited France and met Gertrude Stein, from whom he acquired a taste for the early twentieth-century masters that she collected and espoused. By 1941 when his collection was exhibited for the first time in its entirety at the Virginia Museum of Fine Arts and the Philadelphia Museum of Art, the catalogue foreword by Tom Colt could rightly claim that "the Chrysler Collection will be recognized as one of the largest, the most important, and remarkable collections of Expressionist Art in the United States. . . . Assembled by a young man with a keen mind, at once aesthetically perceptive and visionary." Included in this monumental collection were paintings by three old masters, El Greco, Goya, and Chardin (who were believed to have had a modern spirit), African art, some paintings of the nineteenth century, and "primitive" American art, but the majority of works were of the twentieth century, with thirteen Arps, fifteen Braques, ten Gris, thirty-one Legers, twenty-two Matisses, and a tremendous group of eighty-nine diverse works by Picasso, which, as the catalogue stated, "ranks by itself in America as a very complete survey of this vital artist's work."[284]

Never content to remain static, Mr. Chrysler then shifted his focus to decorative arts, particularly glass, of which he formed a major collection, and to paintings by the Dutch and Flemish old masters, of which he would later claim to have owned over one thousand examples. A portion of these were shown in 1951 at the Lowe Art Museum of the University of Miami, Coral Gables.[285] It was, however, just at this time that, through Mr. Manning, new interests had again taken the collector's fancy. Throughout the 1950s the Chrysler collection became most famous for two diverse areas—the large-scale and previously unfashionable French academics and landscapists and Italian paintings of the seventeenth and eighteenth centuries. There is no doubt that, like other collectors of this era, Mr. Chrysler was pleased to find that with these paintings he could get the maximum amount of size and quality for the minimum of outlay. Being a passionate man with a taste for rich food and an occasional backer of Broadway shows, he genuinely responded to the bold exuberance of these Baroque works. The gallery he created for them while he was director of the museum in Norfolk was a remarkable theatrical treat, a cross between the approaches of those earlier single-minded collectors who formed private museums, Isabella Stewart Gardner and Henry Clay Frick. With the walls painted in shades of

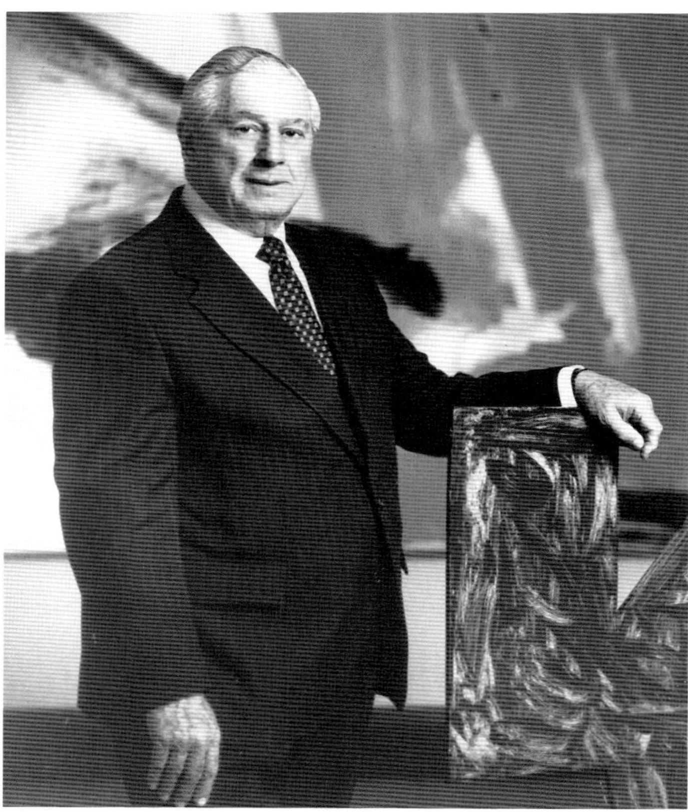

FIGURE 15

Walter P. Chrysler, Jr. Photograph courtesy of the Chrysler Museum, Norfolk, Virginia.

yellow and purple, the gallery was dominated by the tremendous Bernini marble *Bust of the Savior.* The great Baroque paintings by Reni, Guercino, Rosa, and others filled the walls, and a set of sculptures by Bertos vied for space with mounted period vestments. Although not to everyone's taste, the grandiose clutter probably gave the best approximation of a Baroque *palazzo* then available in America.

Mr. Chrysler often bought on impulse, so it was fortunate that he had such knowledgeable advisors in his pursuit of the Italian Baroque as Robert and Bertina Manning, who assisted by directing pictures his way, providing suggestions on purchases, and even researching and writing catalogues of the collection. The bulk of the Chrysler Italian Baroque paintings was acquired during the fifties from the small circle of New York dealers who specialized in such works. In 1950 he began auspiciously with two quintessential Guido Renis from Koetser, the *St. Cecilia* and the *Meeting of David and Abigail.* From the same source came in succeeding years two Guercinos, an equally classic *Samson Bringing Honey to his Parents,* formerly in the Barberini collection, in 1953, and a *Lot and his Daughters* in 1954. That same year Koetser also sold Chrysler the great Ashburnham pair of Rosas, as well as a Ricci *Apollo and Pan,* a large *Concert* attributed then to Creti but now sometimes to Muratori, as well as works by Castiglione, Dolci, and Liss; shortly thereafter came two paintings by Giordano and an impressive *Portrait of Paolo Raggio* by Strozzi. In the years 1953 to 1954 a number of major acquisitions were made from Weitzner. These included the enormous Valerio Castello *Legend of St. Geneviève of Brabant* (the curious pendant to the *Diana with Nymphs* in the Norton Gallery), which Mr. Manning convinced Chrysler was a worthwhile painting despite the then high price of $10,000. (His conviction was proven when this work sold for over one million dollars in the auction the year after the collector's death.) Also from Weitzner came Strozzi's *Martyrdom of St. Dorothy,* Renieri's *Death of Sophonisba,* and Preti's monumental *Belisarius Receiving Alms.* As previously noted, Chrysler purchased from Acquavella in these same years the beautiful Crespi *Continence of Scipio,* and this dealer also sold him Rosa's *Hagar and Ishmael* and a Cavallino school *Marriage of Tobias.* A truly fine Cavallino was the *Procession to Calvary* from Newhouse Gallery in 1957. Frederick Mont supplied a Magnasco *Landscape with Monks,* Solimena *Portrait of a Nobleman,* and a version of Annibale Carracci's *Venus, Cupid, and Satyr.* From Central Picture Galleries Mr. Chrysler obtained a Tiberio Titi *Portrait of a Nobleman,* a Giordano *Descent from the Cross,* a Pietro Liberi *Mercury and Venus,* and in 1969 the large Paolo de Matteis *Olindo and Sophronia Rescued by Clorinda.* As late as 1976 they supplied a Sassoferrato *Madonna and Child.* That same year the collector also received, as part of one of his many multi-faceted deals, a version of Andrea de Leone's *Tobit Burying the Dead* from French & Co. A few works came from farther afield—like the fine Giordano *Bacchus and Ariadne* and Magnasco *Arcadian Landscape* from German sources. A *Portrait of a Seated Gentleman* once attributed to Caravaggio was obtained from Jean Nager of Paris in 1954. Other pictures that passed through the Chrysler collection but whose origins were not recorded include Beinaschi's *Neptune with a Triton and Nereides,* Lanfranco's *Stratonice,* and Domenichino's *St. Catherine of Alexandria.*[286]

The first major showing of many of these works was the 1956 exhibition *Paintings from the Collection of Walter P. Chrysler, Jr.,* organized by the Portland Art Museum in Oregon, which traveled to eight other museums, including those of Boston, Detroit, Kansas City, Los Angeles, and Minneapolis. The unexpected richness of Chrysler's Baroque and Rococo paintings both Northern and Italian was a startling and memorable revelation. In 1962-63, another touring exhibition, *1550-1650. A Century of Masters from the Collection of Walter P. Chrysler, Jr.,* was sent to Austin, Fort Worth, and Tulsa. This included the two Cavallinos, two Luca Giordanos, two Guercinos, two Renis, and the Renieri *Death of Sophonisba.* Bowdoin College hosted in 1963 *Baroque Paintings from the Collection of Walter P. Chrysler, Jr.,* with the *Portrait of a Man* attributed to Caravaggio, as well as the Crespi, Creti, Dolci, Lanfranco, Liss, Preti, Renieri, the pair of Rosas, and Della Vecchia's *Philosopher.* To commemorate the opening of the new wing of the Norfolk Museum in late 1967 was staged the richest selection yet, *Italian Renaissance and Baroque Paintings from the Collection of Walter P. Chrysler, Jr.,* for which Mr. Manning prepared the catalogue. This great array of works must have helped convince the city's art lovers that the Chrysler collection as a whole was worth bringing to the city even if the cantankerous collector also had to become a presence in their affairs.

Certain paintings in the Chrysler collection, especially those of the early twentieth century by Picasso and Braque, were never brought to Norfolk but remained sequestered in the collector's famous New York warehouse. There also was stored a most notable Baroque painting, a version of Caravaggio's *Supper at Emmaus* that he had purchased from Central Picture Galleries in 1957 and later quietly sold.[287] The Chrysler collection of Italian Baroque paintings was kept fairly intact until the late 1960s, when he began again selling and trading these works to build up his holdings of American and earlier old master paintings. Feeling he needed only one representative work by an artist, Mr. Chrysler disposed of the Reni *St. Cecilia* (now in the Norton Simon Museum), Guercino *Lot and his Daughters,* and Renieri *Sophonisba.* Even sadder was his splitting the pair of Rosas (with one going to St. Louis). Nevertheless, many fine works still remained in the Chrysler Museum, and, as he repeatedly employed the threat of removing his loans to get his way in running the museum, it was expected that he would bequeath them all. But instead, perhaps, in one last effort to mastermind events and revenge himself on the often critical Norfolkians, he never signed his much-discussed will to that effect, and all his loans were left to a distant relative, who promptly sent them to auction at Sotheby's in New York.[288] In this way, many important works such as the Valerio Castello, the Solimena and Caravaggio school portraits, the Sassoferrato, and the Andrea de Leone, to name only those of the Italian Baroque school, were returned to the market that Mr. Chrysler so dearly loved.

THE BOB JONES UNIVERSITY COLLECTION

At almost exactly the same time that Mr. Chrysler began his accumulation of Italian Baroque paintings, another major collection was launched in Greenville, South Carolina. It was created by Dr. Bob Jones, Jr. at the university founded in 1927 that bears his father's name. Like the Chrysler Museum, the collection was to be a survey of Western European painting, but, unlike any other, this university museum, as Dr. Jones has stated:

> is unique in that it is composed exclusively of religious paintings, primarily those which illustrate scriptural events or portray Biblical characters. The collection should be regarded as an attempt to gather a well-rounded assemblage of fine paintings which serve at the same time as a record of the history and development of European religious art from the Gothic through the Baroque.[289]

Dr. Jones's first artistic interest was in archaeology, but then, at the age of twelve, he was taken by his parents to Europe and discovered old master paintings. He was encouraged by the longtime collector Carl Hamilton, who was then involved in advising the new museum of art in Raleigh. A devout man, despite all his escapades,[290] Hamilton saw a need at the evangelical university for an art museum and was able to both inspire young Jones and introduce him to some of the leading experts and art dealers. Thus Dr. Jones was to receive advice from such scholars as Suida, the Tietzes, and later, Federico Zeri and Anthony Clark. Of the New York dealers, Julius Weitzner and Mitchell Samuels were especially solicitous and were to have galleries in the museum named for them. Gradually, however, as he has modestly stated, Dr Jones came to rely on his own "eye for quality."[291] He had visited the Ringling Museum and met on a few occasions his fellow collectors, Walter Chrysler, Jr. and Paul Ganz. Unlike them, however, he was not a rich man; his purchase funds were limited to an annual budget of $30,000 allotted by the University. As for his taste in collecting, Dr. Jones has said that if he had a choice, he would have preferred to concentrate on the small, highly finished Netherlandish works, but the big Italian Baroque pictures were less costly and more readily available from the dealers of the time. It should also be added that with his mastery of oratory, skill as an actor, and love of opera, Dr. Jones is, in fact, temperamentally suited to respond to the glories of Baroque art. Despite relatively limited means, he has been able through acquisitions, gifts, and upgrading to assemble a remarkable collection of all periods, but one particularly strong in the Italian Baroque.

The Bob Jones University Collection of Religious Art was begun in 1951, and the gallery to house it was dedicated on Thanksgiving Day of that year. The collection then consisted of some forty paintings displayed in two rooms. By the time the first museum

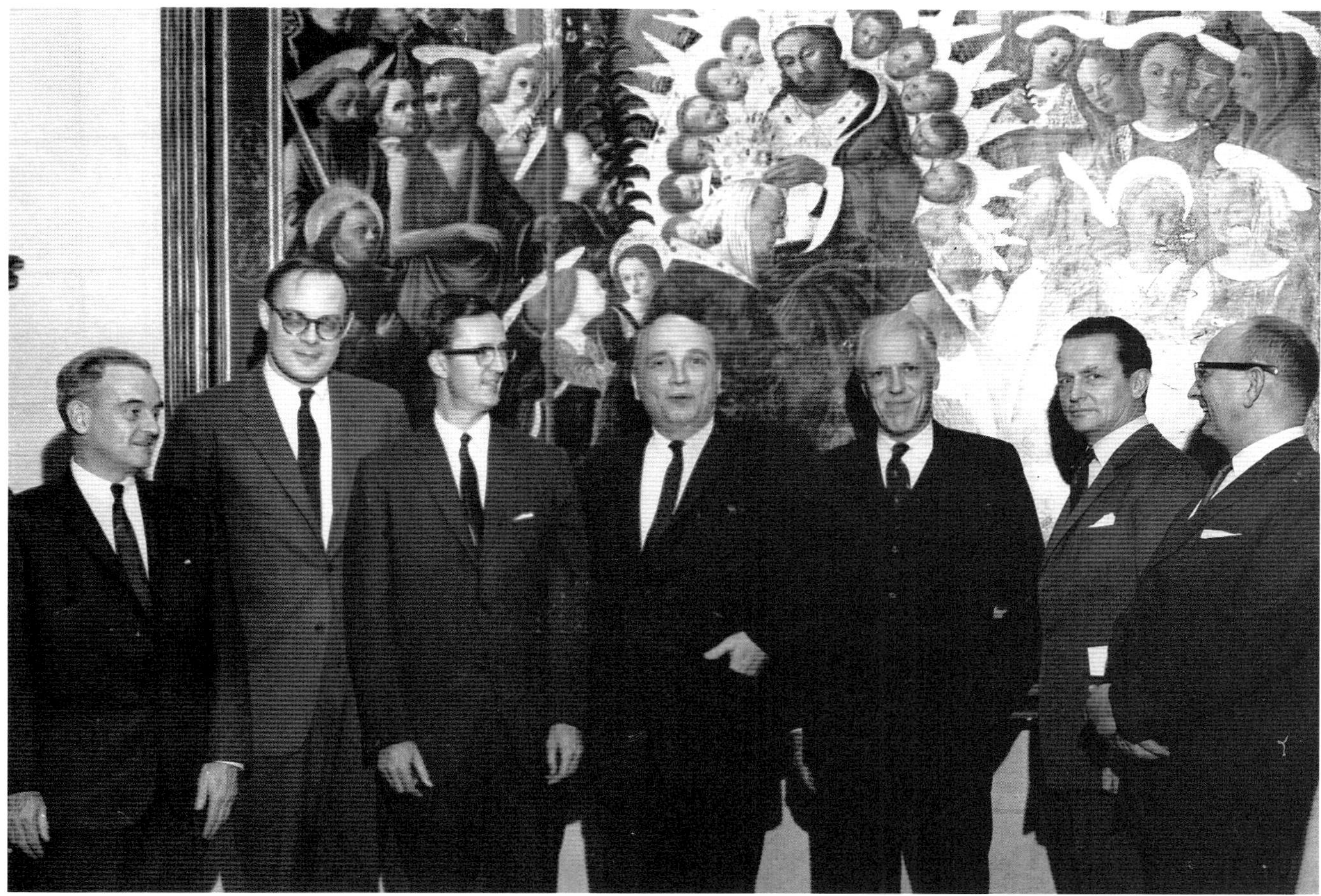

catalogue appeared in 1954, there were nearly seventy paintings, and Dr. Jones could proudly write that the collection "contains fine examples of a wide variety of schools and periods and a number of pictures of particular importance. One or two artists are represented in no other public collection on this side of the Atlantic; and in some instances the Bob Jones University Collection contains what is possibly the finest example of an artist's work to be seen in this country." The Tietzes in their foreword to the catalogue seconded this view, writing that "the university program has resulted in a distinguished collection *without* centering all its attention on the accepted great masters."[292] Already a number of Baroque works figured prominently among the paintings. A Solimena *Ecce Homo* (now Francesco de Mura; cat. no. 36) had been purchased from John Levy of New York in 1951. Through the intervention of Carl Hamilton, a monumental Luca Giordano of *Christ Driving the Merchants from the Temple* was obtained from the London dealer Tomás Harris (cat. no. 24). Harris, who specialized in Spanish paintings

FIGURE 16

Dignitaries in 1965 at the opening festivities inaugurating the new galleries at Bob Jones University, which featured the symposium "Culture and the Visual Arts." From left to right are: John Coolidge, Director of the Fogg Art Museum; Anthony Clark, Director of the Minneapolis Institute of Arts; David Carter, Director of the Montreal Museum of Fine Arts; Bob Jones, Jr.; John Walker, Director of the National Gallery of Art; Theodore Rousseau, Chief Curator of the Metropolitan Museum of Art; Charles Parkhurst, Director of the Baltimore Museum of Art. They stand in front of the important altarpiece of the *Coronation of the Virgin* by Antonio da Imola, signed and dated 1470. Photograph courtesy of Bob Jones University.

and died before Dr. Jones had a chance to personally thank him, also donated in 1952 a pair of large scenes from the story of Joseph by Giovanni Battista Carlone, formerly in the Duke of Norfolk's collection. Dr. Jones did, however, become acquainted with the circle of New York dealers, and a Maratta of the *Martyrdom of St. Andrew* was purchased from Koetser in 1951 (cat. no. 26) and, from Weitzner in 1953, the fine Preti of *Christ Seating the Child in the Midst of the Disciples* (cat. no. 25), which had been shown at the Oberlin exhibition. From E. and A. Silberman Galleries came in 1954 a *Judith with the Head of Holofernes* then attributed to Guercino but now given to Flaminio Torre. Given as a Matteo Rosselli by Mrs. W.D. Neves in 1952 was a *St. Margaret* now called Mario Balassi. There was also a Carlo Dolci *Ecce Homo* no longer in the collection.

The Fine Arts Building was erected at the University in 1956 adjoining the original museum, which increased the number of available galleries, but this soon proved too small for the rapidly growing collection, and a new art museum consisting of thirty galleries was created by remodeling a former dining hall. With over 250 paintings now on the walls, it opened on Thanksgiving Day in 1965. The occasion was celebrated by a two-day symposium on the theme of "Culture and the Visual Arts" at which six prominent museum directors and curators, including John Coolidge, Ted Rousseau, John Walker, and Tony Clark, delivered papers. The distinguished panel was photographed with Dr. Jones (Figs. 16, 17). Among the many other guests was the editor of *The Art Journal,* Henry R. Hope, who reported in his magazine:

> Of the many aspects of the current boom in the Fine Arts, this new art museum is in some ways the most unusual and the strangest.... It is absolutely extraordinary that such a collection has been acquired in the last fourteen years.... The director and plenipotentiary of the collection is unquestionably Dr. Bob Jones, Jr.... Dr. Jones is an ordained minister, a Baptist, a brilliant evangelical speaker, and he is not a rich man. But he is a man of urbanity, tact, wit, and generosity of spirit, and he is possessed of a profound knowledge of human nature.... A word should be said about the decoration of the galleries ... [which is] not so much period installation as a colorful treatment of walls, floors, and ceilings.... Settings like these of gold moiré walls, green or purple carpets are a little heady.... There was even background music.[293]

The growth of the collection had been documented in a catalogue published in 1962, with entries on the Italian paintings written by Alfred Scharf.[294] By this time Julius Weitzner and Dr. Jones were in close contact, and their friendship is commemorated by a portrait of Weitzner by the fashionable New York painter John Koch that the

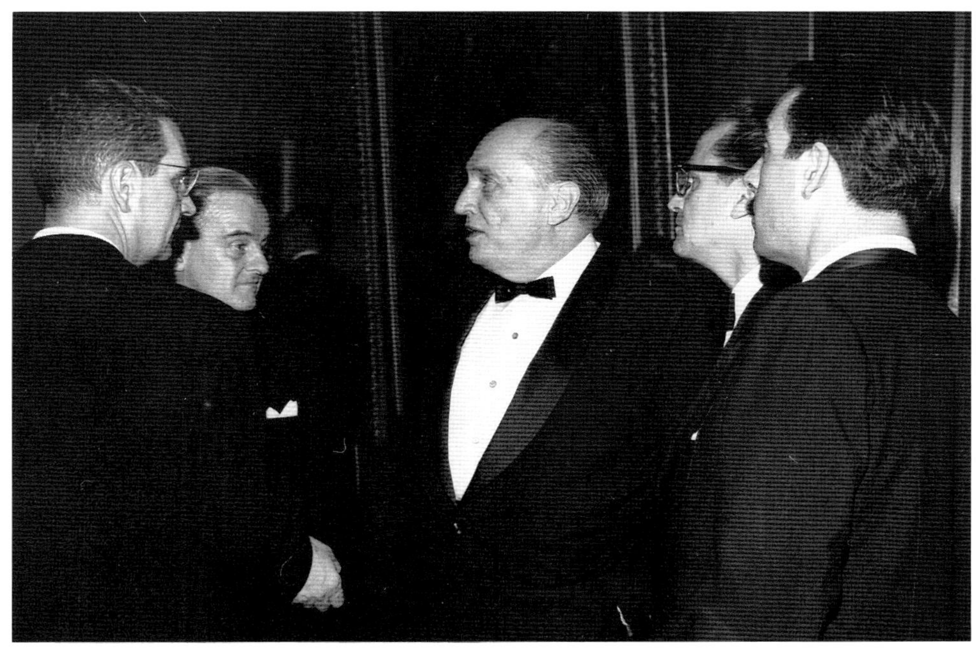

FIGURE 17

Also present at the November 1965 opening, seen on the far left speaking with Dr. Bob Jones, Jr. and John Coolidge, is Federico Zeri, the Italian connoisseur and scholar who supplied many opinions on paintings in the collection. Photograph courtesy of Bob Jones University.

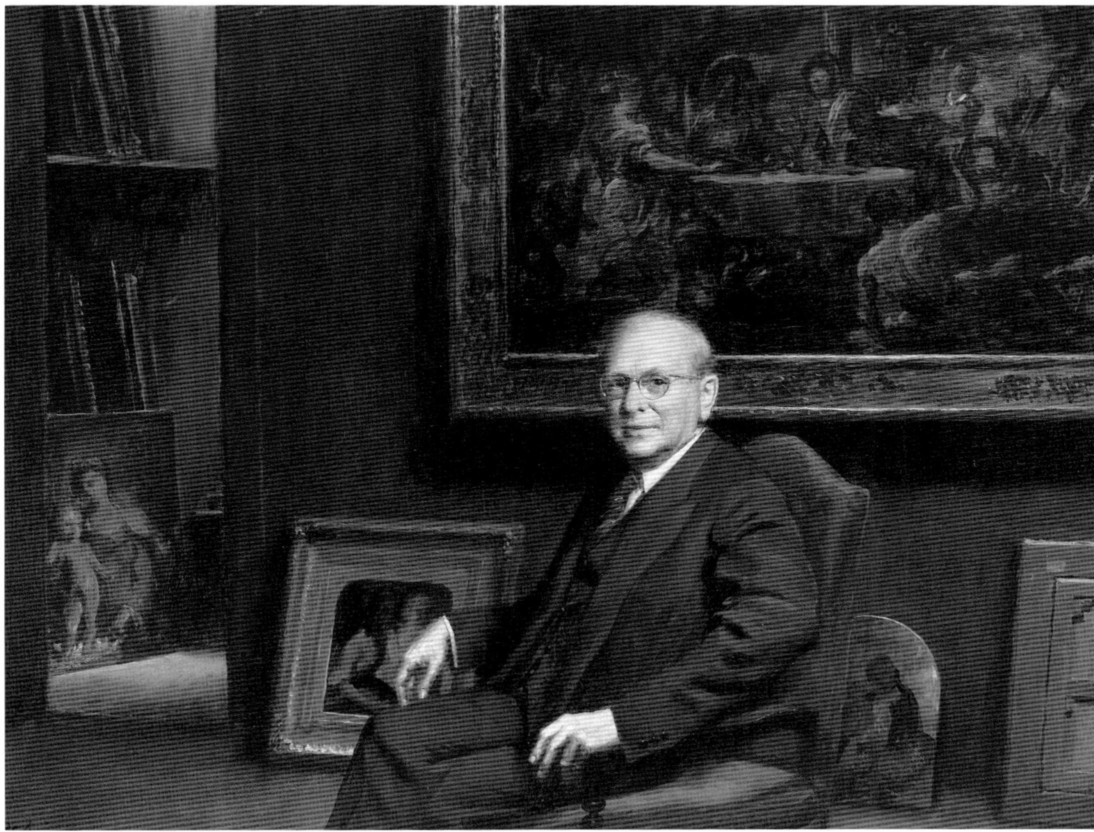

FIGURE 18

JOHN KOCH, *Portrait of Julius Weitzner in his Gallery,* Art Gallery, Bob Jones University, Greenville. Photograph courtesy of Bob Jones University.

dealer characteristically traded to Dr. Jones as part of one of their exchanges (Fig. 18). From Weitzner during these years came paintings by the following Italian Baroque masters: Chiari, Rosa, and Strozzi (cat. no. 32) in 1956, Guercino in 1957, and Fiasella (cat. no. 31) in 1958. Also in that year the dealer offered the *Christ in the Garden of Gethsemane* attributed to Spadarino. Since many of the works were by obscure artists and the scholarship of this period was in its infancy, a number of the original attributions have changed. The *Triumph of David* that came from Weitzner as a Rosselli in 1961 is now identified as by Vignali (cat. no. 29), as is the *Moses and the Burning Bush,* formerly given to Lorenzo Lippi, which had been supplied by Weitzner the preceding year. An *Entombment* that was acquired in 1961 as Ribera is considered by some as a workshop production. Mr. and Mrs. Weitzner themselves gave the impressive Sabatini *Circumcision* and the diminutive oil on copper by Pasquale Ottini (cat. no. 14) to the museum in 1959.

Two more gifts to the growing collection were Rosa's *Landscape with the Baptism of Christ* (Fig. 1) from Mr. and Mrs. Henry Simpson in 1955, and Giordano's *Song of Miriam* from Harry and Oscar Dwoskin in 1961.

Following his November 1965 visit to the museum, Henry Hope sent the young scholars Donald and Kathleen Weil-Garris Posner to provide a more thorough review of the collection for *The Art Journal.* They remarked on the lack of the great early Roman masters Caravaggio, the Carracci, Domenichino, and Pietro da Cortona, but did note that other Italian schools were well represented, particularly the Bolognese with the large Denys Calvaert of *St. Francis of Assisi Adoring the Christ Child* (cat. no. 15) and the Genoese with the huge *Samson,* then given to Assereto. For them the Guercino *Christ on Mount of Olives* was the best of the Baroque paintings, but this was later sold and is now in the North Carolina Museum of Art at Raleigh; also notable to the Posners were the two Giordanos, *Christ Driving the Merchants from the Temple* (cat. no. 24) and the *Song of Miriam,* as well as Maratta's *Martyrdom of St. Andrew* (cat. no. 26) and Sassoferrato's *Virgin.*[295]

A supplemental catalogue of the collection, published by the University in 1968,[296] reflected the considerable growth of Italian Baroque paintings since

Hope and the Posners visited Greenville in 1965. Many of the works added in the sixties came from Weitzner, including Sassoferrato's *Virgin* and Reni's *St. Paul* in 1966; the latter's set of *Four Evangelists* (formerly in the Duke of Beaufort's collection) in 1967 (see cat. nos. 18, 19); Baglione's *Entombment* (cat. no. 11), Turchi's *Madonna and Child with St. John,* and Carlo Francesco Nuvolone's *St. Joseph and the Christ Child* in 1968; and Romanelli's *Marriage of St. Catherine* and Baciccio's *Lot and his Daughters* in 1969. The Kleins of Central Picture Galleries provided the *St. Michael Overcoming Satan* as a Reni follower (later given to G.A. Sirani) in 1960, Orazio de'Ferrari's *Samson* in 1965, Langetti's *Joseph Interpreting Pharaoh's Dreams* in 1966, and Rosa's *Blind Bartimaeus* in 1967. From Schaeffer Galleries came a Francesco Ruschi in 1963 and, in 1967, the collaborative work representing *The Sacrifice at Lystra* by Giovanni Coli and Filippo Gherardi. Sestieri of Rome produced a Giovanni Domenico Piastrini in 1966, and, in addition to the Maratta that he sold to Dr. Jones in 1951, David Koetser also supplied paintings by Pietro Montanini and Francesco Montemezzano in 1967.

The Bob Jones University Collection today has over four hundred paintings. Many more Italian Baroque works were acquired in the seventies and eighties, as is evident in the 1984 catalogue by D. Stephen Pepper.[297] The highlights from these years include Magnasco's *Monks* from Jack Tanzer in 1970; Nuvolone's *Madonna and Child with St. Dominic and St. Catherine* and Pignoni's *St. Dorothy,* both from Weitzner in 1972; Giuseppe Simonelli's *Rest on the Flight* from Central Picture Galleries in the same year; and from Weitzner again, Luca Saltarello's *Christ in the House of Simon* in 1977 and Pietro della Vecchia's *Christ before Caiaphas* in 1983.

In 1984 a selection of the Baroque paintings from Greenville was exhibited at the North Carolina Museum of Art and the Colnaghi gallery in New York City.[298] That showing, and even more so the present exhibition held ten years later, reveal that the Bob Jones University Collection of Religious Art is the most extensive of the great Italian Baroque collections in the United States.

THE GANZ COLLECTION

In New York City a collection was formed beginning in the mid-1950s that, unlike the more universal approach of Mr. Chrysler or Dr. Jones, was devoted almost exclusively to Italian Baroque painting. This was the achievement of Paul and Eula Ganz. The Ganz family's fortune came from Bohemian costume jewelry, and it allowed the two brothers, Victor and Paul, to indulge their taste for art. Victor collected works by Picasso and other modern masters; Paul, after a brief interest in contemporary art and in Dutch and Flemish paintings, turned to the Baroque period. Some have speculated that this was in part because Ganz identified with these undervalued and undiscovered painters, and delighted in seeing them returned to acclaim. Another factor was his attending classes at Columbia University taught by Professor Wittkower, to whom Mr. Ganz became devoted. Wittkower's students, as well as those from the Institute of Fine Arts, and other young art historians, curators, conservators, and collectors on the New York scene, such as Donald Posner, Alan Rosenbaum, Everett Fahy, Gaby Kopelman, Ian Kennedy, George Wachter, the Mannings, and Morton and Mary Jane Harris—many of whom eventually acquired works from the Ganz collection—often gathered in the evenings for intense viewing sessions at the collector's Upper East Side apartment at 1130 Park Avenue (Fig. 19). All have a vivid memory of the small, eccentric Mr. Ganz passionately declaiming in his raucous voice on his latest discoveries, as he wielded an old-fashioned electric lamp on a long cord through the dusty spaces, the windows boarded over to make room for the paintings, which were also stacked in the spare rooms and even filled the bathtub. Meanwhile, his brilliantly organized wife Eula would provide exact data, no matter how obscure, on the artists, as well as information about other related works. When a fellow fanatic such as Denis Mahon visited, the lively talk could last all night. Mr. Ganz bought his pictures at auction and from dealers in New York, Paris, London, and even Boston. But most especially he would search them out all over Italy, where he and his wife traveled every summer visiting churches, museums, and galleries. They went not only to Rome and Florence (with daily trips to the Uffizi), but also to Genoa, Venice, Milan, and Padua. At the end of the summer, their booty would be rolled and folded into their luggage.

Although Mr. Ganz on occasion spoke of having an exhibition drawn from his collection at the Knoedler gallery in New York, this never came to pass, and the vision of the collection as a whole thus exists only in the memories of those fortunate enough to have seen it over the years as paintings came and went in the apartment. It was a remarkable collection, for it covered so many different schools. Responsive to the sensuous content of Italian Baroque painting, as well as to its ecstatic sensibility, Ganz acquired both nudes and unusual religious subjects, often by lesser-known artists. To name a few, there were Caracciolo's *Magdalen at the Foot of the Cross,* Carpioni's *Death of Leander,* Giordano's *Annunciation,* Balestra's *Scene of Martyrdom,* Fracanzano's *Ecce Homo,* Liberi's *Finding of Moses,* Mastaletta's *Landscape with Balaam and the Angel,* Guercino's *St. Jerome,* Scarsellino's *Madonna Giving the Scapula to St. Simon Stock,* Assereto's *Mary Magdalen,* Valerio Castello's *Samson and Delilah,* and Castiglione's *Bacchanal.*

The Ganzs were generous with loans, and a large number of their best paintings were displayed in the first major exhibition of Baroque art in America at the Detroit Institute of Arts held in 1965 (discussed below). These included the Caracciolo, Carpioni, Guercino, and Mastaletta, as well as Turchi's *Bacchus and Ariadne,* Balestra's *Martyrdom of St. Cosmas and St. Damian,* Cerano's *Madonna and Child with St. Francis,* Schedoni's *Rest on the Flight,* Morazzone's *Flagellation of Christ,* Del Cairo's *Herodias,* and Andrea de Leone's *Tobit Burying the Dead.*

The collection, which at its peak had well over a thousand paintings, was very fluid, as Mr. Ganz delighted in buying and selling his works at a profit. The *Herodias* by Francesco del Cairo was given by him to the Metropolitan Museum in memory of Professor Wittkower, and the Andrea de Leone was usually on loan to the same institution. Other works were sold or exchanged with the dealers or others of the committed and knowledgeable devotees of Baroque paintings. The largest group was sold to Don Luis Ferré from Puerto Rico, to form the core of the Italian section of the European paintings collection he was making for his museum in Ponce. Several other paintings, most notably, the Baglione, Guercino, Fracanzano, and Scarsellino went to Morton and Mary Jane Harris of New York. A collector from western Massachusetts, Channing Blake, also acquired several works, including two small Giuseppe Bazzanis, a Valerio Castello, G.M. Crespi, Gaetano Gandolfi, Manfredi, and Turchi, most of which eventually were given to the museum in Springfield.

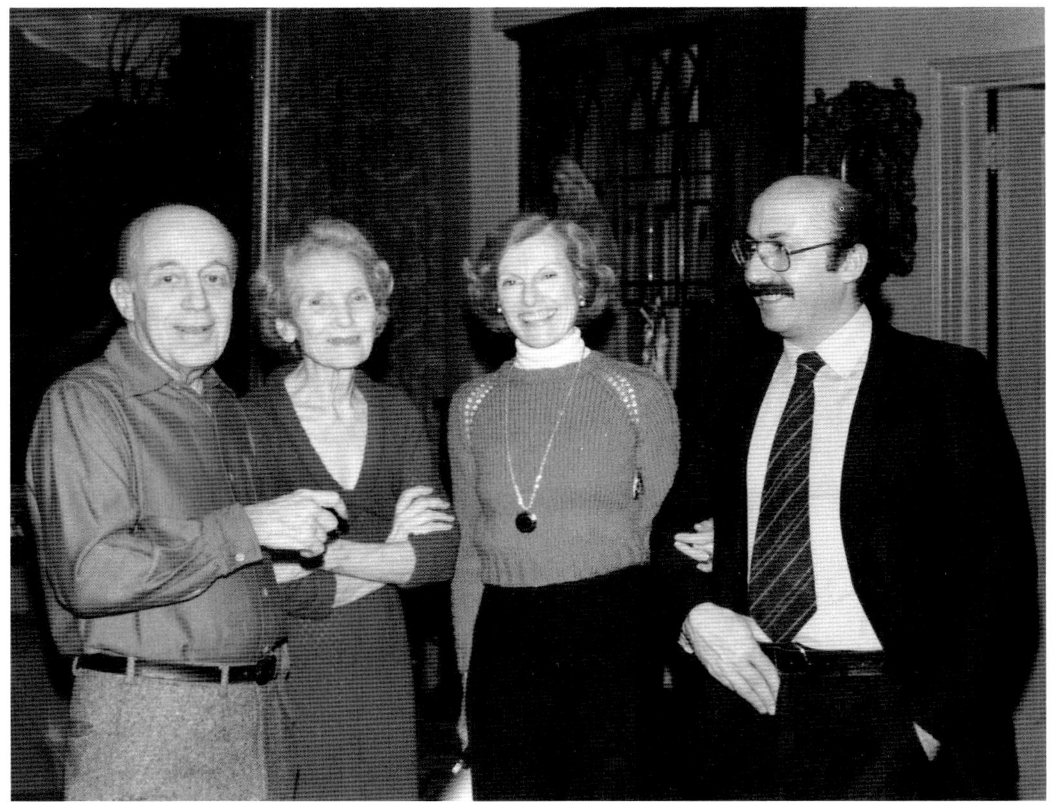

FIGURE 19

Paul and Eula Ganz at home; to their right are Mary Jane Harris and Nicola Spinosa, noted Neapolitan scholar. Photograph courtesy of Mary Jane Harris.

Following the tragic death of Mr. Ganz in 1985, a great many works from the collection were sold in 1987 and 1988 at both Christie's and Sotheby's in New York.[299] Among these were a Bartolomeo Passerotti *Portrait,* as well as paintings by Anselmi, Barbelli, Bononi, Ippolito Borghese, Orazio Borgianni, Cantarini, Carneo, Carpioni, Francesco da Castello, Cerano, Chiari, Cittadini, Creti, Dolci, Ferri, Furini, Luigi Garzi, Gaspare Gasparini, Giacinto Gimignani, Giordano, Filippo Lauri, Loth, Mazzoni, Francesco Monti, Giovanni Odazzi, Lorenzo Pasinelli, Pellegrini, Camillo Procaccini, Giovan Camillo Sagrestani, Solimena, and one by Coli and Gherardi.

Another group, including a Mastaletta and an Annibale Carracci *Head of an Old Man,* entered the stock of Mr. Ganz's niece Kate, who became a prominent art dealer. A pair of Giacomo del Pos were given in memory of Mr. Ganz by his widow, Eula, to the museum at Princeton in 1986; to the Metropolitan Museum of Art in 1987 she donated Testa's *Alexander the Great Saved from the River Cadmus.* This was, as Everett Fahy wrote her at the time, a fitting memorial, for "it has the slightly unconventional quality that first drew Paul to Baroque art."[300]

DON LUIS FERRÉ AND THE MUSEO DE ARTE DE PONCE

The last of the great collections of Italian Baroque art launched in the 1950s was that of Luis A. Ferré. From a Puerto Rican family of Cuban ancestry, he was educated as an engineer at the Massachusetts Institute of Technology and returned to his homeland where he became first a successful industrialist, making a fortune from the production of cement and glass, and then an active politician, eventually being elected governor of the island. Having studied the piano with distinguished teachers, he was long interested in European culture, but did not make his first trip there until 1950. This, plus the friendship of the New York collectors of Dutch and Flemish paintings, Mr. and Mrs. Salomon van Berg, who had a diamond-cutting business in his hometown of Ponce,[301] inspired Ferré and his wife,

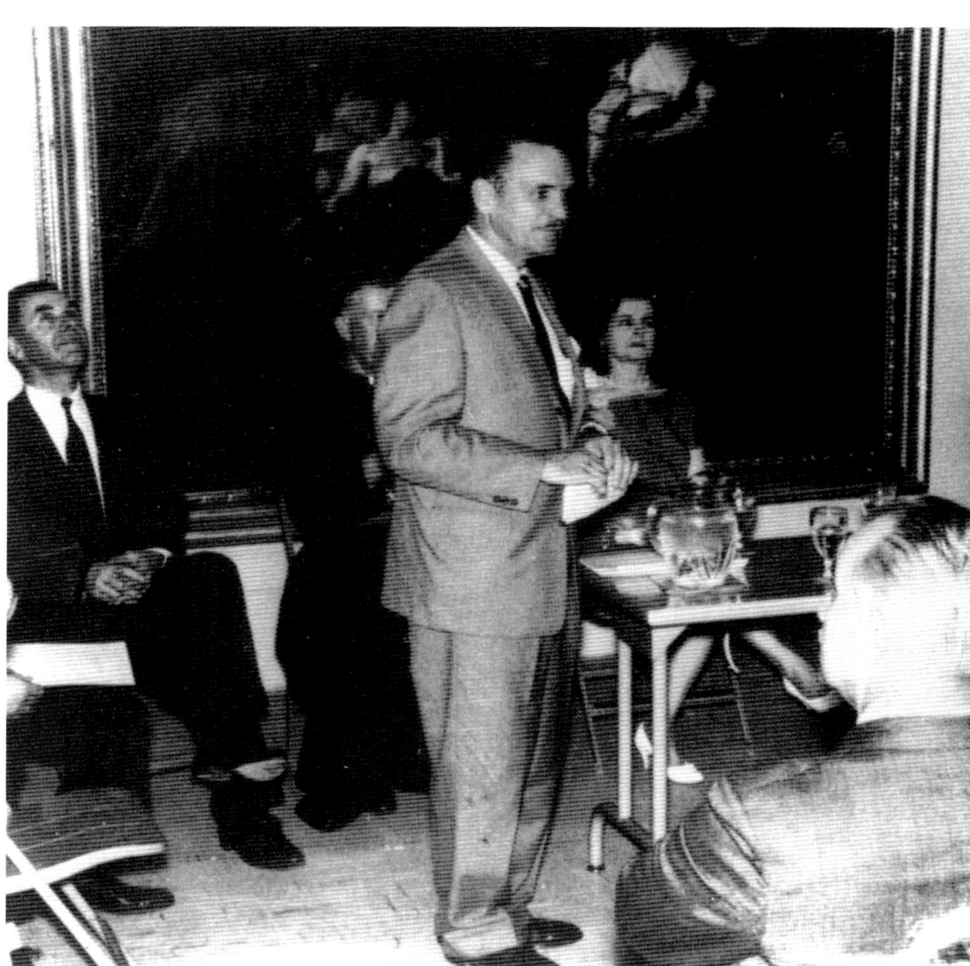

FIGURE 20

Don Luis A. Ferré (standing) at the inauguration of the Museo de Arte de Ponce in 1959. Seen sitting on the far left is his close advisor, Professor Julius S. Held. Reproduced from *Treinta Años del Museo de Arte de Ponce,* Ponce, 1989.

Doña Lorencita, to begin collecting themselves and, ultimately, to create the first art museum in Puerto Rico. According to Ferré, he attended an auction at the Savoy Gallery in New York in 1956, and, carried away by the excitement, bought more than twenty-five paintings. He then decided it would be wise to have the Van Berg's friend, the distinguished art historian, Julius S. Held of Barnard College, review these purchases. Professor Held remembers visiting the warehouse in Queens where the paintings were stored and finding that "as the result of good luck there were six decent works that still remain in the collection." Held became both an advisor and friend of Ferré and helped mold the quality of the collection.[302]

By 1959 seventy-one paintings had been assembled, and in January of that year, with the support of the Luis A. Ferré Foundation, the museum opened in a charming colonial house in Ponce, the island's second largest city, which had long been a cultural center independent of the capital of San Juan. Following the example set by Andrew Mellon at the National Gallery of Art in Washington, Ferré chose not to name the institution after himself, but, in honor of the strong regional ties he felt, to call it instead the Museo de Arte de Ponce (Fig. 20). To find the works he desired for the museum, Ferré became a regular visitor to the New York dealers and auction rooms. During the late 1950s and into the 1960s, he and Professor Held often went together, and on one memorable visit to Julius Weitzner in 1962 Ferré purchased about eight paintings, including Rubens's *Head of the Old King.* The Kleins of Central Picture Galleries, who also became good friends of Ferré, sold and donated so many works—including one especially close to their hearts, a portrait of a girl by the Czech painter Jaroslav Czermak—that one large gallery in the museum was dedicated to Oscar Klein.

Ferré has written that the Ponce art museum "is meant to be a place where the people of Puerto Rico may enjoy the exhilarating experience of admiring the works of art of the major schools of our Western civilization....In assembling the collection we were not seeking names...we preferred always paintings of high quality, even if by minor painters....We have also specialized in certain schools which have been long out of vogue but are now coming back into favor because of their intrinsic esthetic value."[303] The result of this policy was that not only the Spanish and Latin American works, which naturally appealed to Ferré, were acquired, but also such remarkably disparate but notable pieces as those by the Russian Konstantin Makovskii and the American Charles Frederick Ulrich, as well as a strong group of English Pre-Raphaelite paintings, notably Burne-Jones's *Briar Rose* series and Lord Leighton's masterpiece, *Flaming June.* There were also to be many Italian Baroque works; the first group consisted of Filippo Napoletano's *Fall of the Rebel Angels* purchased from a private collection in Naples in 1957, a *St. Sebastian* by Guido Reni, and other works by Giordano, Guercino, Pignoni, and Solimena, all acquired in 1957; a Brandi, a wonderful Furini *Cephalus and Aurora* (formerly identified as a Vignali), and Magnasco all from 1958; and another Giordano and a Romanelli in 1959.

In 1962 the Kress Foundation, through the efforts of Mr. Manning who had become friendly with Ferré, donated a group of Italian works, among which was a *Head of Christ* attributed to Elisabetta Sirani.[304] That same year Dr. René Taylor was appointed museum director and contributed greatly to its further development. Reviewing this growth, Professor Julius Held noted in 1964:

> It is well known that the art market is still generously offering paintings by Italian Baroque artists, especially those whose names are not making the "front pages" of art-historical handbooks. As one would expect, Ponce has bought a fair share of such works, among them pictures of superior merit such as the dramatic canvas, the *Torture of Ixion* by Langetti. Others represented include Bassetti, Pompeo Batoni, Cignani, Gaulli, de Mura, Pellegrini, Ricci, Sassoferrato, Sorbi, and Vignali. Luca Giordano is represented with several canvases, among them a fascinating and monumental *Death of Seneca.*[305]

With so many large additions, the collection soon outgrew its space, and thus in January of 1966 a major event in Puerto Rican cultural history took place—the opening in Ponce of a new museum building designed by Edward Durell Stone and incorporating the ideas of its founder, Ferré. The "keynote" of this museum, according to the Wittkowers, who had also become friends of the collector, was "clarity," and the galleries were arranged thematically.[306] The collection of Italian Baroque paintings continued to grow in the 1960s and 1970s with purchases from dealers and at auction of works by Bononi, Cagnacci, Chiari, Cignani, Placido Costanzi, Cesare Dandini, Dolci, Francesco Gessi, Guercino, Paolo de Matteis, and Pietro Paolini. From the Central Picture Galleries was acquired a fine example by Strozzi, and another by Ricci that was given to the museum by the Phillips Petroleum Company in 1971.

The New York circle of Baroque advocates whom Ferré knew included not only Professor Held, Wittkower, and the Mannings, who even donated works, but also most importantly Paul Ganz, who often vacationed in Puerto Rico. It was in 1966-68 that Mr. Ganz sold to Ferré some twenty-five of his finest Italian pictures, including paintings by Sisto Badalocchio, Bianchi, Caracciolo, Castiglione, Cerano, Chiari, Cigoli, Francesco Curradi, Fontebasso, Furini, Gaulli, Gimignani, Giordano, Mastaletta, Morazzone, Nuvolone, Ricci, and Pacecco de Rosa as well as four monumental canvases by Pietro della Vecchia representing the Ages of Man. The Museo de Arte de Ponce thus became, as Professor Held attests,[307] what Dr. Taylor described as "one of the most remarkable assemblies of baroque paintings in the Western hemisphere."[308]

MUSEUM ACQUISITIONS IN THE 1950S

The decade of the 1950s not only witnessed the launching of these great private collections of Baroque paintings, but also was one in which a tremendous amount of activity in this field occurred in American museums, with many new institutions entering the fray. Perhaps the biggest splash of the early fifties was made by the Metropolitan Museum of Art when it purchased Caravaggio's *The Concert.* The dealer David Carritt had apparently discovered it in an obscure English country house and brought it to the attention of Denis Mahon, who published it with full scholarly apparatus in the *Burlington Magazine.*[309] As the National Gallery in London had balked at the asking price of $70,000, finding the picture "not their cup of tea," Mahon contacted Ted Rousseau, the Metropolitan's curator of paintings, and urged him to act quickly to acquire it, which he did. The museum earlier had an opportunity to buy another Caravaggio, the later and very beautiful *St. John the Baptist,* but ostensibly turned it down because it did not have enough figures. With *The Concert* they got what they wanted, and the Nelson-Atkins in Kansas City, on the recommendation of one of their trustees who had spotted the *St. John* at Agnew's, was able to secure this painting by the master, so that two new works by Caravaggio joined the *St. Francis* in Hartford as the only authentic examples in America.

In subsequent years of the decade the Metropolitan obtained a Romanelli in 1954 from Kleinberger and the Strozzi *Tobias Curing his Father's Blindness* from Koetser in 1957. In 1959 a Stanzione *Judith* was given by Edward Carter, the large, previously mentioned Reni *Immaculate Conception* was purchased from Acquavella, and a Preti also entered the collection.

Of the other major museums, Boston in 1950 enhanced its Baroque collection with a presumed Caravaggio *Still Life with Poppies in a Wine Flask* and then in 1959, with an Italian seventeenth-century *Still Life with Peaches and Pears* "under the full sway of Caravaggio's concept of violent contrasts of light and shade."[310] The Baltimore Museum of Art purchased Strozzi's *St. Apollonia* in 1951 from Adolph Loewi of Los Angeles, and Philadelphia acquired three Magnascos in 1957 and 1958. The National Gallery received a work then identified as a Mastaletta *Allegorical Landscape* as a gift of Duncan Phillips in 1952.

In the Midwest, the Cleveland Museum of Art, under its director William Milliken and curator Henry Francis, substantially increased its holdings with a Langetti in 1951, a Strozzi *Pietà* in 1953, and a Rosa in 1958. Cincinnati acquired a supposed Annibale Carracci *Clytie* in 1952, and Chicago, the Strozzi portrait in 1958 (that was exhibited earlier by Wildenstein), as well as works by Crespi and Guercino in 1956. Indianapolis obtained a Magnasco in 1950, Carlone and Lanfranco in 1956, and a Carbone and the *Sleeping Eros* attributed to Caravaggio from the Clowes collection,[311] both in 1959. In Detroit the Strozzi *Street Musician* was purchased for the museum by the Italian Americans of Detroit in 1951; the museum added a Mainardi in 1953, and as a gift from Mr. Leslie H. Green in 1952, Artemisia Gentileschi's *Judith and Holofernes,* described at that time as her "only great work in America."[312] St. Louis obtained a Balestra *Still Life* in 1954.

On the West Coast, Seattle made a number of additions with Magnasco's *Christ on the Water* in 1950, a school of Cavallino in 1951, a supposed Valerio

Castello *Fantastic Shipwreck* in 1952, Luca Giordano's *Triumph of Neptune* the following year, and the Carbone *Madonna and Child* and Rosa *Mock Funeral* in 1954. Los Angeles added a Magnasco and Caravaggio follower in 1950, a pair of Rosas in 1951 from Hearst, and through the courting of William Valentiner a *Misery* by Schedoni was donated in 1954 by Sam Weisbord of the William Morris Agency. To the San Diego Museum of Art went a Strozzi *Madonna and Child with St. John* in 1951.

In North Carolina, the General Assembly had appropriated a million dollars in 1947 for the purchase of old master paintings for a state museum to be opened in Raleigh. The state senator Robert Lee Humber, who was responsible for this unusual legislation, was then able to convince Mr. Kress to provide a matching grant, which eventually was given in the form of paintings. Humber and his commission enlisted as their consultant the collector Carl Hamilton, who was familiar with the New York dealers. They sought to achieve a broad range of works, but as Baroque paintings were readily available and reasonably priced, seventeen of the original group of 139 paintings purchased in 1952 were Italian.[313] These included a Bocchi, Castiglione, G.M. Crespi's *Resurrection,* Giordano's *Finding of Moses,* and two Sebastiano Riccis, as well as an Agostino Carracci and Strozzi's *St. Lawrence Distributing the Goods of the Church.* From 1955 until his death in 1958, William Valentiner, one of America's most seasoned museum professionals, was director of this new state museum.[314] During his tenure were added, through a gift arranged by David Koetser in 1955, a fine Guido Reni *Virgin and Child* formerly in the Woodburn and Holford collections. Another major gift was Ludovico Carracci's altarpiece of *The Assumption of the Virgin* in 1957, and still later Strozzi's *Portrait of a Gentleman* and Solimena's *Christ Appearing to St. Martin,* both in 1959.

The J.B. Speed Art Museum in Louisville, Kentucky, acquired a Rosa *Landscape* from Koetser in 1955. Farther south, the Ringling Museum in Sarasota was reopened, and, with Chick Austin as its director, sought to complement the collection of its founder with a Strozzi from Weitzner in 1950 (believed then to represent *Elijah and the Widow of Zarephath* but now called *An Act of Mercy*), a Magnasco *Stormy Sea* from Schaeffer in 1952, and a Schedoni *Sleeping Christ Child* from Mont in 1954.

A great many smaller institutions were also adding seventeenth-century Italian pictures. The Washington County Museum of Fine Arts in Hagerstown, Maryland, was given in 1954 by Hughs Dallas of New York an unusual *Self-Portrait* by Lorenzo Lippi. That same year, Richmond's Virginia Museum of Fine Arts hired Pinkney Near as curator; later he became chief curator, overseeing acquisitions until his death in 1990. He was able to buy from Durlacher's in 1958 Mola's *Diana and Endymion,* Magnasco's *Peepshow* from Duveen, and from Agnew's, a major Salvator Rosa of the *Death of Regulus* and then later Strozzi's *Charity* and Magnasco's *Quaker Meeting* in 1960. The Norfolk Museum in 1956 was given a supposed Reni *St. Peter* (sold in 1978) and also, partly by gift and purchase from Gabarty, an enigmatic *Portrait of a Man,* then called Guercino but still not definitely identified.[315] The New York collector Emile Wolf, who for a time had lived in Norfolk, presented in 1952 Balestra's *Juno Placing the Eyes of Argus in the Peacock's Tail.* In Atlanta the High Museum of Art acquired in 1955 a *Boy Playing the Violin* attributed to Fetti. Later it was assigned to Simon Vouet, but in a letter of 1988 Mina Gregori made the persuasive attribution of Martinelli. Then in 1958 from Wildenstein the High Museum bought a "Caravaggio" *Boy with Flowers* that was endorsed by Venturi and Voss and also (from photographs) by both W.G. Constable and Berenson,[316] but it has since been identified as a copy by a follower.

The Wadsworth Atheneum in Hartford, now under the directorship of Charles Cunningham, added a Domenichino *Landscape* bought from Colnaghi's in 1950. Springfield purchased a *Portrait of a Bishop* by Strozzi and was given a Solimena *Presentation of Christ* in 1956. To Rochester also went a Strozzi of *Two Musicians* in 1953 and a Magnasco *Exorcism of the Waters* in the previous year. The Lyman Allyn Museum in New London, Connecticut, received a Rosa in 1953 and a Magnasco in 1958.

Dayton Art Institute's director from 1957-75, Thomas C. Colt, Jr. was, as we have seen, also interested in the Baroque and arranged for the purchase or gift of many remarkable works commencing with a *Christian Charity* by Guercino from Schaeffer Galleries and a Ludovico Carracci *Portrait of a Widow* (as Annibale) from Seligman in

1958. In Omaha, the Joslyn Art Museum acquired a Strozzi *Erminia* in 1952 and a Magnasco in 1957.

In 1957 Hugo M. Dixon, a leading citizen and collector of Memphis, donated to that city's Brooks Museum of Art two paintings by Luca Giordano, the *Massacre of the Children of Niobe* and the *Slaying of Medusa,* bought by him from Agnew's earlier that year. In Texas the collector Kay Kimbell purchased a Stanzione *Madonna and Child* in 1956 (later sold) that would be one of the nearly two hundred paintings he would bequeath to the museum bearing his name in Fort Worth. Yet another collector who was to be responsible for founding an even richer museum, J. Paul Getty, Jr., in 1953 also acquired from Agnew's the only Italian Baroque painting he was personally to buy, Orazio Gentileschi's *Rest on the Flight,* which had been given by the Duke of Buckingham to the Countess of Shrewsbury.[317] Despite this provenance, the work was later deaccessioned by the Getty Museum.

The college and university museums of America also continued to keep up with the busy pace of collecting. John Maxon, a flamboyant man with a fondness for things Baroque, served during this decade as director at both the Spencer Museum of the University of Kansas in Lawrence and the museum of the Rhode Island School of Design. For the former, between 1948 and 1952, he acquired a Guercino from Spencer Samuels, a Sebastiano (now Marco) Ricci from Koetser, Elisabetta Sirani and Giordano from Weitzner, and a Strozzi from Kleinberger. His successor Edward Maser added an Empoli and two works of the school of Solimena. At Providence, Maxon had from 1955 as his curator Anthony Clark, who became a leading scholar in the field, and together they made the school's museum exceedingly active. In that same year were acquired an Annibale Carracci *Landscape,* a Gaulli *Portrait of Cardinal Cybo,* and Guido Reni's *St. Sebastian* of which Maxon wrote, "It is only in the last generation (the last five years in some places) that fashionable opinion will once more admit the virtues of Guido."[318] The year 1956 brought another Reni school work, a *Lucretia,* along with a Manfredi *Flagellation;* to these were added a Ludovico Carracci in 1957, Muratori's *Death of Cleopatra* and a Guercino in 1958, as well as Francesco Vanni's *Vision of St. Francis,* a Cavaliere d'Arpino, Maratta's *Cleopatra,* and a Dolci *Trinity* from Koetser all in 1959.

Given to the Snite Museum of the University of Notre Dame by Mr. and Mrs. Samuel J. Schatz in 1954 was a Luigi Garzi *Judah and Tamar.* Other gifts received by that institution included: a Maratta *Virgin Reading* in 1951 and a studio of Maratta *Cleopatra* in 1959; Francesco Trevisani's *Martyrdom of St. Andrew* and Federico Bianchi's *Mystic Marriage of St. Catherine* from Mr. Busch in 1954; a Sebastiano Conca *Adoration of the Magi from* Mr. Snite in 1957; Mola's *Solomon* and a Vincenzo Spisano *Noli me Tangere* in 1958 from Mr. David Findlay; and Solimena's *Erminia among the Shepherds* in 1959.

The art museum at Wellesley College began receiving a series of Italian Baroque gifts from Dr. and Mrs. Arthur K. Solomon. These included a Domenichino *Christ and the Woman of Samaria* given in 1953 in honor of the art faculty's Professor Sydney Freedberg, and in 1959 they likewise honored the museum's director, John McAndrew, with a Guercino school work of the same subject purchased from Weitzner. The Solomons also gave a beautiful Strozzi *St. Francis in Ecstasy* in 1952, and a study for Giordano's *Triumph of David* and Preti's *Youth in a Plumed Hat* in 1958. That same year, the museum itself purchased a Dolci *Penitent Magdalen* from Colnaghi's.

Princeton received a Reni *Sleeping Christ Child* in 1952, Yale a Rosa *Landscape with Bathers* in 1957, and Columbia a Caracciolo in 1954 from John del Drago as well as a Giordano *Salvator Mundi* in 1959. Wells College in Aurora, New York, obtained a Giordano *Holy Family with St. John* in 1958. Georgetown University received from Hans Wyman of New York a pair of still lifes by Michelangelo del Campidoglio and a Solimena of *Rebecca's Departure* in 1957, and in addition acquired two paintings attributed to Guercino also in 1957, as well as a supposed Gherardini *Prophet* in 1959. An *Assumption of the Virgin* by an artist from the circle of Carlo Saraceni was given to Bowdoin by Mr. and Mrs. John Halford in 1957. Baldwin Wallace College in Berea, Ohio, was given two Fettis identified as "Roman Emperors" (but probably poets) by Dr. and Mrs. Oscar Costa, although these were later sold. A Ligozzi was acquired by Oberlin in 1958 and the Ackland Art Museum at Chapel Hill, North Carolina, was given a Vaccaro in 1959. To Marquette University in Milwaukee, Marc B. Rojtman gave two Sassoferratos in 1958 and a Trevisani *St. Francis* in 1959. That same year, Stanford University received two works by Albani.

EXHIBITIONS IN THE 1960S

The net result of all the lively collecting of Italian Baroque art in the fifties was that the sixties could begin with a series of exhibitions devoted to the regional schools of seventeenth-century Italy. The first was organized for the Sarasota Ringling Museum by its curator Creighton Gilbert. In 1960 he had already arranged for an unusual exhibition *Figures at a Table,* which incorporated a number of Baroque works such as a Cecco del Caravaggio from the New Orleans Museum of Art, Detroit's Pensionante del Saraceni, and an Empoli from Los Angeles (now given to Tarchiani), as well as the Ringling's own Renieri. Then in 1961 Gilbert conceived the show *Baroque Painters of Naples.* In a review, Robert Enggass wrote that:

> the exhibition on view too briefly (4th March to 4th April) at the Ringling Museum in Sarasota, is by its existence alone an event of some significance in the history of taste. To the best of my knowledge, no museum outside of Italy has ever held an exhibition of Neapolitan Baroque paintings before. In organizing what becomes in a sense a pioneering project, Creighton Gilbert has drawn chiefly on American collections. . . . An exhibition such as this both reflects and stimulates new interests. The next decade may well see Neapolitan baroque painting at last s*provincializzarsi* — becoming of interest not merely to Naples but to the West as a whole.[319]

Even more significant because it traveled to several locations, was the next large Baroque exhibition, this time devoted to Genoese art. It was the idea of Tom Colt at the Dayton Art Institute, and he enlisted as willing partners his fellow directors, Charles Cunningham at Hartford and Kenneth Donahue, then at Sarasota. To organize the exhibition he wisely chose the country's leading experts, Bertina Suida Manning and Robert Manning. They visited Genoa in the fall of 1961 and with great patience and fortitude made the rounds of both public and private collections. To secure the loans they wished took, what Bertina in a letter to Tom Colt described as "prodding in a flowery but extremely firm manner, by the American Embassy in Rome, emphasizing that the Italian ambassador would attend the opening in Dayton."[320]

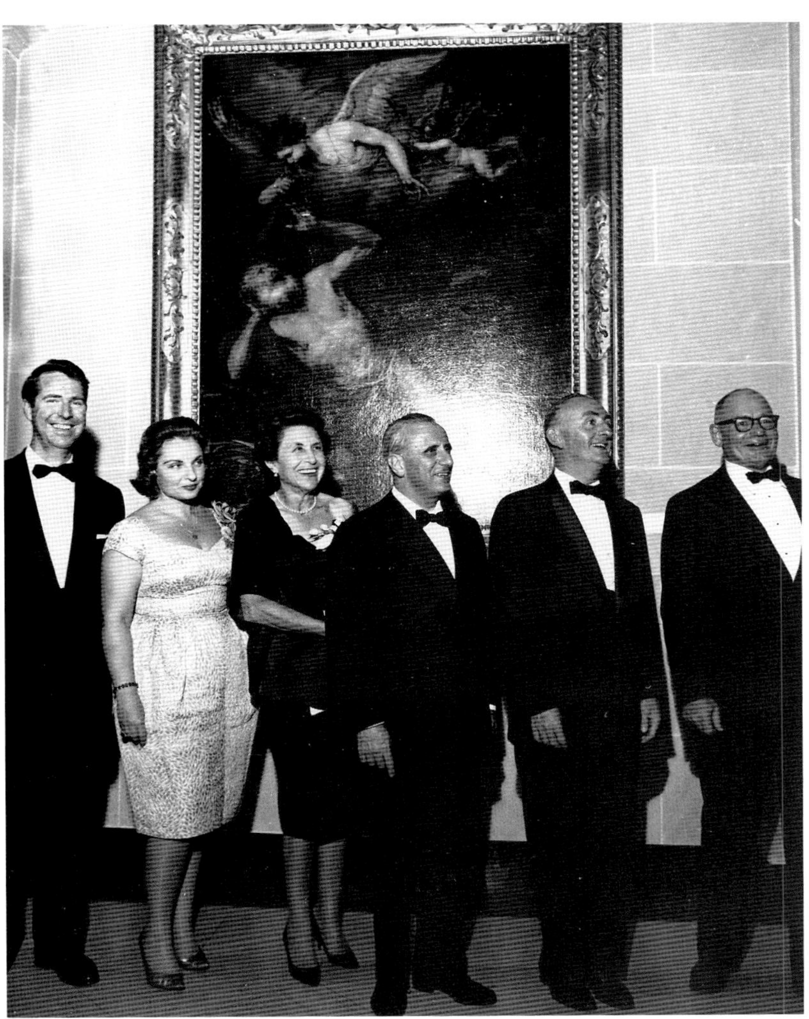

FIGURE 21

The opening of the exhibition, *Genoese Masters: Cambiaso to Magnasco, 1550-1750,* at the Dayton Art Institute in October 1962. From left to right are: Robert L. Manning and Bertina Suida Manning; His Excellency and Signora Sergio Fenoaltea, Italian Ambassador to the United States; John Sullivan, Jr., President of the Dayton Art Institute; and its director, Thomas C. Colt, Jr. Behind them hangs one of the show's most important paintings, Langetti's *St. Jerome* from The Cleveland Museum of Art. Photograph courtesy of Robert L. Manning.

This approach succeeded, and the resulting exhibition, *Genoese Masters: Cambiaso to Magnasco, 1550-1750,* which opened in Dayton in October 1962 and traveled to the Ringling and then the Wadsworth Atheneum, was a rich selection of both paintings and drawings (Fig. 21). A great many works were familiar from American collections. There were Fiasellas from both Bob Jones University (cat. no. 31) and the Ringling, the Cleveland Langetti, and the Chrysler and Norton (of Palm Beach) Castellos, reunited; Mr. Chrysler also lent his two Strozzis and Castiglione, and the Mannings supplied from their own extensive collection a Castiglione, Piola, and Cambiaso. Of the dealers, Acquavella contributed a Giovanni Andrea de'Ferrari, and Schaeffer, a wonderful *Circe Mulling Wine* by Assereto, which the Dayton Art Institute would later appropriately purchase. When the exhibition was at the Ringling, it had an important consequence, for there on a rainy day, the vacationing Mary Jane and Morton Harris from New York took cover and discovered Baroque painting, of which they were to become devoted and significant collectors in the following decade (see Fig. 19).

Since the Kress Foundation had transferred ownership of most of its paintings to museums around the country in 1961, Mr. Manning was free to accept an invitation that year from Roland de Marco, the enlightened president of Finch College in New York City, to be director of its museum of art at 62 East 78th Street. Mr. Manning quickly launched a series of now historic exhibitions, which, with their slim but informative catalogues selling for one dollar, were devoted to a variety of themes, but especially the Italian Baroque. The loans came not only from the Manning's personal collection, but also from those of Chrysler, Ganz, and many other New York area collectors and dealers. First in late 1961 was the *Loan Exhibition of Venetian Paintings of the Eighteenth Century,* which included the Chrysler Sebastiano Ricci of *The Contest Between Apollo and Pan.* In February of 1962 opened *Baroque Painters of Bologna and Neighboring Cities.* This time Mr. Chrysler lent his Guercino *Samson* and Reni *David and Abigail* and *St. Cecilia,* as well as a *St. Cecilia* by Domenichino, a Giovanni Andrea Sirani *Apollo,* a G.G. dal Sole *Magdalen,* his Crespi and Creti, a supposed Annibale, and as a Lanfranco the *Neptune* later attributed to Beinaschi. The collection of Paul Ganz supplied a Scarsellino *Madonna Giving the Scalpula to St. Simon Stock* on copper, the Mastaletta *Landscape with Balaam and the Angel,* and Guercino's *St. Jerome.* The Kress Foundation lent a Cagnacci and an Albani. Then in October 1962 appeared *Neapolitan Masters of the Seventeenth and Eighteenth Centuries.* This time the familiar Chrysler pictures were his three Rosas, Solimena portrait, and Preti, along with Giordano's *Dream of St. Joseph* and Stanzione's *Lot and his Family;* from Mr. Ganz came the Caracciolo *Magdalen,* Fracanzano *Ecce Homo,* and the Del Po pair of *Scenes from Ovid.* The Mannings anonymously supplied a Guarino, Cavallino, and Preti, while of the dealers, Mont provided two exceptional works, Vaccaro's *Martha Rebuking Mary Magdalen* and Andrea de Leone's *Tobit Burying the Dead;* Schaeffer, a Rosa *Jason Poisoning the Dragon;* Newhouse, a Solimena *St. Joseph and the Christ Child;* and Spark, a Conca *Annunciation.*

Next in 1964 the Finch College Museum mounted *Venetian Baroque Paintings.* The enormous painting by Langetti representing *Ixion Chained to the Wheel* was shown in the exhibition before being sent to Ponce by Ferré, who had recently purchased it from Oscar Klein. The latter himself lent a Liberi *Fortitude,* Della Vecchia *David,* and Padovanino *Athena and Venus.* Of the established collectors, Mr. Chrysler this time lent both his Renieris, two Della Vecchias, a Liss, the Strozzi *St. Dorothy,* Ricci's *Continence of Scipio,* and Pietro Bellotti's *Sleeping Hunter;* and Ganz provided the Turchi *Creation of Eve,* Liberi's *Finding of Moses* and *Venus and Amor,* Carpioni's *Death of Leander,* Giordano's *Annunciation,* and a ceiling sketch by Gianantonio Fumiani. From Bob Jones University came the Ruschi *Expulsion of Hagar.* The Mannings contributed their Forabosco (now Ponzone) *Cleopatra* and Fetti *Artemisia,* while Mr. and Mrs. J. O'Connor Lynch lent a Scarsellino *Madonna and Child.* Mr. Manning was also to develop for Finch College a permanent collection of paintings, and in this exhibition was the museum's *Charity* by Giovanni Coli and Filippo Gherardi.

Featured in the last major Italian exhibition in 1965 at Finch College, which recycled Dayton's title *Genoese Painters: Cambiaso to Magnasco, 1550-1750,* were from the Finch collection a pair of Carlones (companions to the set in the Bob Jones University Collection) of incidents from the life of Joseph. Naturally, to this exhibition the Mannings also lent several paintings by Cambiaso and Castiglione, as well as Assereto's *Magdalen,* Castello's *St. Francis,* Gaulli's *Rinaldo and Armida,* Domenico Piola's *Allegory of Youth,* Sinibaldo Scorza's *Orpheus,* and Antonio Travi's *Rest on the Flight.* From the Chrysler collection there were the Castello, Strozzi portrait, and Magnasco *Arcadian Landscape.* Also of special note were the Strozzi *Elijah and the Widow of Zarephath* from the O'Connor Lynch collection and an Ansaldo *Deposed Christ* from Robert Draper. Sadly, the museum and college were both eventually closed and the paintings sold,[321] but the memory of the brilliant and eye-opening exhibitions remains.

An unusual monographic exhibition of a type not seen since those of the Durlacher gallery's prime was *Luca Giordano in America,* organized in 1964 by Michael Milkovich for the Brooks Memorial Art Gallery in Memphis, Tennessee. The impetus for the show was the donation of the two paintings by Mr. and Mrs. Dixon to the Brooks; to complement these, paintings were lent from the museums in Hartford, Sarasota, Worcester, Boston, Oberlin, Raleigh, and Seattle, as well as those of Vassar, the University of Kansas, the Metropolitan, and Bob Jones University; the private collectors represented were Mr. and Mrs. Ganz, the Mannings, the Wrightsons, and several dealers. Memphis followed this up the next year with the exhibition *Sebastiano and Marco Ricci in America,* which was also shown at the University of Kentucky in Lexington.

A number of smaller exhibitions, often of private collections, were also presented in a variety of locations in the sixties. A modest group of Baroque works from the collection of Hugh Gordon Miller shown at the Norfolk Museum in 1960 contained a supposed Guercino *Legendary Scene with Figures* and a Sebastiano Ricci *Massacre of the Innocents.* In May of 1964 the Washington County Museum of Fine Arts in Hagerstown, Maryland, and the E. and A. Silberman Galleries collaborated on an exhibition of *Old Masters of the Italian Baroque,* held in New York City. Of works sold by Silberman to the museum, there were a presumed Strozzi *Portrait of a Scholar* and, more importantly, the Lorenzo Lippi *Self-Portrait;* on loan was a *St. John the Baptist in the Desert* attributed to Caravaggio. The Spencer Museum of Art of the University of Kansas in 1964 showed the Salzer collection of trompe l'oeil and still-life paintings of which two, by Paolo Porpora and G.B. Ruoppolo, were of the Baroque era. The following year the Mitchell Gallery of Southern Illinois University in Carbondale presented *Masterpieces of Renaissance and Baroque Art from the Collection of Colonel Frank W. Chesrow,* in which a number of works had impressive attributions: there were two supposed Caravaggios, a so-called *Portrait of Galileo* by Giordano, as well as paintings given to Castiglione, Dolci, Guercino, and Rosa.

Much of the collecting and exhibition activity during the fifties and sixties may be said to have culminated in the largest American presentation of Baroque art to that date, which included 214 works at the Detroit Institute of Arts in 1965 (Fig. 22). *Art in Italy, 1600-1700* was organized by the museum's director Frederick Cummings and had a catalogue introduced by Rudolph Wittkower with contributions on the paintings by most of the leading young American scholars—Robert Enggass, the Mannings, Donald Posner, Alfred Moir, and Dwight Miller—as well as a listing of previous exhibitions by Stephen Pepper. The mixture of paintings, sculpture, and drawings came from thirty-five American and Canadian museums and eighteen private collections. Added to this were twelve paintings lent by the English scholar Denis Mahon. The exhibition, as Cummings explained in the preface, sought to represent not just the famous artists—Caravaggio, Reni, Guercino, Rosa, and Strozzi—but also the lesser-known ones such as Manfredi, the two Gentileschi, Sassoferrato, Pietro da Cortona, Domenichino, Schedoni, Lanfranco, Crespi, and so forth. It was not intended "to define Baroque" but "to demonstrate the multiplicity and variety in the art of the age." The exhibition lasted only six weeks and was reviewed in detail by Wittkower's Columbia colleagues, Howard Hibbard and Milton Lewine. They wrote:

> One's first and essential reaction to the exhibition... is one of immense pleasure at the sight of so many notable paintings, drawings, and sculptures assembled to create America's first major exhibition of seicento art... no previous exhibition had been so ambitious in range and scope, but none could have taken place much earlier because, on the whole, American collectors have had no appreciation of the Italian Baroque.... The Detroit exhibition may therefore herald a new spirit in

FIGURE 22

Entrance to the 1965 Detroit Institute of Arts exhibition, *Art in Italy, 1600-1700,* showing Giovanni Battista Beinaschi's *St. Cecilia* (cat. no. 24) from the Bob Jones University Collection flanked (on the left) by Orazio Gentileschi's *Judith with the Head of Holofernes* from the Wadsworth Atheneum, Hartford, and (on the right) by Annibale Carracci's *Coronation of the Virgin* now in The Metropolitan Museum of Art, New York. Photograph courtesy of Bob Jones University.

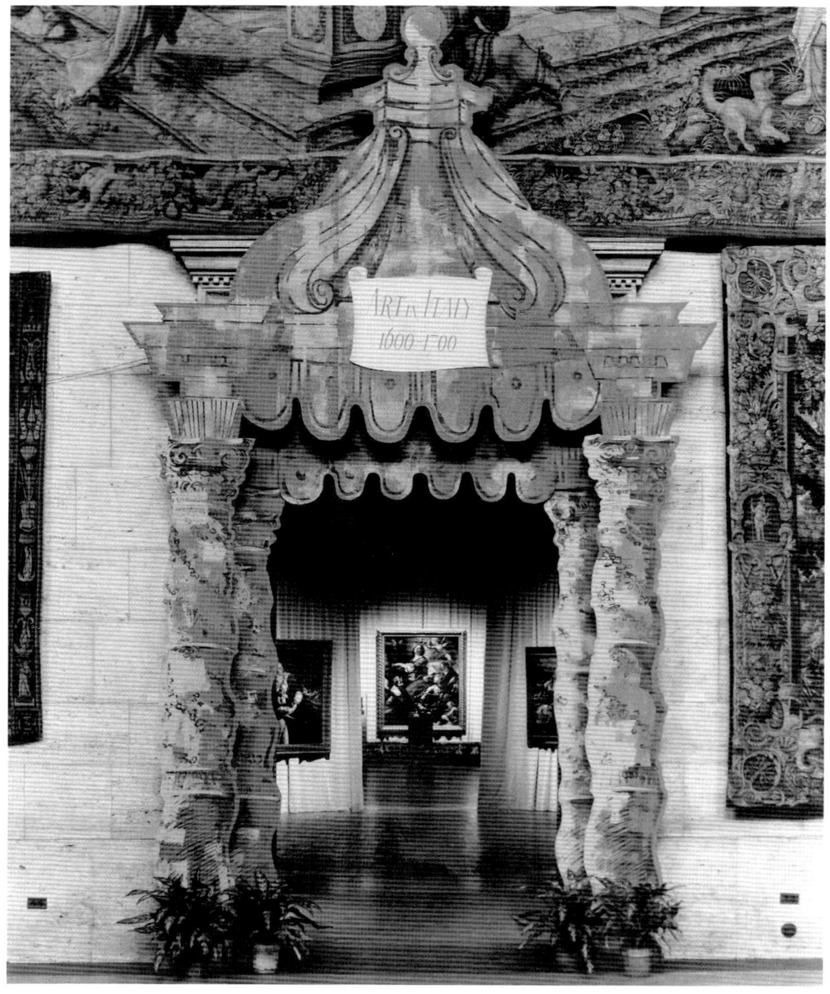

> American collecting. . . yet it remains symptomatic of American taste that, despite excellent publicity, the show was not reviewed by *The New York Times.*

For Hibbard and Lewine, the highlight was the work of Reni, "which gave the American public a chance to understand Reni's central position in the seicento—his virtuosity and range, his cool detachment in the midst of violence and emotion. Seeing these works one could understand why Reni's style held such fascination for younger artists and why Guercino all but destroyed himself in vain emulation." They also found "the Milanese paintings were outstanding thanks to the perspicacious collecting of Mr. and Mrs. Ganz," whose works included Cerano's *Madonna and Child,* Morazzone's *Flagellation,* and Del Cairo's *Herodias.*[322] Another major Baroque exhibition, *Le Caravage et la peinture italienne du XVIIe siècle,* also took place that year at the Louvre, and Denis Mahon reviewing both it and the Detroit show, observed, "The mere existence of these two exhibitions. . . testifies to a remarkable recovery of status in the reputation of the Seicento, after it had plumbed the depths during the second half of the nineteenth century as a consequence of widespread misunderstanding and ensuing neglect."[323]

The continued interest of Columbia University's Department of Art History in Baroque works of art resulted in 1967 in the exhibition *Masters of the Loaded Brush: Oil Sketches from Rubens to Tiepolo* held in New York at M. Knoedler & Co. A wide-ranging survey with loans from America and abroad, it included a good selection of Italian Baroque works, most notably the G.M. Crespi *Peasant Scene with Street Musicians* from Mrs. Agnes Rindge Claflin, a Rosa and De Mura from Professor Milton and Carol Lewine, a Carlo Carlone from David Rust of Washington, D.C., and the Ricci *Assumption* from the Springfield Museum of Fine Arts.

Mounted that same year were two monographic exhibitions devoted to the long-esteemed masters of the Genoese school. For the opening of the University Art Gallery at the State University of New York at Binghamton, Michael Milkovich arranged the loan show *Bernardo Strozzi: Paintings and Drawings,* and all of the favorite works from American museums were assembled, as well as two from Walter Chrysler, Jr. and one from Mr. and Mrs. J. O'Connor Lynch. The J.B. Speed Art Museum in Louisville and the University of Michigan Museum of Art were host in 1967 to *Alessandro Magnasco (1667-1749),* with loans from both Europe and America. Organized by the university's Professor Paul Grigaut, it made "no effort to be comprehensive or to present definitive conclusions," but rather "to encourage serious study of the evolution and development of Magnasco's style in all its complex and puzzling manifestations." The familiar museum examples were drawn from Boston, Dayton, Detroit, Hartford, Kansas City, Los Angeles, Oberlin, St. Louis, San Francisco, Springfield, and Worcester.

In 1968 the Heckscher Museum in Huntington, New York, presented an exhibition called *The Last Flowering of Religious Art,* which included a small number of Italian Baroque works. These were Giordano's *Presentation in the Temple* from the Mannings, Solimena's *Birth of the Virgin* from the Metropolitan, and Tavella's *Magdalen* from Victor Spark.

A more major Baroque exhibition that toured nationally opened in 1968 at the Museum of Art of the Rhode Island School of Design. Organized by the museum's curator Stephen E. Ostrow and circulated by the American Federation of the Arts, it was titled *Baroque Paintings: Italy and her Influence.* Among the works were Detroit's Cavallino and Giordano; Hartford's so-called Caravaggio *Still Life;* the Rhode Island School of Design's own Cavedone *St. Anthony,* Leone *Portrait,* and Maratta *Cleopatra;* the Ringling's Sassoferrato, Mola, and Furini; Boston's Del Cairo; Kress's Cagnacci and Gentileschi; Minneapolis's Assereto; Bob Jones's Serodine *St. Jerome* (now attributed to Pietro Paolini; cat. no. 12) and Chiari *Rest on the Flight* (cat. no. 35); Mr. Chrysler's Beltrami and Dolci; and finally, from the New York dealer Herman Shickman, a Castiglione, Forabosco, G.C. Procaccini, and Elisabetta Sirani.

Just two years after their inaugural exhibition, the University Art Gallery in Binghamton showed in 1969, *The Lynch Collection,* a group of paintings acquired in the previous decade by Mr. and Mrs. J. O'Connor Lynch of New York, which, as was evident from loans to the Finch exhibitions, included several notable Italian Baroque works. There were examples attributed to Barocci, Carlone, Crespi, Matteis, Camillo Procaccini, Scarsellino, Strozzi, as well as a Coli and Gherardi collaboration, Antiveduto Grammatica's *Lute Player,* and other works given to Domenichino and Vaccaro.

Completing the cycle of those exhibitions devoted to a single school from the earlier years of the decade was *Florentine Baroque Art in America,* held at the Metropolitan Museum of Art from April to June of 1969. This show was inspired by the discovery at Columbia University of a lovely Furini *Youth in a Hat* (later considered a Cecco Bravo) of unknown provenance. It was originally intended by Professor Howard Hibbard to be a modest campus exhibition, but the Metropolitan's flamboyant director, Thomas Hoving, was intrigued by the idea and brought it to the Museum, where it was presented in an enlarged format accompanied by a scholarly catalogue prepared by Joan Nissman, a Columbia graduate student. Significant loans for this specialized theme came from the established collections of Mr. Ganz, the Museo de Arte de Ponce, Bob Jones University, the Mannings, Mr. and Mrs. J. O'Connor Lynch, the Hibbards, and the Lewines, as well as from those at the University of Kansas, Vassar, Rhode Island School of Design, Atlanta, Los Angeles, Sarasota, and Phoenix. Anne Sutherland Harris, reviewing this Florentine show, wrote, "the exhibition will be a controversial one...on grounds of taste... no other school of Italian seicento painting provokes the range of judgment from outright dismissal to almost unreserved enthusiasm. And perhaps these reactions are a fair assessment of Florentine seicento paintings—partly delightful, partly dreadful."[324]

MUSEUM ACQUISITIONS IN THE 1960S

It is not surprising that the string of specialized exhibitions in the sixties both fostered and drew upon continued museum acquisitions of Baroque paintings. At the Metropolitan Museum of Art, Giordano's *Flight into Egypt,* which had been in the New York World's Fair in 1940, was given in 1961 by Mr. Harold M. Lincoln. A Rosa *Dream of Aeneas* was purchased from Agnew's in 1965; and in 1969 two notable works came as gifts: a Dandini *Charity* from Mr. and Mrs. Ralph Friedman and Artemisia Gentileschi's *Esther Fainting* (which Acquavella had acquired in Rome in 1959) from Elinor Dorrance Ingersoll. To the National

Gallery in Washington came an Orazio Gentileschi *Lute Player* in 1962.

The Cleveland Museum of Art, with Sherman Lee as director and Ann Tzeuschler Lurie as curator, was now extremely active, acquiring a Giordano in 1966 from Heim, a Guercino in 1967 from Weitzner, as well as works by Cavallino, Dolci, and Sassoferrato in 1968, and those of Castiglione, Gaulli, Preti, and Reni in 1969. Also in Ohio, the Dayton Art Institute under Tom Colt continued to collect vigorously with, in 1961, a major Preti of *The Roman Empress Faustina Visiting St. Catherine of Alexandria in Prison* from Weitzner. Manfredi's *Allegory of the Four Seasons* was acquired from Schaeffer in 1960, a Reni *Magdalen between Two Angels* from Central Picture Galleries and a Ricci *Lucretia* in 1961, a Cambiaso from Mont in 1962, a Guercino school *St. Paul* from Schaeffer in 1963, Saraceni's *Judith* from Mont in 1964, and a Pittoni and the beautiful Assereto *Circe* that was featured in the Genoese exhibition in 1965. Toledo under Otto Wittmann and William Hutton moved into the Baroque area with, in 1960, a Pietro da Cortona *Virgin with a Carmaldolese Saint* purchased, as were most of these works, from Colnaghi's of London with funds donated by the museum's leading patron, Mr. Libbey. A magnificent Preti representing *The Feast of Herod* came to the museum in 1961, a Sebastiano Ricci *St. Paul Preaching* in 1966, and a Maratta *Holy Family* in 1967.

The Detroit Institute of Arts got a Solimena *Alexander the Great* from Colnaghi's in 1965 (now attributed to Vaccaro), Rosa's *Self-Portrait* in 1966, Orazio Gentileschi's *Young Woman with a Violin* in 1968—giving it "the distinction shared only with two other museums in the world of possessing paintings of undoubted authenticity by both the Gentileschi"[325]—and a Reni *Angel Appearing to St. Jerome* in 1969. Indianapolis added another Genoese master with a Valerio Castello in 1966, as well as a Solimena, and Pietro Ricchi's *Adoration of the Magi.* Pittsburgh's Carnegie Institute was given a Nuvolone *St. Agatha* in 1961. That same year Kansas City acquired a major Castiglione and a Guercino fresco in 1968.

The Ringling Museum acquired its very impressive Francesco del Cairo *Judith with the Head of Holofernes* in 1966. Also in Florida, the Cummer Gallery of Art in Jacksonville received a Pietro della Vecchia of *David Called from his Flock* in 1961 and purchased a Sassoferrato *Praying Madonna* in 1968.

San Francisco and Los Angeles both added Guercinos, the *Samson Bringing Honey to his Parents* in 1965 and *St. Jerome in the Wilderness* in 1968 (sold in 1986), respectively. The Getty Museum, now established in Malibu and with Federico Zeri advising Mr. Getty, purchased a Lanfranco *Moses and the Messenger from Canaan* from Hallsborough Gallery in 1969 and from Spark, a Vaccaro *Judith with the Head of Holofernes.* In addition were acquired from various sources works by Cecco Bravo, Dolci, Nuvolone, Paolini, and Preti, although most of these were later sold.

The Minneapolis Institute of Arts, now under the directorship of Anthony Clark, a passionate devotee of seventeenth- and eighteenth-century Italian art, replaced the works deaccessioned earlier and broadened the collection with many rarer artists. His additions included Assereto's *St. Augustine and St. Monica* in 1960; a Schedoni, Cavaliere d'Arpino's *Virgin and Child,* and Guercino's magnificent *Erminia and the Shepherds* in 1962; Rosa's *St. Humphrey* in 1964; works by Pietro da Cortona and Solimena in 1965; Castiglione's *Immaculate Conception* and examples by Della Vecchia, Reni, and Ricci in 1966; and Gaulli's *Diana* in 1969.

At the Art Institute of Chicago during the sixties, John Maxon had become associate director and Joseph Rishel, assistant curator of paintings. Both were friends of Anthony Clark and shared his enthusiasm for the Baroque, so that in 1960, when the Institute was given through the generosity of Mr. and Mrs. Frank Woods Reni's *Salome with the Head of St. John the Baptist* formerly in the Colonna collection, Clark wrote the bulletin article titled, "A Late, Great Guido Reni."[326] In the same year, the museum received Empoli's *Young Woman of the Medici Family.* Other gifts that served to fill out the Baroque holdings were a Magnasco and Turchi from the Worcester collection in 1961 and 1964, a Della Vecchia *Epiphany* from Mr. and Mrs. Morris Kaplan in 1965 (whose other notable Baroque paintings were sold at Sotheby's, London, on 12 June 1968), and a *Self-Portrait* by Preti from Mrs. Sterling Morton in 1968.

The Saint Louis Art Museum in 1961 was given the Sassoferrato bought in Europe in 1890 by John Hay, and in 1962 acquired a supposed Rosa of *Jason Poisoning the Dragon* from Schaeffer Galleries; then came two ceiling sketches by Luca Giordano, a *Judith* from Wildenstein in 1965 and the other in the same year from a Paris private collection. Another Rosa was added in 1966.

To Boston in 1964 came what was described as "a splendid example of Italian Baroque painting," the *Still Life of Musical Instruments* by the seventeenth-century master of Bergamo, Evaristo Baschenis.[327] One of director Perry Rathbone's most outstanding acquisitions was the Crespi *Lute Player* bought from Vitale Bloch in 1969. Hartford's already distinguished collection was enhanced by Mola's *Barbary Pirate* in 1968.

A wider range of smaller museums also were now entering this field. Richmond added a Magnasco and Strozzi in 1960, a Santagostino and a Giordano in 1963, and a Solimena in 1968. The Mint Museum in Charlotte was given in 1959 a Sisto Badalocchio *Christ and the Samaritan Woman* and then, from its Woman's Auxiliary, Valerio Castello's *Christ and the Little Children* and Domenichino's *Portrait of a Prelate* in 1962 and 1963. In Columbus, Ohio, the Museum of Art added works by Lanfranco in 1962, Reni in 1964, and Solimena in 1967, and received from the Schumacher collection an Artemisia Gentileschi in 1967 and a Giordano in 1968. The Milwaukee Art Museum in Wisconsin was given Magnasco's *Landscape with Monks* by Dr. and Mrs. Alfred Bader in 1965 and obtained Solimena's *Madonna and Child with Saints* in 1966. Louisville had Maratta's *Holy Family* donated by Mr. Garbaty in 1961 and purchased a Lanfranco *Mystic Marriage of St. Catherine* in 1966. At the Phoenix Art Museum, director Dr. F.M. Hinkhouse sought to expand the collection with a Solimena school work *St. Anthony* in 1960, a Furini in 1961, a Dolci *Salome* in 1964, and a Guercino *Madonna and Child* in 1965, the latter two both from Agnew's. Seattle got as gifts a supposed Mola *Holy Family* in 1967 and a De Mura *Christ and the Woman of Samaria* in 1968. In Oregon, the Portland Art Museum was given Strozzi's *Madonna* in 1966.

Works by Magnasco continued to be popular at this time: the Honolulu Academy of Arts purchased the artist's *Stormy Sea* in 1964 and a pair went to Springfield in 1967. In 1960 the Worcester Art Museum acquired from Weitzner a follower of Caravaggio *St. Jerome* once owned by Giulio Briganti and in 1962 a *Galatea* by Giordano. The Frick Art Museum in Pittsburgh acquired its only Italian Baroque painting in the sixties—a Luca Giordano in 1965. The Washington County Museum of Fine Arts in Hagerstown received as gifts both a Strozzi *Portrait of a Scholar* in 1963 and Stanzione's *Joseph and Potiphar's Wife* in 1964. The Lyman Allyn Museum in New London was given a supposed Annibale Carracci *St. Jerome* in 1960.

In Houston, then director Philippe de Montebello made it a policy to add large seventeenth-century paintings to the collection of the Museum of Fine Arts. The chief Italian example was Mattia Preti's *Decollation of St. Paul* acquired in 1969 from F. Kleinberger & Co., New York. This was one of an important set of three paintings commissioned from Preti by a Flemish merchant in Naples. One of the others, the *Martyrdom of St. Bartholomew*, coincidentally appeared on the art market and, after being rejected by Houston, was purchased by the Currier Gallery of Art in Manchester, New Hampshire, from the Heim Gallery of London in 1970.[328]

The active university museums now included that at Ann Arbor, Michigan, which acquired a Magnasco *Landscape with Washerwomen* in 1960, another Magnasco in 1962, and Guercino's *Esther Fainting before Ahasuerus* from Agnew's in 1963. The Elvehjem Museum of Art at the University of Wisconsin in Madison received as gifts during this decade a Preti and a Paolini *Conversion of the Magdalen* from Dr. and Mrs. Henry R. Hope, a Luca Ferrari, and Paolo de Matteis's *Apollo Pursuing Daphne* from Mr. and Mrs. Marc B. Rojtman; the school also purchased a *St. John the Baptist* attributed to Giacinto Brandi in 1961 and a Rosa *Landscape with Bridge* in 1966.

At Oberlin College several works added to the collection clearly reflected the influence of the school's distinguished specialist in Bolognese Baroque painting, Richard Spear. These included paintings by Mola in 1961, Gaulli in 1966, Domenichino's *Landscape* in 1968, and a Cavaliere d'Arpino in 1969. The Ackland museum at Chapel Hill added a work attributed to Sagrestani in 1960 and one after Domenichino in 1966; a Luca Giordano *St. Sebastian* was purchased from Central Picture Galleries in 1969 during the directorship of Joseph Sloane.

The University of Indiana Museum at Bloomington purchased a Giordano in 1961 and a Luca Ferrari in 1966. Notre Dame bought a Ceresa

Young Girl in 1964, a Grammatica in 1965, and was given a Turchi *Adoration of the Magi* by Morris Kaplan, a Giordano *Adoration of the Shepherds,* and another Maratta studio work. Stanford received a Guidobono *Sibyl* in 1965, a Negretti S*t. John the Baptist* in 1966, and Solimena's *Holy Trinity* in 1969. The University of California at Berkeley obtained an important Caracciolo, the Y*oung St. John in the Wilderness,* in 1968, and the University of Missouri in Columbia also acquired a Caracciolo *David with the Head of Goliath* in 1969, as well as Giordano's *Apparition of the Virgin to St. Bernard of Clairvaux* in 1967. The Washington University Gallery of Art in St. Louis purchased in 1968 a *Glaucus and Scylla* by Rosa.

The Art Museum of Princeton University received a copy of Caravaggio's *Cardsharps* in 1961, a Carlo Coppola in 1963, and a Sebastiano Ricci in 1964; Rhode Island School of Design, a Reni copy and a Magnasco in 1963; and Vassar College, works by Sacchi and Empoli in 1967. The Williams College Museum of Art bought from F. Kleinberger & Co. of New York in 1966 a Stanzione *St. John the Evangelist Exorcizing a Demon from the Cup.* The Fogg was given from the Kress Foundation in 1962 a painting of *Joseph and Potiphar's Wife* then attributed to Artemisia Gentileschi but now to Paolo Domenico Finoglia. The Smith College Museum of Art received as a gift of Stanley S. Wulc in 1967 a *St. Peter* now attributed to Giacinto Brandi and to Bowdoin went a Castiglione in 1961. The University Art Gallery in Binghamton received from Dr. Adolph Posner a Zanchi *Death of Seneca* in 1969. The new Rose Art Museum of Brandeis University in Waltham, Massachusetts, was given several notable Baroque works during these years, including the Strozzi *Allegory of Sculpture* that had been in the Gladys Lloyd Robinson collection, a Paolo de Matteis *King Hezekiah in Prayer* from Lauritz Melchior, and a school of Caravaggio *David with the Head of Goliath,* all unfortunately sold in 1978.[329]

EXHIBITIONS IN THE 1970S

In 1971 two exhibitions featured Italian Baroque art—a Castiglione show at the Philadelphia Museum of Art was devoted to works on paper,[330] but the inaugural fall exhibition of the Denver Art Museum, *Baroque Art: Era of Elegance,* included a number of Italian paintings lent from all around the country. Among these were the Ringling's Annibale Carracci, Stanzione, and Del Cairo; from Hartford the *Medea* by Castiglione; the Kansas City Strozzi; the Dayton Manfredi; Rhode Island School of Design's Maratta; Indianapolis's Solimena and Carbone; the Joslyn's Magnasco of *Two Monks;* Rochester's Strozzi; and Worcester's Sebastiano Ricci. From Mr. Chrysler came Reni's *David and Abigail,* Cavallino's *Marriage of Tobias,* and a work by Creti; of former Kress paintings there were the Tanzio from Tulsa and a supposed Annibale Carracci *Crucifixion* (subsequently identified as by Pedro Orrente) from the High Museum in Atlanta; and from Denver's own collection a Paolini (formerly given to Reni) of *Esther at the Feast* purchased by Helen Dill in 1932 and left by her to the museum.

A groundbreaking exhibition of 1970 that encapsulated much of the scholarly research and acquisitions of the previous decades was *Painting in Italy in the Eighteenth Century: Rococo to Romanticism,* organized by John Maxon and Joseph Rishel and shown in Chicago, Minneapolis, and Toledo. Despite the show's title, a good many artists still fell within the category of the Baroque, represented by Magnasco, with works from Chicago and St. Louis; Crespi, with examples from Boston, Hartford, and Chrysler; and Chiari, with one from the Walters Art Gallery.

Another significant exhibition, which was seen only in Cleveland in 1971-72 but became widely known through its catalogue prepared by Richard Spear, was *Caravaggio and his Followers.* An international loan show, it was certainly the largest held to date devoted specifically to the Caravaggisti, including those of Dutch, French, and Spanish origin, as well as Italian. Among the American loans were a Baglione *Ecstasy of St. Francis* from the Davidson collection, now in Santa Barbara, as well as the Cecco del Caravaggio from Chicago, Orazio Gentileschi's *Sibyl* from the Kress collection in Houston and the *Danae* from Cleveland, the Pensionante del Saraceni from Detroit, a Saraceni from Hartford, Pretis from Wellesley College and the Park Ridge Public Library of Park Ridge, Illinois, and an anonymous *St. Matthew and the Angel* from Sarasota.

In London, Thomas Agnew & Sons presented in late 1973 *England and the Seicento: A Loan Exhibition of Bolognese Paintings from British Collections.* This had particular relevance for the United States, for, although its purpose was to aid the National Art-Collections Fund, a number of the paintings from English private collections and country houses had already been or were shortly to be bought by Americans. Thus, the Guercino *Suicide of Cleopatra* belonged to Norton Simon, Reni's B*acchus and Ariadne* went to the Los Angeles County Museum of Art, Annibale's *Butcher's Shop* was purchased by the Kimbell Art Museum in Fort Worth, and Mola's *Rest on the Flight* has come recently to the Metropolitan Museum; another work by Reni of *Liberality and Modesty* passed from Wildenstein's to the late New York collector Peter J. Sharp, and Albani's *Rest on the Flight* entered the collection of Mr. and Mrs. Stewart Resnick of Los Angeles.

Also exhibited in London in 1973 and sold there the following year was the considerable collection of the Marshall family of Chicago.[331] Its most notable Italian Baroque item was certainly the large Guercino *Toilet of Venus* formerly in the Minneapolis museum, but there was also by the same artist a sketch for his *Vision of St. Jerome,* as well as a Fetti *Melancholy,* and works attributed to Valerio Castello, Lauri, Maffei, Mola, Preti, Sagrestani, Solimena, Stanzione, and Volterrano.

Back in America, a collection of works that received a showing was that formed by the Getty Museum. *Baroque Masters from the J. Paul Getty Museum* took place at the Fine Arts Gallery of the California State University at Northridge in 1973, and included paintings by Cavaliere d'Arpino, Castiglione, Cecco Bravo, Cigoli, Falcone, Garzi, Nuvolone, Sebastiano Ricci, and Pietro della Vecchia, all accumulated during the sixties and early seventies. On the East Coast another exhibition in an academic setting was *Major Themes in Roman Baroque Art from Regional Collections* held at Amherst College in April of 1974. This mélange of paintings, sculpture, and drawings, nominally drawn from the region, was actually more wide ranging, with the Caracciolo *Lot and his Daughters* from Columbia University, a Gaulli from Cleveland, Pretis from the Fogg and Manchester, a Strozzi from Worcester, Mola from Hartford, and Domenichino from the Fogg, among others. Then in 1979 was presented at the Wellesley College Museum the exhibition *Salvator Rosa in America,* which included prints, drawings, and paintings by the Italian master, as well as paintings by Americans inspired by his romantic style. As the catalogue introduction noted, "fortunately a number of Rosa's most interesting and successful pictures are in American collections." A highlight of the show was the reuniting of Wellesley's own *Nurture of Jupiter* with the Getty's *Allegory of Fortune;* the pair had formerly been in the collection of the Duke of Beaufort at Badminton. Other paintings by Rosa were lent from the Pennsylvania Academy of the Fine Arts, the Ringling, the Metropolitan Museum, and the museums of Hartford and Minneapolis.

A major exhibition at the Detroit Institute of Arts in 1974 was *The Twilight of the Medici: Late Baroque Art in Florence, 1670-1743.* This sumptuous array of all the arts was drawn primarily from European sources, but of the few notable examples from American collections there were the Magnasco *Hunting Scene* from Hartford, the pair of Gherardinis from Jacksonville, the Dolci *Salome* from Phoenix, and the Ferretti *Moses and the Brazen Serpent* from Mary Jane and Morton Harris.

MUSEUM ACQUISITIONS IN THE 1970S

The pace of acquisitions slowed somewhat across the country in the seventies, but there were still some very notable purchases, such as Caravaggio's *Crucifixion of St. Andrew* by the Cleveland Museum of Art in 1976. That same museum continued to be active, obtaining its Gentileschi and Solimena in 1971, Trevisani in 1974, and Rosa in 1977.

The painter Mattia Preti was especially popular during these years. The purchase in 1970 of the *Martyrdom of St. Bartholomew* by the Currier Gallery of Art in Manchester, New Hampshire, from Marshall Spink of London has already been noted, and at the Metropolitan Museum of Art, Sir John Pope-Hennessy bought a large *Pilate Washing his Hands* from Somerville & Simpson in 1978. The Metropolitan had also added a Guidobono in 1970 and a Saraceni in 1971, but its acquisition of Baroque paintings was particularly enhanced during this decade by the involvement and generosity of Charles and Jayne Wrightsman, who had begun collecting seriously in 1952.[332] Already in 1957 they had acquired Guercino's large altarpiece depicting *The Vocation of St. Luigi Gonzaga* from Agnew's for only $15,000, which price made Mr. Wrightsman wonder if an "0" had been left off the bill. Even Berenson in a letter to the collector had courteously written, "The Guercino is as good as the master ever did,"[333] and the painting was given to the Metropolitan in 1973 along with a

Giordano *Annunciation* they had purchased in Paris in 1958. Reni's lovely *Charity* they acquired from Wildenstein in 1968 and gave to the Metropolitan in 1974. Then in 1976, at Everett Fahy's urging, the Wrightsmans bought at auction Domenichino's *Landscape with Moses and the Burning Bush.* Later in 1979, when another major Guercino, *The Capture of Samson,* of the painter's earlier, bolder period was discovered in a collection in Lebanon, it was to the Wrightsmans that Sir John Pope-Hennessy turned, and they kindly complied, giving it in 1984. The Metropolitan also acquired Annibale Carracci's *Coronation of the Virgin* from Denis Mahon's collection in 1971; the Del Cairo *Herodias* was given by Mr. Ganz in memory of Professor Wittkower in 1973; and Francesco Curradi's *Narcissus* was given by Mr. and Mrs. Nathaniel Spear, Jr. in 1978.

On the other coast, the Ahmanson Foundation of Los Angeles began contributing substantial sums for purchases by that city's museum in 1972. Director Kenneth Donahue, who—since his days as a graduate student with Walter Friedländer had a fondness for and knowledge of the Italian Baroque—was able to acquire the Morazzone *St. Francis's Vision of an Angel* in 1973 from Mont and Reni's *Bacchus and Ariadne* from Agnew's in 1979.[334]

Meanwhile, the National Gallery of Art received two of its few non-Kress Baroque paintings, a Cantarini *St. Matthew and the Angel* as a gift from Mr. James Belden in 1972 and from Emily Floyd Gardiner a Magnasco of *The Choristers* brought to this country by her ancestors about 1825. Also still actively adding works was the museum in Toledo with a Giordano and a Ricci in 1971, Reni in 1972, and Solimena in 1973. Worcester joined in with a Gaulli in 1974, Solimena in 1978, and Vaccaro in 1977, all from Colnaghi's; earlier in 1971 the museum had purchased Giulio Cesare Procaccini's *St. Catherine* from Schickman. Procaccini was, in fact, one of the other great discoveries of the era, and from the late sixties into the eighties many of his paintings were added to American museums. Dallas acquired an *Ecce Homo* in 1969; Princeton, its *Martyrdom of St. Justina* in 1975 from Colnaghi's; the Metropolitan, a *Madonna and Child with Saints and Angels* in 1979; and Kansas City, a *Holy Family with St. John and the Angel* in the same year. Boston's Procaccini, the large *Scourging of Christ,* came in 1981 and the Getty's *Coronation of the Virgin* in 1983.

Still other museums acquired Baroque works during the seventies. The Museum of Fine Arts in Boston at the beginning of the decade under Perry Rathbone purchased Strozzi's *St. Sebastian* in 1971 from the Hallsborough Gallery, and near the end of the decade, with John Walsh and Scott Schaefer as curators, bought in 1978 from Agnew's the *St. Stephen Mourned by St. Gamaliel and St. Nicodemus* by Saraceni or a close follower, and a Fetti *Penitent Magdalen* at auction in 1979. To the Berkshire Museum in Pittsfield, Josephine Boardman Crane, the sister-in-law of its founder, bequeathed in 1977 an *Apollo and Marsyas* that had been exhibited as an Annibale Carracci at the Royal Academy in 1878 but is now identified as by Giovanni Antonio Burrini. In 1979 Springfield received three gifts from Channing Blake—Trevisani's *Allegory of Architecture* and *Allegory of Painting* and Turchi's *Bacchus and Ariadne.* Manchester was given a Magnasco *Monks on a Stormy Shore* by an anonymous donor in 1972, while Rochester added a Paolini *Portrait* in 1977 and received a Solimena in the same year. Philadelphia added a Pacecco de Rosa *Massacre of the Innocents* in 1973, and in 1976 the Walters Art Gallery in Baltimore received as a gift from Carlton M. Slagle, Jr. a painting by Vignali of *St. Gregory the Great.*

To Indianapolis came Romanelli's *Finding of Moses* in 1972, Giordano's *Dream of St. Joseph* in 1977, as well as works by Marco Ricci, Onofri, Loth, and Conca. The Detroit Institute of Arts under Frederick Cummings purchased a Guercino *Assumption of the Virgin* directly from the Marquess of Bute in 1971,[335] Giordano's *Entombment* in 1972, Caravaggio's *Conversion of the Magdalen* in 1973, and Langetti's *Giant* and Manfredi's *Fortune Teller* both in 1979. Cincinnati added an impressive Guercino of *Mars with Cupid* in 1977. The Saint Louis Art Museum under director Charles Buckley continued to grow with a Rosa *St. John Preaching,* one of the pair formerly in the Chrysler collection purchased from Eugene V. Thaw in 1970, and an *Annunciation* by Paolo de Matteis from Heim in 1973. Seattle purchased a Bettera *Still Life,* later attributed to Francesco Fieravino.

In California, San Francisco received an unusual Strozzi *Market Scene with Still Life* in 1977[336] (deaccessioned in 1993). At the Getty Museum, the Gentileschi that Mr. Getty had purchased in 1953 was formally given in 1971, and that same year the museum acquired the important Rosa *Allegory* from

Marlborough Gallery. Burton Fredericksen had joined the Getty as curator of paintings in 1969, and to fulfill Mr. Getty's desire for big pictures at reasonable prices, he naturally looked to the Italian Baroque. In the 1970s, therefore, the Getty added several large Lanfrancos, and works by Castiglione, Cigoli, Conca, Luigi Garzi, Magnasco, Piola, Preti, and Ricci (two), as well as Ludovico Carracci's *St. Sebastian Thrown into the Cloaca Maxima,* a *Supper at Emmaus* from Heim formerly attributed to Falcone, but now to Crescenzi, and a Dolci bought from a local collector that turned out to have been previously owned by Lucien Bonaparte.

Also commencing serious pursuit of Baroque pictures during this period was another Californian, Norton Simon, who established his own museum in Pasadena. Already in 1968 he had acquired a school of Caravaggio *Geographer,* and Solimena's *Garden of Eden* and Trevisani's *Apelles Painting Campaspe* from Sotheby's. The next year, in the tradition of John Ringling, he bought a set of large-scale tapestry cartoons representing the story of Dido and Aeneas by Giovanni Romanelli. In 1973 he went on to buy Baciccio's *St. Joseph and the Infant Christ* from Heim, Magnasco's *Interior with Monks* from Edward Speelman, and Guercino's *Suicide of Cleopatra* from Agnew's. A second Guercino was added in 1984, a *Portrait of a Dog* from the David Koetser gallery of Zurich. Two Giordanos were purchased: first in 1975, the *Birth of the Virgin* from Trafalgar Galleries and then a *Battle Scene* at Sotheby's in 1976. That same year Simon bought Tanzio da Varallo's *David with the Head of Goliath* from a French collection, and from Wildenstein the Reni *St. Cecilia* , formerly in the Chrysler collection. Another Solimena, the *Personification of Faith,* was purchased at Christie's in 1979 and, lastly, the remarkable, large Cagnacci of *Martha Rebuking Mary for her Vanity* from Colnaghi's in 1982.

In the South, the Cummer Gallery in Jacksonville received a pair of Alessandro Gherardinis, the *Forge of Vulcan* and the *Triumph of Neptune* in 1972, and purchased Solimena's *St. Joseph and the Christ Child* in 1973; Louisville, a Paolo de Matteis *Expulsion of Hagar* in 1970 from Newhouse, a Cavarozzi in 1971, and a Magnasco in 1972; Richmond, a Matteis in 1979; and New Orleans a Giordano *Baptism of Christ* in 1974. The Kimbell Art Museum acquired Rosa's *Pythagoras Emerging from the Underworld* in 1970; Houston gained Giordano's *Allegory of Prudence* in 1975 and was given Strozzi's *Guardian Angel* in 1976. Also in Houston throughout the 1970s, the Sarah Campbell Blaffer Foundation, advised by the dealer Spencer Samuels, was creating a survey collection of Italian painting from 1300 to 1800 to be shown throughout Texas and then other parts of the country in the 1980s. Of the Baroque period, the notable examples are Guercino's *Madonna and Child with St. John,* Bonzi's *Fruit Market,* Cavarozzi's *Virgin and Child with Angels,* a circle of Lanfranco *Gregory the Great,* Pietro da Cortona's *St. Constantia's Vision,* Mola's *Erminia and Vafrino Mourning Tancred,* Ciro Ferri's *Moses and the Daughters of Jethro,* Rosa's *Witches' Sabbath,* Giordano's *Battle of Israel and Amalek* (once owned by the Mannings), and a wonderful Paolo de Matteis *Allegorical Self-Portrait.*[337]

University museums continued to add Italian Baroque paintings to their collections during this period as well. In addition to the Procaccini already mentioned, Princeton—where Alan Rosenbaum became assistant director in 1975 and later director—purchased an Albani *Assumption* in 1977 and was given by Joseph McCrindle, Rosselli's *Christ the Redeemer* in 1977, and by Mrs. Douglas Delano, Padovanino's *Tobias and the Angel* in 1978. Mr. McCrindle in 1979 also gave paintings to Yale, a G.B. Crespi *St. Ambrose* and a Sacchi *Baptism of Christ.* Of other eastern schools, Harvard's Fogg Museum of Art received in 1976 from Mr. William Coolidge an outstanding Orazio Gentileschi that he had purchased from Agnew's.[338] The Hood Museum of Art at Dartmouth was given Giordano's *Martyrdom of St. Lawrence* in 1971 and a *St. Paul the Hermit* then attributed to Giacinto Brandi but later to Beinaschi in 1976. In 1977 to the Mead Art Museum at Amherst, Spadarino's *Christ and the Samaritan Woman* and a follower of Solimena *Rebecca and Abraham's Servant* were given in 1978; Trevisani's *Crucifixion* was purchased in the same year. The Palmer Museum of Art at Pennsylvania State University acquired a G.B. Vanni *Holy Family* from the O'Connor Lynch collection in 1973 and a Giuseppe Ghezzi *Marriage of St. Catherine* from Newhouse in 1976. In North Carolina, the Duke University Museum of Art in 1971 was given a fine Mola representing a *Philosopher with a Youth,* and the Ackland Art Museum at Chapel Hill added a Chiari *Swooning Virgin* in 1979.

Other college museums that added Baroque works during the seventies included Madison's Elvehjem Museum of Art, which acquired a Solimena *Adoration of the Shepherds* in 1970. The Snite Museum at Notre Dame purchased in 1972 from Heim Francesco de Mura's *Bacchus and Ceres;* the Indiana University Art Museum in Bloomington was given a Codazzi in 1974 and then in 1975 a Solimena *Flight into Egypt* from Nicholas Acquavella. The Krannert Art Museum of the University of Illinois received in 1972 from Mrs. Krannert a Sebastiano Ricci *Christ and the Woman Taken in Adultery.* Also in Illinois, the Martin D'Arcy Gallery of Art at the Loyola University Museum in Chicago during this decade was given a Guercino school *Rest on the Flight* and acquired a Sassoferrato *Madonna and Child with Cherubs.* At the Washington University Gallery of Art in St. Louis, Solimena's *King Ratchis Renouncing his Crown* was purchased in 1976. The University of Minnesota's Gallery in Minneapolis received by bequest in 1970 a collection formed by Professor Hylton A. Thomas that included a pair of paintings by Matteo Bonechi and a *Charity of St. Elizabeth* attributed to Solimena. The Utah Museum of Fine Arts at the University of Utah in Salt Lake City was given a Magnasco *Landscape* in 1970, and finally, on the West Coast, Stanford added a Dolci *Madonna in Glory* in 1970.

AMERICAN SCHOLARSHIP TRIUMPHANT

Before proceeding to the most recent period of twentieth-century collections and exhibitions, it would be worthwhile to briefly survey the achievements of American scholars in publications on the Italian Baroque painters. While acknowledging the contribution in this field of foreign—especially Italian and English—art historians, it is fair to say that the generation of young American scholars from the 1950s has emerged from the shadows of the grand old men Friedländer and Wittkower to produce works that have had a truly dramatic impact on our appreciation and knowledge of several of the major Baroque artists. Already in 1964 Robert Enggass had written his definitive study of Il Baciccio (Giovanni Battista Gaulli). Several scholars have been intrigued by Caravaggio. Alfred Moir, who taught for many years at the University of California at Santa Barbara produced his first study on *The Italian Followers of Caravaggio* in 1967; then came *Caravaggio and his Copyists* in 1976, and a book devoted to the master himself in 1989. Howard Hibbard of Columbia University, whose untimely death was a sad blow to the field, did publish in 1983 his monograph on Caravaggio. That same year Harvard's distinguished professor, Sydney J. Freedberg, wrote a trenchant study of the triumph of the Baroque in *Circa 1600: A Revolution of Style in Italian Painting.* Richard Spear of Oberlin College, who had produced the important 1971 exhibition catalogue *Caravaggio and his Followers* for the Cleveland Museum of Art, then turned his attention to the significant figure of Domenichino and wrote the monograph and catalogue on this artist in 1982. Equally important was D. Stephen Pepper's *Guido Reni* of 1984. Donald Posner, who inherited Friedländer's mantle at the Institute of Fine Arts in New York City, has introduced several succeeding generations of students, including the present writer, to the wonders of Baroque painting, and in 1971, authored the classic catalogue on the works of Annibale Carracci. Then, in 1979, he prepared the Italian section in a survey of Baroque art written with Professor Julius Held (see Fig. 20). Another fine survey of the era is that of 1977 by John Rupert Martin, professor of art history at Princeton (see Fig. 13). The Gentileschi have come in for closer scrutiny by Ward Bissell on Orazio (1981) and Mary Garrard on Artemisia (1989). Other recent studies have been Michael Stoughton's 1983 dissertation on Caracciolo; Dwight C. Miller on Franceschini (1991), and Thomas Willette on Stanzione (1992). Serious review of Carracci and Testa has been undertaken by Charles Dempsey, and Caravaggio studies have been carried on more recently with great insight in a brilliant series of articles and catalogue texts by Keith Christiansen of the Metropolitan Museum of Art.

ACQUISITIONS FROM 1980 TO 1994

From 1980 to the time that this study was written, significant additions to American public collections have been made, reflecting the taste of a new, younger generation of museum curators and directors. The present author was responsible for a Paolo de Matteis of the unusual subject *St. Nicholas of Bari Felling a Tree Inhabited by Demons* from Newhouse Gallery and a Conca *Annunciation* from Victor Spark being acquired by the High Museum in Atlanta in

1982 and 1984, respectively, and then, in 1988, for the exquisitely beautiful Guido Reni *Penitent Magdalen* from Piero Corsini coming to the Walters Art Gallery in Baltimore.[339]

In Kansas City, curator Roger Ward made among other distinguished purchases that of a major Guercino *St. Luke Painting the Virgin,* formerly in the Spencer collection at Althorp in 1983, as well as Reni's *St. Francis Adoring a Crucifix* in 1986, and a Cavaliere d'Arpino *Virgin and Child with Saints* in 1990. The Ahmanson funds allowed the curators at the Los Angeles County Museum of Art, Scott Schaefer and then Philip Conisbee, to continue outstanding Baroque acquisitions with Manetti's *Dido and Aeneas* and Tanzio da Varallo's *Adoration of Shepherds and Saints* both from Matthiesen in 1981, Mazzanti's *Death of Lucretia* in 1982, Reni's *Portrait of Cardinal Ubaldino* in 1983, Castiglione's *Noah's Sacrifice* from Wildenstein and Preti's *St. Veronica* from French & Co. in 1984, and Domenichino's *St. Ignatius's Vision* from Matthiesen in 1989.[340] Through other sources they obtained a Magnasco *Temptation of Christ* in 1981, an anonymous gift of a Turchi *St. Agnes* in 1983, a Sebastiano Ricci from Colnaghi's in 1990, and two works on copper, Romanelli's *St. John and St. Peter Preaching* in 1981 and Giordano's *St. John the Baptist Preaching* in 1990. In Cincinnati, director Millard Rogers chose a lovely Rosa *Finding of Moses* in 1980, a monumental Bernardino Mei *Alexander and the Fates* in 1988, and a Preti of *St. John Chrysostom* in 1989. The Milwaukee Art Museum received in 1982 from Mr. and Mrs. Myron Laskin a Colonna *Architectural Fantasy* and in 1985 a Pellegrini *Roman Triumph.* Then, in 1988, as a centennial gift, they and many other individuals contributed to purchase Castiglione's *Noah and the Animals Entering the Ark* from the Piero Corsini gallery.

The Metropolitan Museum of Art bought in 1981 the remarkable Andrea Sacchi depicting the castrato, *Pasqualini Crowned by Apollo.* The extensive collection of Jack and Belle Linsky donated in the following year contained a Magnasco *Nuns at Work* and, by the Neapolitan painter called the Master of the Annunciation to the Shepherds, an *Allegory of the Sense of Sight.*[341] Another Magnasco, *The Tame Magpie,* was purchased in 1984, the same year that the large Guercino *Samson* was given by the Wrightsmans. Sebastiano Ricci's *Holy Family with Angels* was the gift of Mr. and Mrs. Piero Corsini in 1986 and then in 1987 Mrs. Ganz, as noted previously, presented the Testa in her husband's memory. In 1989 the Metropolitan acquired the Andrea de Leone formerly in the Ganz collection from Channing Blake. Most recently, Fetti's *Parable of the Mote and Beam* was purchased from Wildenstein in 1991, and Mario Modestini has made a promised gift of his Giuseppe Chiari *Bathsheba at her Bath.*

At the Museum of Fine Arts in Boston, John Walsh, Theodore Stebbins, Scott Schaefer, and Laurence Kanter over the course of these years were responsible for bringing a small but tasteful work by Scarsellino in 1982, Maratta's *Flagellation of Christ* in 1983, a Creti in 1984, Giordano's *Venus Giving Arms to Aeneas* formerly in the Chrysler collection and purchased from French & Co. also in 1984, a striking large Carlo Dolci *David with the Head of Goliath* in 1985, and a Cavaliere d'Arpino in 1987. Springfield received in 1991 as a gift from Channing Blake *The Conversion of Saul* by Filippo Lauri.

The National Gallery also added a Cavaliere d'Arpino in 1984, and now that Sydney Freedberg was chief curator, even more remarkably, purchased the pair of Guercinos representing *Joseph and Potiphar's Wife* and *Amnon and Tamar* in 1986 that had been in the collection of the Marquess of Londonderry. Both a Luca Giordano *Diana and Endymion* given by Joseph McCrindle, and a Ribera *St. Bartholomew* came in 1991 as part of the Gallery's fiftieth anniversary celebration. On the same occasion, the Mannings gave in honor of William Suida a *Lamentation* by Palma Giovane. Also in Washington, a brand new institution, the National Museum of Women in the Arts, opened in 1987; in the collection donated by its founders, Wilhelmina and Wallace Holladay, is a fine Elisabetta Sirani *Virgin and Child.*[342]

The museum in St. Louis added in 1981 Orazio (now Artemisia) Gentileschi's *Danae* from Morton Morris & Co., London. In Detroit, the curator J. Patrice Marandel wisely saw to the purchase of a haunting *St. Francis Comforted by an Angel* by Assereto from Colnaghi's in 1990. Yet another Assereto, *Christ Healing the Blind,* was acquired that year by Pittsburgh's Carnegie Institute from Piero Corsini. Also in Pennsylvania, the museum in Allentown had acquired from Piero Corsini in 1986 Annibale Carracci's *The Bean Eater.* Chicago in 1991 purchased

Luca Giordano's impressive *Rape of the Sabines.* Cleveland's director Evan Turner acquired a Tanzio portrait from Patrick Matthiesen in London in 1986, and before retiring in 1993, a Strozzi *modello* of *The Healing of Tobit.*[343] Most recently, at the sale of Peter Sharp's collection in January 1994, Cleveland acquired the Annibale Carracci *Boy Drinking.*

Richmond bought Giordano's *St. Paul the Hermit* in 1982 from Heim. The following year saw New Orleans acquire works by Dolci and Solimena, while the Joslyn in Omaha added a Stanzione *Susannah and the Elders.* A Guercino formerly in the Bob Jones University Collection of *Christ in the Garden of Gethsemane* was bought from a collector in Tulsa by the Raleigh museum in 1984. The Birmingham Museum of Art in Alabama was made a promised gift of Dandini's *Miracle of the Pears* in 1981 and received a Sebastiano Ricci *Hagar and Ishmael* in 1993. To the already substantial Ringling Museum collection in Sarasota, Anthony Janson added in 1985 a Preti *Salome with the Head of St. John the Baptist* from Matthiesen. The Cummer Gallery in Jacksonville bought at auction in 1988 a *Pietà* by Assereto.

The Kimbell Art Museum in Fort Worth under Edmund P. Pillsbury was active with purchases of Annibale Carracci's *Butcher's Shop* in 1980, a Cavallino in 1981, Domenichino in 1982, Pietro da Cortona in 1984, the rediscovered, original Caravaggio *Cardsharps* in 1987, and a Guercino portrait in 1991. Dallas received as a gift Paolini's *Bacchic Concert* in 1987. Phoenix was given their Strozzi portrait of Doge Francesco Rizzo in 1981.

On the West Coast, in addition to the many acquisitions in Los Angeles and those already noted by Norton Simon in Pasadena, San Francisco, with Tommy Lee as curator, bought from Heim a major Preti of *St. John the Baptist Preaching* in 1981 and a Rosa in 1987. The Timken Art Gallery of San Diego purchased Guercino's *Return of the Prodigal Son* from Matthiesen in 1981, and the Santa Barbara Museum of Art, the beautiful Baglione of *St. Catherine of Alexandria Carried to her Tomb by Angels* in 1984 from the Corsini Gallery, as well as acquiring two Concas as gifts, and a Cantarini *St. Barbara.* Most importantly, the newly gained wealth of the Getty Museum in Malibu allowed it to make some outstanding acquisitions of Italian Baroque art. These included in 1983 two elegant works on copper, Cavallino's *Shade of Samuel Invoked by Saul* and Domenichino's *Christ Carrying the Cross,* the latter purchased from Sir John Pope-Hennessy. Then the following year came a pair of Solimenas, Lanfranco's *Madonna and Child with St. John,* and Guido Reni's *Virgin and Child with St. John.* In 1985 was acquired a pair of paintings, also on copper, by Francesco Maffei of scenes from the *Gerusalemme Liberata;* in 1986, a Luca Forte *Still Life,* Ricci's *Perseus with the Head of Medea,* and another copper, by G.M. Crespi; and in 1987, Guercino's *Portrait of Pope Gregory XVI,* which had been in America since 1908, from the Smithsonian's old National Gallery collection. A lovely Mola, the *Vision of St. Bruno,* was one of the chief purchases by the museum in 1989, and most recently, in 1993, a long-lost Fetti *Portrait of a Musician* and a previously unknown Guido Reni *Joseph and Potiphar's Wife* have been added to the ever-growing collection.

Once again the college collections have been among the busiest in the country with regard to Baroque painting. Princeton acquired Ludovico Carracci's *Kiss of Judas,* a rare Domenichino oil on copper of *The Mocking of Christ* in 1987,[344] and a wonderful Giordano of a *Pasta Eater* from Piero Corsini in 1985. Since the museum's director Alan Rosenbaum had been a friend of the Ganz family, Mrs. Eula Ganz donated in 1986 a pair of paintings by Giacomo del Po in memory of her husband, and then in 1991 Princeton added two anonymous Italian works and a Luti *Supper at Emmaus* formerly in the Bob Jones University Collection. Other gifts to Princeton were from Charles Scribner III, a Michele Regoglia in 1983; Marco Grassi, a Vignali in 1985; Joseph McCrindle, a Rosa in 1986 and Conca in 1987; and Mrs. Edith Goldner, a Pietro da Cortona in 1991.

Of other eastern college collections, Harvard's Fogg Museum received as a gift the impressive Renieri *Self-Portrait* in 1984, and the Yale University Art Gallery, Trevisani's *Crucifixion* from Mr. McCrindle and Sebastiano Ricci's *Pope Gregory the Great* in 1991. Other gifts included Dartmouth's studio of Strozzi *Berenice* and a Della Vecchia *St. Cecilia* in 1983 and 1984 from Julia and Richard Rush, and Smith College's Cantarini *Penitent St. Peter* from Mr. and Mrs. A.C. Michel in 1985. Wellesley was given in 1991 an *Abraham and the Angels* attributed to Jacopo Vignali. Amherst purchased a Solimena *St. Bernard* in 1982 and a Carlone *Triumph of Christ* in 1985, and the Picker

Art Gallery of Colgate University, Tavella's *Adoration of the Angels* in 1986. Cornell University was given a Falcone and a Luti in 1985, a Rosa *Landscape* in 1986, and acquired an Elisabetta Sirani *Portia Wounding her Thigh* in 1990. As a gift, the Palmer Museum of Art at Pennsylvania State University received a Pietro della Vecchia *Sacrifice of Jeptha's Daughter* from Mr. and Mrs. Morton Harris in 1993. Ackland at Chapel Hill added a Domenico Piola in 1981 and Guercino's *Assumption of the Virgin* from Matthiesen in 1982, and in 1987 curator Dean Walker obtained from the Corsini Gallery a Creti sketch of the *Cumaen Sibyl.*

In the Midwest and beyond, the Snite Museum's curator Steven Spiro added a number of paintings to the University of Notre Dame, including a fine Dolci *Virgin Annunciate* in 1983, works by Ferri, Solimena, and Gandolfi all purchased from Colnaghi's, and, as a gift from Gaby Kopleman, a Conca in 1990. To the University of Indiana went a Strozzi *St. Dorothy* in 1980. The Spencer Museum of Art at the University of Kansas obtained a pair of mythological subjects by Luti. The Elvehjem Museum of Art in Madison purchased in 1993 *Christ's Charge to St. Peter* by Strozzi. At Oberlin, Larry Feinberg saw to the purchase of a Tanzio da Varallo *St. John the Baptist* from Robert Dance, and the same dealer supplied a Solimena *Death of St. Joseph* to the University of Utah in 1990. The University of Michigan Museum of Art got a Carpioni *Hero and Leander* in 1984. To the Huntington Art Gallery at the University of Texas in Austin came in 1984 a Giordano *Presentation of the Virgin* as well as an *Allegory of Astrology* by Guercino. In 1980 Stanford was given Cigoli's *Salome with the Head of St. John* and purchased the wonderful *Circe* by Guidobono and, more recently, was given Rosa's *Torment of Tityus* by Mr. McCrindle in 1992. Finally, Santa Barbara added Cristoforo Roncalli's *St. Domitilla* in 1985.

EXHIBITIONS IN THE 1980s

The 1980s began with a retrospective view of recent New York collectors of Baroque art, held at the Art Museum of Princeton University and organized by John T. Spike. His catalogue introduction noted that, unlike Tietze in 1944, he did not have to justify Baroque art, for "the reputations of the Italian contemporaries of Rembrandt and Velazquez have been thoroughly rehabilitated in the intervening decades," and he further added that for compiling this group of forty-seven paintings, New York is "today one of the few cities in the world that could support an exhibition of this kind." It was also clear from the results that "New York collectors harbor a decided preference for figure paintings, with, interestingly, the absolute exception of portraiture."[345] At this time, the three leading lenders who were identified were of course the Mannings, who supplied, among others, works by Baciccio, Carpioni, Castiglione, Daniele Crespi, Dolci, Fetti, and Preti; Mr. and Mrs. Ganz, with examples by Annibale Carracci, Dandini, Forabosco, Del Po (two), and Testa; and Mr. and Mrs. Morton Harris, who lent their Badalocchio, Baglione, Codazzi, Fracanzano, Lupicini, and Scarsellino. Professor and Mrs. Hibbard also lent a Pignoni, and the dealer Richard Feigen sent from his private collection a Dolci and a Lanfranco.

The success of this exhibition led to Spike's organizing throughout the 1980s a series of outstanding and enlightening exhibitions on different specialized aspects of Italian art with great emphasis on the Baroque. The first of these was *Italian Still-Life Paintings from Three Centuries* shown in 1983 at the National Academy of Design in New York, the Philbrook Museum of Art in Tulsa, and the Dayton Art Institute. Most of the loans came from Europe, but there were also the National Gallery's Pensionante del Saraceni and Vassallo, and the Ringling's Luca Forte. Next was *Baroque Portraiture in Italy: Works from North American Collections* shown at the Ringling Museum and the Wadsworth Atheneum in 1984-85. All media were included, and of the paintings, there were a Ludovico Carracci from Dayton; Pietro da Cortona from Minneapolis; Gaulli from the Walters Art Gallery; the Guercino still then in the Smithsonian; Paolini from Rochester; Reni from Los Angeles; Renieri from the Fogg; Rosas from Hartford and the Metropolitan; the Ringling's Sassoferrato; Solimena from the Metropolitan; Strozzi and Tinelli from the National Gallery; a Della Vecchia from the Chrysler Museum; and several loans from the Mannings' collection. Then in 1986 Spike organized a very lovely exhibition *Giuseppe Maria Crespi and the Emergence of Genre Painting in Italy* for the Kimbell Art Museum in Fort Worth. Although there were many loans from abroad, one of the purposes of the exhibition was, as he stated in the introduction, "to call attention to several important works by Crespi in American collections."

Those to be seen were the *Lute Player* from Boston, *Tarquin and Lucretia,* a Kress picture from the National Gallery, *The Wedding at Cana* of the Art Institute of Chicago, and the Chrysler Museum's *Continence of Scipio.*

Also presented at the country's major museums during the 1980s were several international blockbuster exhibitions devoted to Italian Baroque art. Accompanied by the now fashionable weighty catalogues, these testified to the absolute acceptance of this once suspect era of art. Thus the National Gallery in Washington shared with London in 1982-83 *Painting in Naples 1606 to 1705: From Caravaggio to Giordano.* Included were the Cleveland Caravaggio, the Kimbell Cavallino, the Codazzi from the Blaffer Foundation, Detroit's Giordano, and both Philadelphia's and Bob Jones, Jr.'s Pacecco de Rosas (cat. no. 22).

From February to April 1985, the Metropolitan Museum of Art hosted in New York a great exhibition *The Age of Caravaggio,* which brought most of the master's accepted works to America, as well as many by his contemporaries such as Baglione, Orazio Borgianni, the Carracci, and Orazio Gentileschi; notable from American collections was the Chicago Manfredi. The following year the Metropolitan and the National Gallery of Art joined forces to present in both New York and Washington the even larger *Age of Correggio and the Carracci: Emilian Painting of the Sixteenth and Seventeenth Centuries.* The Baroque section of this included from American collections Annibale's *Boy Drinking* from the late Peter Sharp (recently sold at auction to the Cleveland Museum), the same artist's *Butcher's Shop* from the Kimbell Art Museum, his *Landscape* and *Venus Adorned by the Graces,* both in the Kress collection at the National Gallery of Art, and the Metropolitan's *Coronation of the Virgin.* From Raleigh came Ludovico Carracci's *Assumption of the Virgin,* and his *St. Sebastian* was lent by the Getty Museum. Among the general survey of seventeenth-century Bolognese artists, there were, to name just a few highlights, the Metropolitan's own Guercino *Samson,* the Ringling's Sisto Badalocchio, the Bob Jones University Denys Calvaert (cat. no. 15), and from private collectors, Nelson Shanks's Cagnacci and Cignani, and Elmar Seibel's monumental *Resurrection* by Cantarini.

A number of smaller, more specialized exhibitions dealing with Baroque art were organized around the country during the eighties and early nineties. In 1981-82 at Gainesville and Jacksonville in Florida was seen *Transformations of the Roman Baroque,* which spanned the period 1590 to 1742, and of paintings, included the Cummer Gallery's own Sassoferrato *Praying Madonna* and from Bob Jones University a Maratta and a Chiari (cat. nos. 26 and 35), the Ringling's Fetti, another Maratta and a Reni from the Rhode Island School of Design, as well as the Rosa and circle of Sacchi from Vassar College. Also seen only in Florida was *Italian Renaissance and Baroque Paintings in Florida Museums* organized by Arthur R. Blumenthal at the Cornell Fine Arts Museum of Rollins College in Winter Park. From its own collection was a Turchi on slate, while other Baroque loans came from the Cummer and the Ringling museums.

The Cleveland Museum of Art presented in 1984 the exhibition *Baroque Imagery* organized by John Schloder, which featured works primarily from the museum's own collection illustrating a number of themes. Later that year, Cleveland joined with the Kimbell Art Museum in Fort Worth to present a remarkable monographic exhibition entitled *Bernardo Cavallino of Naples, 1616-1656.* This reunited a beautiful pair of paintings on copper divided between the Kimbell and the Getty and also, of works from American collections, included the examples from Kansas City and Hartford, as well as one owned by the restorer Mario Modestini of the *Angel Liberating St. Peter from Prison.* The Kimbell had become one of the chief supporters of the unusual monographic exhibition, presenting, in addition to that of Cavallino, *Jusepe de Ribera, Lo Spagnoletto,* his first retrospective organized by Professor Craig Felton in 1982, and in 1988, in collaboration with the Los Angeles County Museum of Art, *Guido Reni, 1575-1642,* a show that revealed to America the full glory of Reni, with loans of two paintings each from Detroit and Bob Jones University, as well as Los Angeles. Others included the recent purchases of the Walters Art Gallery and Kansas City, and from Richard Feigen, a *Martyrdom of St. Apollonia.*

Traveling shows were also organized in the 1980s from two of the great American collections of Baroque art. In 1984 the North Carolina Museum of Art in Raleigh presented *Masterpieces of Baroque Paintings from the Bob Jones University Collection,* which included all the various European schools but naturally featured many of the outstanding Italian works assembled by Dr. Jones, with all four of the Guido Reni *Evangelists* (cat. nos. 18, 19), as well as the Nuvolone, Maratta (cat. no. 26), and Guidobono (cat. no. 33), among others. This exhibition was also seen at Colnaghi's in New York and nearly the same show was repeated in Austin in 1990. Likewise, in 1986 the National Gallery of Art in Washington showed *Baroque Paintings from the John and Mable Ringling Museum of Art,* in which the sensuous works of Del Cairo, Pietro da Cortona, Mola, and Sassoferrato invaded the usually staid halls.[346] This same experience was repeated in 1990 when the National Gallery without much fanfare hosted a remarkable group of Baroque works belonging to Italian banks.[347]

In 1988 an exhibition devoted to the prints and drawings of Pietro Testa was shown at the Philadelphia Museum of Art,[348] and included were two of the rare paintings by this artist—*Aeneas on the Banks of the River Styx* from a private collection and *Alexander the Great Saved from the River Cyndus,* the ex-Ganz painting that now belonged to the Metropolitan Museum of Art. Circulating during that same year to Yale, the Ringling, and Kansas City was the large-scale exhibition, *A Taste for Angels: Neapolitan Painting in North America, 1650-1750.* Pictures for this came from both private and public collections and included, of the Baroque era, such old favorites as Giordano's *Hymn of Miriam* from Bob Jones University and the *Rape of Europa* from Hartford, the Bob Jones Preti of *Christ Seating the Child in the Midst of the Disciples* (cat. no. 25), the Matteis *Self-Portrait* from the Blaffer Foundation, and Solimena's *Lot and his Daughters* from Ponce; newer acquisitions that appeared were the Preti *St. John Preaching* from San Francisco, *Herodias with the Head of St. John the Baptist* from the Ringling, and the Matteis scene of *St. Nicholas* from the High Museum in Atlanta.

The decade concluded with a more old-fashioned assemblage of interesting paintings that oddly recalled that very first American exhibition at Harvard sixty years earlier in 1929. This time the location was the Smith College Museum of Art in Northampton, Massachusetts, which presented from November 1989 to February 1990, in conjunction with a course taught by Professor Craig Felton, *Baroque Painters in Italy.* As in the case of the early Fogg exhibition, there was no published catalogue, but there were explanatory texts on the works prepared by students.[349] The works on view included the school's own Brandi and Cantarini, several paintings from the collection of Dr. Carlo Croce of Philadelphia—especially a fine Caracciolo *St. John the Baptist*—and also loans from the Harrises and Mannings, as well as from the dealers Newhouse, Corsini, and Wildenstein.

COMMERCIAL EXHIBITIONS

The 1980s witnessed a great surge in the art market, and this was reflected not only by more Baroque pictures in the auction houses, but also in the number of exhibitions at commercial galleries, often accompanied by scholarly catalogues. The English firm of P. & D. Colnaghi opened a branch in New York in 1982 and proceeded to organize an exhibition almost every year that featured a number of Italian Baroque works. *Discoveries from the Cinquecento* in 1982 had paintings by Annibale and Ludovico Carracci, Empoli, Mastaletta, and Scarsellino. *European Baroque Paintings* in 1984 included, among many Italian examples, Crespi's *Portrait of Farinelli* and the Lanfranco bought by the Getty Museum. In Colnaghi's exhibition of European paintings in 1985 was the Dolci *David with the Head of Goliath* that was acquired by the Boston Museum of Fine Arts. The gallery's *Master Paintings* of 1989-90 included the Assereto purchased by Detroit and a recently discovered, large *St. Bartholomew* by Bernardo Cavallino (see Fig. 23). *A Collectors Miscellany* presented in 1990-91 featured two Rosas and two Sebastiano Riccis, one of which went to the Los Angeles County Museum of Art.

The New York gallery of Richard Feigen, who also collects Baroque paintings, has mounted several noteworthy exhibitions, in particular, *Landscape Painting in Rome, 1595-1675,* organized in 1985 by Ann Sutherland Harris, as well as one in 1992, devoted to Guercino. The Piero Corsini gallery's annual exhibition also became during these years a highlight of the art season, offering a great many newly discovered Baroque paintings.

Other galleries also now mounted special exhibitions with Baroque pictures. Didier Aaron presented *A Timeless Heritage* in 1987 that featured a Dolci *Adoration of the Shepherds;* Stair-Sainty Matthiesen included in *An Aspect of Collecting Taste* in 1986 a Sebastiano Ricci *Hagar and Ishmael,* and in their 1992 general presentation was a striking G.C. Procaccini of *Venus with Cupid.* At M. Knoedler & Co. in 1981 an *Exhibition of Old Masters* in collaboration with I. & G. Fine Arts International of London included Domenichino's *Expulsion of Adam and Eve,* and many other Baroque works. The old firm of Newhouse Gallery, now under new management, presented in 1987 in collaboration with the Matthiesen Gallery of London *Paintings from Emilia, 1500-1700,* and then in 1989, an exhibition of *Old Master Paintings,* among which was the recently cleaned Valerio Castello of *St. Geneviève* acquired at the Chrysler sale.

Although most of the Baroque commercial activity was in New York City, there was an occasional showing elsewhere, and one that contained a substantial number of unusual paintings was *The Wealth of Cities: Italian Painting in the 17th and 18th Centuries,* held in early 1982 at the Osuna Gallery in Washington, D.C.

PRIVATE COLLECTIONS: 1980 TO THE PRESENT

Several collectors, who emerged during the previous decades and have already been noted as donors or lenders, continue to maintain significant Baroque holdings, and of these should be mentioned Joseph McCrindle, David Rust, Nelson Shanks, Channing Blake, and Mr. and Mrs. Morton Harris. Of the great pioneers of the 1950s, Dr. Jones is happily still pursuing works of this period, and the magnificent Suida Manning collection is still intact.

Some other subsequent collections formed more recently have for various reasons already been dispersed. The Fellowship of Friends of Renaissance, California, had acquired a notable group of fine paintings in the eighties, including such Baroque gems as Guercino's *Toilet of Venus* and an unusual pair of Old Testament scenes of drunkenness by Cavallino, but reversals in the wine industry led to their being sold soon after.[350] In San Francisco, David B. Goodstein had accumulated a remarkable group of Italian Baroque paintings, which, following his death, were sold in London in 1986.[351] Among these works were notable examples by Cantarini, Castello, Pietro da Cortona, Ferri, Gaulli, Guercino, Magnasco, and Preti. Another significant West Coast collection was that of Frederick W. Field of Beverly Hills. His paintings, auctioned off for personal reasons at Christie's, London, 5 July 1991, included those by Guercino, Giordano, Solimena, Rosa and Reni. Peter Jay Sharp, a real-estate tycoon, who owned the Carlyle Hotel in New York, assembled a small but choice selection of paintings over a decade that were auctioned a year after his death in New York in 1994.[352] The Italian Baroque highlights of this collection were the pair of Cavallinos formerly owned by the Fellowship of Friends, Annibale's *Boy Drinking,* a pair of Crespi peasant scenes, and, one of Mr. Sharp's first major purchases, the enormous Reni *Liberality and Modesty.* One year earlier in January 1993, New York had also seen the auction of the more extensive collection of paintings formed in the 1980s by Dr. Carlo Croce of Philadelphia.[353] A selection of these had been exhibited at Smith College and at the Delaware Art Museum in Wilmington in 1992. Among the well-known names were Cambiaso, Caracciolo, Castiglione, Fetti, Guercino, G.C. Procaccini, Reni, and Stanzione, as well as many more unusual ones such as Giovanni Balducci, Giovanni Do, Pietro Faccini, Carlo Francesco, Antiveduto Grammatica, and Bartolomeo Passante.

FIGURE 23

BERNARDO CAVALLINO, *St. Bartholomew,* Private Collection, New York. Photograph courtesy of Colnaghi Gallery, New York.

A new group of collectors fortunately still pursue Italian Baroque paintings. By far the most extensive group has been accumulated by Barbara Piasecka Johnson at her estate in Princeton, New Jersey. Only the religious works collected in the seventies and eighties have so far been published,[354] and they present a powerful array of images, with two attributed to Caravaggio, two by Castiglione, and others by Cantarini, Ludovico Carracci, Desubleo, Orazio Gentileschi, Manfredi, Saraceni, Sassoferrato, and the Master of the Annunciation to the Shepherds.

Several recent collectors have also emerged in New York City. The well-known businessman Saul Steinberg has built a collection of extraordinarily high quality in which are to be found some of the Baroque era's most famous painters such as Cavallino *(Triumph of Galatea),* Annibale (*St. Francis),* and Domenichino *(Adam and Eve),* in addition to Caracciolo, Castello, and Liss. Also active has been Damon Mezzacappa,

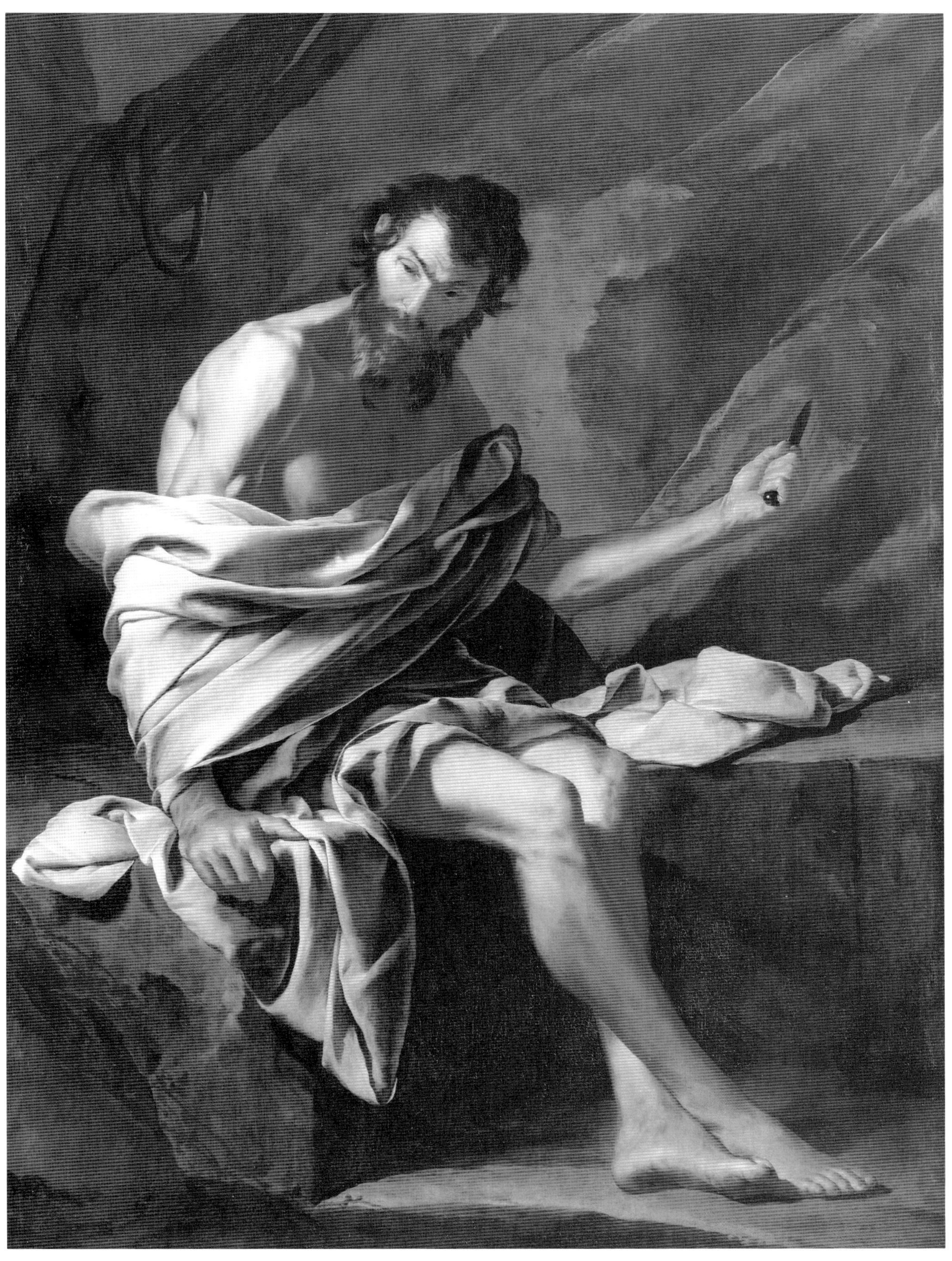

who in a little over ten years has brought together about twenty works, primarily Baroque paintings with allegorical, historical or religious subjects. Among these are the Testa *Aeneas,* which had been lent to the Testa exhibition, and paintings by Cignani, Franceschini, Guercino, Ligozzi, and Mola. Another noteworthy collector is Alexis Gregory, who owns the remarkable *Christ Crowned with Thorns* by Manfredi, formerly in the Colyer collection of Bennington, Vermont.

Outside of New York there are other growing regional collections. Dr. and Mrs. Alfred Bader, who are primarily known for their seventeenth-century Dutch and Flemish paintings, also have amassed some Italian ones of the same period, and these were exhibited at the Union Gallery of Purdue University, West Lafayette, Indiana, in 1987.[355] They included a *Portrait of a Man* attributed to Passerotti, a version of Fetti's *Dream of Jacob* and the same subject by Paolo de Matteis, Paolini's *Portrait of a Young Man,* Fracanzano's of an old man, a Bellucci *Caritas Romana,* and Guidobono's *Departure of Tobias.* In Boston, Elmar and Azita Seibel own, in addition to the Cantarini shown in Washington and New York, a large Pietro Novelli, and works by Daniele Crespi, Paolo de Matteis, and Giaquinto.[356] Another couple, who live in Washington and are advised by the staff of the National Gallery, have brought together large-scale works by Castello, Franceschini, G.C. Procaccini, Sebastiano Ricci, and Scarsellino. Very active within a restricted area are two brothers in Houston, Texas, Kurt and Mark Haukohl, who collect works of the Florentine school, in particular those of the Dandini family, and who also have a fine Dolci *St. Agnes* and Ficherelli *St. Sebastian Tended by St. Irene.* Residing also in Houston are Mr. and Mrs. Harris Masterson III, who do not especially pursue the Baroque, but did purchase from French & Co. one of the most touching pictures to appear in recent times, Guido Reni's *St. Joseph and the Christ Child.*[357]

CONCLUSION

Judging by the summer loans displayed at the Metropolitan Museum of Art in 1993, it seems clear that the taste for seventeenth-century paintings has not abated. There, for example, was to be seen the large Cavallino *St. Bartholomew* formerly with Colnaghi (Fig. 23),[358] and other paintings such as a Cavarozzi *Still Life,* G.B. Ramenghi *Holy Family and Saints,* G.C. Procaccini *Baptism,* Franceschini *Triumph of Venus,* and Tiarini *Madonna and Child with Saints.*

Likewise, exhibitions that celebrate the seventeenth century and our passion for it continue into this last decade of the twentieth century. In 1992 the National Gallery of Art in Washington marked the Guercino quadricentennial with a large international loan exhibition orchestrated by Sir Denis Mahon,[359] and in early 1994 a survey of works by Ludovico Carracci was shown at the Kimbell Art Museum in Fort Worth. In addition, two major retrospectives of famous collections known for their Italian Baroque paintings are circulating in a number of American cities. The first, which opened in February 1994 at the North Carolina Museum of Art in Raleigh, is devoted to the Kress collection,[360] and the second is the present exhibition of the ever-surprising and still-growing collection of Bob Jones University. These, it is hoped, will inspire continued American interest in and further collecting of Italian Baroque painting well into the twenty-first century.

This essay, which has grown to somewhat ungainly proportions, could not have been written without the cooperation of many people. First of all I must thank Richard P. Townsend, Ruth G. Hardman Curator of European and American Art at the Philbrook Museum of Art, who conceived the present exhibition and was kind enough to invite me to write something dealing with the collecting of Italian Baroque paintings in America, little suspecting that the result would be so gargantuan. It is to his and the Philbrook's credit that this study appears substantially as it was written. Despite the vast array of collectors, paintings, exhibitions, and institutions mentioned, it is possible that some works or individuals have been overlooked, or that paintings have had attribution changes of which I am unaware. Nevertheless, it is hoped that the main value of this text will reside in the documenting of the sheer quantity of material, which evidences the evergreen popularity of Italian Baroque painting in this country. In fact, much more could be written about the influences from abroad, but it has seemed practical to focus here primarily on the United States. Furthermore, the designation "Italian Baroque" is intended throughout to refer to Italian-born artists active during the seventeenth century.

Naturally, I am especially indebted to those individuals who gave time to be interviewed on their recollections of collecting and collectors in the 1950s and subsequent decades. Dr. Bob Jones, Jr., in particular, was most gracious in making time in his still busy schedule to talk about his early days as a collector. In addition, I spoke with Robert L. Manning, Morton and Mary Jane Harris, Donald Posner, Everett Fahy, Alan Rosenbaum, Joseph Rishel, Gaby Kopleman, Jan Klein, Robert Samuels, Pamela Askew, Julius Held, Jack Tanzer, William Acquavella, Joan Nissman, Mort Abromson, Kate Ganz, Maggie Fitch, and Sir Denis Mahon.

I received information from many museum and gallery colleagues whom I wish to thank for their time and trouble: Donna Antoun, Colin Bailey, Frederic M. Bancroft, Bernard Barryte, Leslie Blacksberg, Caryl Burtner, Susan Caroselli, Dawson Carr, Alan Chong, Keith Christiansen, Mary Frisk Coffman, Janet Comey, Judith Dressel, Craig Felton, Stephen Fisher, Joe Giuffre, Mary Gristina, Nicholas Hall, Jefferson Harrison, Erica Hirshler, Karen C. Hodges, Chiyo Ishikawa, Sona Johnston, William Johnston, Ian Kennedy, L. Lippincott, Janet Manahan, Judith Mann, J. Patrice Marandel, Linda Muehlig, Nancy Netzer, Andrea Norris, Melissa Owens, Roxana Pagés, Karen Quinn, Richard Rand, Matthew Robinson, Betsy Rosasco, Donald Rosenthal, Kathryn Rothkopff, Irene Roughton, Eliot W. Rowlands, Donna di Salvo, Alan Salz, Spencer Samuels, J.J. Schlegel, Sarah Schroth, Elmar Seibel, George Shackelford, Louana Skorupa, Abigail Smith, Kimberly Spence, Stephen Spiro, David Steel, Tom Styron, Dominique H. Vasseur, Olga M. Viso, George Wachter, Karin J. Walker, Sally Weiner, Sarah Weiner, Michael Wentworth, Marjorie E. Wieseman, Susan Wiggins, Gloria Williams, Alan Wintermute, Martha Wolff, and Karen Zukowski.

In Boston, I had the benefit of the resources of the Museum of Fine Arts, especially its Archives under the direction of Maureen Melton, and I was assisted in reviewing this material by a most skilled intern, Sydney Resendez. I was also fortunate to have time at the Getty Center in Santa Monica as a visiting Getty Museum fellow to make use of their extraordinary facilities, including the Library, Special Collections, and Provenance Index; I am most grateful for all the kind assistance provided by their staff, and also to my fellow Getty Museum scholar A.D. Coleman, who provided vital help with the Center's computer system.

The manuscript was reviewed in whole or in part and helpful comments made by Pamela Askew, Efraín Barradas, Edgar Peters Bowron, Burton Fredericksen, Mary Jane Harris, Robert L. Manning, and Robert Simon. The difficult job of preparing the first draft of the manuscript was carried out with great dedication by my assistant Regina Rudser, and the most understanding editor has been Elizabeth Allen.

NOTES

1. W. Dunlap, *History of the Rise and Progress of the Arts of Design in the United States (1834),* eds. F. Bayley and C. Goodspeed, Boston, 1918, I, p. 24.
2. H.W. Foote, *John Smibert, Painter,* Cambridge, Massachusetts, 1950, pp. 11, 13, 53, 58.
3. Dunlap 1918 (as in note 1), I, p. 118.
4. *The Journal of Dr. John Morgan of Philadelphia,* Philadelphia, 1907, pp. 241-43; C. and J. Bridenbaugh, *Rebels and Gentlemen: Philadelphia in the Age of Franklin,* Cornwall, New York, 1942, p. 214.
5. R.T.H. Halsey, "Benjamin Franklin: His Interest in the Arts," in *Benjamin Franklin and his Circle,* Metropolitan Museum of Art, New York, 1936, pp. 5, 146.
6. R. Peale, *Notes on Italy Written During a Tour in The Years 1829 and 1830,* Philadelphia, 1831, p. 4; C.C. Sellers, *Charles Willson Peale,* New York, 1969, pp. 222, 463; and C.E. Hevner, "Rembrandt Peale's Dream and Experience of Italy," in *The Italian Presence in American Art, 1760-1860,* ed. I.B. Jaffe, New York, 1989, p. 9.
7. Quoted in M. Benisovich, "The Sale of the Studio of Adolphe-Ulrich Wertmüller," *Art Quarterly,* XVI, 1953, p. 21.
8. H. Dickson, " TH. J. Art Collector," in *Jefferson and the Arts: An Extended View,* National Gallery of Art, Washington, D.C., 1976, p. 110; and S. Howard, "Thomas Jefferson's Art Gallery for Monticello," *Art Bulletin,* LIX, 1977, pp. 593-95.
9. S.R. Stein, *The World of Thomas Jefferson at Monticello,* New York, 1993, pp. 32-33, 76, 146; Dickson 1976 (as in note 8), pp. 111-12.
10. Stein 1993 (as in note 9), p. 38; and W.H. Adams ed., *The Eye of Th. Jefferson,* National Gallery of Art, Washington, D.C., 1976, p. 195.
11. Stein 1993 (as in note 9), pp. 69-70. After Jefferson's death, his collection was sent to Boston for exhibition and then sale at the Athenaeum in May 1828, but as only one picture sold at this time, they were offered again in July 1833 at Chester Harding's Gallery on School Street in Boston. See Dickson 1976 (as in note 8), p. 127.
12. C. Codman Wolcott, *A History of the Codman Collection of Pictures,* Brookline, Massachusetts, 1935, pp. 1-2, 10, 13, 63-65.
13. J. Gault, *The Life and Studies of Benjamin West Prior to his Arrival in England,* Philadelphia, 1816, pp. 105-106; R.C. Alberts, *Benjamin West. A Biography,* Boston, 1978, pp. 49, 53.
14. M.B. Amory, *The Domestic and Artistic Life of John Singleton Copley, R.A.,* Boston, 1882, p. 57.
15. I.B. Jaffe, *John Trumbul: Patriot-Artist of the American Revolution,* Boston, 1975, pp. 172-78.
16. Dunlap 1918 (as in note 1), II, p. 49, and III, pp. 270-71; Jaffe 1975 (as in note 15), p. 208.
17. *A Catalogue of Eight Most Valuable Pictures the Property of John Trumbull,* sold by Peter Coxe, London, 12 June 1812, lot 19. See also *The Autobiography of Colonel John Trumbull,* ed. T. Sizer, New Haven, 1953, p. 294.
18. C.A. du Fresnoy, *The Art of Painting with Remarks and also a Short Account of the Most Eminent Painters both Ancient and Modern by Richard Graham,* London, editions of 1716 and 1750. M. Pilkington, *A General Dictionary of Painters,* London, 1798. Between this first edition and the later one of 1829, there were considerable changes, including the addition of an entry on Caravaggio. A good guide to the range of books on art available to well-educated Americans in the first half of the nineteenth century is provided by the extensive library of English, French, and Italian texts sold from the library of James Thomson, New York, 22 March 1848. See also L.B. Miller, "An Influence in the Air, Italian Art and American Taste," in Jaffe ed. 1989 (as in note 6), p. 26. At a slightly later moment, a correspondent for *The Crayon,* I, 7 March 1855, p. 152, reported from Florence in January 1854 on a collection in Rome that had about one hundred and fifty works, "ranging through all the great names, Raphael, Michelangelo, Titian, Correggio, Guido, Domenichino, Claude, Salvator Rosa, etc., etc."
19. A.W. Rutledge, "Robert Gilmor, Jr., Baltimore Collector," *Journal of the Walters Art Gallery,* XII, 1949, pp. 19-22; *The Taste of Maryland: Art Collecting in Maryland, 1800-1934,* Walters Art Gallery, Baltimore, 1984, pp. 1-2; Dunlap 1918 (as in note 1), III, pp. 272-75.
20. H. Johnson, *Descriptive Catalogue of the Bowdoin College Art Collection,* Brunswick, 1895, pp. 3, 38-39; W.G. Constable, *Art Collecting in the United States of America: An Outline of a History,* London, 1964, p. 16; *Handbook of the Collection: Bowdoin College Museum of Art,* ed. M.R. Burke, Brunswick, 1981, pp. 35-36, 61.
21. *The Vernon Mona Lisa,* Otis Art Institute of Los Angeles, 1964, n.p.
22. Information supplied by Helen Rutherford Meade in 1935, preserved in the files of the Frick Art Reference Library, New York. The sale by Thomas & Sons in Philadelphia was on 15 March 1853. See also E. Larsen, "Highlights from the Georgetown University Art Collection," *Apollo,* LXXII, December 1960, pp. 201-202; and E. Larsen, *Georgetown University. Catalogue of the Art Collection,* Washington, D.C., 1963, pp. 40-41.
23. According to information supplied by the Art Institute of Chicago.
24. See E.M. Woodward, *Bonaparte's Park and the Murats,* Trenton, 1829, p. 58; and the catalogue of the sale organized by Thomas Birch, Jr. at Bordentown on 17-18 September 1845. One of the Giordano still lifes has recently appeared on the New York art market; see *Master Paintings,* Colnaghi, New York, 1994, no. 9. Two other large Giordanos recently on the New York art market are also supposed to have come from the Bonaparte collection; see Ferrari and Scavizzi 1992, pp. 288-89, nos. A228 c and d.
25. R. Spear, *Caravaggio and his Followers,* Cleveland Museum of Art, 1971, no. 50; the painting is now in the Park Ridge Public Library, Park Ridge, Illinois.
26. According to correspondence of March 1951 from W.G. Constable to Denis Mahon in the files of the Department of Paintings in the Museum of Fine Arts, the Lowell family archives have a letter dated Florence 24 May 1852 that confirms the attribution to Giordano.
27. The information is in the painting's file in the archives of the Harvard University Art Museums.
28. See Pepper 1984a, pp. 100-101; and the files of the Metropolitan Museum of Art, Department of European Paintings. The Thomson auction organized by Dumont & Hosack took place in New York on 22 March 1848. The Rosa "Self-Portrait" was lot 55 and the two landscapes were lots 13 and 66. The portrait has more recently been

identified as depicting a literary friend of the painter, Giovanni Battista Ricciardi; see J.T. Spike, *Baroque Portraiture in Italy,* John and Mable Ringling Museum of Art, Sarasota, 1985, p. 188.

29. Transcript of a letter of 17 June 1837 in the archives of the Museum of Fine Arts, Boston.
30. M. Benisovich, "Sales of French Collections of Paintings in the United States during the First Half of the Nineteenth Century," *Art Quarterly,* XIX, 1956, pp. 288-300. The only copy of the Jumel sale catalogue is in the Museum of Fine Arts, Boston. See also W. Craven, "Introduction: Patronage and Collecting in America 1805-1835," in *Mr. Luman Reed's Picture Gallery,* ed. E.M. Foshay, New York Historical Society, New York, 1990, p. 13.
31. See Craven in E.M. Foshay ed. 1990 (as in note 30), pp. 17, 203.
32. See E.M. Foshay, "Luman Reed, A New York Patron and His Picture Gallery," in E.M. Foshay ed. 1990 (as in note 30), pp. 19, 41, 45, and pl. 47; and R.W.G. Vail, *Knickerbocker Birthday,* New York, 1954, p. 108.
33. Dunlap 1918 (as in note 1), III, p. 275. See also Craven in E.M. Foshay ed. 1990 (as in note 30), p. 16.
34. The Michael Paff collection was sold in New York City by Mr. Platt's auction house under the direction of A. Levy on 25 March 1838.
35. L.B. Miller, *Patrons and Patriotism,* Chicago, 1966 (reprint 1974), p. 90.
36. Miller 1966 (as in note 35), p. 92.
37. Miller 1966 (as in note 35), p. 97.
38. *A Catalogue of Italian, Flemish, Spanish, Dutch, French, and English Pictures which have been collected in Europe and brought to this country by Mr. Richard Abraham of New Bond Street, London, and are now exhibited at the American Academy of Fine Art,* New York, 1830; and the J.W. Brett sale at the American Academy of Fine Art, 18 May 1835.
39. *Catalogue of the Exhibition of the New York Gallery of the Fine Arts,* National Academy of Design, New York, 1844, no. 5; and 1850, nos. 5, 9, 38, 55, 60, 63, 80.
40. H.W. Henderson, *The Pennsylvania Academy of the Fine Arts and Other Collections of Philadelphia,* Boston, 1911, p. 1.
41. See A.W. Rutledge, *Cumulative Record of Exhibition Catalogues: The Pennsylvania Academy of the Fine Arts, 1807-1870,* Philadelphia, 1955, pp. 43-44, 62, 179, 262; and P.H. Falk, ed., *The Annual Exhibition Record of the Pennsylvania Academy of the Fine Arts, 1807-1870,* I, Madison, Connecticut, 1988, pp. 187, 349-50.
42. Henderson 1911 (as in note 40), pp. 15, 153-54.
43. Henderson 1911 (as in note 40), p. 159. The attribution to Loth was rejected by G. Ewald, *Johann Carl Loth,* 1965, nos. 631, 633.
44. Christie's, New York, 11 January 1989, lot 78. See N. Hall, *Colnaghi in America,* New York, 1992, pp. 10, 13.
45. Christie's, New York, 11 January 1989, lots 88, 89.
46. *Celebrated Gallery of Paintings from England,* Pennsylvania Academy of the Fine Arts, Philadelphia, 1833.
47. *Exhibition at the Pennsylvania Academy of the Fine Arts,* Philadelphia, 1843.
48. M.M. Swan, *The Athenaeum Gallery, 1827-1873,* Boston, 1940, pp. 7-8, 18.
49. *Catalogue of the First Exhibition of Painting in the Athenaeum Gallery,* Boston, 10 May 1827.
50. Swan 1940 (as in note 48), pp. 18, 34, 111.
51. J.P. Harding, *The Boston Athaeneum Collection: Pre-Twentieth Century American and European Painting and Sculpture,* Boston, 1984, p. 78.
52. Swan 1940 (as in note 48), pp. 118, 34, 89, 122, 90-93.
53. Swan 1940 (as in note 48), pp. 95-97. Brett, who was to become more famous as the developer of underwater telegraph transmission, had two sales of the works from his collection in London at Christie's on 23 April 1847 and 5 April 1864.
54. Inv. no. Res. 15.87. Information in the file of the Department of Paintings.
55. Swan 1940 (as in note 48), pp. 127-28.
56. N. Hawthorne, *Passages from the French and Italian Notebooks,* Boston, 1902, p. 208.
57. Swan 1940 (as in note 48), p. 127.
58. M. Wentworth, " 'The Flaying of Marsyas,' An Athenaeum Masterpiece," *Athenaeum Items,* 97, 1991, pp. 5-9. Harding 1984 (as in note 51), p. 81. The sale of the Maratta and Cignani was at Sotheby's, New York, 30 May 1979, lots 232, 236.
59. Swan 1940 (as in note 48), p. 128. See also J.P. Harding, "The Painting Gallery," in *A Climate for Art: The History of the Boston Athenaeum Gallery, 1827-1873,* Boston Athenaeum, 1980, pp. 13-14.
60. Swan 1940 (as in note 48), p. 128; and letter of Brimmer in the files of the Boston Athenaeum dated 24 April 1838.
61. Originally given to the museum by George Peabody Gardner in 1920, the work was then sent to the Childrens Hospital and reacquired by the museum in 1986. See P. Bagni, *Benedetto Gennari e La Bottega del Guercino,* Milan, 1986, p. 205, no. 98; and Salerno 1988, pp. 280-81.
62. Swan 1940 (as in note 48), p. 100.
63. See W.G. Constable, "Some Unpublished Baroque Paintings," *Gazette des Beaux-Arts,* XXIII, 1943, pp. 227-28. See also *Twenty-Sixth Exhibition of Painting and Statuary,* Athenaeum Gallery, Boston, 1853, no. 160.
64. Harding 1984 (as in note 51), p. 85.
65. Inv. no. 26.167. Constable 1943 (as in note 63), p. 222.
66. *Catalogue of Pictures Lent to the Sanitary Fair for Exhibition,* Boston, 1863; and *Catalogue of Paintings and Statuary Exhibited for the Benefit of the National Sailors' Fair,* Boston, 1864.
67. See *"The Spirit of Genius": Art at the Wadsworth Atheneum,* Wadsworth Atheneum, Hartford, 1992, pp. 11-14.
68. *"The Spirit of Genius"* 1992 (as in note 67), p. 15.
69. See W.H. Hunter, Jr., *The Story of America's Oldest Museum Building: Peale's Baltimore Museum,* Peale Museum, Baltimore, 1952, p. 2. See also the listings in J.L. Yarnall and W.H. Gerdts, *The National Museum of American Art's Index to American Art Exhibition Catalogues from the Beginning through the 1876 Centennial Year,* Boston, I, 1986, pp. 11-12.
70. Yarnall and Gerdts 1986 (as in note 69), pp. 9, 17, 37, 45. See also Miller 1966 (as in note 35), pp. 121, 202-203.
71. Paintings from the same collection were offered at Christie's, London, 30 June 1853. Burton Fredericksen has pointed out in oral communication that the name is probably a corruption of that of a family of Neapolitan collectors, Capecelatro.
72. Yarnall and Gerdts 1986 (as in note 69), p. xxviii, and pp. 20-30.
73. Collection of Thomas Thompson, sold Leeds Art Gallery, New York, 7 February 1870.
74. Miller 1966 (as in note 35), p. 113.

75. Yarnall and Gerdts 1986 (as in note 69), pp. 12-16.
76. Sales at Howe, Leonard & Co., Boston, on 14 July 1843 and 13 May 1846.
77. See E. Foucart-Walter, "Paintings Granted to Churches in the United States," in *France in the Golden Age,* Metropolitan Museum of Art, New York, 1982, p. 382; G. Hersey, "The Critical Fortunes of Neapolitan Painting: Notes on American Collecting," in New Haven 1987, pp. 69-70; and Fredericksen and Zeri 1972, p. 559.
78. See note 22.
79. Information supplied by Nancy Netzer, director of the Boston College Museum of Art.
80. See C. Gilbert, "Italian Paintings at St. Meinrad Archabbey," *Gazette des Beaux-Arts,* LII, 1958, pp. 355-68; and *Catalogue of 16th- and 17th-Century Italian Oil Paintings of the Neapolitan School from the Collection of St. Meinrad Archabbey,* St. Meinrad, 1968.
81. Information supplied by Donald Rosenthal, director of the Chapel Art Center, St. Anselm College.
82. Information supplied by Melissa Owen, registrar of the Mabee-Gerrer Museum. See also Fredericksen and Zeri 1972, p. 638.
83. See E. Clark, *History of the National Academy of Design, 1875-1953,* New York, 1954, pp. 27-28; and *Samuel F.B. Morse: Educator and Champion of the Arts in America,* National Academy of Design, New York, 1982, pp. 25-27. On the influence of Italian Baroque art on Morse, see W. Kloss, *Samuel F.B. Morse,* New York, 1988, pp. 26-28.
84. "Picture-Buying," *The Crayon,* I, 4 February 1855, p. 100.
85. R. Peale, "Reminiscences," *The Crayon,* I, 10 January 1855, p. 23.
86. Hevner in Jaffe ed. 1989 (as in note 6), pp. 14, 18. A letter from Rembrandt Peale dated Boston, 3 November 1832, to Mr. Benjamin Bussey thanks him for purchasing several of his copies done in Italy, including one after Domenichino's *St. Cecilia;* this letter is in the Special Collections of the Getty Center, Santa Monica.
87. Peale 1831 (as in note 6), p. 97.
88. Peale 1831 (as in note 6), pp. 141, 150-51.
89. Dunlap 1918 (as in note 1), II, p. 310.
90. Miller 1966 (as in note 35), p. 48.
91. *The Crayon,* I, 6 June 1855, p. 355.
92. Miller 1966 (as in note 35), p. 150.
93. Miller 1966 (as in note 35), p. 150.
94. H. James, *William Westmore Story and His Friends,* New York, 1903, p. 10.
95. For Browning's poem "The Guardian Angel" on the painting in the Museo Civico, Fano, see *The Complete Poetic and Dramatic Works of Robert Browning,* Boston and New York, 1896, p. 194. Shelley's verse tragedy "The Cenci" was published in 1819. According to the tale, popular in art and literature of the nineteenth century, Reni was allowed into the cell of Beatrice Cenci to paint her portrait on the night before she was hanged for killing her incestuous father. The painting in the Barberini palace gallery (now the Galleria Nazionale d'Arte Antica) then believed to be by Reni is probably by a Reni follower; see Pepper 1984b, p. 304. A letter of Shelley on the power of Reni is quoted in Osbert Sitwell's introduction to the exhibition catalogue, *Italian Art of the Seventeenth Century,* Burlington Fine Arts Club, London, 1925, p. 8.
96. Byron's praise of Guercino's *Abraham and Hagar* in the Brera gallery, Milan, is mentioned in G.S. Hillard, *Six Months in Italy,* Boston, 1853, I, p. 18.
97. Hawthorne 1902 (as in note 56), pp. 87-89. Mrs. Hawthorne was equally enthralled with the *Cenci* and noted, "This is a masterpiece which baffles words," but nevertheless she managed to expatiate on it at length. She also spoke warmly of the works of Guercino and wrote of Reni's *Magdalen delle Radice,* "one of the pictures that can be looked at forever without weariness or satiety, It is forever new, and forever more expressive, eloquent, and pathetic." See Mrs. N. Hawthorne, *Notes in England and Italy,* New York, 1872, pp. 212-14, 245, 263.
98. Hawthorne 1902 (as in note 56), pp. 91, 96.
99. N. Hawthorne, *The Marble Faun* (1859), Meridien Classic edition, 1987, pp. 107, 137, 253-54.
100. H. James, *Roderick Hudson,* New York, 1907, p. 183.
101. E. Wharton, *Old New York, False Dawn (The Forties),* New York, 1924, p. 78. On her sources, see Van Wyck Brooks, *The Dream of Arcadia,* New York, 1958, p. 241.
102. B. Berenson, *Aesthetics and History in the Visual Arts,* New York, 1948, p. 234. The *Portrait of Beatrice Cenci* had been warmly mentioned, for example, in a popular text by H.T. Tuckerman, *The Italian Sketch Book,* Boston, 1837, p. 42.
103. See H. Melville, *Journals,* chapter 15, Evanston and Chicago, 1989, p. 108.
104. Brooks 1958 (as in note 101), p. 14.
105. W.M. Gillespie, *Rome as Seen by a New Yorker,* New York and London, 1845, pp. 110, 113.
106. Hawthorne 1859 (as in note 99), p. 50.
107. J.J. Jarves, *Italian Sights and Papal Principles Seen through American Spectacles,* New York, 1856, p. 105.
108. *Catalogue of the Permanent Collection: Arnot Art Museum,* Elmira, 1973, p. 125. The copy is by Jalumzo Rasaiglini.
109. See *Collegiate Collections, 1776-1876,* Mount Holyoke College, South Hadley, 1976, p. 24, no. 4. The Amherst *Aurora* was painted by Luigi Cazolari(?) in 1865.
110. Reproduced in *Artistic Houses,* New York, 1883, II, part 2, following p. 103.
111. Reproduced in W. Seale, *The Tasteful Interlude: American Interiors through the Camera's Eye, 1860-1917,* New York, 1975, p. 98, pl. 71.
112. W.C. Bryant, *Letters of a Traveller,* 2d series, New York, 1859, 259-60.
113. See Vail 1954 (as in note 32), pp. 126-28; Miller in Jaffe ed. 1989 (as in note 6), pp. 54-55; Constable 1964 (as in note 20), p. 29.
114. R.G. White, *Companion to the Bryan Gallery of Christian Art,* New York, 1853, p. v.
115. White 1853 (as in note 114), pp. 36-42; and *Catalogue of the Gallery of Art of the New York Historical Society,* New York, 1915, pp. vii, 63-67.
116. Sales at Parke Bernet, New York, 2 December 1971, and Sotheby's, New York, 9 October 1980.
117. A.F. Bye, "The Lea Collection," *Philadelphia Museum Bulletin,* XXI, May 1926, pp. 156-62; and "Notes on Current Art," *International Studio,* July 1926, pp. 82-83; see also the *Checklist of Paintings in the Philadelphia Museum of Art,* Philadelphia, 1965.
118. *European Paintings in the Collection of The Worcester Art Museum* (text volume), Worcester, 1974, p. 376.
119. Constable 1943 (as in note 63), p. 220.
120. See *Ruskin in Italy: Letters to his Parents, 1845,* ed. H.I. Shapiro, Oxford, 1972, pp. 144-45. See also

Ruskin's disparaging comments on Guido Reni (p. 63) and Rosa (p. 105).

121. *The Crayon,* II, 4 July 1855, p. 8.

122. Jarves 1856 (as in note 107), pp. 92, 102.

123. Jarves 1856 (as in note 107), pp. 102-103.

124. J.J. Jarves, *Art Hints: Architecture, Sculpture, and Painting,* New York, 1855, pp. 256, 259-61.

125. J.J. Jarves, *The Art-Idea* (1864), ed. B. Rowland, Jr., Cambridge, Massachusetts, 1960, p. 75.

126. In a letter to his Boston supporters of December 1861, Jarves wrote that his collection was formed "to illustrate the rise and progress of painting from A.D. 1000 to the 17th century. . . . Some of my most important paintings are still in Europe, but I have just received a very fine specimen of Guido, lately belonging to Lord Fleetwood, the subject of which is the 'Three Graces Disarming Cupid.' " See F. Steegmuller, *The Two Lives of James Jackson Jarves,* New Haven, 1951, p. 202.

127. Miller in Jaffe ed. 1989 (as in note 6), p. 41.

128. On Norton and Ruskin, see Brooks 1958 (as in note 101), pp. 122-27; and Constable 1964 (as in note 20), p. 44. See also D.A. Brown, *Berenson and the Connoisseurship of Italian Painting,* National Gallery of Art, Washington, D.C., 1979, p. 38.

129. J. Bell, *Observations on Italy,* London, 1825.

130. C.E. Norton, *Notes of Travel and Study in Italy,* Boston, 1860, pp. 177, 312.

131. T.G. Appleton, *Boston Museum of Fine Arts: A Companion to the Catalogue,* Boston, 1877, p. 56.

132. H. James, *Transatlantic Sketches,* Boston, 1875, p. 177.

133. In Boston auctions were held at Leonard & Co., with works by Reni and Guercino, on 4-5 February 1898 and 16-17 November 1900; in New York City a major sale of paintings from the Ehrich Galleries took place at the Waldorf Astoria on 24 March 1905, with pictures attributed to Caravaggio, Guercino, Dolci, Rosa, and others.

134. M.F. Sweetser, *Guido Reni,* Boston, 1878, pp. 3-4.

135. *Artistic Houses* 1883 (as in note 110), II, part 1, p. 33.

136. Catalogue cards of the Shaw loans are in the Department of Paintings of the Museum of Fine Arts and indicate that the paintings were returned to the Shaw family in 1941.

137. H.L. Peabody, "Samuel Longstreth Parrish," in *The Story of the Parrish Art Museum,* Southampton, 1962, pp. 13, 18-31; and *Catalogue of Renaissance Paintings: Parrish Art Museum,* Southampton, 1967, n.p.

138. *Catalogue of Paintings, Sculpture, and Contemporary Arts and Crafts,* Detroit Institute of Arts of the City of Detroit, 1920, pp. 7-12. According to information supplied by the Detroit Art Institute in 1993, most of these works were deaccessioned in 1991.

139. Henderson 1911 (as in note 40), pp. 294-95, 309.

140. *Catalogue of the W.P. Wilstach Collection,* ed. C.H. Beck, Philadelphia, 1893; *Catalogue of the W.P. Wilstach Collection,* Philadelphia, 1922.

141. The sale at Memorial Hall, Fairmount Park, Philadelphia, conducted by Samuel T. Freeman, was from 25-30 October 1954. For the remaining Wilstach paintings in the museum, see *Checklist of the Philadelphia Museum of Art,* 1965.

142. *A Collection Rediscovered: European Paintings from the Tweed Museum of Art,* Minneapolis Institute of Arts, 1986, pp. 2-3, 66-70, 77.

143. R.H. Adams, *The Walker Art Galleries,* Minneapolis, 1927, pp. 53-54, 124-25. The sales were at Parke Bernet, New York, on 22 October 1970 and 20 January 1971.

144. *Crocker Art Museum: Handbook of Paintings,* Sacramento, 1979, pp. 7-18.

145. Constable 1964 (as in note 20), p. 94.

146. See Mrs. A.C. Doyle, *Catalogue of Paintings in the E.B. Crocker Art Gallery,* Sacramento, 1925; and also *Handbook* 1979 (as in note 144), nos. 8, 13, 17, 25, 35, 38, 42.

147. Swan 1940 (as in note 48), p. 110.

148. *Catalogue of Pictures Belonging to H.R.H. The Duke de Montpensier and of Other Pictures also Loaned to the Museum of Fine Arts,* Boston, 1874, p. 6, nos. 25-26, and p. 9, no. 60.

149. See the museum's annual reports for the years 1877, pp. 16-19; 1878, p. 15; and 1890, p. 57.

150. On the Sumner collection, see Constable 1964 (as in note 20), p. 92; and W.G. Constable, "A Cranach from the Sumner Collection," *Museum of Fine Arts Bulletin,* XLI, December 1943, pp. 64-68.

151. On the Brimmer gift, see *Museum of Fine Arts Boston: Annual Report for the Year 1883,* pp. 7, 18; and Constable 1943 (as in note 63), pp. 223-24, fig. 4.

152. Correspondence of 1891 detailing the history of the painting is in the file of the Department of Paintings. See J. de Wolf Addison, *The Boston Museum of Fine Arts,* Boston, 1910, p. 62.

153. See the annual reports for the years 1894, pp. 7, 44, and 1910, p. 91; and Constable 1943 (as in note 63), p. 223.

154. Inv. nos. 17.575, 20.1630, and 21.751, 21.752. See Constable 1943 (as in note 63), pp. 224-25.

155. *The Metropolitan Museum of Art: Catalogue of the Pictures,* New York, 1872, pp. 3-4, 6, 49, 52, 68.

156. See "Principal Accessions, Paintings," *Bulletin of The Metropolitan Museum of Art,* I, April 1906, p. 72; and B. Burroughs, *The Metropolitan Museum of Art: Catalogue of Paintings,* New York, 1926, pp. 10, 49, 125, 220, 287, 291-92, 297, 313, 373.

157. The *Head of a Hermit* and a *Landscape with Figures* by Rosa were both lent by Church to *Pictures by the Old Masters,* an exhibition held at the Metropolitan Museum of Art, New York, in March 1873 and October 1874. These two supposed Rosas, as well as paintings Church believed to be by Reni, Guercino, and Magnasco are, according to curator Karen Zukowski, still in Olana, Church's home in upstate New York.

158. *The Art Institute of Chicago: General Catalogue of Painting and Sculpture and other Objects in the Museum,* Chicago, 1914, p. 114.

159. See E.M. Zafran, "Introduction," *Fifty Old Master Paintings from The Walters Art Gallery,* Baltimore, 1988, pp. 11-12.

160. *The Walters Collection,* Baltimore, 1919.

161. Zeri 1976.

162. W. Macleod, *Catalogue of the Corcoran Gallery of Art,* Washington, D.C., 1889, p. 67.

163. See "The Ralph Cross Johnson Collection," *American Magazine of Art,* II, August 1920, p. 346; and W.H. Holmes, *Smithsonian Institution, The National Gallery of Art: Catalogue of Collections,* I,

Washington, D.C., 1922, p. 62.
164. D. Mahon, "Guercino as a Portraitist and his Pope Gregory XV," *Apollo,* CXIII, April 1981, pp. 230-35; and "Acquisitions," *J. Paul Getty Museum Journal,* 16, 1988, p. 161.
165. *The Berkshire Museum: A Guide to the Collection,* Pittsfield, 1968, pp. 3-4. Information also supplied by the acting museum curator, Judy Dressel.
166. J. Watrous, *A Century of Capricious Collecting, 1877-1970,* Madison, 1987, pp. 3, 6; R. Panczenko, "Development of the Collection," in *Handbook of the Collection: Elvehjem Museum of Art,* University of Wisconsin, Madison, 1990, p. 1.
167. *Handbook of the Collection: Art Gallery, University of Notre Dame,* Notre Dame, 1967, pp. 32-33, 40-41, nos. 16, 20; D.C. Miller, *Seventeenth- and Eighteenth-Century Paintings from the University of Notre Dame,* Krannert Art Museum, University of Illinois, Urbana, 1962, nos. 16, 24, 28, 34. These works could be from a descendant of the family of Giannangelo Braschi, Pope Pius VI (d. 1799). See E. Ricci, *Palazzo Braschi,* Rome, 1989, p. 33.
168. *Cyclopedia of Painters and Painting,* eds. J.D. Champlin, Jr. and C.C. Perkins, New York, 1885-86, p. 70. *Catalogue of the Gallery of Art of the New York Historical Society,* New York, 1915, includes four Rosas from the Bryan collection (pp. 66-67, nos. B67-70), a *Landscape with Monks at their Devotions* bequeathed by T.W. Moore in 1872 (p. 27, no. 223), and another *Landscape* given with the Louis Durr collection in 1882 (p. 104, no. D14).
169. R. Brimo, *L'Évolution du goût aux États-Unis d'après l'histoire des collections,* Paris, 1938, pp. 80-124.
170. E. Strahan, *The Art Treasures of America,* Philadelphia, 1882, II, p. 90; III, p. 64.
171. Quoted in Pepper 1984b, p. 49.
172. B. Berenson, *Caravaggio: His Incongruity and His Fame,* New York, 1953, pp. 13, 45, 77.
173. *John G. Johnson Collection: Catalogue of Paintings,* Philadelphia, 1941, p. 7, no. 49.
174. See the deluxe publication by J. La Farge and A.F. Jaccaci, *Noteworthy Paintings in American Private Collections,* New York, 1907, pp. 392-93; and the reference to it in L. Bénédite, "Les Collections d'art aux États-Unis," *Revue de l'art,* XXIII, March 1908, p. 172.
175. Letter of 26 July 1926 in the files of the Philbrook Museum, supplied by Richard P. Townsend. Furini's *Judith* was given to the museum by family members in 1979.
176. *Illustrated Handbook of the W.A. Clark Collection,* Corcoran Gallery of Art, Washington, D.C., 1928, p. 34.
177. *Comune di Firenze: Mostra della pittura italiana del Seicento e del Settecento. Catalogo,* Florence, 1922.
178. W. Milliken, " 'Minerva' by Bernardo Strozzi," *Bulletin of the Cleveland Museum of Art,* 16, April 1929, p. 63.
179. W. Stechow, "Exhibition of Italian Paintings of the Seventeenth Century," *Allen Memorial Art Gallery Bulletin,* IX, 1952, p. 36.
180. S. Sitwell, *Southern Baroque Art,* London, 1924, p. 36.
181. O. Sitwell in *Exhibition of Italian Arts of the Seventeenth Century,* Burlington Fine Arts Club, London, 1925, p. 9.
182. F. Kimball, "The Baroque and the Primitives: The Lea Collection," *Pennsylvania Museum Bulletin,* XXI, May 1926, pp. 160-62; see also "Notes on Current Art," *International Studio,* July 1926, pp. 128-30.
183. The importance of Wölfflin's analysis of the Baroque in his *Kunstgeschichtliche Grundbegriffe* was recognized by Roger Fry in his essay "The Seicento," reprinted in *Transformations,* Garden City, New York, 1956, pp. 128-30.
184. H. Voss, *Die Malerei des Barock in Rom,* Berlin, 1924; N. Pevsner and O. Grautoff, *Barockmalerei in der romanischen Ländern,* Potsdam, 1928.
185. See K. Donahue, *Oral Memoir: Collections and Programs at the Los Angeles County Museum of Art,* interviewed by G. Goodwin, University of California, Los Angeles, 1987, pp. 102-103.
186. See "John Ringling the Collector," in P. Tomory, *Catalogue of the Italian Paintings before 1800: The John and Mable Ringling Museum of Art,* Sarasota, 1976, pp. ix-xiii; and the thorough recent study by D.C. Weeks, *Ringling: The Florida Years, 1911-1936,* Gainesville, 1993, pp. 170-96.
187. See note 186 above and D. Sutton, "A Voyage of Discovery," in *Masterworks from The John and Mable Ringling Museum of Art,* Wildenstein & Co., New York, 1981, pp. 7-9.
188. Constable 1964 (as in note 20), pp. 138-39.
189. Constable 1964 (as in note 20), pp. 139-40. Also critical of Hearst as a collector are D. and E. Rigby, *Lock, Stock, and Barrel: The Story of Collecting,* Philadelphia, 1944, pp. 286-87.
190. See B.B. Fredericksen, *Handbook of the Paintings in the Hearst San Simeon State Historical Monument,* 1976.
191. H. Wehle, "Some Italian Baroque Paintings," *Bulletin of The Metropolitan Museum of Art,* XXIV, July 1929, pp. 187-90.
192. Milliken 1929 (as in note 178), p. 66. The painting was acquired from the Venetian dealer Italico Brass through the museum's agent Harold Parsons.
193. "A Painting by Guercino," *Bulletin of The Minneapolis Institute of Arts,* XVIII, 5 January 1929, pp. 26-28.
194. On the sale of old masters from the Minneapolis collection, see J.A. Hess, *Their Splendid Legacy: The First 100 Years of the Minneapolis Society of Fine Arts,* Minneapolis, 1985, p. 64. For the Reni, see Pepper 1984b, p. 247, no. 92.
195. H.E.S., " 'St. Stephen' by Domenico Fetti," *Bulletin of the Memorial Art Gallery,* I, May 1929, pp. 1-3.
196. E.A. Safarik, *Domenico Fetti,* Milan, 1990, p. 312, no. A108.
197. A.K. McComb, "A Painting by Caravaggio," *Fogg Art Museum Notes,* 1930, p. 199.
198. D.C.R., "Four Paintings by Alessandro Magnasco," *Bulletin of The Art Institute of Chicago,* XXIII, April 1929, pp. 42-43.
199. The original typed text is in the archives of the Harvard University Art Museums, kindly shown to me by archivist Abigail Smith.
200. *Art News* of 26 January 1929; and *Parnassus* of 15 February 1929.
201. E.S. Siple, "Art in America—Italian Baroque Painting," *Burlington Magazine,* IV, 1929, pp. 105-106.
202. For background on Austin's life, see *A. Everett Austin, Jr.: A Director's Taste and Achievement,* Wadsworth Atheneum, Hartford, 1958, pp. 7-8; and more recently, N.F. Weber, *Patron Saints,* New York, 1992, pp. 140-46.
203. A.K. McComb, "Exhibition of Italian Art of the Sei- and Settecento,"

Bulletin of the Wadsworth Atheneum, VIII, January 1930, p. 4.
204. Quoted in Cadogan 1991, p. 13.
205. McComb 1930 (as in note 203), p. 5.
206. See K. Askew, "The Old Master Acquisitions of A. Everett Austin, Jr.," in *Director's Taste* 1958 (as in note 202), p. 21.
207. J.R.S., "Two Large Canvases by Luca Giordano," *Bulletin of the Wadsworth Atheneum,* VIII, January 1930, pp. 2-3.
208. H.R. Hitchcock, Jr., "Salvator Rosa," *Bulletin of the Wadsworth Atheneum,* VIII, April 1930, p. 22.
209. Askew in *Director's Taste* 1958 (as in note 202), p. 24. The story of how Brass tried to hoodwink Austin by at first sending a different version of the painting has been told in several places, most recently in Weber 1992 (as in note 202), p. 170.
210. Cadogan 1991, pp. 19-20; and Weber 1992 (as in note 202), p. 345.
211. A.K. McComb, *The Baroque Painters of Italy: An Introductory Historical Survey,* Cambridge, Massachusetts, 1934, pp. 25, 30-33.
212. McComb 1934 (as in note 211), pp. 34, 50, 56, 90, 94.
213. F.J. Mather, *Venetian Painters,* New York, 1936, pp. 426-47.
214. E. Singleton, *Old World Masters in New World Collections,* New York, 1929.
215. L. Venturi, *Italian Paintings in America,* New York, 1933, III, pls. 580-84.
216. *Catalogue of A Century of Progress: Exhibition of Paintings and Sculpture,* Art Institute of Chicago, 1933, pp. 23-25.
217. H. Tietze, *Masterpieces of European Painting in America,* New York, 1939, pp. 101, 112, 116.
218. G.H. McCall and W.R. Valentiner, *Catalogue of European Paintings and Sculpture from 1300 to 1800: Masterpieces of Art,* New York World's Fair, May to October 1939.
219. W. Pach, *Catalogue of European and American Paintings 1500-1900: Masterpieces of Art,* New York World's Fair, May to October 1940.
220. F. Kimball and L. Venturi, *Great Paintings in America,* New York, 1948.
221. H. Gardner, *Art Through the Ages,* 2d edition, New York, 1936, p. iii, and pp. 434-35.
222. H. Gardner, *Art Through the Ages,* 4th edition, New York, 1959, pp. 402-405.
223. H. Gardner, *Art Through the Ages,* 9th edition, New York, 1991, pp. 765-74.
224. Cadogan 1991, p. 16; and Weber 1992 (as in note 202), p. 181.
225. This information is drawn from an interview conducted by Burton Fredericksen with Mr. Weitzner in London on 6 June 1984 and from the reminiscences of Mr. and Mrs. Weitzner as recorded by Jack Tanzer. I thank both of them for making these materials available to me.
226. Letter in the files of the Art Institute of Chicago dated 21 May 1967 from Weitzner to Charles Cunningham.
227. *Exhibition of Italian Paintings of the Late Renaissance and Baroque Periods,* Portland Art Museum, 1936, p. 6.
228. *Alessandro Magnasco ca. 1677-ca. 1749,* Springfield Museum of Art, 1938, n.p.
229. *A Loan Exhibition of Paintings by Alessandro Magnasco, 1667-1749,* Durlacher Brothers, New York, 1940.
230. E.S. Siple, "Recent Acquisitions in America," *Burlington Magazine,* LX, 1932, p. 110.
231. *Art Digest,* 15 May 1935, p. 7.
232. Information from the files of the Metropolitan Museum of Art, Department of European Paintings.
233. M.M. Salinger, " 'Christ and the Woman of Samaria' by Caracciolo," *Bulletin of The Metropolitan Museum of Art,* XXXII, January 1937, pp. 4-6.
234. See *Battistello Caracciolo,* Naples, 1991, pp. 35-36, fig. 34.
235. Information supplied by Eliot Rowlands of the Nelson-Atkins Museum of Art, Kansas City, in a letter of 18 May 1993.
236. W.H. Siple, "An Unpublished Painting by Bernardo Strozzi," *Bulletin of the Cincinnati Art Museum,* IX, October 1938, pp. 106, 109, 112.
237. Letter in the archives of the Museum of Fine Arts.
238. *Museum of Fine Arts, Boston. Sixty-First Annual Report for the Year 1936,* p. 34.
239. Correspondence and information in the Department of Paintings file. Weitzner's letter to Charles Cunningham is dated 28 April 1936, and that to James Plaut, 24 September 1936.
240. *Worcester Art Museum Bulletin,* XXV, Spring 1934, pp. 18-21.
241. See *An Exhibition of Italian Paintings Lent by Mr. Samuel H. Kress of New York,* Los Angeles Museum of History, Science, and Art, 1934, pp. 37, 52-53.
242. R.P. Townsend, *The Samuel H. Kress Collection at Philbrook,* Tulsa, 1991, p. 6.
243. F.R. Shapley, *Paintings from the Samuel H. Kress Collection: Italian School, XVI-XVIII Century,* New York, 1973.
244. Mary Berenson in a letter of 1932 provided a telling observation of Walker, writing: "... the most talented and delightful pupil we have ever had, the young man from Pittsburgh—of all places! named John Walker. When he was sent to us a year and a half ago from Harvard, B.B. was too busy to direct his work, so I took him into this scheme thinking it would be good training for his taste. To my surprise and delight his taste needed very little training. We united independently upon almost every picture. What he needs training in is writing, and I am putting him to a severe course of sprouts, as we used to call it, in that respect." See *Mary Berenson: A Self-Portrait from her Letters and Diaries,* eds. B. Strachey and J. Samuels, New York and London, 1983, p. 289.
245. T.C. Howe, Jr., *Exhibition of Italian Baroque Painting, 17th and 18th Centuries,* California Palace of the Legion of Honor, San Francisco, 1941, p. 5.
246. N.S. Trivas, "Italian Baroque Painting in San Francisco," *Apollo,* XXXIV, August 1941, p. 44.
247. A.M. Frankfurter, "Baroque Reading on the Barometer of Today's Taste," *Art News,* 1-14 February 1942, p. 23.
248. A. Breeskin, "Foreword," in *Three Baroque Masters: Strozzi, Crespi, and Piazzetta,* Baltimore Museum of Art, 1944, p. 3.
249. H. Tietze, "Introduction," in *Three Baroque Masters* 1944 (as in note 248), pp. 5, 8.
250. D. Phillips, "Magnasco," in *Six Loan Exhibitions,* Phillips Memorial Gallery, Washington, D.C., 1943, n.p.
251. W.R. Valentiner, "Baroque Painting," *Bulletin of the Art Division of the Los Angeles County Museum,* I, Spring 1947, p. 9.
252. See M. Sterne, *The Passionate Eye: The Life of William R. Valentiner,* Detroit, 1980, pp. 315-16.
253. *Fine Arts Society of San Diego:*

Catalogue of European Paintings, 1300-1870, San Diego, 1947, p. 32.

254. Correspondence between Weitzner and the museum's director, Harold Edgell, is in the archives of the Museum of Fine Arts.
255. See Constable 1943 (as in note 63), p. 225.
256. Letter from Constable to Schaeffer in the files of the Department of Paintings.
257. *Museum of Fine Arts Boston. Annual Report for the Year 1948,* p. 38.
258. See Hall 1992 (as in note 44), p. 33; and D. Garstang, "Colnaghi 1760-1984," in *Art, Commerce, Scholarship,* Colnaghi, London, 1984, p. 24.
259. Letter of 27 September 1948 from Denis Mahon to W.G. Constable in the files of the Department of Paintings. The book was the seminal *Studies in Seicento Art and Theory,* London, 1947.
260. Correspondence and memos in the file of the Department of Paintings. See also Cadogan 1991, p. 148.
261. Information supplied by Eliot Rowlands of the Nelson-Atkins Museum in a letter of 18 May 1993.
262. See P.L. Grigaut, " 'The Finding of Moses' by Salvator Rosa," *Bulletin of The Detroit Institute of Arts,* XXVII, 1948, pp. 63-67; E.P. Richardson, "Foreword," in *Catalogue of the Paintings and Sculpture Given by Edgar B. Whitcomb and Anna Scripps Whitcomb to The Detroit Institute of Arts,* Detroit, 1959, and p. 99.
263. J. Spargo, *A Descriptive List of the Colyer Collection of Paintings and Sculpture in the Bennington Historical Museum and Art Gallery,* Bennington, 1952.
264. See C.H. Shell and J. McAndrew, *Catalogue of European and American Sculpture and Painting at Wellesley College,* Wellesley, 1964; and L. Flint-Gohlke, *Davis Museum and Cultural Center, Wellesley College,* Wellesley, 1993, pp. 22-24.
265. *Mostra del Caravaggio e dei caravaggeschi,* Palazzo Reale, Milan, 1951.
266. Stechow 1952 (as in note 179), pp. 36-37.
267. See K. Christiansen, *A Caravaggio Rediscovered: The Lute Player,* Metropolitan Museum of Art, New York, 1990.
268. See M.R. Waddington, "Introduction," in *The Paintings of The Betty and David M. Koetser Foundation,* Zurich, 1988, pp. 7, 10, 15.
269. I am indebted to Jan Klein for supplying this information on the Central Picture Galleries.
270. William Acquavella kindly provided this information on his father.
271. See C. Eisler," 'Kunstgeschichte' American Style: A Study in Migration," in *The Intellectual Migration,* eds. D. Fleming and B. Bailyn, Cambridge, Massachusetts, 1969, pp. 575-76.
272. W. Suida, *Genua,* Leipzig, 1906.
273. Galerie Sanct Lucas, *Ausstellung Italienische Barockmalerei,* Palais Pallavicini, Vienna, 1937.
274. W. Suida, *A Catalogue of Paintings in The John and Mable Ringling Museum of Art,* Sarasota, 1949.
275. W. Suida, "Die Sammlung Kress, New York," *Pantheon,* XXVI, July-December 1940, pp. 273-82.
276. See E.P. Bowron, "The Kress Brothers and Their 'Bucolic Pictures': The Creation of an Italian Baroque Collection," in *A Gift to America: Masterpieces of European Painting from the Samuel H. Kress Collection,* North Carolina Museum of Art, Raleigh, 1994, pp. 41-59.
277. See Shapley 1973 (as in note 243).
278. Bowron 1994 (as in note 276), p. 540.
279. See C. Chester, "The Suida Manning Collection," in *Sotheby's Preview,* November-December 1989, pp. 12-15.
280. B. Hannegan, *Eighteenth-Century European Paintings from the Collection of Robert and Bertina Suida Manning,* Duke University Gallery, Durham, 1969.
281. See the obituary in *The New York Times,* Monday, 19 September 1988; and D.L. Goodrich, *Art Fakes in America,* New York, 1973, pp. 205-206.
282. See the catalogue *Chrysler Art Museum of Provincetown: Inaugural Exhibition,* Provincetown, 1958.
283. M.N. Carter, "The Chrysler Museum," *Art News,* 75, February 1976, pp. 56-62.
284. T.C. Colt, Jr. and F. Kimball, *Collection of Walter P. Chrysler, Jr.,* Richmond, 1941, pp. 5-6.
285. *Chrysler Collection of Dutch Old Masters,* Art Gallery of the University of Miami, Coral Gables, 1951.
286. See *Chrysler Museum at Norfolk, Newsletter,* I, March 1972, p. 1; and IV, July 1975, p. 2.
287. See M. Marini, "Equivoci del Caravaggismo 2," *Artibus et Historiae,* IV, 1983, pp. 143, 153, fig. 31.
288. Sotheby's, New York, 1 June 1989.
289. Quoted in H.R. Hope, "The Bob Jones University Collection of Religious Art," *Art Journal,* XXV, 1965-66, p. 154.
290. On Hamilton, see S.N. Behrman, *Duveen,* Boston, 1972, pp. 211-12; M. Secrest, *Being Bernard Berenson,* Harmondsworth, 1979, pp. 320-23; and C. Simpson, *Artful Partners,* New York, 1986, pp. 193-202.
291. This quote and much of the biographical information derives from an interview with Dr. Jones held in Greenville on 29 April 1993.
292. B. Jones, Jr., "Introduction," and H. Tietze and E. Tietze-Conrat, "Foreword," in Greenville 1954, pp. 7-11.
293. Hope 1965-66 (as in note 289), pp. 154, 156, 162.
294. Greenville 1962 (vol. 1, *Italian and French Paintings*).
295. D. Posner and K. Weil-Garris Posner, "More on the Bob Jones University Collection of Religious Art," *Art Journal,* XXVI, 1966-67, pp. 146-48.
296. B.A. Jones, *Supplement to the Catalogue of the Art Collection: Paintings Acquired 1963-1968,* Greenville, 1968.
297. Pepper 1984a.
298. Raleigh 1984.
299. The sales that contained Ganz paintings were at Christie's, New York, 3 June 1987, 16 October 1987, 8 April 1988; those at Sotheby's, New York, were on 4 June 1987, 15 October 1987, 14 January 1988, 7 April 1988, and 3 June 1988.
300. File in the Metropolitan Museum of Art, Department of European Paintings.
301. It is worthwhile noting that in addition to their better-known Dutch and Flemish paintings, the Van Bergs also had two Italian Baroque works—a Domenichino *St. John the Evangelist* (now in the Bob Jones University Collection; see cat. no. 17) and a Sassoferrato *Holy Virgin.* See *The Van Berg Collection of Paintings,* New York, 1947, pp. 12, 28. The sale of the Van Berg collection took place at Sotheby's, London, 25 June 1969.
302. The best history of the museum is to

be found in R. Ferré, *Memorias de Ponce: Autobiografía de Luis A. Ferré,* Barcelona, 1992, pp. 76-80. Also see R. Taylor, *El Museo de Arte de Ponce,* Ponce, n.d.; *Treinta Años del Museo de Arte de Ponce: Exposición en Honor A.D. Luis A. Ferré,* Ponce, 1989, pp. 1-13. I am also grateful to Professor Held for sharing his reminiscences with me.

303. Ferré quoted in R. Taylor, "The Ponce Art Museum, Ponce, Puerto Rico," *Antiques,* 90, November 1966, p. 681.
304. J.S. Held, *The Samuel H. Kress Collection of Italian and Spanish Paintings: Museo de Arte de Ponce,* Ponce, 1962.
305. J.S. Held, "The New Museum in Ponce," *Art Quarterly,* XXVII, 1964, p. 26.
306. R. and M. Wittkower, "Puerto Rico's Museum," *Apollo,* LXXXV, March 1967, p. 191.
307. Held 1984.
308. Taylor 1966 (as in note 303), p. 684.
309. D. Mahon, "Addenda to Caravaggio," *Burlington Magazine,* XCIV, 1952, pp. 3-7.
310. See the annual reports for the Museum of Fine Arts, 1950, p. 35; and 1959, p. 50.
311. For the supposed Caravaggio, see *Paintings from the Collection of George Henry Alexander Clowes: A Memorial Exhibition,* John Heron Art Museum, Indianapolis, 1959, no. 13.
312. E.P. Richardson, "A Masterpiece of Baroque Drama," *Bulletin of The Detroit Institute of Arts,* XXXII, 1952-53, p. 83.
313. For the fullest account of this, see E.P. Bowron, "The North Carolina Museum of Art and Its Collections," in *The North Carolina Museum of Art. Introduction to the Collection,* Raleigh, 1983, pp. x-xi.
314. Sterne 1980 (as in 252), pp. 334-49.
315. *Norfolk Museum Bulletin,* X, March 1960, n.p.
316. Copies of the letters with the opinions of Berenson and Constable are in the files of the High Museum of Art.
317. J.P. Getty and J.S. Held, *The Joys of Collecting,* New York, 1965, pp. 31, 104-105.
318. J. Maxon, "Three Baroque Figure Paintings," *Bulletin of the Rhode Island School of Design, Museum Notes,* March 1956, p. 11.
319. R. Enggass, "Neapolitan Seicento in Sarasota," *Burlington Magazine,* CIII, 1961, pp. 199-200.
320. Letter of Bertina Suida Manning to Tom Colt of 1 August 1962 in the files of the Dayton Art Institute.
321. Some of the paintings in the Finch College collection were sold at Parke-Bernet, New York, 22 October 1970.
322. Hibbard and Lewine 1965, pp. 370-71.
323. D. Mahon, "Stock-Taking in Seicento Studies," *Apollo,* LXXXII, November 1965, p. 378.
324. A.S. Harris, "Florentine Sunset," *Art News,* May 1969, p. 32.
325. R.W. Bissell, "Orazio Gentileschi's 'Young Woman with a Violin,' " *Bulletin of The Detroit Institute of Arts,* XLVI, 1967, p. 75.
326. A. Clark, "A Late, Great Guido Reni," *Art Institute of Chicago Quarterly,* 54, April 1960, pp. 2-7.
327. *Annual Report 1964. Museum of Fine Arts Boston,* pp. 16, 57.
328. C. Wright, "Preti's 'Martyrdom of St. Bartholomew', " *Currier Gallery of Art Bulletin,* 3, 1972, pp. 3-9.
329. Sotheby's, New York, 7 June 1978.
330. *Giovanni Benedetto Castiglione: Master Draughtsman of the Italian Baroque,* Philadelphia Museum of Art, 1971.
331. *The Marshall Collection,* Sotheby's, London, 3 December 1973 to 8 January 1974. The actual sale took place at Bonham & Sons, London, 28 March 1974.
332. See J. Walker, "Introduction," in *The Wrightsman Collection,* V, New York, 1973, p. 5.
333. Letter from Berenson of 28 August 1957 to Mr. Wrightsman in the files of the Metropolitan Museum of Art, Department of European Paintings.
334. Donahue 1987 (as in note 185), p. 196.
335. F.J. Cummings, " 'The Assumption of the Virgin' by Guercino," *Bulletin of The Detroit Institute of Arts,* LI, 1972, pp. 53-62.
336. B. Suida Manning, "A Panorama of Italian Painting," *Apollo,* CXI, March 1980, p. 187.
337. See T. Pignatti, *Five Centuries of Italian Painting 1300-1800 from the Collection of The Sarah Campbell Blaffer Foundation,* Houston, 1985; and G.T.M. Shackelford, *Masterpieces of Baroque Painting from the Collection of The Sarah Campbell Blaffer Foundation,* Museum of Fine Arts, Houston, 1992.
338. See S.J. Freedberg, "Gentileschi's 'Madonna with the Sleeping Christ Child'," in *A Dealer's Record: Agnew's 1967-81,* London, 1981, pp. 45-49.
339. E.M. Zafran, "A Newly Acquired Masterpiece by Guido Reni," *Walters Art Gallery Bulletin,* 41, January 1988, pp. 1-2.
340. P. Conisbee et al., *The Ahmanson Gifts,* Los Angeles County Museum of Art, 1992.
341. *The Jack and Belle Linsky Collection in The Metropolitan Museum of Art,* New York, 1984, pp. 44-47.
342. *National Museum of Women in the Arts,* New York, 1987, pp. 18-19.
343. A. Chong, "Bernardo Strozzi: 'The Healing of Tobit'," *Bulletin of The Cleveland Museum of Art,* 80, April 1993, pp. 154-57.
344. See G. Feigenbaum, "The 'Kiss of Judas' by Ludovico Carracci," and R. Spear, "Notes on Two Copper Paintings by Domenichino and Guido Reni," in *Record of The Art Museum, Princeton University,* 48, 1989, pp. 3-17.
345. J.T. Spike, *Italian Baroque Paintings from New York Private Collections,* Art Museum, Princeton University, 1980, pp. 11-14.
346. Substantially the same group of works had been shown in Sarasota from 15 January to 2 March 1986 as *Great Paintings from the John and Mable Ringling Museum of Art.*
347. *Selected Baroque Paintings from Italian Banks,* National Gallery of Art, Washington, D.C., 1990.
348. *Pietro Testa, 1612-1650: Prints and Drawings,* Philadelphia Museum of Art, 1988.
349. A typescript of the explanatory texts on the works in the exhibition was kindly sent to me by the museum's curator, Linda Muehlig.
350. See E. Young, "Old Master Paintings in the Collection of the Fellowship of Friends at Renaissance, California," *Apollo,* CXXI, June 1985, pp. 373-78; and Salerno 1988, p. 177, no. 93. Some of the paintings were sold privately, others appeared in the Sotheby's, New York, sale of 12 January 1989.
351. A privately printed catalogue of the David B. Goodstein and Edward W. Goodstein collection was published in 1983. The sale at Sotheby's, London, was on 10 December 1986.
352. Sotheby's, New York, 13 January 1994.

353. Christie's, New York, 14 January 1993.

354. *Opus Sacrum from the Collection of Barbara Piasecka Johnson,* ed. J. Grabsky, Royal Castle, Warsaw, 1990.

355. See *Italian Baroque Paintings: Selections from the Bader Collection,* Union Gallery, Purdue University, West Lafayette, 1983.

356. See *Prized Possessions: European Paintings from Private Collections of Friends of the Museum of Fine Arts,* Boston, 1992, nos. 18, 87, 58.

357. See *Bulletin of the Houston Museum of Fine Arts,* XIII, Fall 1989, p. 29.

358. See Hall 1992 (as in note 44), p. 68.

359. *Guercino: Master Painter of the Baroque,* National Gallery of Art, Washington, D.C., 1992.

360. Raleigh 1994 (as in note 276).

BOTTICELLI TO TIEPOLO

THREE CENTURIES OF ITALIAN PAINTING

THE CATALOGUE

~ 1 ~

SANDRO BOTTICELLI AND STUDIO

Florence 1445-1510 Florence

Madonna and Child with an Angel, c. 1490-1500

Oil on panel

38 inches in diameter

PROVENANCE: Florentine collection, c. 1890; Douglas Freshfield, England; Agnew's, London, 1902; T.J. Blakeslee, London; Catholina Lambert, New York; Boice Thompson, Yonkers, New York; Julius Weitzner, New York, 1952

EXHIBITIONS: Memphis 1963-64

REFERENCES: Pepper 1984a, no. 4.1

This composition, showing the Madonna and Child accompanied by an angel holding a book open to the text of the Magnificat, exists in an almost identical version last known to be in the collection of Lord D'Abernon, which was sold in 1929. Ronald Lightbown lists the D'Abernon picture under Botticelli workshop and school works and mentions the Bob Jones *tondo* in connection with it, along with similar studio productions, one (with a second angel, who also holds lilies) in the Chigi-Saracini collection, Siena, and the other (with John the Baptist depicted on the right) documented in the Van Buuren sale in Amsterdam in 1925. The present picture relates compositionally to still others catalogued by Lightbown as workshop and school. For example, the depiction of the Madonna is closest to the panel in the National Gallery, London, while the manner in which the Child grasps his mother's neck resembles the same gesture in the Dresden version. Both of these paintings are rectangular in format.[1]

The felicitous design of this *tondo* belongs to Botticelli's late devotional works. Especially characteristic of the master is the tension introduced into the composition through the motifs of the Child's foot and fingers caught in the folds of cloth, as well as the tenderness conveyed by his touch on his mother's neck. Despite these elements, many scholars have discounted Botticelli's participation in the painting. Yet one has only to look closely at the high quality of painting in the Virgin's face, with its subtle gradations of light, and her expressive hands, with their stylized positioning typical of Botticelli's mannered late works, to realize that the master himself was responsible for the important passages of the *tondo.* Stephen Pepper wrote in his 1984 catalogue that an attribution to Botticelli should be considered and noted that Everett Fahy and Philip Pouncey favored this opinion.[2] Recently, Fahy confirmed the work's autograph status and dated the *tondo* to around 1490. [3]

1. Lightbown 1978, no. C50, p. 142. For the National Gallery and Dresden works, see pp. 126-27.
2. Pepper 1984a, p. 7.
3. Written communication, 17 November 1992.

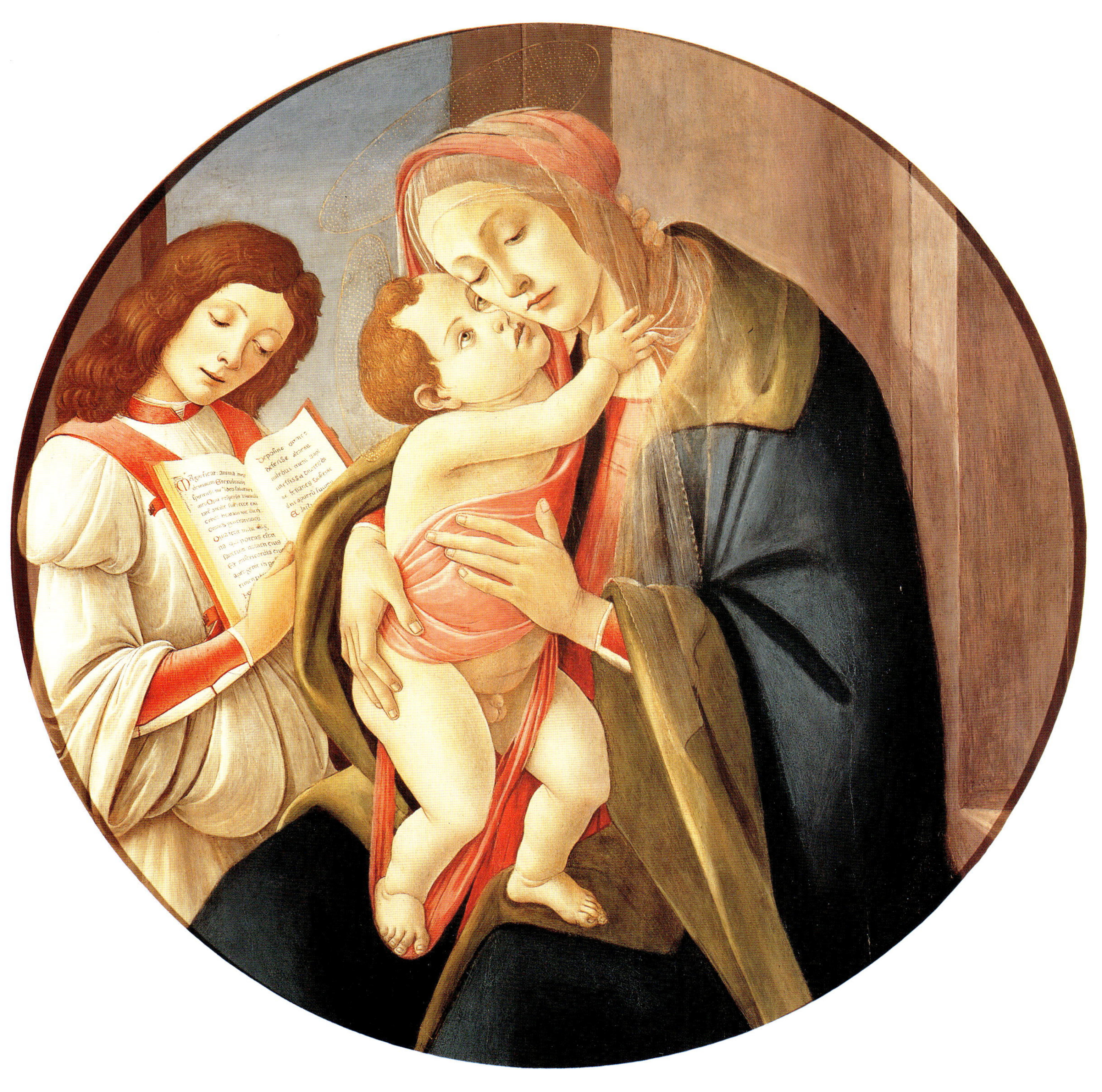

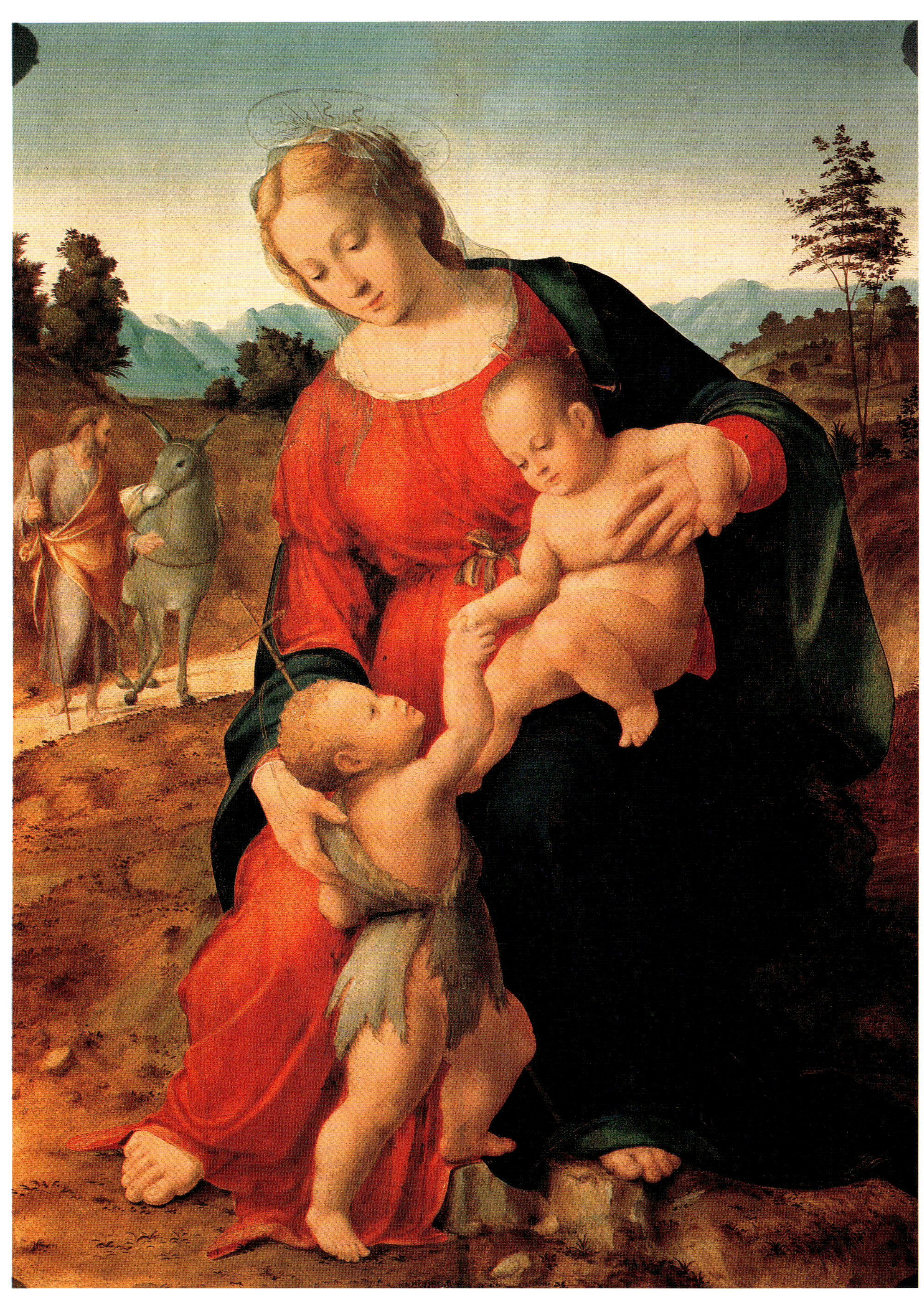

~ 2 ~

FRANCESCO GRANACCI

Florence 1469-1543 Florence

The Rest on the Flight into Egypt, c. 1500

Oil on panel

38¾ x 28¼ inches

PROVENANCE: Sotheby's, London, 30 July 1969, lot 34, sold to Mr. Holstein; Julius Weitzner, London, 1970

REFERENCES: Pepper 1984a, no. 61.1

The young Francesco Granacci is said to have encouraged an even younger, aspiring artist named Michelangelo Buonarroti to draw (Granacci was sixteen and Michelangelo about ten). Both were in the workshop of Domenico Ghirlandaio around 1488 and there began a lifelong friendship. Understandably, early art historians have connected the present composition with Michelangelo.[1] Mary Logan Berenson first proposed Granacci's name in 1903. [2] Christian von Holst in his monograph on the artist enumerated seven versions and copies of the prime version in the National Gallery of Ireland, Dublin. The Bob Jones painting is one of three autograph replicas of the Dublin panel; Von Holst has suggested that the Dublin picture's cartoon was used for the panels at Boughton House, Northamptonshire, the Palazzo Spinola, Genoa, and Bob Jones University, all of which share similar dimensions. [3] Everett Fahy has attributed the present painting to Granacci, noting as well the existence of numerous autograph variants. [4] While Von Holst dated the Dublin composition to the last decade of the fifteenth century, [5] Stephen Pepper has written, "it is very likely that the BJU painting dates from the XVI century, considerably later than the Dublin work."[6]

Granacci's graceful and noble composition—clearly one he favored and one much admired by others, given the many versions and copies—may be compared to Michelangelo's works of around the same time. From the latter's marble relief, the *Madonna of the Steps* of around 1489-92 in the Casa Buonarroti, Granacci took the monumentality of the Virgin's figure. The liveliness of the Christ Child and the young St. John is analogous to that in Michelangelo's composition. In particular, the way in which Granacci's Child grips Mary's hand with his arm resembles the much noted "heroic" Child's arm in the Michelangelo relief. St. John descends the stairs in the sculpture, the left arm resting on the banister above him, the other, below him; Granacci's figure is similarly posed, but in reverse, as he steps up and reaches above with his right arm to grasp Christ's hand. There are affinities with still other Michelangelo works in the sculptural quality of the interwoven forms. Like Michelangelo, Granacci here employed the motif of St. John moving between the legs of the Virgin and linking hands with Christ, who nestles in the crook of the Virgin's left arm. She, in turn, completes the group's embrace by reaching down with her right arm to touch John's shoulder. [7] David Steel has suggested that the panel may not represent the Flight into Egypt, but rather the moment when the Holy Family returned to Judea and were greeted by the young St. John the Baptist. [8]

1. Von Holst 1974, pp. 129-30.
2. Von Holst 1974, pp. 129-30.
3. Von Holst 1974, p. 130. It should be noted that the version listed as no. 4 under cat. no. 3, formerly at Kirtlington Park, is now in the Ponce museum, Puerto Rico (see Held 1984, pp. 136, 138). This panel and its variants differ from the Dublin painting and its replicas as Joseph is seen seated on the ground, rather than standing next to the ass.
4. Written communication, 17 November 1992.
5. Von Holst 1974, p. 130.
6. Pepper 1984a, p. 64. Held (1984, p. 138) dated the Dublin picture "early, c. 1505, on stylistic grounds," while placing the Ponce picture about 1515-20.
7. Compare the *Bruges Madonna* (Nôtre Dame, Bruges; also noted in Von Holst 1974, p. 130), the *Taddei Madonna* (Royal Academy, London), and the *Pitti Madonna* (Bargello, Florence), all from the first years of the sixteenth century.
8. Written communication, November 1993. See cat. no. 35 by Chiari for one such example.

~ 3 ~

ATTRIBUTED TO FRANCESCO MORANDINI CALLED IL POPPI

Poppi c. 1544-c. 1597 Florence

The Meeting of Abraham and Melchizedek, c. 1570

Oil on panel

23⅜ x 17⅛ inches

PROVENANCE: Ospedale degli Innocenti, Florence, until the mid-19th century (?);[1] Panciatichi collection, Florence, until 1902;[2] Havemeyer collection, New York, until 1927; Julius Weitzner, New York, from c. 1952 to 1958

EXHIBITIONS: Baltimore 1961, no. 74 (as Vasari); New York 1967, no. 32 (as Vasari); Notre Dame 1970, no. P21 (as Vasari); Charlotte 1982, no. 20 (as Vasari)

REFERENCES: Pepper 1984a, no. 80.1; Corti 1989, pp. 83-84

Until recently, this small panel executed in jewel-like colors seemed to fit naturally within Giorgio Vasari's oeuvre. It bears a strong similarity to Vasari's cycle in S. Pietro, Perugia, of *The Three Miraculous Feedings*.[3] In particular, emulated in the present picture are the angelic apparition seen in the upper right of the *St. Benedict and his Monks* and the architectural elements of the staircase and arched pediment of the portal in *The Wedding at Cana,* two of the three paintings in S. Pietro. The figures in the *Abraham and Melchizedek* are generally disposed in the manner of those in Vasari's cycle. Laura Corti has most recently discussed the Bob Jones panel in the context of the decoration of the De Monte chapel in S. Pietro in Montorio, Rome, and Vasari's painting of the *Baptism of Saul.*[4] However, Paola Barocchi in 1964 published the Bob Jones panel as by Vasari's early student, Francesco Morandini, and correctly identified the subject.[5] It has continued to be exhibited as a work by Vasari, but Barocchi's opinion has gained increased acceptance.[6]

A further issue is the existence of the probable pendant to the Greenville picture, the *Christ Carrying the Cross* in the Spencer Museum of Art, University of Kansas, Lawrence. The two panels share identical dimensions, the same provenance, [7] and replicate Vasarian models. [8] Charles Davis has suggested that both works once belonged to Vincenzo Borghini (prior of the Ospedale degli Innocenti and friend of Vasari), were part of the same commission, and are based on designs by Vasari. [9]

There is a plausible iconographical connection between the Bob Jones and Spencer paintings. The story of Abraham the biblical patriarch and Melchizedek the ancient king of Salem (Jerusalem) is told in Genesis, chapter 14. Abraham pays a call on Melchizedek, "a priest of God," who furnishes bread and wine. The priest-king blesses Abraham and the latter tithes a tenth of recently acquired war booty to him. The bread and wine, according to traditional Christian interpretation, foreshadow the Eucharist, and Melchizedek the priest-king is a prefiguration of Christ. [10] Thus, the pairing of this Old Testament scene with that of Christ on his way to Calvary makes sense, for the New Testament panel emphasizes Christ's sacrificial, that is, Eucharistic, nature. There are, in fact, four panels assigned by Federico Zeri to the workshop of Vasari depicting Eucharistic themes: our subject here, the *Sacrifice of Isaac,* the *Fall of Manna,* and the *Last Supper.*[11] The existence of these panels underscore the association of Old Testament passages with Christ's Passion in Vasarian works, as seen in the Bob Jones and Spencer panels.[12]

1. Cherici (1926, p. 44) records in his guide to the Innocenti: "il March[ese] Federigo Panciatichi, acquirente di tre quadri su tavola di Giorgio Vasari...."
2. Marchese Ferdinando Panciatichi Ximenes d'Aragona sale, Galardelli e Mazzoni auction house, Florence, 3-5, 7-12, 14-16 April 1902, 14th year, cat. no. 5, lot 31.
3. Riedl (1963, pp. 14-19) discusses the cycle in S. Pietro, particularly the *Wedding at Cana,* and the role of certain drawings and *bozzetti,* connecting the Bob Jones panel to Vasari's program.
4. Corti (1989, p. 83) regards the Bob Jones painting as a replica of this work. However, despite the strong compositional similarities between the foreground figures, different subjects appear to be represented. The Saul of the picture in Rome is appropriately young. The figure with the same pose in the Greenville panel is old and thus represents Melchizedek, whose attendant at the lower left carries the bread and wine. The younger standing figure presumably is Abraham, and the kneeling figure in the lower right may be the king of Sodom mentioned in Genesis, chapter 14. The war booty mentioned there may be the objects seen carried in procession down the staircase in the background. Corti's misidentification of the subject may have also have been caused by its description in the Panciatichi sales catalogue (see note 2 above) as a "conversion of St. Paul after recovering his sight" (p. 8).
5. Barocchi 1964, p. 142.

6. Pepper 1984a, p. 79; Fredericksen and Zeri 1972, p. 144.
7. Barocchi (1964, p. 142) was the first to associate two of the three Panciatichi panels referred to in note 1 with those formerly in the Havemeyer collection, the present picture, and that in the Spencer Museum. The pair's modern history is recounted by Bob Jones, Jr.: Julius Weitzner bought them at auction around 1952 and thereafter offered both to the Spencer Museum. The museum's director John Maxon could afford only one and purchased the panel of *Christ Carrying the Cross.* Several years later, Dr. Jones acquired the other, present painting. Oral communication, 13 July 1993.
8. The Spencer picture has been compared to Vasari's altarpiece of the same subject in S. Croce; see Broun 1978, p. 38. Corti (1989, p. 84) has remarked that the painting at Lawrence was probably produced in Vasari's workshop.
9. Written communication to William Hennessey, 25 January 1979, on file at the Spencer Museum of Art, University of Kansas. It is quite possible that the two panels are not by the same hand; while similar in figural types and composition, the Spencer panel is executed in a more precise and brilliant manner. The differences, it should be noted, are not due to condition, as the Bob Jones panel is in a pristine state. Davis first suggested two separate hands in the letter cited above. The idea of two Vasari pupils producing paintings based on the master's designs for a common commission does not seem farfetched.
10. See Psalm 110 and Hebrews 7.

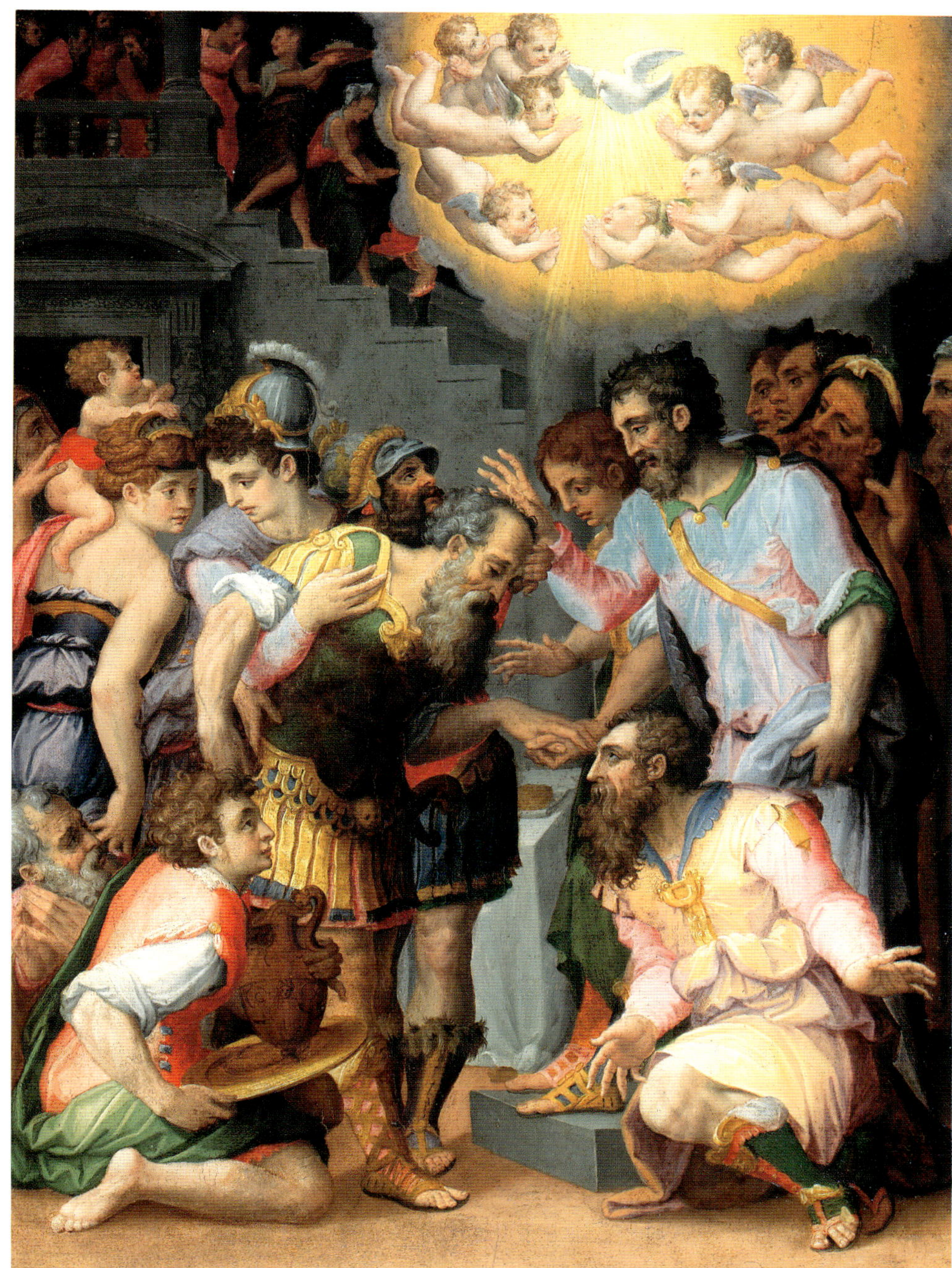

11. These are in the Walters Art Gallery, Baltimore (Zeri 1976, pp. 333-34). The Vasarian compositions (a series of small panels) that the Walters panels appear to derive from are mentioned in Corti 1989, pp. 63, 64; closest are an *Abraham and Melchizedek* at Avignon and a *Last Supper* at Troyes.
12. My thanks to Kerry Morgan and Mark White for their help with this entry.

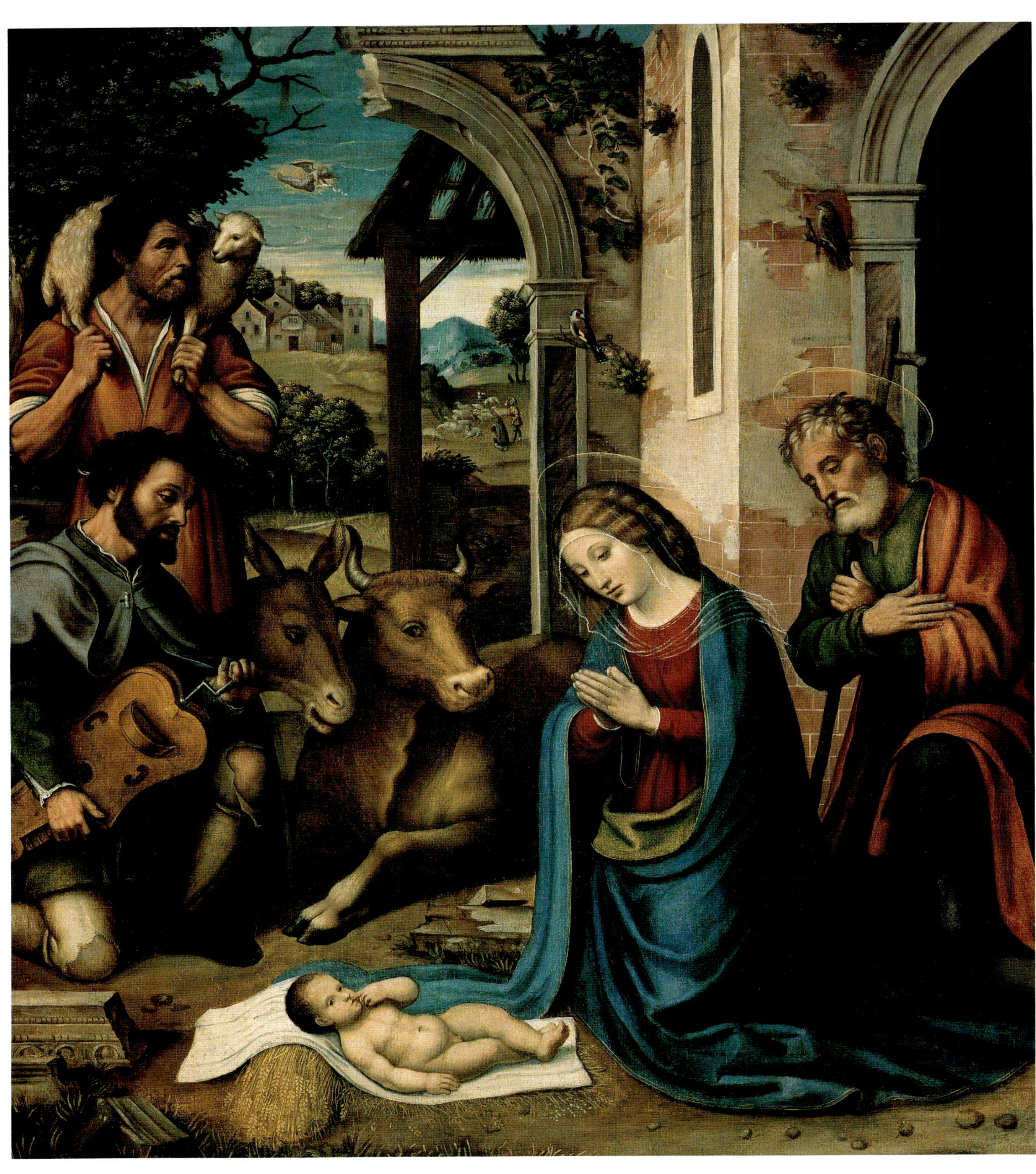

– 4 –

PIER FRANCESCO SACCHI CALLED IL PAVESE

Pavia 1485-1528 Genoa

The Adoration of the Shepherds, c. 1518

Oil on panel transferred to canvas

43 x 37⅞ inches

PROVENANCE: Julius Weitzner, New York, 1956

REFERENCES: Dufour 1970, p. 172; Pepper 1984a, no. 105.1; Gregori 1988, p. 241, fig. 112

This *Adoration* is rich in Quattrocento symbolism filtered through the latest stylistic innovations brought to Milan by Leonardo and propagated by his followers such as Andrea Solario or Marco d'Oggiono (see cat. no. 5). Pier Francesco Sacchi, whose nickname derives from his birthplace of Pavia in the northern region of Lombardy, worked in Milan and later in Genoa from 1501 until his death. He infused his subjects with a *morbidezza,* or the atmospheric, soft modeling of Leonardo's style fashionable in Milan, while his art, at the same time, evoked an earlier age.

The painting was convincingly attributed to Sacchi, first by William Suida in 1956, and then by Erica Tietze-Conrat, Lionello Venturi, and Gian Vittorio Castelnovi.[1] Francesco Frangi dates it to around 1518 based on comparison with the *Holy Family* in Strasbourg, signed and dated 1518, and a slightly earlier, lost lunette of the *Lamentation* of 1516.[2]

In this idyllic pastoral scene, man and nature, in the form of the music-making shepherd and the goldfinch, serenade the Christ Child. Sacchi's panel is touchingly simple in its natural depictions of St. Joseph, the rustics, and the beautiful landscape. Further emphasizing the *retardataire* quality of this composition is the scene played out in the middleground: the Annunciation to the Shepherds. In fact, the two adoring onlookers in the foreground are the very figures to whom the angel appears. Thus, the passage of time is conflated into one scene as in the medieval tradition to which the painting alludes. The symbolism in the picture is extensive. The classical ruins refer to Antiquity, and are a sign of the bankrupt past and the primacy of the new covenant in Christ. The goldfinch, whose diet reputedly consisted of thorns, is consequently a symbol of Christ's crucifixion. The sheaf of wheat used for the Child's headrest prefigures Christ's later presence in the Eucharist as the Bread of Life, and refers as well to the site of Bethlehem, or the "House of Bread." Finally, the motif of the shepherd with the lamb draped over his shoulders is a potent symbol of Christ the Good Shepherd, employed by artists since the Early Christian period.

1. Opinions on file at the Art Gallery, Bob Jones University. Castelnovi lists it under attributed works in Dufour 1970, p. 172. Everett Fahy has called it a "characteristic" work of Il Pavese (written communication, 17 November 1992).
2. Frangi in Gregori 1988, p. 240.

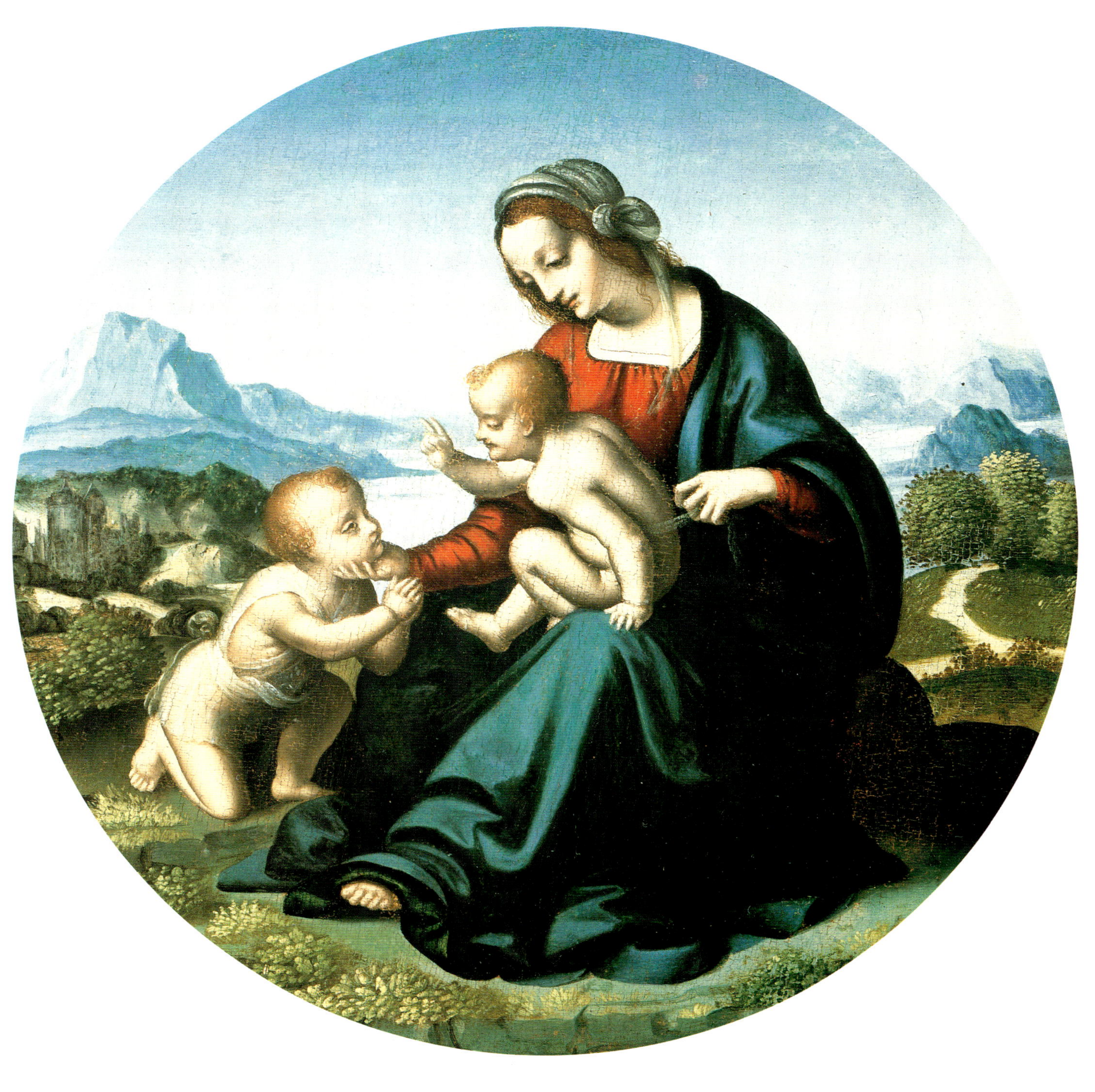

– 5 –

MARCO D'OGGIONO

Milan c. 1477-1530 Milan

La Madonna del lago

(The Madonna of the Lake), c. 1520

Oil on panel

10¼ inches in diameter (sight size);

11 x 10½ inches (panel size)

PROVENANCE: Galerie Brunner, Paris; Gentile di Giuseppe, Paris; F. Kleinberger, New York, 1956 [1]

REFERENCES: Pepper 1984a, no. 9.1; Sedini 1989, no. 45, pp. 66, 158, 220 (with earlier references)

This exquisite and rare little panel in pristine condition is one of only four or five autograph works by Marco in the United States (one attributed to him is at Seattle, two panels are at San Simeon, California, and the last is in a private collection).[2] The design of the composition probably derives from the artist's teacher, Leonardo da Vinci,[3] whose presence in Milan from 1483-99 and again from 1506 on, also informs the preceding work by the Pavese painter Pier Francesco Sacchi (cat. no. 4). At minimum, Marco assembled various parts of Leonardo's paintings to form his composition. Overall, the *tondo* is somewhat reminiscent of the triangular arrangement in Leonardo's *Virgin and Child with St. Anne and the Lamb* in the Louvre. In both, Mary extends her leg and leans to one side toward Christ, or St. John in the present picture.[4] The mountainous landscape with water and trees in the distance is also analogous. Marco lifted the poses of the children out of another composition in the Louvre, the *Madonna of the Rocks.*[5] Leonardo's kneeling St. John, with hands clasped in supplication, and Christ, with his right hand raised in benediction, are transformed in Marco's copy of *The Madonna of the Rocks* and in *La Madonna del lago* into his peculiar figural types.

The above-mentioned work in Seattle, the *Virgin with Child and St. John,* duplicates the pose of the Christ Child seated on the Virgin's lap as seen in the Bob Jones painting. However, this panel is in reverse of the present composition, its figures are situated within an interior, and it is executed in a harder style; thus scholars have not reached a consensus on the attribution to Marco.[6]

While it is possible that the Bob Jones *tondo* was intended simply as a private devotional work, its form and size led Domenico Sedini to suggest that it may once have formed the central part of the predella of a polyptych. He places it generically in the artist's full maturity, implying a date of sometime after 1515-20, and notes the earlier opinions of Suida and Baroni, who dated the panel to around 1510. [7]

1. Domenico Sedini's assertion that Robert Lehman donated the picture to Bob Jones University in 1962 is incorrect (Sedini 1989, p. 120). While Lehman donated three pictures in 1957 and a remarkable Fiorenzo di Lorenzo *Crucifixion* in 1960, the panel by Marco d'Oggiono was not among the financier's gifts to the University.
2. Earlier, the attribution to Marco was confirmed by Zeri (1957) and Suida (1958). Opinions on file at the Art Gallery, Bob Jones University.
3. The *tondo*'s relationship to a composition by Leonardo is noted in Budny 1983, pp. 40, 50, and Sedini 1989, pp. 66, 120-21.
4. Budny (1983, p. 40) points out that, as echoed in the *tondo* here by Marco, Leonardo several times depicted a swaddling band, a symbol of the Incarnation. In a drawing in the British Museum and in the well-known cartoon in the National Gallery, London, the Virgin appears to pull the Christ Child back from St. John, or to steady him, by grasping this band. Sedini (1989, p. 121), acknowledging Budny, discusses the impact of Leonardo's designs on the present picture and others by Marco, Cesare da Sesto, and Raphael (in particular, in his *Alba Madonna*).
5. Marco made a copy of Leonardo's famous work, but square in format, which is now in the Castello Sforzesco, Milan. See Sedini 1989, pp. 59-60.
6. See Sedini 1989, pp. 158-59.
7. Sedini 1989, pp. 120-21.

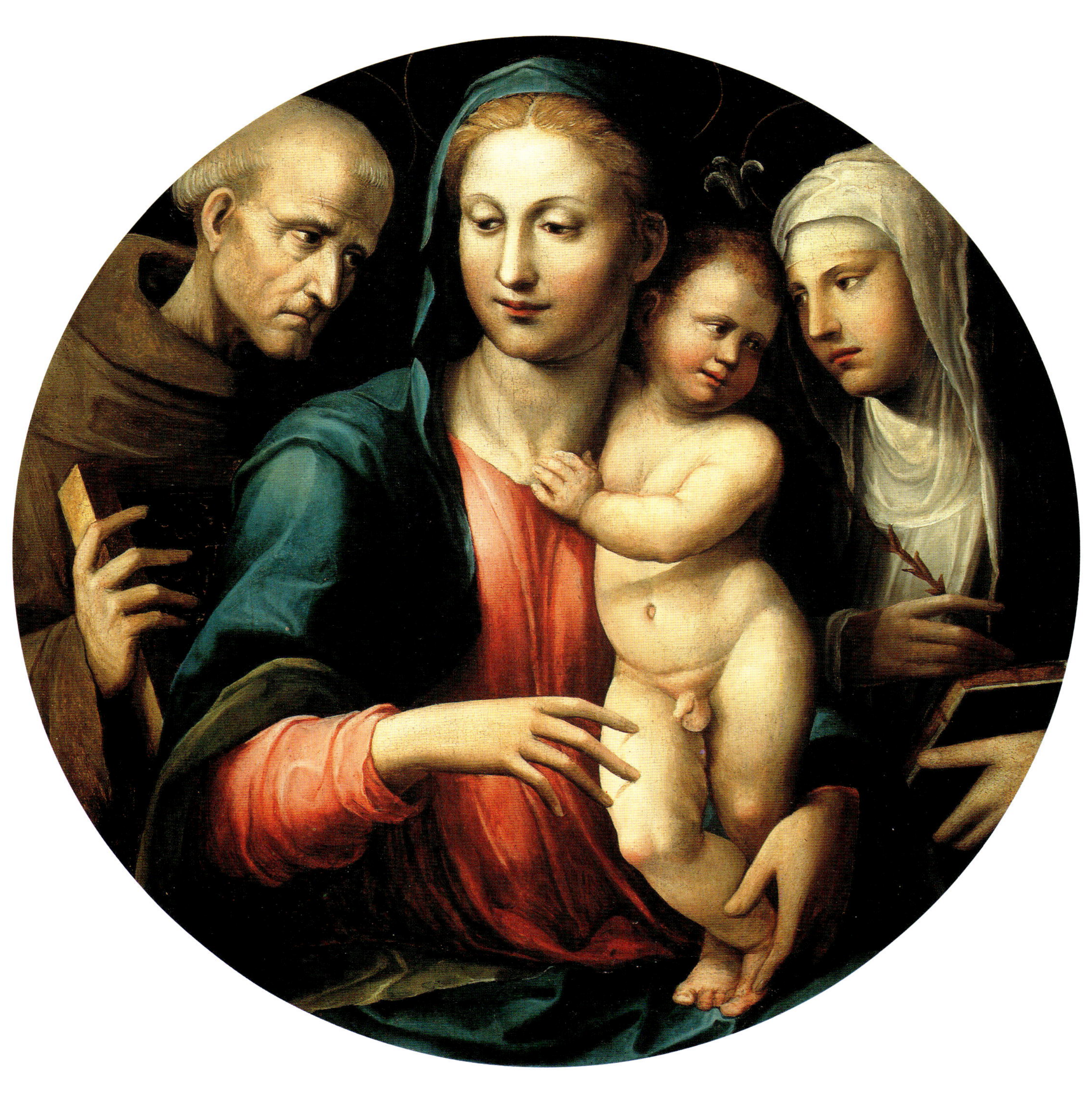

- 6 -

BARTOLOMMEO NERONI CALLED IL RICCIO

Siena, active 1532-1571 Siena

Madonna and Child with St. Bernardino and St. Catherine of Siena, c. 1550

Oil on panel

24⅜ inches in diameter

PROVENANCE: Count Braciaforte; Luigi Grassi, Florence; Jacob Heimann, Los Angeles; French & Co., New York, 1954

EXHIBITIONS: Los Angeles 1949, no. 63A (as Sodoma)

REFERENCES: Pepper 1984a, no. 84.1; Bianchi and Giunta 1988, p. 330 (as Follower of Sodoma)

Although this *tondo* was attributed to Sodoma for many years, Stephen Pepper listed it correctly in 1984 as the work of Bartolommeo Neroni at the suggestion of Federico Zeri and Everett Fahy.[1] In the present composition, the Virgin and Christ are flanked on either side by Bernardino and Catherine, the patron saints of Siena. Innumerable works of this sort by Sienese painters feature rather crowded compositions of the Virgin and Child shown half-length with various saints. Such popular devotional images from the fifteenth century by Pellegrino di Mariano, Neroccio di Landi, and Guidoccio Cozzarelli, depict Bernardino and Catherine at the left and right of the Virgin and Child, in the usual rectangular panel format.[2] By the Cinquecento, these images often took the form of *tondi,* such as our fine example here, and those by Beccafumi, Sodoma, Marco Pino, and others.

St. Bernardino and St. Catherine of Siena figure prominently in the paintings of Beccafumi [3] and Sodoma, the two leading artists of Siena in the first half of the sixteenth century, both of whom profoundly influenced Neroni. Bernardino was known for his preaching to the Sienese in the piazza outside the cathedral and Catherine for her mystical experiences. In the Bob Jones *tondo,* the former holds a book inscribed with the initials IHS (the name of Christ in Greek), while the latter wears her order's garb, and holds a book and a lily, symbol of purity. The devotion to the two Sienese patrons had reached new heights with the canonization of Bernardino in 1450 and Catherine eleven years later. [4]

1. Pepper 1984a, p. 82. Earlier, Morassi, Venturi, Fiocco (1939), and Suida (1953) all concurred regarding the ascription to Sodoma. In Bianchi and Giunta 1988, p. 330, the Bob Jones picture is catalogued as by a Follower of Sodoma; within the entry, however, it is suggested that Neroni might be partially responsible for the painting.
2. See, for example, Bianchi and Giunta 1988, nos. 151, 153, 160, and 176.
3. For example, the S. Spirito altarpiece of 1528 (Chigi-Saracini collection, Monte dei Paschi, Siena) represents Catherine's supernatural marriage to Christ; among the company of saints looking on is Bernardino. Its predella—the panels of which are now scattered between Tulsa, Boston (in contemporary copies), and Cambridge—depict, among other subjects, Catherine's vision of Christ offering her a crown of thorns or one of roses (Philbrook Museum of Art, Tulsa) and St. Bernardino preaching to the people (Fitzwilliam Museum, Cambridge).
4. For the history of Catherine of Siena's cult and her iconography, see Bianchi and Giunta 1988.

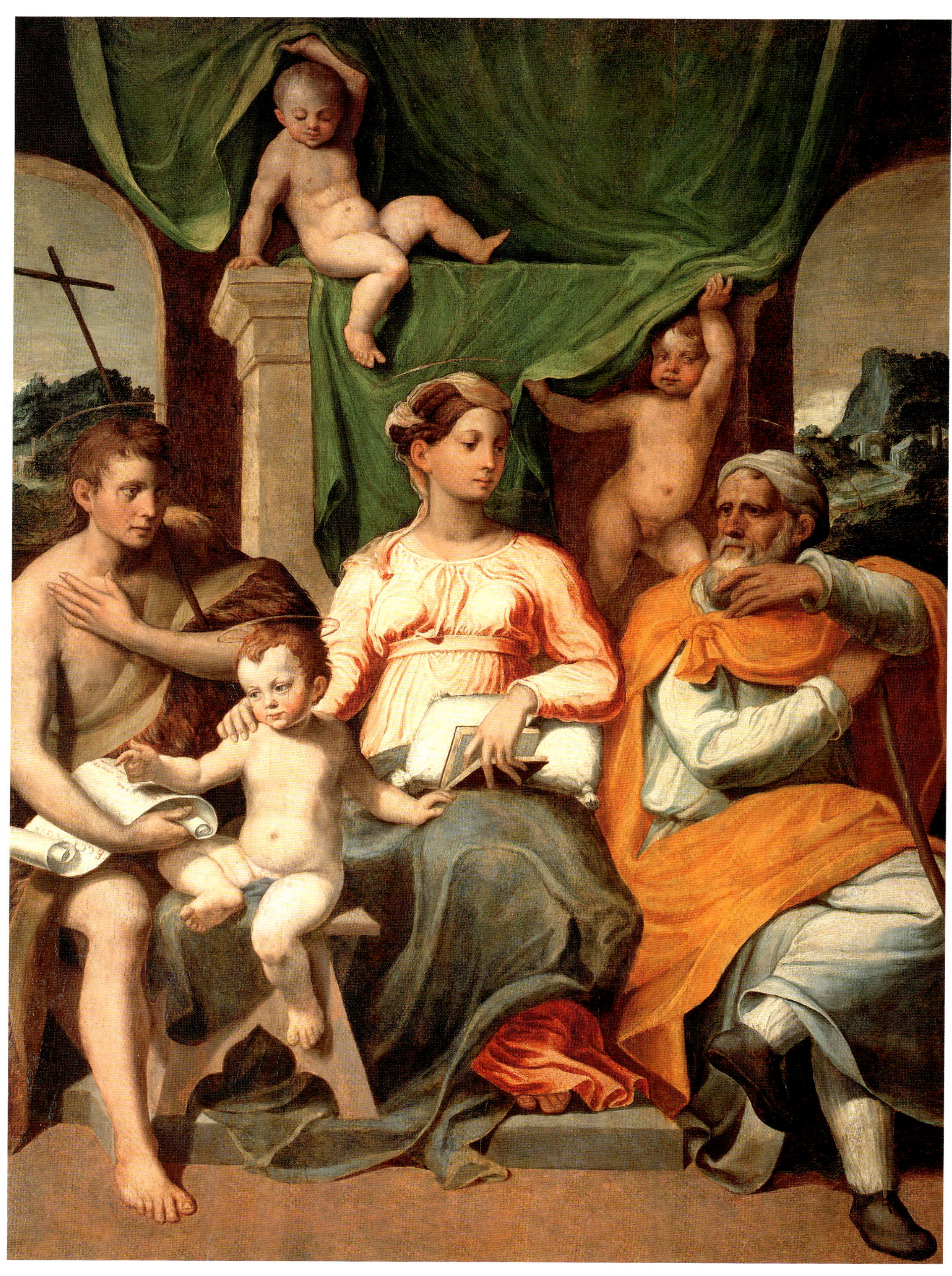

- 7 -

FRANCESCO MENZOCCHI

Forlì 1502-1574 Forlì

Holy Family with St. John the Baptist and Putti, c. 1550

Oil on panel

64½ x 47⅜ inches

PROVENANCE: Seymour Maynard; Sotheby's, London, 22 February 1956, lot 82 (as Girolamo Genga); Julius Weitzner, New York, 1958

REFERENCES: Pepper 1984a, no. 76.1; Scrase 1991, pp. 773, 775

In this altarpiece, seated upon an architectonic throne, are the Virgin and Child, flanked by St. Joseph and John the Baptist. Here John is not represented as Christ's little cousin, but as the youthful saint about to go into the wilderness to prepare his Lord's way. The figures framing the composition suggest balance, but Joseph's mannered, cross-legged pose offsets it. The disposition of the putti contributes further to this asymmetry, for while both hold up the brilliant green cloth of honor, one is seated on the top of the throne and the other stands below.

David Scrase recently published the altarpiece's preparatory drawing on the occasion of its acquisition by the Fitzwilliam Museum, Cambridge, in honor of the late Philip Pouncey.[1] This tribute was fitting, for it was Pouncey who first assigned the Bob Jones picture to Menzocchi in the late 1950s.[2] It was later published as such by Ferdinando Bologna.[3] Of the very few drawings now given to Menzocchi, one other also relates closely to the central figures in the Greenville composition, that is, the *Virgin and Child with St. Anne and St. John the Baptist* in the Ashmolean Museum, Oxford.[4] The Virgin in the Oxford drawing is posed almost precisely as her counterpart is in the painting: her legs are positioned to her right while her torso is oriented to the left, and her right arm rests on Christ's shoulder, her left on a book. But only in the Cambridge sheet does the Virgin turn her head to the right as in the Bob Jones altarpiece. In the Oxford drawing, a putto on the right lifts up a curtain, similar to the corresponding passage in the altarpiece; two putti perform the same function in the Cambridge drawing. Yet another variation between the latter sketch and the painting may be observed: the two arches in the painting that reveal the landscape beyond are reduced to one on the left in the Cambridge drawing. This sheet bears an old inscription at the lower right, "del Parmigiano," which underscores Menzocchi's proximity to this major figure of Italian Mannerism. In particular, the stylized "wet" drapery of Menzocchi's Virgin and her graceful attenuated features, neck, and hands, recall the wise virgins in Parmigianino's frescoes in S. Maria della Steccata, Parma.

1. See Scrase 1991. Stephen Pepper is responsible for alerting the dealer, Kate Ganz—from whom the Fitzwilliam Museum acquired the sheet—to Menzocchi's authorship.
2. Both Federico Zeri and Julius Weitzner record Pouncey's initial impressions of the panel as being by Menzocchi (opinions on file at the Art Gallery, Bob Jones University). The painting had been formerly attributed to Menzocchi's teacher Girolamo Genga and Raphael's Bolognese follower, Pellegrino Tibaldi.
3. Bologna 1971, p. 155.
4. Discussed and reproduced in Macandrew 1980, no. 290-1, pl. XXVII.

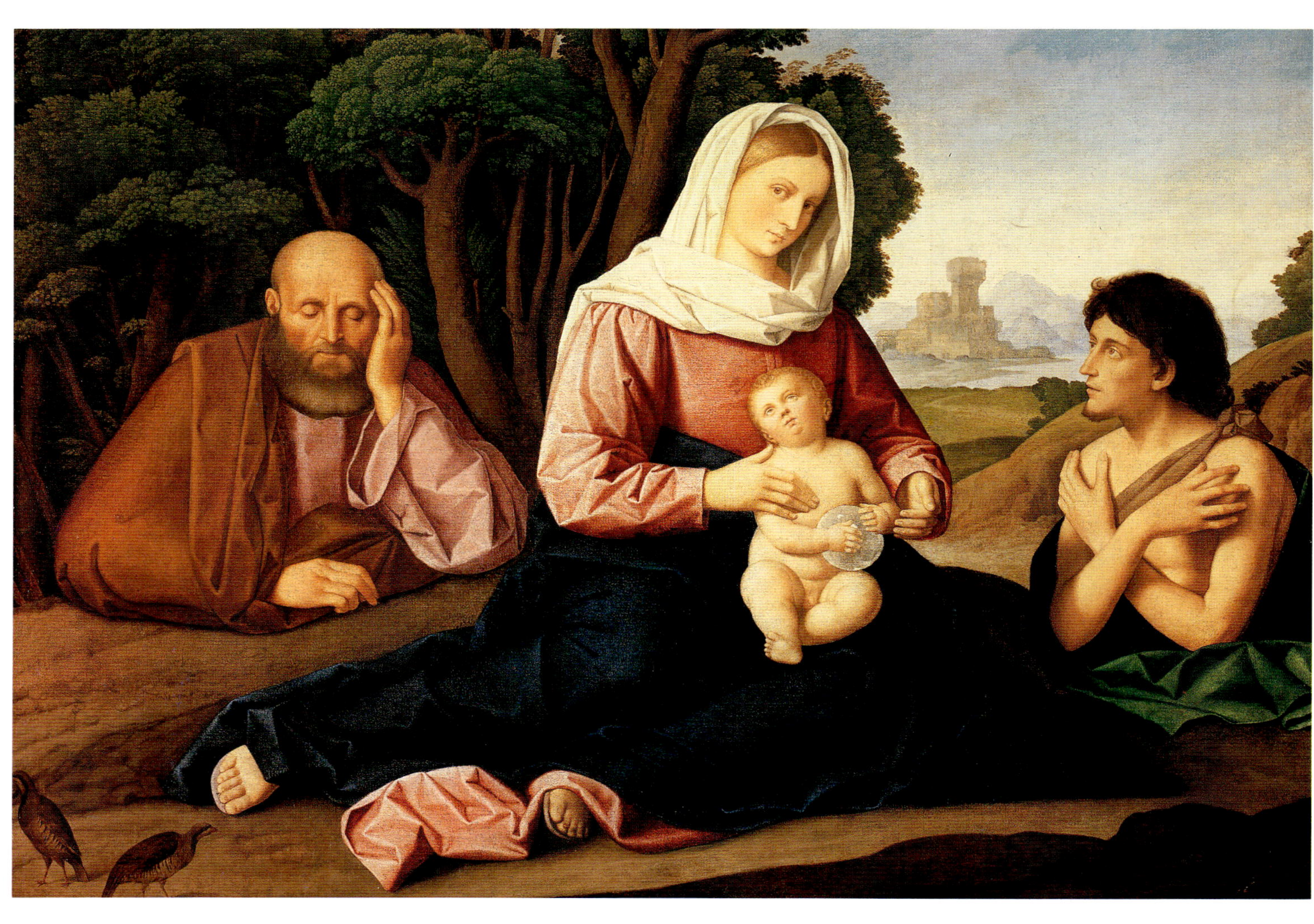

- 8 -

VINCENZO CATENA

Venice c. 1480-1531 Venice

Holy Family with St. John the Baptist, c. 1518

Oil on canvas

44 x 62 inches

PROVENANCE: Earl of Caledon, London; Christie's, 9 June 1939, lot 9, sold to William Permain, London (as Giovanni Bellini); David Koetser, New York, 1965

REFERENCES: Pepper 1984a, no. 39.1

Many pictures now attributed to Vincenzo Catena have long been associated with other artists, such as Giovanni Bellini, Giorgione, Palma Vecchio, and their followers. This is due to Catena's dependence on the compositions of Bellini and the stylistic innovations of Giorgione, as well as the occurrence of Palma's signature on pictures subsequently given to Catena. The same has been true for this painting. Given the obvious influence of these major Venetian painters seen in this beautiful (if slightly abraded) *Holy Family,* and the fact that it shares certain motifs with a number of works correctly ascribed to or associated with Catena, the attribution to the artist is convincing.[1]

Of the paintings depicting the Holy Family by or given to Catena that contain shared elements, three have virtually the same composition: that in the Martin von Wagner-Museum, Würzburg; one in the Norton Simon Museum in Pasadena, California (formerly in the Sawbridge-Erle-Drax collection); and the finest of the three, the present picture. The pensive St. Joseph, head in hand, is also seen, full-length, in the *Holy Family in a Landscape* formerly with Knoedler's and in the *Holy Family with a Warrior Adoring the Christ Child* in the National Gallery, London.[2] The quails seen in the London picture and in the Dresden *Holy Family with St. Anne,* also appear in the Pasadena and Greenville paintings.[3] The Bob Jones version differs from those in Würzburg and Pasadena as it includes a half-length figure of St. John the Baptist. Another useful comparison may be made with the slightly smaller canvas depicting the same subjects in the Museum of Fine Arts, Houston. While there the figures are shown in three-quarters-length and set in front of an interior wall with a cloth of honor bisecting the field in back of the Virgin and Child, the nature of the picture as a *sacra conversazione,* like the Greenville example, is evident. Stylistically, the two paintings share a crispness of execution (compare, for example, the sleeve of the Virgin in the present canvas with that of her counterpart in the Houston picture) and the figures a common physiognomy (particularly in the Christ Child and St. John).

The Pasadena and Würzburg pictures, which exhibit a softer approach to the painting of the features and a fussier treatment of drapery, are probably studio productions.[4] Given the high quality of the Greenville *Holy Family,* it is not surprising that Giles Robertson reversed his earlier opinion, saying the Bob Jones picture is "certainly by Catena."[5]

1. Strong traces of underdrawing on the canvas in black chalk delineating the folds in the sleeve of St. Joseph, the upper garment of the Virgin, and the neck of the Child were seen upon examination with an infrared light scope on 14 July 1993. This evidence of the picture's preliminary stages confirms recent opinion that it is by Catena as opposed to a workshop copy of a Bellini or Catena painting. St. Joseph's brown sleeve, more clumsily developed than the crisp folds typical of Catena, may be early overpainting, as during the technical examination this passage fluoresced differently than other areas.
2. Robertson 1954, p. 61.
3. Quails are symbols of God's providence; during their forty years in the wilderness, the Israelites were fed with manna from heaven in the morning and quail in the evening (Exodus 16). This is an apt parallel for a scene that has associations with the Rest on the Flight into Egypt, since the Holy Family was fed by angels at that time.
4. A conclusion reached by Robertson and Pepper. See Pepper 1984a, p. 41.
5. Pepper 1984a, p. 41. In 1954 Robertson suggested that both the Bob Jones painting and that formerly in the collection of J.C.W. Sawbridge-Erle-Drax in Kentshire (now in Pasadena) were by the same hand, an imitator of both Catena and Palma. Suida and Zeri, in 1946 and 1967 respectively, attributed the present picture to Catena (opinions on file at the Art Gallery, Bob Jones University), while Fritz Heinemann (1959, p. 26) has dissented, calling it "in the manner of Catena," although knowing it only through a photograph.

~ 9 ~

PARIS BORDON

Treviso 1500-1570 Venice

Christ the Redeemer, c. 1545

Oil on panel

8 x 5½ inches (shown actual size)

PROVENANCE: E.D. Levinson, New York; Julius Weitzner, New York, 1954

EXHIBITIONS: Little Rock 1959, no. 16 (as Titian); East Lansing 1959 (as Titian)

REFERENCES: Pepper 1984a, no. 124.1 (as Titian)

The attribution of this impressive, if diminutive panel has been problematic. William Suida published it as Titian in 1943,[1] but this proposal has not found favor with most scholars, with the notable exception of Pepper, who concurred with Suida's opinion in his 1984 catalogue. However, comparison with similar compositions by Titian—that in the Palazzo Pitti dated to the 1530s by Harold Wethey and the later *Christ Blessing* of the 1550s-1560s in the Hermitage, St. Petersburg,[2] or a bust-length portrayal of Christ on the New York art market recently given to Titian [3]—does not support this attribution.

David Rosand has called the present picture the product of a Venetian painter of the second quarter of the sixteenth century, "a painter in or around the circle of Titian," while noting that "One particularly striking feature of the picture is the hand; it is rendered with an articulateness suggestive of the tension to be found in hands by Titian."[4]

The most convincing name put forward for this Titianesque painting, first proposed by Carlo Volpe, is that of Paris Bordon. [5] Terisio Pignatti recently concurred, writing that the overly sweet face, gentle hand, and colors recall Bordon in his early years when he was influenced by Titian. [6] Other versions by Bordon of this subject may be found in the Galleria dell'Accademia, Ravenna; [7] National Gallery, London;[8] Mauritshuis, The Hague; [9] Musée Rolin, Autun (a copy after the master); [10] and a Milanese private collection.[11] The pose of Christ varies slightly in these works, and there are small differences in the details; Christ holds a book in the Bob Jones and Mauritshuis pictures, a scroll in the Ravenna, London, and Autun paintings, an orb in the Milan version.

When Suida originally attributed the Bob Jones panel to Titian, he compared it stylistically to the master's *Temptation of Christ* in Minneapolis.[12] Suida may have had in mind the position and nature of Christ's hand in the Titian and the similar passage in the Bob Jones panel; this would accord with Rosand's observation about the hand noted above. Interestingly, Giordana Mariani Canova, in her Bordon exhibition catalogue, compared the pose of the hand of Christ in the Ravenna Bordon to that in the Minneapolis Titian.[13] She dated the Ravenna picture to around 1545, soon after Bordon's portrait of Hieronimus Kraffter in the Louvre dated 1540 (x-radiographs reveal a composition depicting a Christ similar to the Ravenna picture underneath the portrait) and in the vicinity of the Titian at Minneapolis (that is, 1544-45). Furthermore, Bordon's version in Milan, which has been dated to 1545-50, shares the same type of support (panel) with that of the Greenville picture. Thus it seems reasonable to date the Bob Jones *Christ the Redeemer* to this period, which would also agree with Rosand's dating of the painting to the second quarter of the sixteenth century. One final piece of evidence supports this dating: a drawing by Bordon in the Pierpont Morgan Library, New York, that is extremely close to the Greenville *Christ* has been dated by W.R. Rearick to approximately the same time, that is, around 1538-40.[14]

The iconography of the Greenville panel has puzzled at least one scholar. Erica Tietze-Conrat rejected the attribution to Titian and was troubled by the presence of the book. She could only recall a Vivarini in the Accademia, Venice, that employed this motif.[15] However, there exists a direct antecedent for this type of representation in the Veneto: the *Christ the Redeemer* by Andrea Mantegna of 1493, in the Congregazione di Carità, Correggio.[16] Mantegna's more melancholy Christ also rests his right hand on a book and even inserts his index finger between its pages, as he does in the Greenville painting.[17] Moreover, this motif also occurs in Bordon's painting in the Mauritshuis, The Hague, as mentioned above.

Like Mantegna, Bordon provided a message in his depictions of the Redeemer. In the London and Ravenna versions, it can be seen on the scroll—"Lux Mundi" ("Light of the World"); in The Hague and Greenville paintings, the artist suggested it through the

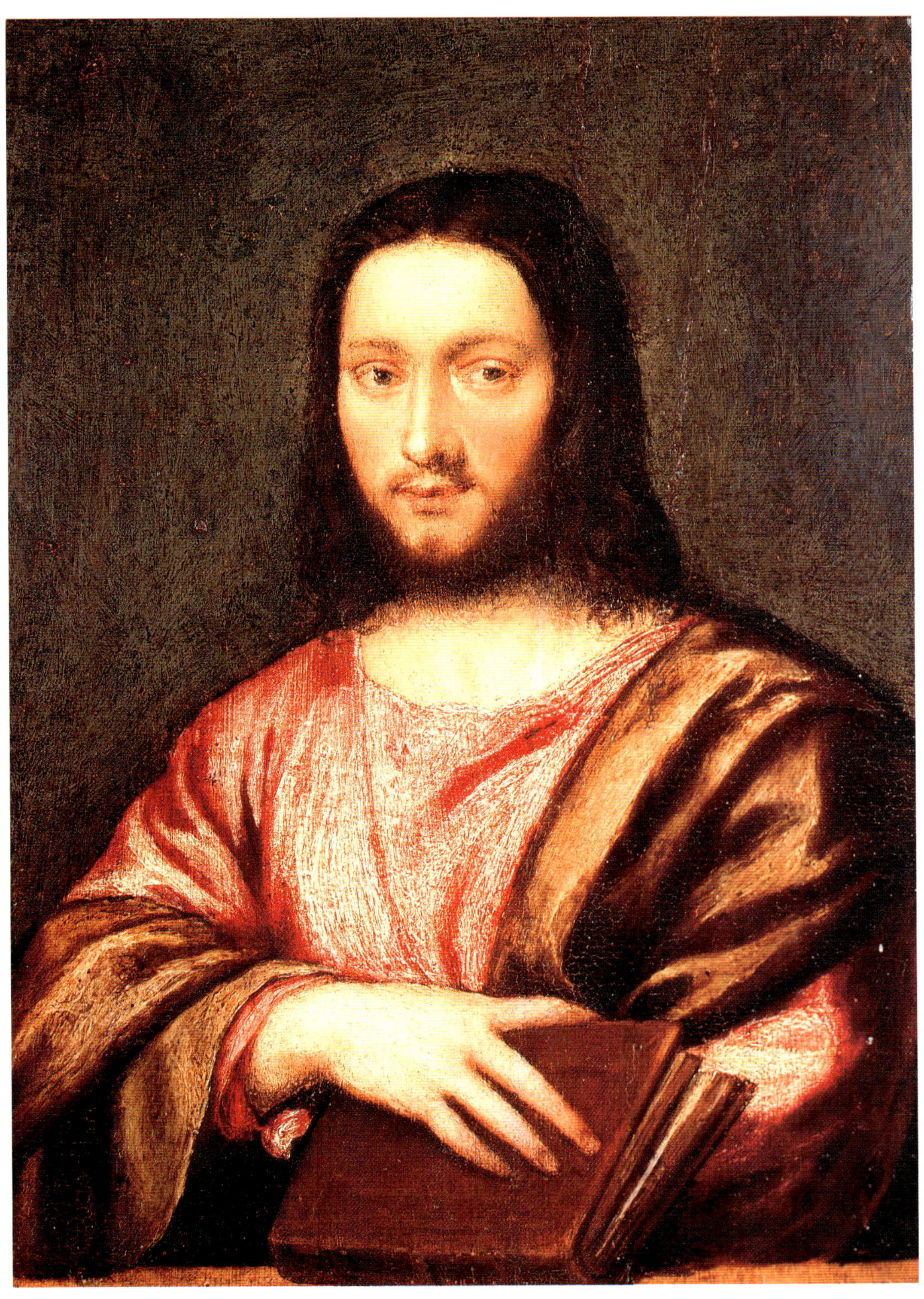

motif of the book. Thus is conveyed the message of salvation and of Christ's eternal presence through the Word.[18] Considering its intimate scale and powerful depiction, the Bob Jones *Christ* must have been intended as a private devotional picture that would impart this assurance to the beholder.

1. Suida 1943, pp. 358-60. He dated the panel to 1550-60.
2. Wethey 1969, pp. 77-78, nos. 18, 19. The Bob Jones panel is listed under related works for the Hermitage picture as by a "follower of Titian."
3. See New York 1991, pp. 10-13. The picture is a strong, but not terribly subtle rendering of Christ in three-quarters view that the late Rodolfo Pallucchini and David Rosand have said is by the master, datable to around 1505; the painting is evidently early sixteenth century and Bellinesque. In contrast, the Bob Jones panel is stylistically much later and reflects Titian's mature phase with its soft brushwork, scumbling, and glazes.
4. Written communication, 14 May 1993.
5. Pepper 1984a, p. 120.
6. Written communication, 3 February 1993. Prof. Pignatti's judgment was rendered solely on the basis of a photograph. Closely analogous stylistically to the Bob Jones *Christ* are two works by Bordon, a *Redeemer* in the Galleria dell'Accademia, Ravenna (see Treviso 1984, p. 71), and the face of Christ in an *Ecce Homo* presently on the art market, New York (see New York 1991, pp. 42-45). In all three, the Savior's tender expression is evoked through the delicate modeling—achieved through glazes—of his eyes, nose, and mouth. This softness is especially apparent in the passage in the present painting where the light moustache fades into the lower cheek.
7. Treviso 1984, p. 71.
8. Canova 1964, fig. 65.
9. Canova 1964, fig. 66.
10. Béguin 1987, fig. 22
11. Sgarbi 1984, p. 255, fig. 4.
12. Suida 1943, p. 359.
13. Treviso 1984, p. 71.
14. Rearick 1987, p. 53, fig. 11. The Morgan Library sheet depicts the Savior a little over bust-length, similar to the Bob Jones panel. Also analogous in the drawing to the present picture, and unlike the other paintings of the Redeemer cited above, Christ's head and upper body are turned to the left, while he gazes directly at the viewer.
15. Opinion on file at the Art Gallery, Bob Jones University.
16. See New York 1992a, pp. 231-32.
17. In the Mantegna canvas, the book bears the inscription, "Ego sum: Nolite timere" or "I am here: have no fear." New York 1992a, pp. 231-32.
18. Recalling John 1:1, "In the beginning was the Word, and the Word was with God, and the Word was God."

- 10 -

JACOPO ROBUSTI CALLED IL TINTORETTO

Venice 1518-1594 Venice

The Visit of the Queen of Sheba to Solomon, 1545-46

Oil on canvas

59½ x 94 inches

PROVENANCE: Pereire collection, Paris; Schaeffer Galleries, New York, from before 1946 to 1952

EXHIBITIONS: Providence 1938; Oberlin 1939; Columbus 1946, no. 20

REFERENCES: Pepper 1984a, no. 122.1

This painting occupies a key place in Tintoretto's early career. Rodolfo Pallucchini has commented on the Bob Jones canvas frequently, [1] summing up its position in the youthful work of Tintoretto in his 1982 monograph on the artist. While Tintoretto painted several versions on the theme of Solomon and Sheba, Pallucchini pronounces this the earliest, first after the *Crucifixion* in Padua, of a series of grand narrative scenes painted under the influence of Andrea Schiavone. Pallucchini then dates the *Christ and the Adulteress* in the Rijksmuseum, Amsterdam, and the *Solomon and Sheba* formerly in a Bolognese private collection to 1546, and the *Solomon and Sheba* at the Château of Chenonceaux, Tours, to late 1546 to 1547.[2] An important motif in these works is the monumental architectural settings inspired by Sebastiano Serlio's *Trattato di architettura* (1537-47). The Bob Jones, former Bolognese private collection, and Rijksmuseum pictures are close in both date and composition; Tintoretto simply rearranged the elements for diversity (the elevated throne, the Serlian portal, the decorated columns, and the perspectival, patterned floors). The Bob Jones canvas prefigures in its overall composition and individual elements the artist's first important commission, for the Scuola Grande di S. Marco of 1548, the *St. Mark Freeing a Christian Slave* (Accademia, Venice).

From its scale and horizontal shape, the painting appears to be a *laterale,* or picture decorating one of the two lateral walls of a side chapel. One such major commission contemporary with the Bob Jones work was undertaken for S. Marcuola in 1547.[3] A leitmotif that recurs from the sixteenth through the eighteenth centuries in Venetian art is found in the present painting. In several of Jacopo Bassano's earliest pictures, such as the *Way to Calvary* of about 1536 (art market, London) and the *Supper at Emmaus* of 1538 (Kimbell Art Museum, Fort Worth), and even into the 1540s in a reprise of the *Way to Calvary* (Fitzwilliam Museum, Cambridge), a distinct ancillary figure appears—an elderly man with a round face and short white hair. The same figure can be seen, holding a cane, in the Bob Jones Tintoretto below and to the right of the enthroned Solomon. This Cinquecento Venetian figural type continues to be employed well into the eighteenth century. (See, for example, at the far right of the *Ecce Homo* by Giambattista Tiepolo and his son Domenico, datable to around 1760 in the Musée des Beaux-Arts, Caen.)[4] This may be evidence of Bassano and Tintoretto using a Venetian type common at the time, with the Tiepolo over two hundred years later quoting their Cinquecento predecessors, as Giambattista was wont to do with Veronese. Or perhaps the old man's presence, as he stares out from Tintoretto's canvas, signals something lost to us now, but recognized by the Tiepolo family in that last golden age of Venetian painting.

1. See Pepper 1984a, p. 118, for these citations.
2. Pallucchini and Rossi 1982, I, pp. 26-30.
3. For an overview of the decoration of Venetian churches with *laterali,* see Hills 1983, pp. 30-43. Hills suggests that these confraternities dedicated to the Holy Sacrament (the Eucharist) were responsible for the proliferation of *laterali* in sixteenth-century Venice and particularly in Tintoretto's oeuvre. The author relates the pietistic and devotional thrust of the confraternities' doctrines and their aspirations reflected in certain subject matter as demonstrated by these paintings by Tintoretto.
4. See Fort Worth 1993b, pp. 292-93.

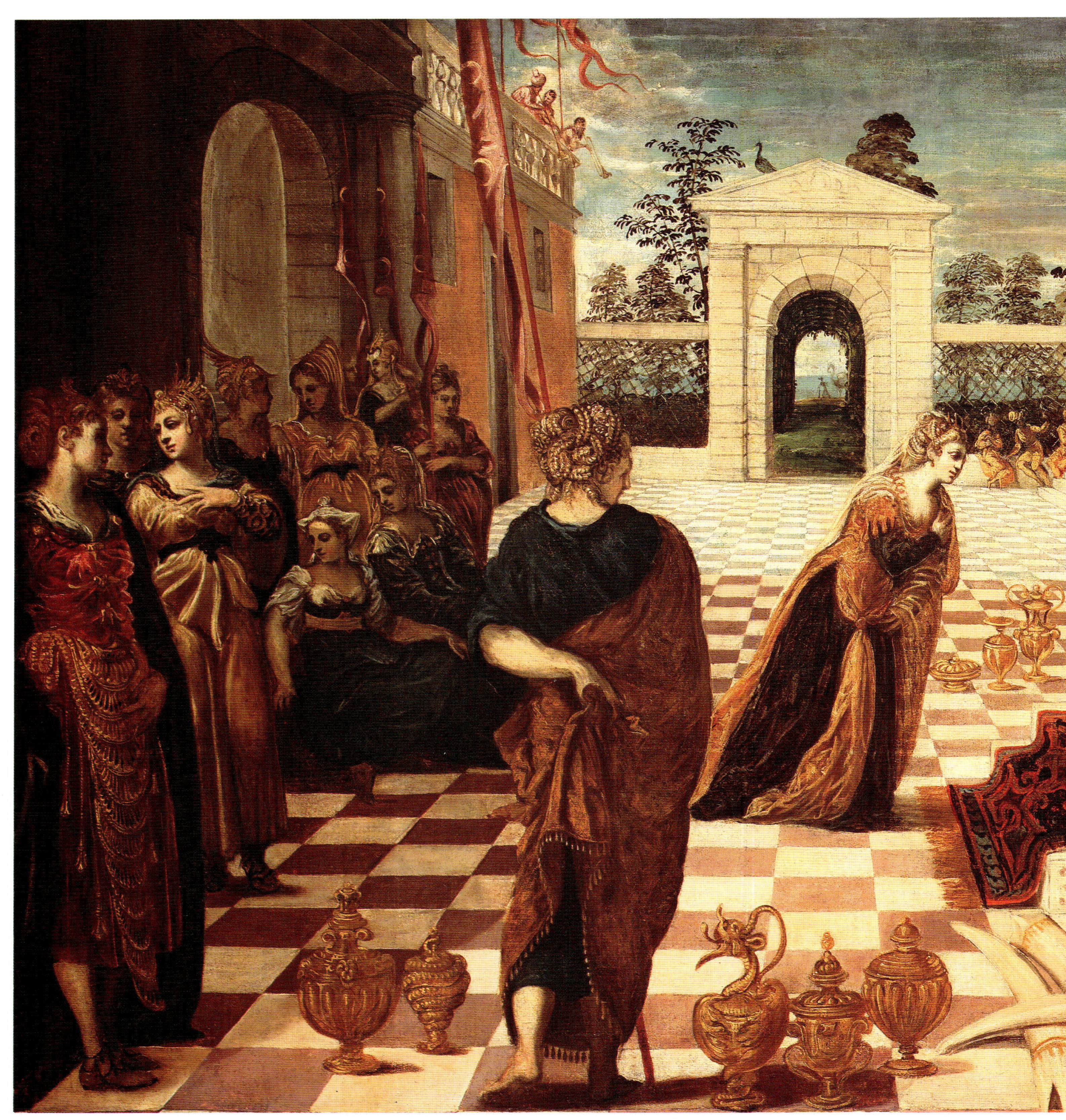

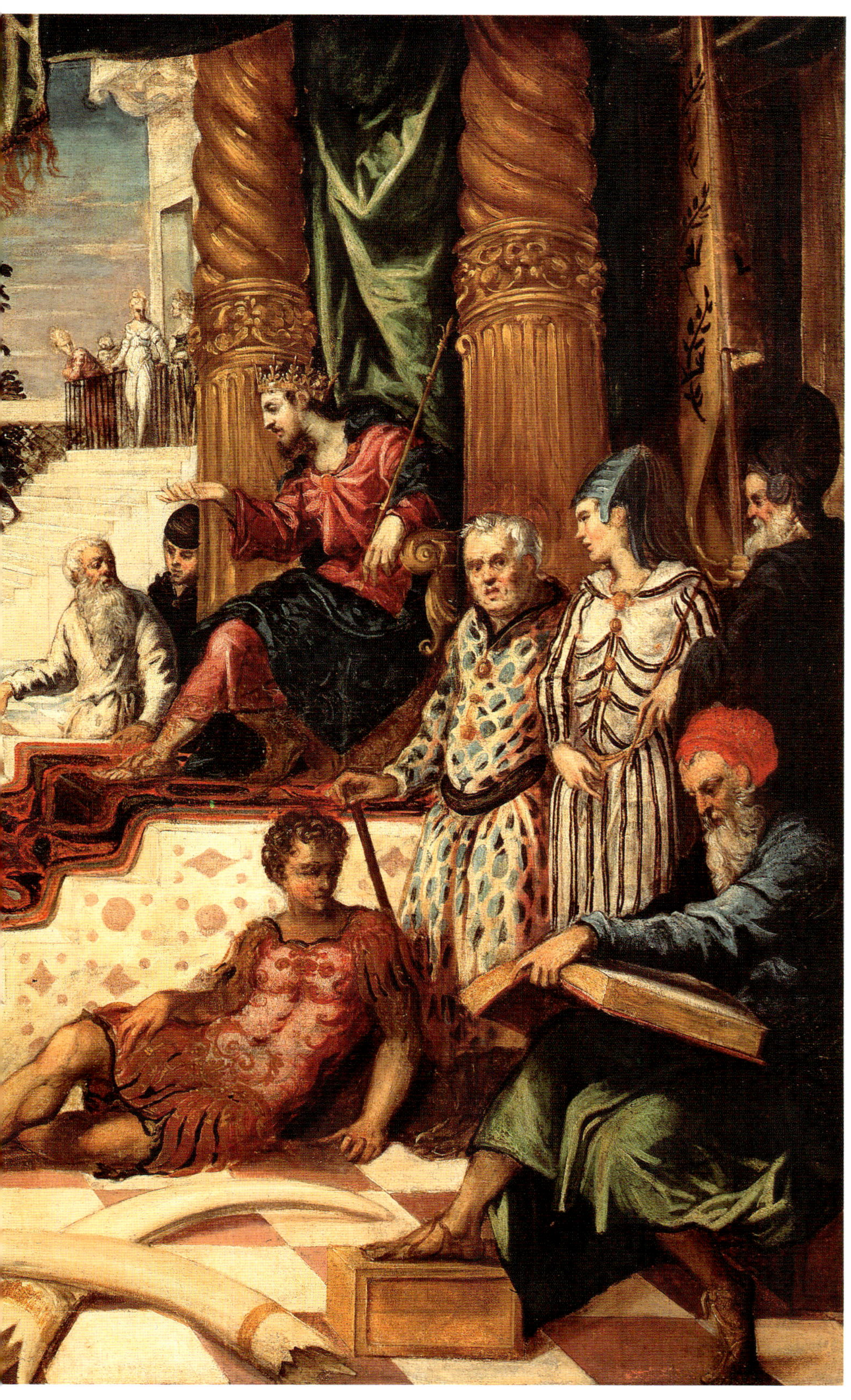

- 11 -

GIOVANNI BAGLIONE

Rome c. 1566-1644 Rome

The Entombment of Christ, 1616

Oil on canvas

90⅜ x 61 inches

Signed and dated:

.EQVS.IO.BAGLIONVS.RO.P.1616

PROVENANCE: private collection, Berlin, 1915; Von Litz collection, Munich, 1954; Christie's, London, 16 June 1967, lot 139; Julius Weitzner, London, 1968

EXHIBITIONS: Raleigh 1984, no. 2

REFERENCES: Pepper 1984a, no. 28.1

This altarpiece depicting the entombment of Christ's body after the crucifixion is inscribed by the artist "Cavaliere Giovanni Baglione, Rome, painted 1616," which alludes to his knighthood conferred on him by Pope Paul V in 1606. Baglione was an extremely accomplished artist for, besides being favored by the pope, he served as president of the Roman academy and wrote an invaluable account of the lives of contemporary artists (1642). Baglione was the first to experiment in 1601 with the revolutionary style introduced to Rome by Caravaggio. The Bob Jones *Entombment* is a rare example of the artist's work in an American public collection and is, in fact, one of his most significant paintings.

An earlier version of the Bob Jones picture exists in the picture gallery of the Pio Monte della Misericordia, Naples.[1] This work is well documented, Baglione having painted and been paid for a "painting of the entombment of the Redeemer" in 1608.[2] Baglione's early Caravaggesque work made the artist a logical choice to produce an altarpiece for the Pio Monte. The church, founded in 1601, first commissioned Caravaggio himself in 1606 to paint his *Seven Acts of Mercy* (the "Nostra Signora della Misericordia").[3] The second altarpiece created for the church was Gian Vincenzo Forlì's *Good Samaritan* and the third, Cavaliere Baglione's *Entombment.* These, and the subsequent works provided by Santafede and Caracciolo, demonstrate the Caravaggesque taste of the governors of the Pio Monte. While Baglione's style here, in terms of its overall effect and palette, is in keeping with late Roman Mannerism, the composition, rather than deriving from the obvious "classical" source of Raphael, is in fact adapted from Caravaggio's great *Deposition* of 1603 for the Chiesa Nuova (now in the Vatican Pinacoteca). In 1658 G.F. Picchiatti initiated renovations for the church of the Pio Monte and commissioned from Luca Giordano in 1669 an altarpiece of the *Entombment* to replace Baglione's. Giordano duplicated the descending diagonal and general disposition of the figures of Baglione's composition, only in reverse. Apparently in 1671 (the year Giordano's work is dated), the Baglione altarpiece was moved to the sacristy, and finally, at the end of the last century, to the picture gallery of the Pio Monte.[4]

The Bob Jones painting of eight years later is similar in composition to the original version in Naples, but the artist has taken care to vary the poses and some of the faces of the foreground figures: the young man standing at the far left, the elderly Joseph of Arimathea, the younger Nicodemus, and the Magdalen at the far right. Nicodemus, supporting Christ's feet, is considerably older in the Naples altarpiece. Finally, in the Naples picture the nails of the cross and the crown of thorns are prominently displayed on the tomb slab, whereas in the Greenville version these elements are relegated to the dark lower left corner. The present painting was probably intended, as David Steel has suggested, as an altarpiece, like its earlier version in Naples.[5]

1. Carla Guglielmi, who first published the Bob Jones painting, quite rightly associates it with later Baglione works on stylistic grounds, as the signature and date were obscured at that time. She is incorrect, however, in believing that the picture in Naples, the prime version, was executed later than the present picture (Guglielmi 1954, p. 321).
2. Causa 1970, p. 31.
3. For full accounts of the context of the commissioning of Caravaggio's altarpiece and the picture itself, see Causa 1970, pp. 13 ff. and the catalogue entry in London 1982, pp. 125-28. In the latter, Mina Gregori notes that while the church was to have an altar each devoted to an Act of Mercy, the Caravaggio over the high altar included all seven Mercies; the remaining altars had paintings by Forlì, Santafede (two), Caracciolo, and the first version of the present picture by Baglione. In his altarpiece, typically, Caravaggio interpreted the Seven Acts of Mercy as events from daily life. The other paintings also depicted "acts of corporeal mercy," while not ignoring "their spiritual

implications, placing the subjects in their sacred context." Thus Baglione's *Entombment,* while a sacred image in itself, is also a representation of the merciful act of burying the dead. In addition to carrying out the initial program established by Caravaggio in his great altarpiece, Baglione, with his interpretation, conveyed one of the very principles of the charitable foundation that commissioned him.

4. Causa 1970, pp. 33, 88. Interestingly, the Giordano *Entombment* that took its place is a variant of an earlier composition that the artist employed in a painting at Detroit and in a signed and dated canvas (165[4?]) in the Philbrook Museum of Art.
5. Raleigh 1984, p. 22.

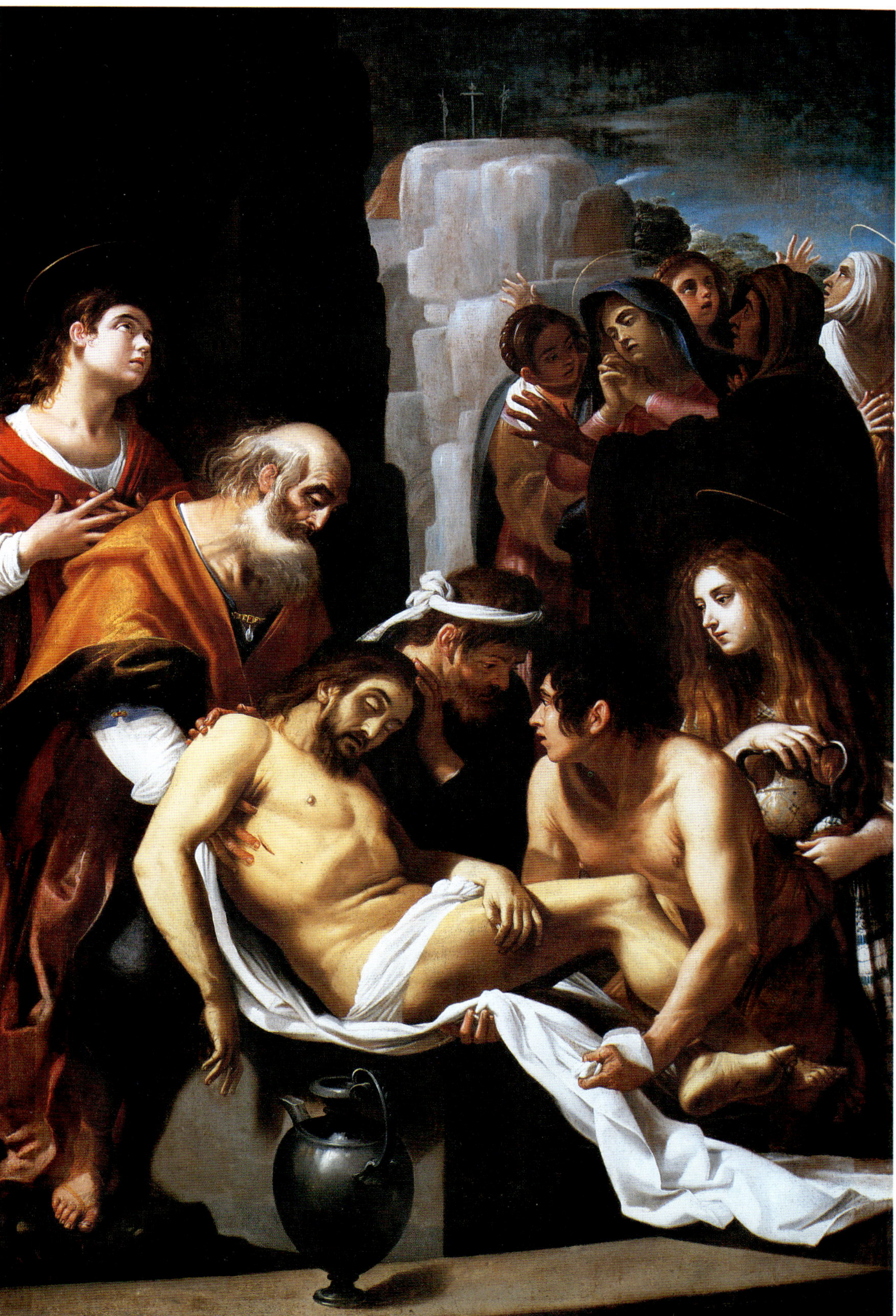

- 1 2 -

ATTRIBUTED TO PIETRO PAOLINI

Lucca 1603-1681 Lucca

St. Jerome, c. 1625

Oil on canvas

34½ x 42½ inches

PROVENANCE: Julius Weitzner, London, 1967

EXHIBITIONS: Providence 1968, no. 5 (as Giovanni Serodine)

REFERENCES: *Art Quarterly,* XXX, 1967, p. 161, under "Accessions" (as Serodine); Nicolson 1979, p. 23 (as by "an associate of Bigot in Rome who might have collaborated on the S. Maria in Aquiro altarpieces"); Nicolson and Vertova 1989, no. 880, repr. (as Circle of Bigot in Rome)

This *St. Jerome* was attributed to Giovanni Serodine since its acquisition by Bob Jones University,[1] until Benedict Nicolson listed it as from the circle of Bigot. Pepper did not include it in his 1984 Italian paintings catalogue as he considered it a Northern work. Leonard Slatkes has suggested the name of Pietro Paolini,[2] which seems quite plausible.

Although the somewhat perfunctory painting of the drapery resembles the broadly illuminated, flat folds typical of the Northern followers of Caravaggio, Slatkes has noted the picture's "rather painterly surfaces . . . characteristically Italian." And while the motif of the lantern also points to a Northerner, Slatkes observes that both Rutilio Manetti (see cat. no. 13) and Paolini were influenced by Northern painters and experimented with artificial illumination.[3] The smooth, almost generalized features, and especially the hands, as well as the highly polished passages of light, or "liquid highlights," are typical of Paolini's style. Moreover, the physical resemblance of the figure of Jerome in the Greenville painting to old men depicted by the artist in later works in Florence and formerly on the art market further reinforces the attribution.[4] A dating to the middle years of the 1620s is here proposed for the present picture, since it was at this time that Paolini worked in Rome and was inspired by Caravaggio, Bartolomeo Manfredi, Angelo Caroselli, Gerrit Honthorst (called by the Italians, Gherardo delle Notti), and the other Northern Caravaggisti.[5]

It has already been noted that this representation of Jerome does not, at first glance, seem "Italian;" rather it resembles the iconographical type as developed in Northern Europe, which generally emphasizes the saint's role of scholar and Church Father.[6] By way of comparison and contrast, it is useful to examine a later work by Paolini, now in a private collection in Lucca, which has been dated to around 1640 by Patrizia Giusti Maccari.[7] Both pictures are horizontal in format and depict Jerome with the large book of his writings (possibly his translation of the Scriptures in Latin called the Vulgate) and skull. However, the later composition is unmistakably Italianate; the saint's torso is bare, revealing a heroic physiognomy, the pose is grander, the composition more airy, and the forms illuminated by natural light, all of which reveals the artist's contact with Bolognese and Venetian art. Moreover, the iconographical type is more typically Italian; after the Council of Trent, images of Jerome in Italy increasingly stressed the penitential aspects of the saint. These portray him as an elderly hermit in the wilderness, sometimes beating himself; in contemplation of a cross or skull (the latter a symbol of the transience of life, or *vanitas*); or visited by the Angel of Judgment. Circulating throughout Italy were prints such as those by Domenico Campagnola in the Veneto (where the tradition of integrating the eremitical Jerome into a landscape probably began in the fifteenth century with Bellini) and those by the Neapolitan Jusepe de Ribera, which show a weathered old man startled by the trumpet of the Last Judgment. Countless paintings, altarpieces, and devotional works depicting the saint by Ribera, Reni, Guercino, and others demonstrate the popular appeal of this devotional Counter-Reformation imagery.[8]

1. Apparently based on opinions furnished to Weitzner by Hermann Voss (1957) and Antonio Morassi. Perhaps the Serodine misattribution stems from comparison to a painting such as the *St. Peter in Prison* (Giovanni Züst collection, Rancate; Nicolson and Vertova 1989, pl. 150), with its similar disposition of the figure, book, and skull, and the illumination by candlelight.
2. Written communication, 21 February 1993.
3. Written communication, 21 February 1993.
4. See Giusti Maccari 1987, nos. 45, 46, and 48.
5. See Giusti Maccari 1987, p. 47.

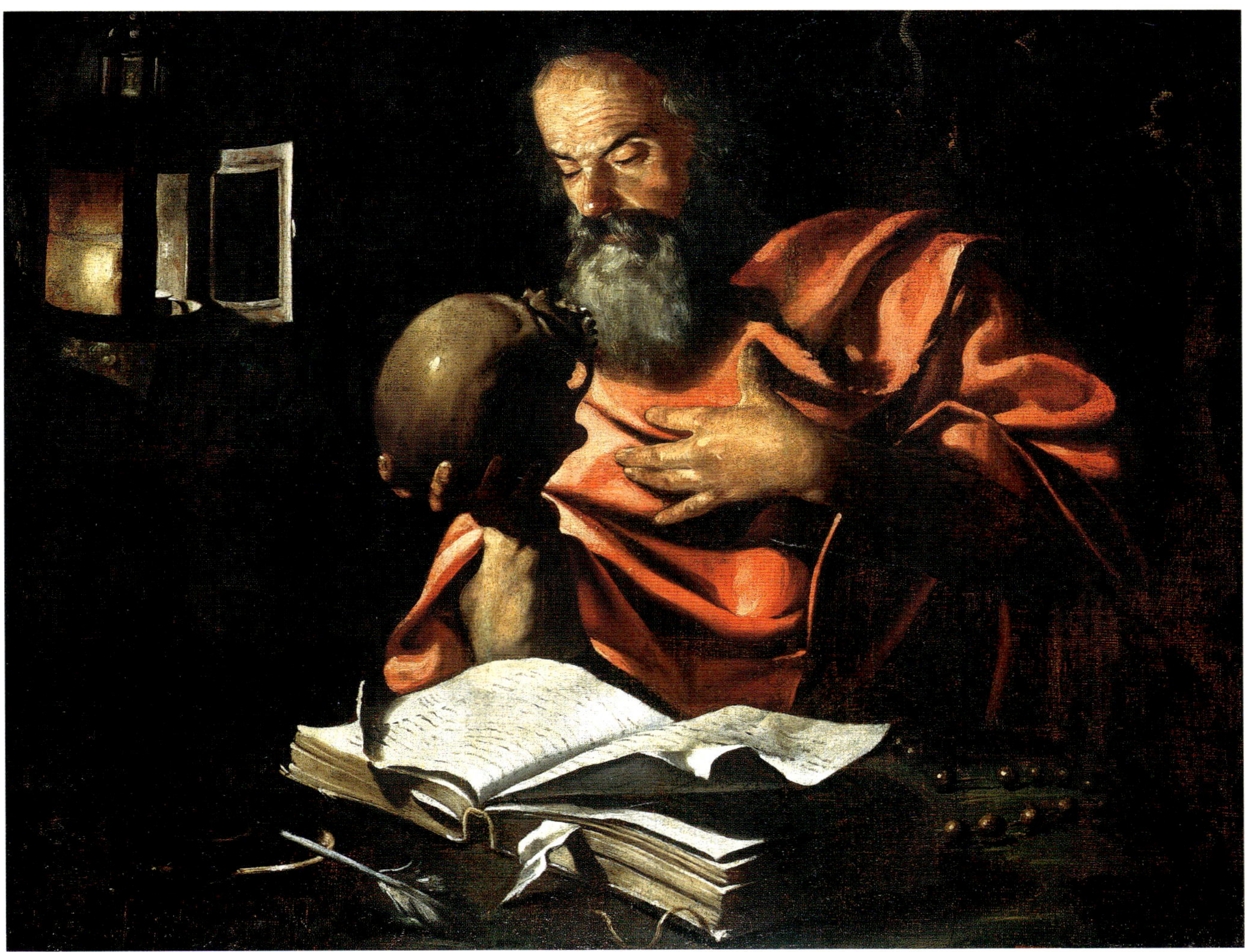

6. For example, Jan van Eyck's painting of 1435 depicting Jerome wearing his cardinal's hat (Detroit Institute of Arts); Dürer's 1514 engraving of *St. Jerome in his Study;* and Joos van Cleve's popular image of the saint in his study contemplating a skull of about 1525 (Harvard University). Northern examples influenced pre-Tridentine Italian depictions of Jerome; see, for example, Antonello da Messina's *St. Jerome in his Study* of about 1475 (National Gallery, London).
7. Giusti Maccari 1987, p. 118. She places the Lucchese painting at that time "because we do not discover in it that dramatic tension typical of the period of stricter adhesion to Northern Caravaggism that characterizes [Paolini's earlier works]."
8. The ubiquitous nature of saintly penitential imagery in the Counter-Reformation has been noted under cat. no. 15. For images of Jerome, there are several useful sources, including Venturi 1924; Friedmann 1980; and Rice 1985.

– 13 –

ATTRIBUTED TO RUTILIO MANETTI

Siena 1571-1639 Siena

Christ Disputing with the Elders, c. 1628-29

Oil on canvas

44¾ x 61¾ inches

PROVENANCE: Charles Brinsley Marlay; his bequest to the Fitzwilliam Museum, Cambridge, 1912; Julius Weitzner, New York, 1958

EXHIBITIONS: Little Rock 1959, no. 19 (as Pietro Bellotti); Hagerstown 1969 (as Bellotti)

REFERENCES: Pepper 1984a, no. 33.1 (as Pietro Bernardi)

This painting depicts the single example of Christ's precocity recorded in the Gospels. The subject, also known as the Dispute in the Temple or Christ among the Doctors, is from Luke 2:41-52. The account tells of the twelve-year-old Christ taken to Jerusalem by his parents for Passover. Having been separated from them for three days, he was found in the temple, debating with the elders or rabbis. When Joseph and Mary questioned him about his behavior, Christ responded, "How is it that ye sought me? Wist ye not that I must be about my Father's business?"

Determining the authorship of *Christ Disputing with the Elders* has been problematic. Comparison with the works of the Veronese Pietro Bernardi, to whom Pepper reattributed this picture in 1984 (from an earlier ascription to Pietro Bellotti), reveals only few and superficial similarities.[1] Rather, the painting should be associated with Rutilio Manetti, the leading painter in early seventeenth-century Siena.[2] It is not a work in the style of Manetti's first manner, when he followed in the tradition of the late sixteenth-century Sienese masters Francesco Vanni and Ventura Salimbeni, but of his second, Caravaggesque phase. Paintings from the early 1620s on display an awareness of Caravaggio's works, at least as seen through his followers. Manetti was commissioned by Cardinal Carlo de'Medici to paint a *Ruggero and Alcina* (Palazzo Pitti) in 1622; he would have seen there in Florence the works of Gerrit Honthorst, Artemisia Gentileschi, and Bartolomeo Manfredi, thereby absorbing the lessons of Caravaggio.[3] Not until Manetti's presumed journey to Rome in 1625 would he have seen originals by the master, whose influence becomes more pronounced in the paintings produced after this date.[4]

The Bob Jones picture must have been executed after that time. Stylistically, it is in the vicinity of Manetti's *Ecstasy of St. Jerome* of 1628 (Monte dei Paschi, Siena) and closer still to the *Two Prophets* of around 1628 (Galleria Nazionale d'Arte Antica, Rome). In particular, the realistic treatment of the old men's beards and the depiction of the books and rich fabrics are analogous. Paintings datable to around 1629-30, such as the *Draughts-players* (Chigi-Saracini collection, Monte dei Paschi, Siena) and the *Temptation of St. Anthony* (S. Agostino, Siena), portray bespectacled figures, which can be compared to the old man with a lorgnette in the Bob Jones painting. The manner in which these figures are posed and illuminated in these three paintings is also similar (most notably, the hand seen *controluce* in the S. Agostino picture resembles Christ's right hand in the present work). In his later years, Manetti was assisted in his pictures by his son Domenico,[5] who may have worked on this painting.[6]

1. Pepper 1984a, p. 38. William Suida was responsible for the earlier attribution in 1958 (opinion on file at the Art Gallery, Bob Jones University).
2. The Sienese origin of this work was first proposed by Mina Gregori in 1968, who recently refined this opinion, suggesting it was "near to Rutilio Manetti and his son" (oral communication, 23 September 1992). Keith Christiansen concurs with this attribution (written communication, January 1993).
3. Pietro Torriti in Siena 1978, p. 16.
4. Pietro Torriti in Siena 1978, pp. 16-17.
5. See, for instance, Siena 1978, pp. 131, 134.
6. It should be noted that Alessandro Bagnoli has expressed reservations about the attribution proposed here, citing differences from Manetti's known oeuvre, including aspects of composition (number of figures and their typology) and style (paint surface and palette), despite his admission of "elements of stylistic affinity with the works of Manetti...." Neither does Bagnoli believe that Domenico Manetti nor the other Sienese painters, Niccolò Tornioli or Bernardo Mei, are responsible for the Greenville picture. Written communication, 4 November 1993.

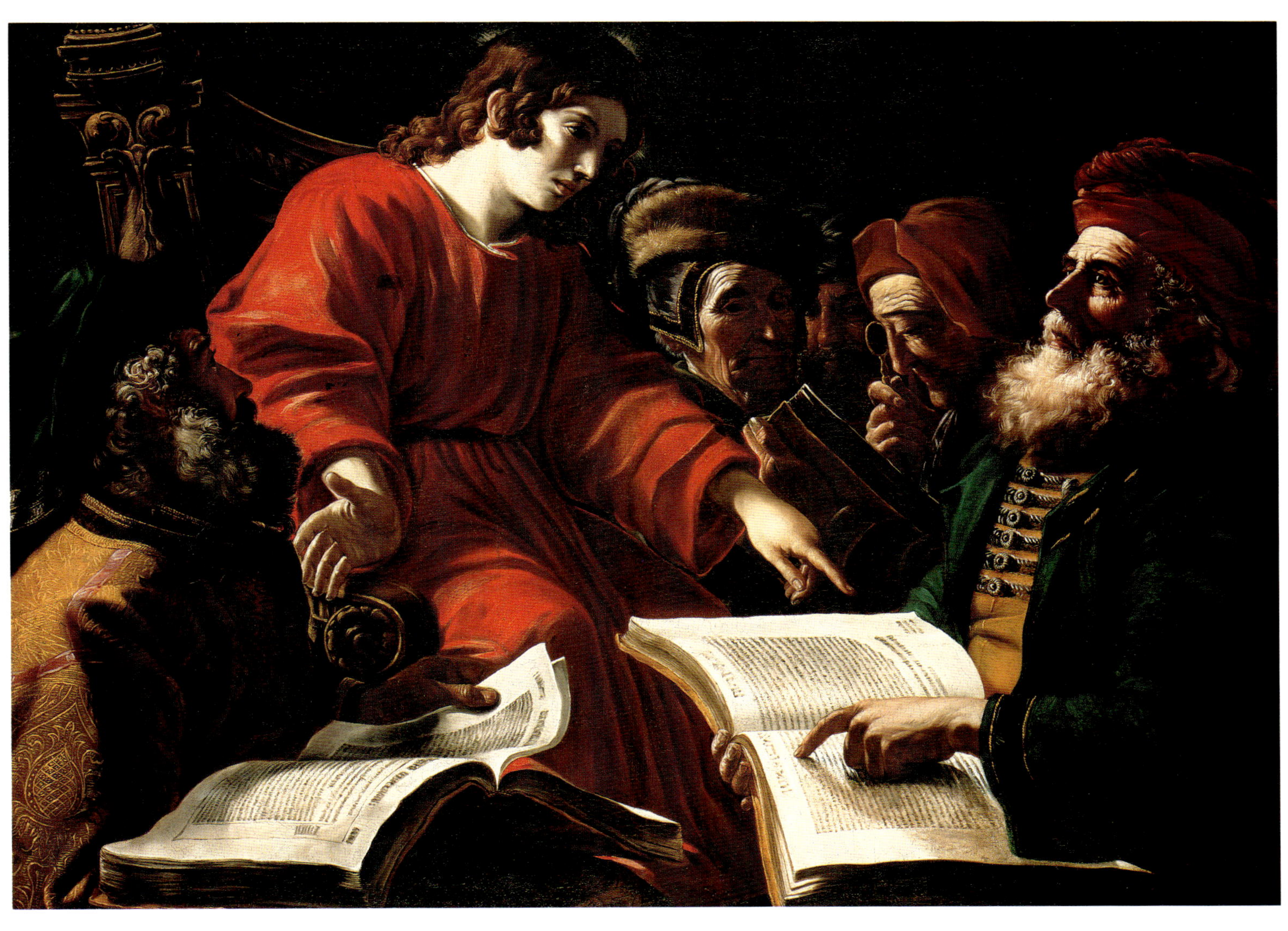

- 14 -

PASQUALE OTTINI CALLED PASQUALOTTO

Verona 1578-1630 Verona

The Conversion of Paul, c. 1613

Oil on copper

10⅜ x 8¼ inches

PROVENANCE: Gift of Mr. and Mrs. Julius Weitzner, 1959

EXHIBITIONS: Montreal 1965, no. 69 (as Felice Ottini)

REFERENCES: Pepper 1984a, no. 86.1

It is not surprising that, given Pasquale Ottini's unfamiliarity, this superb little oil on copper has been confused earlier with the work of a yet another obscure painter, Felice Ottini (d. 1697).[1] Pasquale's artistic production was first examined by Roberto Longhi in 1926, when he addressed the work of "il trio dei veronesi," namely, Marcantonio Bassetti, Alessandro Turchi, and the junior member of the three, Pasquale Ottini.[2]

Pepper placed this painting early in Ottini's career, around 1613, by comparing it to Pasquale's earliest dated work, the *Mysteries of the Rosary* for the church at Engazzà.[3] Evident in this early work is the influence of Bassetti on the figural types, which as Annamaria Conforti has noted, are painted with a *morbidezza* (softness), and whose spatial relationships are conveyed through graduated, "almost monochromatic" blue-gray tones—a technique recalling Ottini's teacher Felice Brusasorci.[4] The same can be observed of the Bob Jones *Conversion.* For example, the middleground figures, some on horseback, are painted *en grisaille* in grayish hues. Furthermore, there are similarities between the present picture and two other works by Ottini, the *Resurrection of Lazarus* in the Borghese Gallery and his engraving of the *Entombment of Christ,* the only print by Pasqualotto known to Bartsch.[5] These three compositions are constructed very much alike: in each, the foreground comprises several persons framed by standing figures on either side; the middleground contains others who are smaller. Observing the left-hand side in all three, the Christ in the Borghese painting parallels the standing elderly man holding the taper in the print and the running soldier in the present picture. As for the right-hand side, the half-reclining Lazarus is echoed by the recumbent body of Christ in the engraving and the stricken Paul in the Bob Jones copper. Indeed, it is this recurring compositional motif representing the idea of physical or spiritual rebirth that links these works. The apparition of Christ to Saul (as he was known before his conversion) on the road to Damascus should be related to a second birth. Just as Lazarus prefigured Christ's Resurrection, and Christ himself lay dead in the tomb three days only to rise again, Saul became Paul and was a new man.[6]

1. The attribution to Felice Ottini was proposed by Federico Zeri in 1960 and maintained by Creighton Gilbert in 1962, while Carlo Volpe, also in 1962, went as far afield as to suggest the name of Bartolomeo Guidobono (see cat. no. 33) "in a moment particularly nourished by Correggesque memories" (opinions on file in the Art Gallery, Bob Jones University). Stephen Pepper correctly attributes the present work to Pasquale Ottini in his 1984 catalogue.
2. "Galleria Borghese: Il trio dei veronesi: Bassetti, Turchi e Ottini" in Longhi 1967, pp. 287-93. More recently, the three artists are examined thoroughly in Verona 1974 and Mullaly 1974.
3. Pepper 1984a, p. 84.
4. Verona 1974, p. 168.
5. Bartsch 1818, XVII, pp. 207-208. Bartsch praises the engraving, writing "Le goût d'une composition ingenieuse y est réuni à l'expression des caractères et à la pureté du dessein." An impression in the British Museum is reproduced in Buffa 1983, p. 49. The Borghese *Resurrection of Lazarus* is reproduced in Longhi 1967, fig. 254.
6. In St. Paul's first Epistle to the Corinthians (1 Corinthians 15: 3-9), he writes of the resurrection of the dead, "For I delivered unto you first of all that which I also received, how that Christ died for our sins according to the Scriptures; and that he was buried, and that he rose again the third day according to the Scriptures: and that he was seen of Cephas, then of the twelve: after that... he was seen of James; then of all the Apostles. And last of all he was seen of me also, as of one born out of due time."

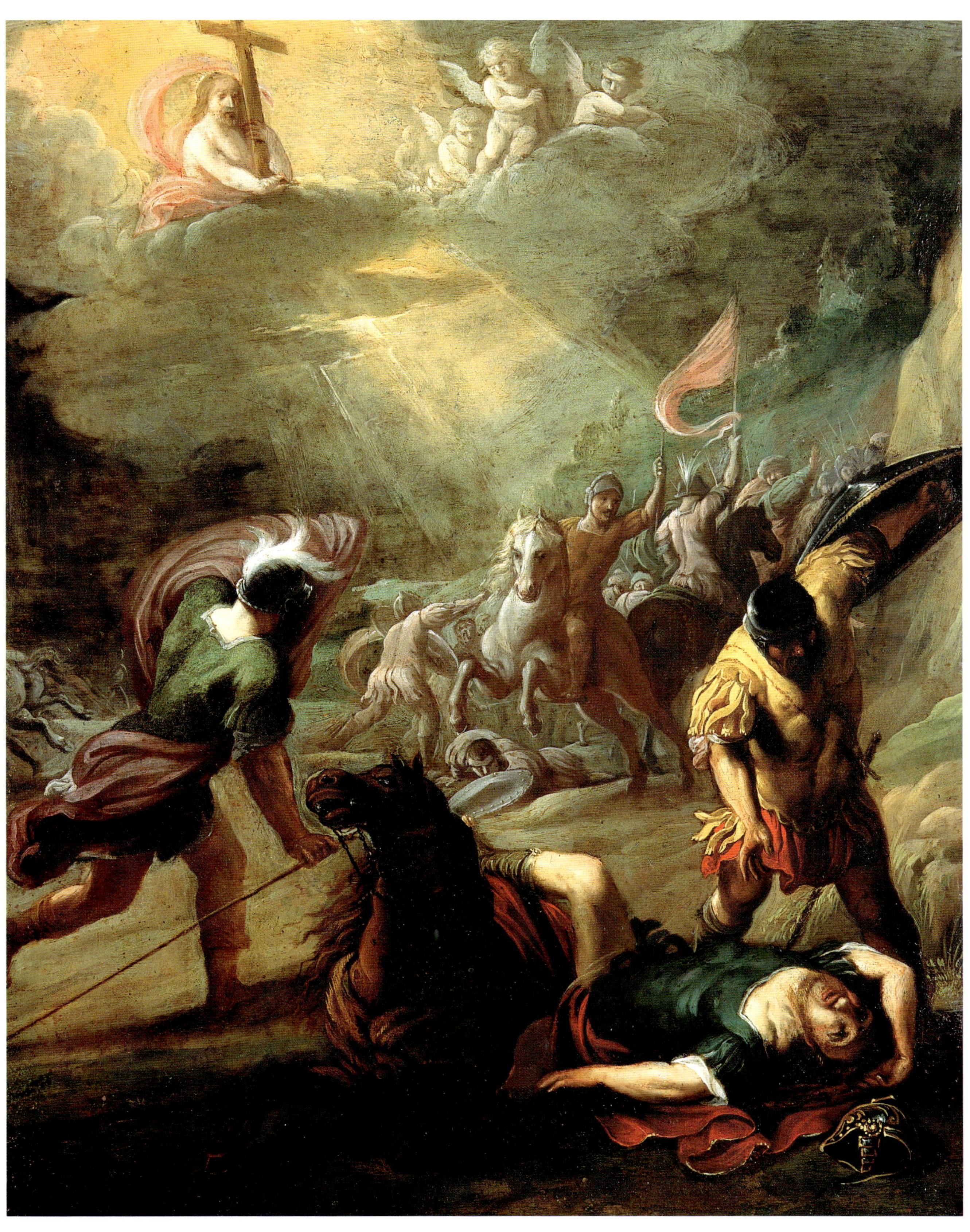

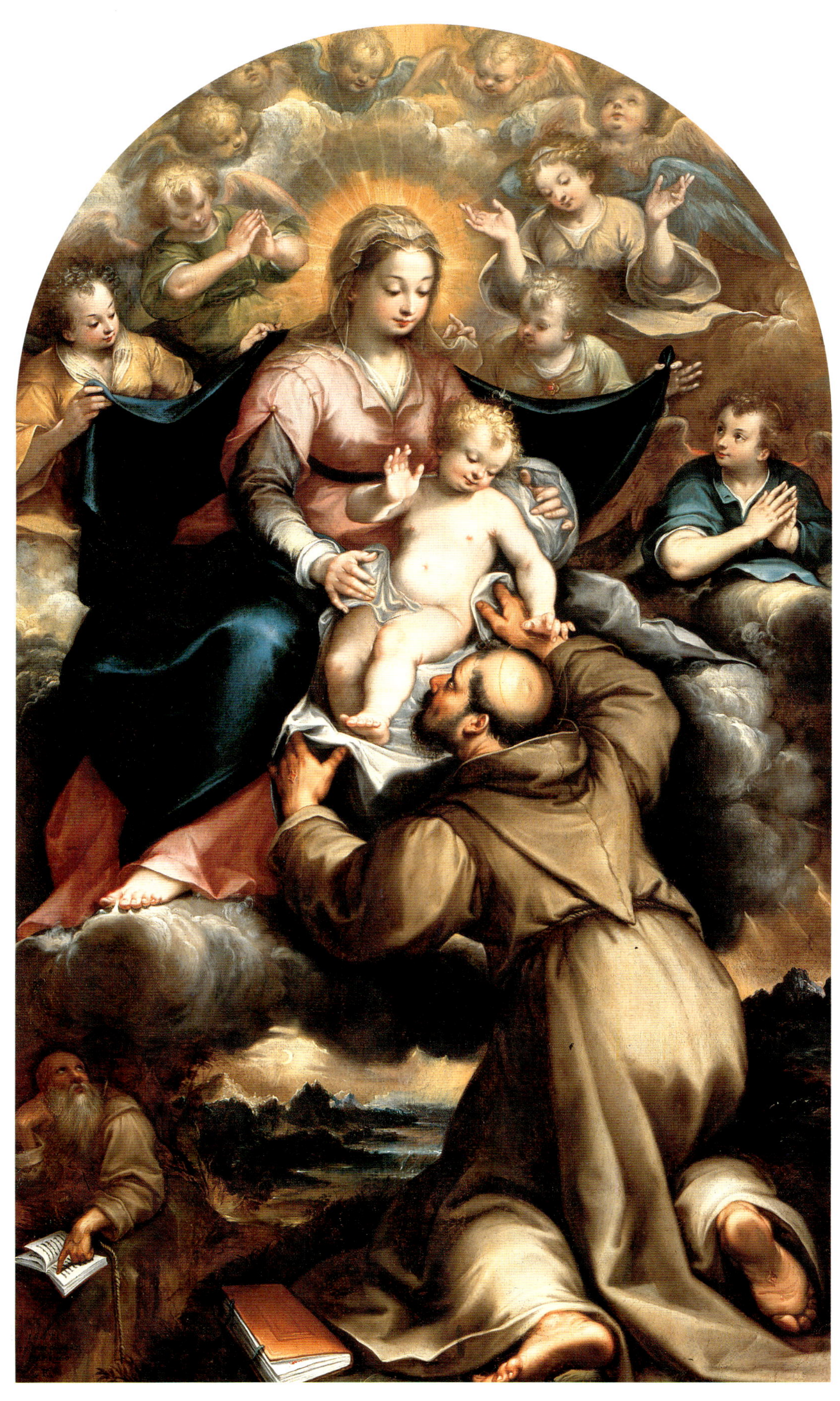

- 15 -

DENYS CALVAERT

Antwerp c. 1540-1619 Bologna

St. Francis of Assisi Adoring the Christ Child, 1607

Oil on canvas

82½ x 49 inches

Signed and dated:

1607/DIONISI CALVART/FIAMENGO/F.

PROVENANCE: Earl of Shrewsbury, Alton Towers, before 1838; Thos. Agnew & Sons, Manchester, between 1851 and 1862; [1] Julius Weitzner, New York, 1958; Gift of Mr. and Mrs. W.J. Greer, 1959

EXHIBITIONS: Raleigh 1984, no. 6; Washington 1986, no. 17

REFERENCES: Pepper 1984a, no. 36.1

Denys Calvaert, in this important and quite beautiful picture (one of the few by him in this country), referred to himself as a Fleming ("Fiamengo"), though by the time it was painted he had lived in Italy for fifty years. Calvaert's Flemish origins are evident in the fantastic landscape with mountains more at home in Joachim Patinir's *weltlandschafts.* However, the painting's iconography is distinctly Italian as are many of the influences reflected in the picture. Although Calvaert studied with the artistic generation preceding the reformers, the Carracci (that is, Prospero Fontana and Lorenzo Sabatini), later influences, such as the Carracci and their interest in Correggio, and the aesthetic of Calvaert's contemporary Federico Barocci, can be discerned in his work. Moreover, Calvaert first trained several of the Carracci's greatest students: Domenichino (cat. no. 17), Guido Reni (cat. nos. 18, 19), and Francesco Albani.

The popularity of St. Francis of Assisi during the Counter-Reformation is demonstrated by innumerable images—usually emphasizing the ecstatic, mystical nature of the saint—produced during the late sixteenth and seventeenth centuries.[2] St. Francis, the alter ego of Christ, was a potent reminder of the Catholic Church's emphasis on piety, self-denial, and contemplation.[3] Painted Franciscan imagery may be placed into at least three groups: the inclusion of the saint with others in a *sacra conversazione;* large-scale depictions of scenes from his life and visions, for example, Francis's stigmatization or the apparition of the Virgin and Child, such as here; and small-scale devotional works.[4] The theme of *St. Francis Adoring the Christ Child* is somewhat uncommon and is not described in the early sources of the saint's life. The story of the Virgin and Child appearing one night to Francis in a vision probably derives from the fourteenth-century *Fioretti di San Francesco,* or *Little Flowers of St. Francis,* but as Steel has noted, in that account the vision occurred to Brother Conrad of Offida.[5] This depiction probably first appeared around 1590 in Bolognese churches of the Capuchins—an independent Franciscan order founded in 1529—as an attempt to "promote the emotional and mystical side of Franciscan spirituality... creat[ing] a new iconography that stressed the ecstatic visions of Franciscan saints."[6]

The Bob Jones painting by Calvaert reflects several decades of pictorial development of this theme in Bologna. While Annibale Carracci treated the subject on a few occasions in the 1590s, his cousin, Ludovico, who exerted as much if not more influence over painting in Bologna, frequently painted Franciscan imagery, beginning with one of the earliest depictions of the subject, his *Vision of St. Francis* of 1583-85 in the Rijksmuseum, Amsterdam. In two later pictures, both in the Pinacoteca, Bologna, Francis appears with three other saints in the *Bargellini Madonna* of 1588 and with St. Jerome in the *Madonna degli Scalzi* of 1590-93. Of these three, the early Amsterdam painting seems to be a close antecedent to the Bob Jones picture, although Ludovico's emphasis is more narrative with its comparatively naturalistic rendering, as contrasted with Calvaert's more iconic, and, admittedly, conventional presentation of the subject. Similar to both works are the appearance in the background of Francis's companion, Brother Leo, and a moonlit landscape.

However, Ludovico's later altarpiece of 1591 for the Capuchin church in Cento (now in the Pinacoteca there) provides the best analogy with the Bob Jones painting. In the Cento altarpiece, the Virgin and Child accompanied by St. Joseph and two angels appear to St. Francis and his companion. The scene takes place outdoors (the façade of a building is visible at left) against a stormy night sky. Indeed, Ludovico's altarpiece is a quintessential example of the hybrid iconography employed in depictions of St. Francis and the Christ Child. The composition conflates three "events": Christ's miraculous appearance to St. Anthony of Padua (in the Cento painting, the Virgin and Child are enthroned on an altar situated on a raised, paved dais);[7] and two accounts from the *Little Flowers of St. Francis*—Brother Conrad's vision and Francis receiving the stigmata.[8]

As the town of Cento is only 17 kilometers northwest of Bologna, Calvaert must have known Ludovico's renowned altarpiece. From this composition, the Flemish artist derived the full-length figure of St. Francis, facing away from the viewer and toward the heavenly vision, the vertiginous perspective, and above all, the unusual subject matter itself, with its inclusion of the two conflated episodes from the *Little Flowers of St. Francis,* the stigmatization and the vision of the Virgin and Child.[9] It should be noted that David Steel has pointed out a preparatory drawing in an American private collection close to the Bob Jones painting.[10]

Calvaert's *St. Francis of Assisi Adoring the Christ Child* may be better understood in light of Bolognese painting of the time and the trend of the Capuchin order to commission paintings that emphasized events from the *Little Flowers,* resulting in an atypical and hybrid iconography. Thus it is likely that Calvaert's altarpiece was painted for a Capuchin church in Bologna. What is striking about the Bob Jones altarpiece is that it shows Calvaert responding to a contemporary theme, probably at the instigation of the patron, but adapting these recently developed ideas to his familiar, more mannerist style.

1. According to a label attached to the relining, which reads in part, "Thos. Agnew & Sons," the style of the firm's name that came into use after 1850 (*Agnew's 1817-1967,* London, 1967, p. 11). The label's inscription includes the royal warrants of Queen Victoria and Prince Albert, the royal consort, who died in 1861, hence providing a *terminus ante quem.*
2. Rome 1982, p. 48: "The imagery of St. Francis in the Counter-Reformation is based on three principal themes: 'withdrawal, meditation and ecstasy.' "
3. The most important overview of Franciscan imagery is given in Rome 1982. See also Askew 1969 for an examination of one particular aspect of Franciscan iconography.
4. The private nature of these devotional images is reinforced by their compositional format, often consisting of bust- or half-length figures. Paintings in this category served as effective vehicles for instilling in the viewer contrition and promoting meditation. Furthermore, Cigoli, Reni, Strozzi, Guercino, and others employed the ubiquitous iconography of the kneeling or reclining saint with the attributes of the cross, skull, and book equally for Francis, the Magdalen, Jerome, and Paul the Hermit, to name just the most prominent (see also cat. no. 12).
5. Raleigh 1984, p. 34. That this source is the origin for the later transposition to Francis has been independently confirmed by Blume (1991, pp. 52, 54).
6. Washington 1984, p. 388. Elsewhere, Charles Dempsey suggests that the theme should be considered in the context of the Capuchin reform of the Franciscan Observance, saying that "Capuchin devotion was rooted in a return to the practical austerity and spiritual unworldliness of Saint Francis himself, and the directness and intensity of Ludovico's portrayal [referring to the Amsterdam picture cited below]. . . blends natural simplicity of representation with a powerful mysticism." New York 1985, pp. 120, 122 (for more on the Capuchins, see also Keith Christiansen, p. 97).
7. See Washington 1984, p. 388. See also cat. no. 20.
8. A contemporary example, Barocci's *Stigmatization of St. Francis* of 1594-95 painted for the Capuchin church in Urbino (now in the Galleria Nazionale delle Marche, Urbino; New York 1985, pp. 97-99), has many of the same elements as Ludovico's and Calvaert's representations of the mystical appearance of the Virgin and Child to St. Francis. Barocci's scene also takes place at night, shows Brother Leo with a book in deep concentration, and shares the source of the *Little Flowers.* It stands to reason that by representing the two parallel incidents in a similar way, the appropriation of Brother Conrad of Offida's mystical experience for Francis was less obvious.
9. Calvaert painted another version of this composition, now in the Bologna Pinacoteca, which has in common several elements with this full-scale altarpiece; see Rome 1982, p. 76, fig. 18. As an easel picture, however, the Bologna painting depicts Francis and his companion in half-length. In this version, Francis's stigmatization is quite prominent.
10. Raleigh 1984, p. 34.

~ 16 ~

GIOVANNI LANFRANCO

Parma 1582-1647 Rome

St. Cecilia, 1620-21

Oil on canvas

28 x 41 inches

PROVENANCE: acquired probably in the 1620s by Natale Rondinini (d. 1627), Rome, remaining with the family until before 1807; [1] Frederick and George Perkins, sold Christie's, 14 June 1890, lot 47 (as Domenichino); V.J. Watney, London by 1915 (as Caravaggio); O.V. Watney, Cornbury Park and Berkeley Square, London, sold Christie's, London, 23 June 1967, lot 19; Christie's, London, 10 March 1978, lot 2; Julius Weitzner, London, 1981

REFERENCES: Mirimonde 1974, p. 150; Pepper 1984a, no. 67.1; De Grazia and Schleier 1994, pp. 73, 77-78; De Grazia forthcoming

The Bob Jones *St. Cecilia,* despite some old damage, has previously been recognized as being by Lanfranco.[2] Recently restored, the artist's intentions, once obscured by dirt, yellowed varnish, and extensive overpainting, are now amply revealed. Not only is the painting a work of the highest quality, it also has a significant place in the popular iconography of St. Cecilia and in the development of painting in Rome in the first half of the seventeenth century.

Schleier dates the picture to 1620-21, placing it and four other works in an "intermediate" period between Lanfranco's painting in a "Borgiannesque phase" in the Buongiovanni chapel (1616) and his "most baroque phase" in the Sacchetti chapel (1623-24).[3] The painting must be considered in the context of the work of other prominent painters in Rome in the 1620s, namely, Domenichino, Reni, and Guercino, all of whom took up with increasing frequency the theme of St. Cecilia. It is, however, closest to the *St. Cecilia* of the same horizontal format and of similar dimensions in the National Gallery of Art, Washington, previously thought to be solely by Orazio Gentileschi, but recently restored in part to Lanfranco's oeuvre.[4] In both works, Cecilia is shown in half-length seated to the left, playing a keyboard. Decorating the sides of the instrument in the Greenville picture are what appear to be scenes from the life of Christ: the short end shows Christ between Mary and Joseph in the carpenter's shop and on the keyboard side, the Nativity. In the Washington painting, this keyboard is a cembalo or virginal (a plucked instrument related to the harpsichord), while in the present work it is an apositif organ (a small portable table version of the pipe organ). The Washington picture shows only one angel, holding a sheet of music; his counterpart in the Greenville canvas looks away and allows the sheet music to fall, while a second angel with a violin regards the paper. In neither composition does St. Cecilia read the musical score, emphasizing the message that her inspiration is divine.

It is instructive to compare the Bob Jones Lanfranco with the treatment of the subject by the artist's great rival Domenichino, with whom, however, he studied in the Carracci academy and worked with in Rome. Domenichino's composition, with a full-length seated Cecilia directing playful putti, was finished by Antonio Barbalonga during the same general period as our picture, that is, in 1623-30. The figure of the saint in the Domenichino/Barbalonga version, in the Palazzo Pallavicini-Rospigliosi, Rome,[5] bears some similarity to the Bob Jones *Cecilia* in pose and physical likeness. However, Domenichino's saint evinces a classical ideal while Lanfranco's portrayal of the young martyr, in its tenebristic composition, is more palpable (indeed, Schleier remarked that it is "decidedly a portrait").[6] In Domenichino's slightly earlier *St. Cecilia* (c. 1617-18) in the Louvre, the saint is seen standing, in half-length, playing a viola da gamba accompanied by a putto holding aloft a book of music. Here she appears in a turban, similar to the headdress seen in the same master's S. Luigi dei Francesi frescoes of 1612-15 and the Persian and Cumaen Sibyls in the Wallace and Borghese collections, respectively. In fact, the headdress, or lack thereof, is one of the chief iconographic differences between Lanfranco's *Cecilia* and other images of the saint popular at the time. While the turban used in depictions of the ancient sibyls (in paintings by Domenichino, Reni, and late works by Guercino) doubtless refers to their Eastern origins, Maryvelma Smith O'Neil has argued that the turban of St. Cecilia results from circumstances surrounding her disinterment.[7] This event in the ancient basilica of S. Cecilia in Trastevere on 20 October 1599 resulted in the cult of St. Cecilia in the seventeenth century, and must be seen within the context of the Counter-Reformation's

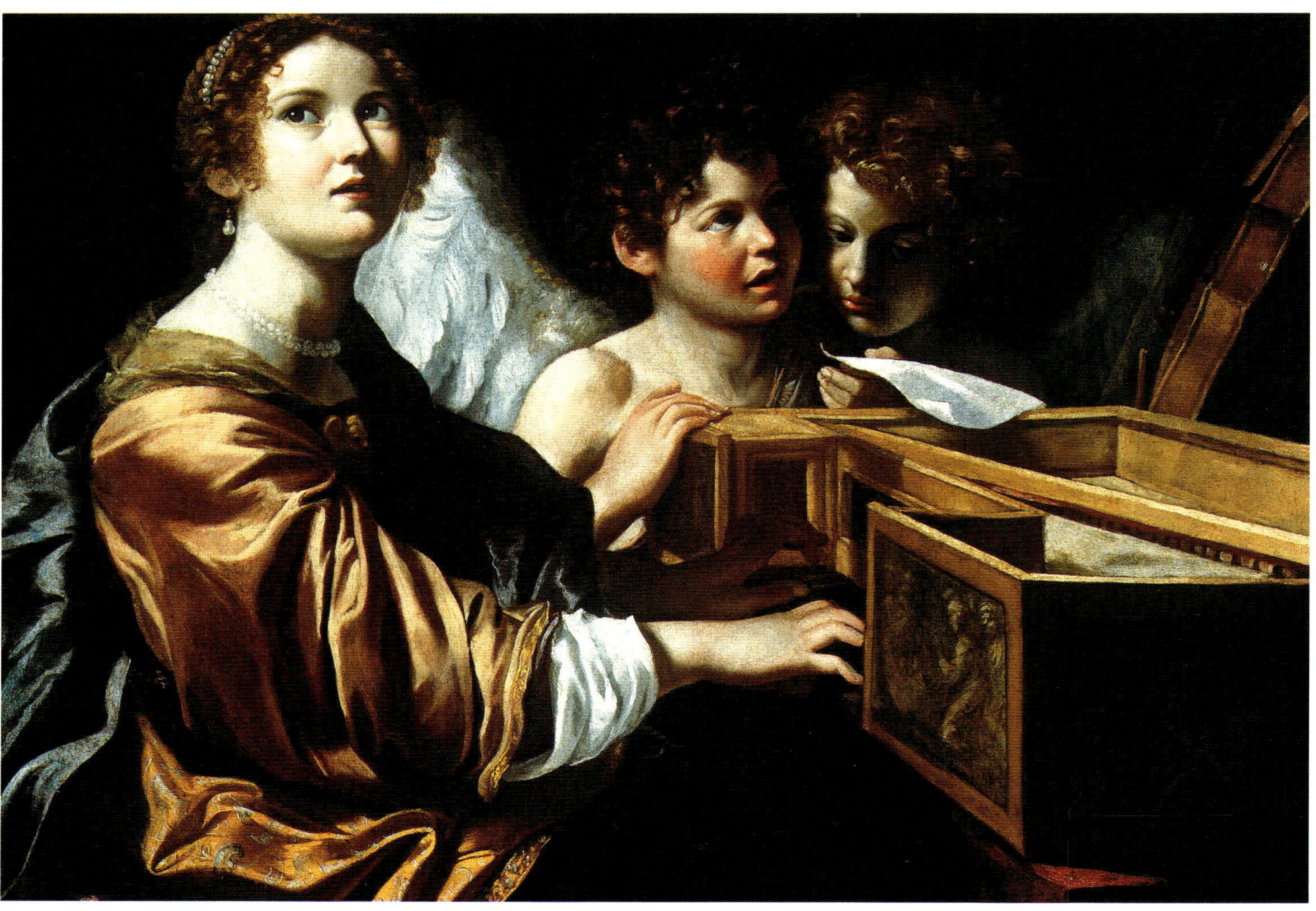

revival of Early Christian churches and saints, an effort led by Cardinal Cesare Baronio and the antiquarian Antonio Bosio. Cardinal Sfondrato, responsible for the exhumation of the saint, had Bosio record the event, which he did with amazement at the miraculous state of preservation of Cecilia's body. Subsequently, in the redecoration of the church, Sfondrato commissioned from Stefano Maderno a sculpture of Cecilia, which was mounted above her new tomb in 1600, and from Francesco Vanni in 1605 a fresco—both of which showed the body as it was discovered in 1599. In each of these images, a veil is wrapped around her head.[8] Thereafter, the turban became associated with St. Cecilia, as is evident from many portrayals by Domenichino and Guercino (the Louvre and Dulwich), as well as, most importantly, from the famous painting of 1606 by Guido Reni, now in the Norton Simon collection, which Reni painted for the same Cardinal Sfondrato. Lanfranco, however, seems not to have employed this motif in his depictions of the saint.

1. Natale Rondinini formed an important collection in early seventeenth-century Rome, which is reflected in an inventory of 1662 included in the will of his daughter-in-law Felice Rondinini, who noted that his wish was to keep the collection intact. Rondinini's taste ran from the Venetians Bellini, the Bassanos, and Titian to contemporary painters in Rome, both the Carracci followers, Reni, Domenichino, and Lanfranco, and the Caravaggesque realists, Gentileschi and Caroselli (Salerno 1965, pp. 31, 35). It is quite possible, given the number of Gentileschi and Lanfranco pictures in the collection, that Natale patronized the artists directly and obtained from Lanfranco himself the painting listed in 1662 as "Un quadro in Tela d'Imperatore per Longo con una S. Cecilia che sona di mano di GIO/LANFRANCO con cornice dorata nelle stanze del Cardinale" (Salerno 1965, p. 280). This picture does not appear in the 1807 valuation (Salerno 1965, pp. 283-301). Franca Camiz has associated an entry in the 1741 inventory of Alessandro Rondinini,

Natale's great-grandson, which lists an "Altro tela d'Imperatore rappresentante s. Cecilia in atto di sonare il Cimbalo con due angeli con cornice liscia dorata di mano del Lanfranco. . . " (De Grazia and Schleier 1994, p. 73). Here the painting described is even more clearly identifiable as the Bob Jones picture.

2. Schleier (1980a, pp. 22-38) discusses it in an article on paintings produced for Tuscan patrons.
3. Schleier 1980a, pp. 25-26.
4. This painting, datable to around 1621, is catalogued in Bissell 1981, p. 166. It has recently been reevaluated by Schleier and De Grazia, who have concluded that the painting is in fact by both Gentileschi and Lanfranco, as, interestingly, it was seen in the seventeenth century. The 1662 Palazzo Rondinini inventory (cited in note 1 above) includes "Un quadro largo Palmi cinque alto tre con una Santa Cecilia con le teste di mano del GENTILESCHI, il resto di GIO/LANFRANCHI con cornice intagliata e indorata nella Galeria del S.r Cardinale" (Salerno 1965, p. 280). Later, the painting is recorded by Giuseppe Ghezzi in 1694 and 1710 (Bissell 1981, p. 166). Salerno (1965, p. 280) implied that the Rondinini entry referred to the Washington picture. Diane De Grazia (oral communication, 29 September 1993) informed me that as a result of her and Schleier's work, they believe Gentileschi was responsible for the heads of Cecilia and the angel and the saint's bodice. Lanfranco painted in the hands (this is borne out by comparison with Cecilia's hands in the Bob Jones picture; in both versions the saint's fingers have the same elastic quality), the blue drapery, the angel's wings, and the organ. This painting will be discussed fully in the forthcoming catalogue of the National Gallery of Art's seventeenth- and eighteenth-century Italian paintings and has just been the subject of an article by De Grazia and Schleier (1994).
5. See Spear 1982, pp. 260-61.
6. Schleier 1980a, p. 26. For an example by Bernardo Strozzi of an instance of a sitter depicted as St. Cecilia, see Rosand 1981.
7. Smith O'Neil 1985.
8. Smith O'Neil (1985, p. 17) proposes that this motif resulted from the linens laying at the top of her headless body, which concealed the fact of her decapitation (the author reminds us that Pope Paschal I in the ninth century had her severed head removed and placed in a reliquary).

- 17 -

DOMENICO ZAMPIERI CALLED IL DOMENICHINO

Bologna 1581-1641 Naples

St. John the Evangelist, c. 1625-28

Oil on canvas

38¾ x 29⅛ inches

PROVENANCE: Chevalier de Lorraine, Paris, 1698; Duc d'Orléans, Palais Royal, Paris, until 1792; Earl of Carlisle, Castle Howard, 1798; Mary van Berg, New York; Sotheby's, London, 25 June 1969, lot 97; Julius Weitzner, London, 1969

EXHIBITIONS: London 1798; London 1851, no. 11; Manchester 1857, no. 341; London 1938, no. 289; Raleigh 1984, no. 13; Austin 1990

REFERENCES: Pepper 1984a, no. 133.1

As well as being one of Domenichino's rare easel paintings,[1] the sheer beauty and expressiveness of the Bob Jones *St. John the Evangelist* make it one of the finest works in the collection, and arguably one of the most important Seicento pictures in America; indeed, it has been received with critical acclaim throughout the centuries.[2]

The classicizing composition—Raphaelesque in its clarity and refinement—depicts the half-length figure of St. John the Evangelist, his eyes turned heavenward, accompanied by his attributes, the eagle and the cup and snake, which allude to his having withstood poison as proof of his faith. The scrolls and book represent his writings, which include the eponymous Gospel and the Book of Revelation.

There exist two other depictions of St. John the Evangelist by Domenichino. One is among four frescoed pendentives in S. Andrea delle Valle depicting the Evangelists, painted between 1622 and 1627. The other is a *St. John* of about 1627-29, formerly belonging to Vincenzo Giustiniani, now at Glyndebourne (presently on loan to the National Gallery, London). The latter derives from the former, particularly in its pose, and, while the Glyndebourne canvas is monumental in its own right, the face of the Evangelist is painted more painstakingly than the visage in the S. Andrea fresco, which is broadly and powerfully developed. The Bob Jones *St. John* owes its design to Domenichino's *Cumaen Sibyl* of about 1616 in the Borghese Gallery and to the other representations of sibyls that descend from it (that in the Wallace collection is datable to 1623-25, also ex-Orléans, and in the same 1798 sale as the present picture; another in the Capitoline Museum is dated to 1620-23).

One drawing in black chalk of the head of St. John in the Royal Library at Windsor Castle has been associated with the Bob Jones picture.[3] Another sheet also at Windsor, which shows studies of hands, has been previously connected only to the Borghese *Cumaen Sibyl.* Although Domenichino may have consulted that picture when painting the Bob Jones composition, so great is the similarity between this sheet of studies and St. John's hand, book, and scroll in the present canvas (and its divergences from it no more significant than those in the Borghese *Sibyl*) that it is possible that the artist referred to the drawing in preparing the Greenville *St. John the Evangelist.*[4]

Domenichino's iconographically traditional, sweet-faced, young St. John also conforms to the figural convention of "lo studio," or the scholar. In his popular emblem book, *Iconologia,* Cesare Ripa describes the scholar as a seated youth with pallid face, open book, and pen in hand.[5] By depicting the ecstatic, revelation-receiving Apostle as this type, Domenichino also alluded to John as the author of Holy Scriptures.

1. Richard Spear (1989a, p. 5) notes the relative rarity of the artist's easel pictures, as Domenichino chose to work more often in fresco.
2. For the picture's *fortuna critica,* see Spear 1982, pp. 114, 262-63.
3. Pope-Hennessy 1948, no. 1428; Spear 1979, p. 255, pl. 26; Spear 1982, no. 93.
4. There are examples of Domenichino returning to drawings after an interval of a year, and sketching out new compositional ideas on them. Spear himself points out just such an instance with this precise sheet, which has studies on it dating from 1615-16, and on whose verso Domenichino drew the hand and book and scroll studies later, in 1616-17 (Pope-Hennessy 1948, no. 100v; Spear 1968, p. 119, pl. 11; Spear 1982, no. 51, pl. 172). It is plausible, then, that the artist reused previously drawn studies for later works.
5. Ripa ed. Buscardi 1618, pp. 193-94.

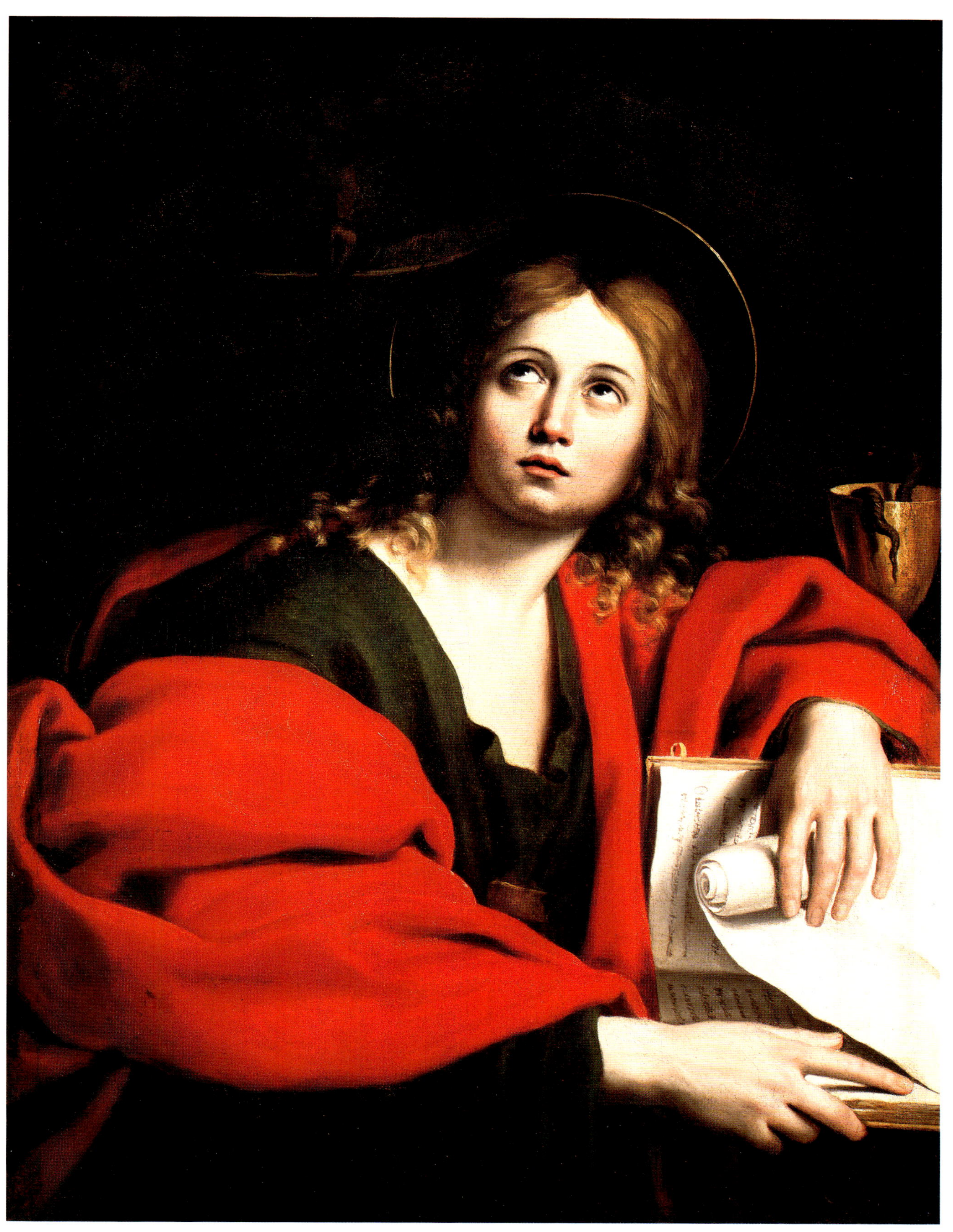

- 18 / 19 -

GUIDO RENI

Bologna 1575-1642 Bologna

St. Matthew and the Angel and *St. Mark, c. 1630s*

Oil on canvas

31¼ x 26 inches each

PROVENANCE: Duke of Beaufort, Badminton; Sotheby's, London, 5 July 1967, lot 75; Julius Weitzner, London, 1967

EXHIBITIONS: Badminton Church, 1908-67 (all four Evangelists by Reni); Raleigh 1984, nos. 31, 32 (all four); Los Angeles 1988, nos. 28, 29 (*Matthew* and *Luke*); Austin 1990 (*Matthew* only)

REFERENCES: Pepper 1984a, nos. 98.1, 98.2; Pepper 1984b, nos. 73-76; Pepper 1988, no. 136; Florence 1989, p. 110; Spear 1989b, p. 371

Guido Reni's depictions of the four Evangelists, Matthew, Mark, Luke, and John (Figs. 1-4), of which the first two are exhibited here, formed a series meant either for devotional contemplation or decoration and very possibly for both. As has been noted, these much copied *Four Evangelists* appear to comprise the only known complete series of such images by the artist.[1] There has been some discrepancy in the dating of these works. While Steel and Pepper in their catalogues of the Bob Jones collection dated the paintings to the early 1630s,[2] Pepper reversed himself later in his monograph on the artist and placed them in the years 1620-21.[3] Giovanna Degli Esposti concurred with a dating in the early 1620s.[4] However, Pepper has recently returned to his initial dating of the Evangelist series, specifying the years 1632-33.[5] This last opinion is the most convincing given the summary technique, broad brushstrokes, and the rich impasto seen in these pictures, all of which point to a date between 1630 and 1635.

Pictorial suites of Evangelists and Apostles were popular in the Sei- and Settecento. A contemporary example is the previously discussed painting by Domenichino of *St. John the Evangelist* (cat. no. 17; although it is not known to be one of four, its format suggests it may have been). Another Bolognese series is Guercino's *Four Evangelists,* formerly in the Este collection and now at Dresden. To the south, Jusepe de Ribera is known to have produced

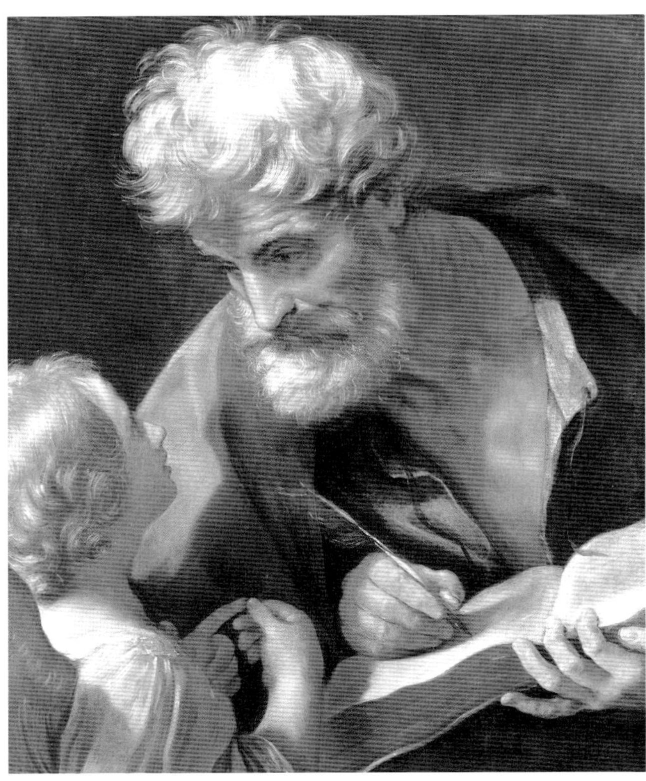

FIGURE ONE. *St. Matthew and the Angel.* Art Gallery, Bob Jones University. Photograph courtesy of Bob Jones University.

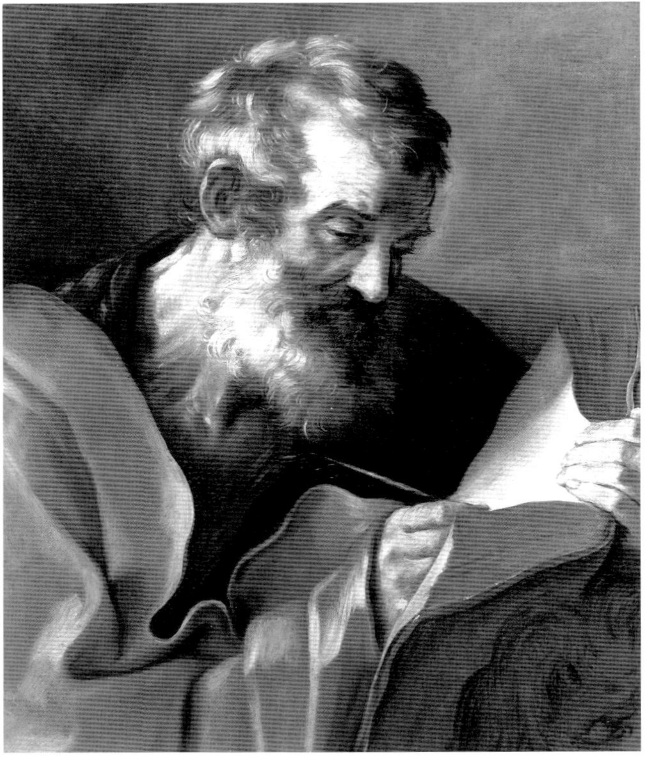

FIGURE TWO. *St. Mark.* Art Gallery, Bob Jones University. Photograph courtesy of Bob Jones University.

an Evangelist series in the years 1616-19 for Prince Marcantonio Doria, as well as several sets of the Apostles, the earliest of which is datable to around the same time as the Doria commission and some of which survive in the Quadreria dei Girolamini in Naples. In the eighteenth century, Benedetto Luti created a series in pastels, and later Pompeo Batoni painted an Apostle series for Count Merenda of Forlì which included the *St. James the Greater* (cat. no. 39).

The origin of Reni's series of half-length figures (which also included sibyls; once again like Domenichino) is reputedly not very exalted. The seventeenth-century biographer Malvasia related that, in order to cope with enormous gambling debts, Guido would paint great numbers of these figures and heads at an hourly rate, and that others would take advantage of this and sell them for twice as much. One such client "contented himself with the *Four Evangelists* and the *Three Sibyls* . . . and when they were scarcely dry . . . sent them off to France under the pretext that they were some of Guido's most excellent work, which was very little to his credit."[6] Steel has rightly pointed out the uneven quality between the four pictures in the Bob Jones collection, which seems to substantiate Malvasia's anecdote.[7] The artist is at his most brilliant in the breathtaking and painterly yet delicate passages seen here in the *St. Matthew* and *St. Mark.*

1. Los Angeles 1988, p. 228. The attraction and influence of Guido's Evangelist series is reflected, for example, in the *St. John the Evangelist* by the still underrated Sienese master, Bernardino Mei (art market, Florence). While Mei's composition borrows the iconographic type established by Domenichino (see cat. no. 17), as Giovanni Pagliarulo has pointed out there are stylistic and pictorial affinities with the *St. Luke* at Bob Jones University (Fig. 3; Florence 1989, p. 110).
2. Steel in Raleigh 1984, p. 110; Pepper 1984a, pp. 97-98.
3. Pepper 1984b, p. 241.
4. Los Angeles 1988, p. 228.
5. Pepper 1988, p. 277.
6. Malvasia trans. Enggass 1678, p. 91.
7. Raleigh 1984, p. 110. Richard Spear (1989b, p. 371) commented on the *Matthew* and *Luke* on the occasion of their exhibition in 1988-89, suggesting that they "are perhaps by two hands" and noting that of the two, only the *Matthew* is on Reni's typical reddish ground.

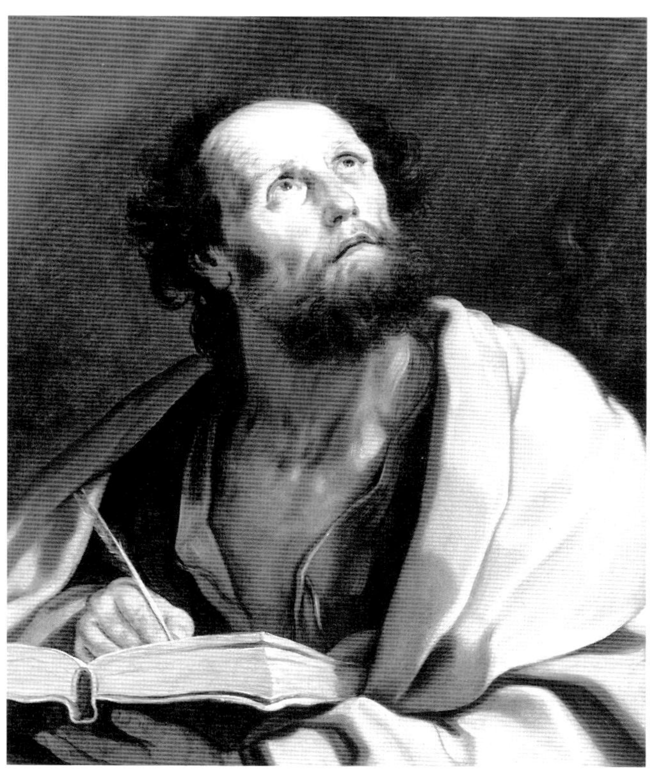

FIGURE THREE. *St. Luke.* Art Gallery, Bob Jones University. Photograph courtesy of Bob Jones University.

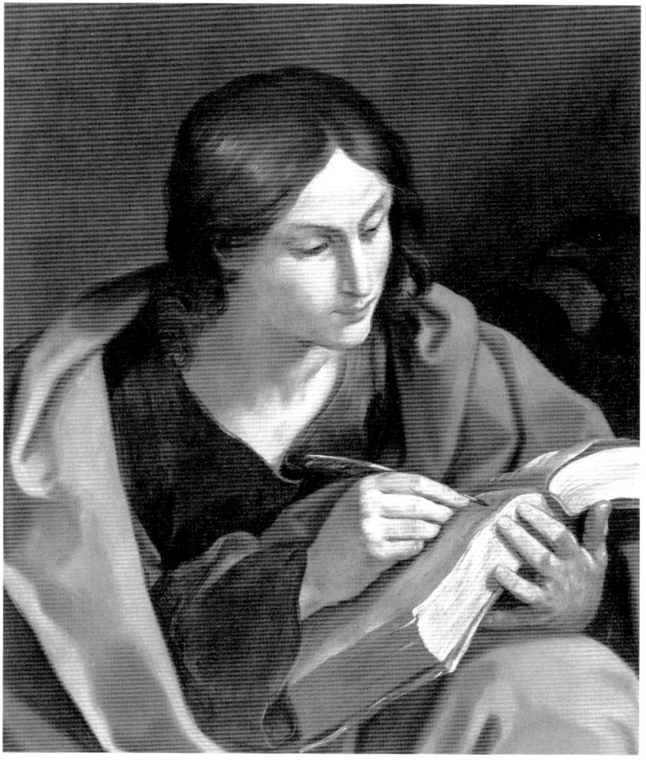

FIGURE FOUR. *St. John the Evangelist.* Art Gallery, Bob Jones University. Photograph courtesy of Bob Jones University.

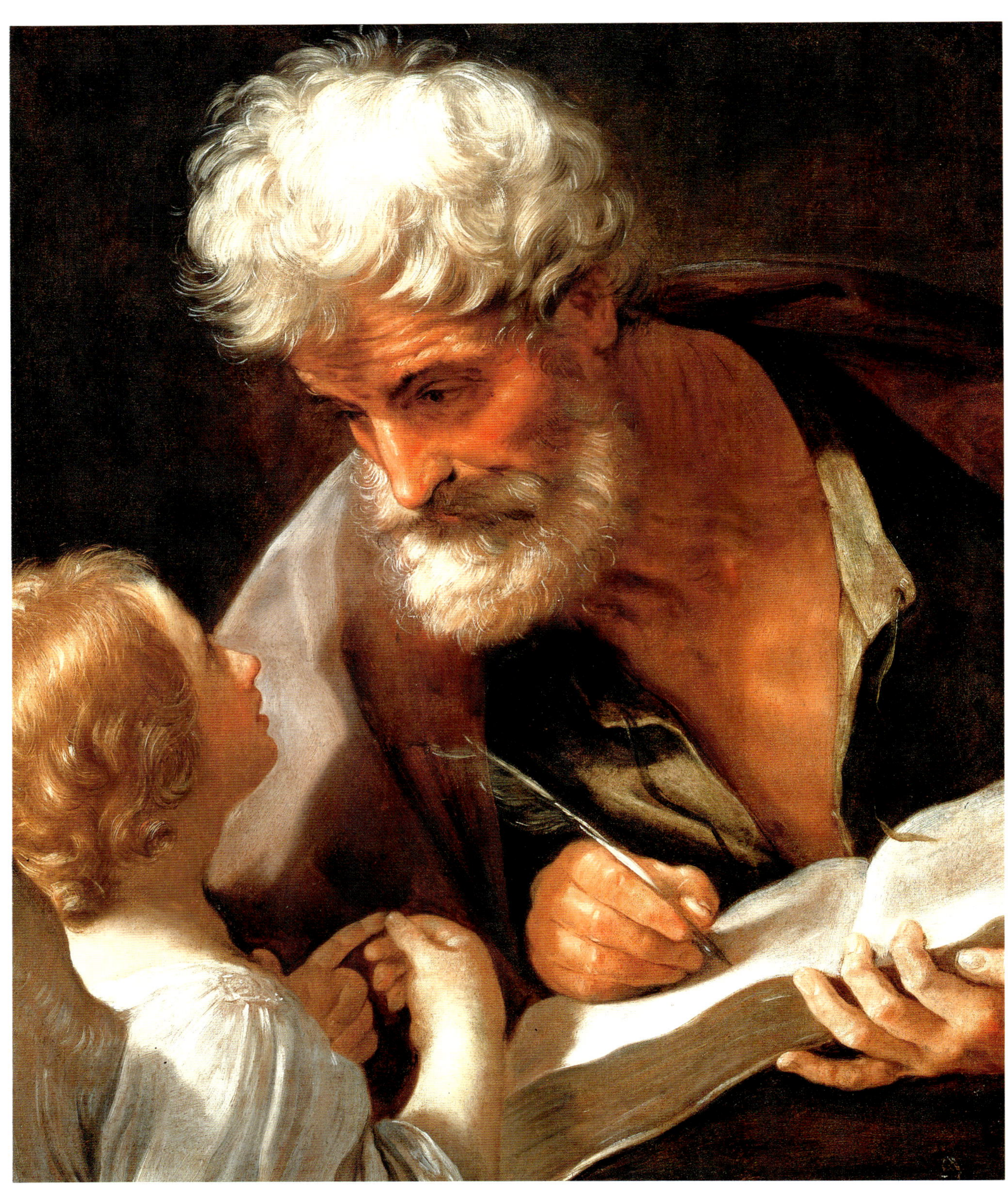

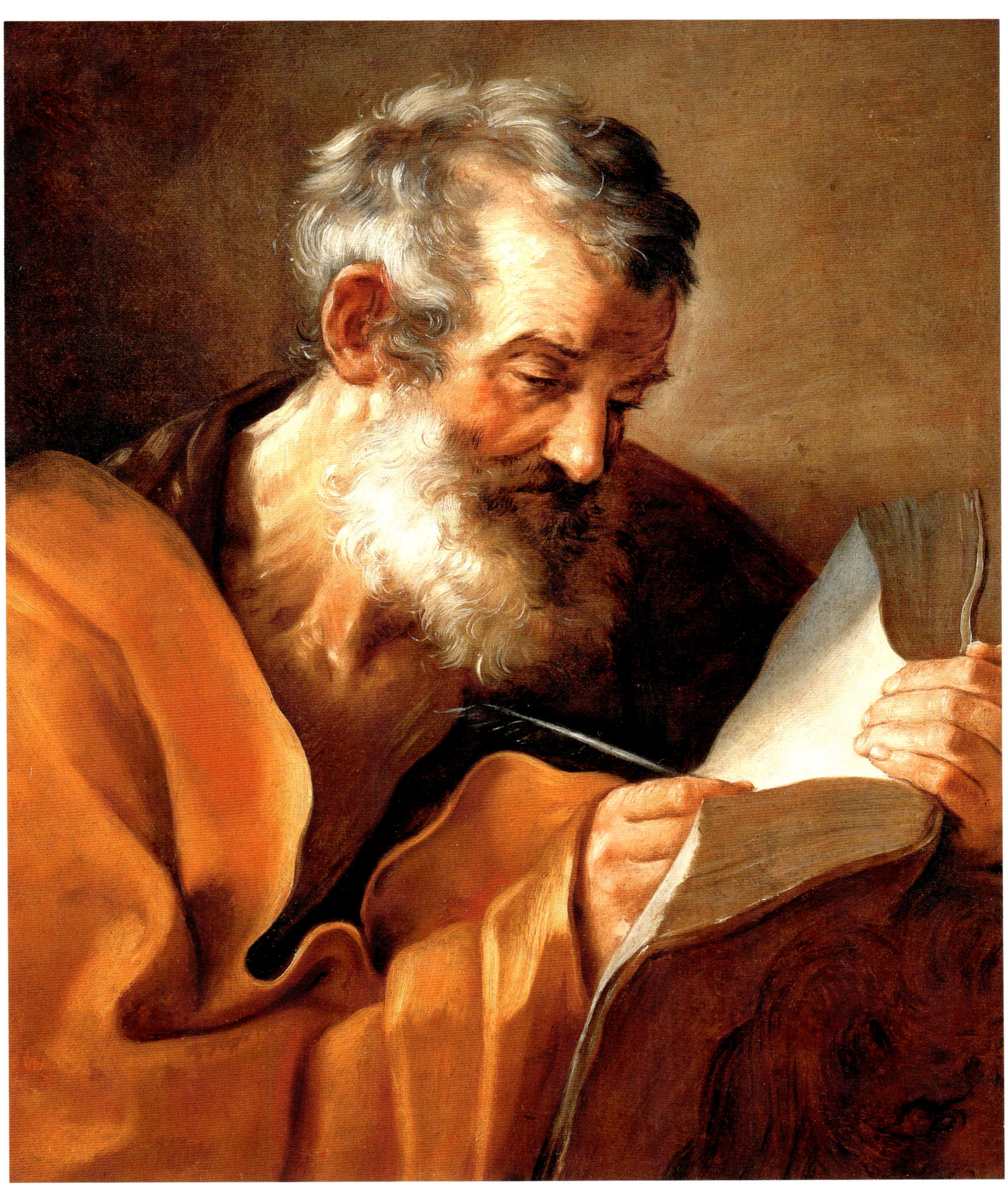

- 2 0 -

GIOVANNI FRANCESCO BARBIERI CALLED IL GUERCINO

Cento 1591-1666 Bologna

St. Anthony of Padua, 1658 or 1663

Oil on canvas

58 x 66¼ inches

PROVENANCE: Pier Luigi Pecana, Verona, 1658, or alternatively, the Chiesa dei Cappucini, Verona, from 1663 until after 1737; Julius Weitzner, London, 1973

REFERENCES: Pepper 1984a, no. 63.2 and p. 318; Salerno 1988, p. 391; Stone 1991, p. 322

The present picture, never before exhibited outside Greenville since its acquisition and only briefly mentioned in the literature, is thus relatively neglected, particularly in comparison with other works in the Bob Jones University collection. Happily, this exhibition provides the occasion to discuss more fully this fine example of a late, large-scale Guercino painting.

To judge from the size of this fragment, the *St. Anthony of Padua* was once part of what must have been a major altarpiece. The first scholar to recognize the work as from Guercino's late production and to associate it with two lost paintings was Sir Denis Mahon.[1] The commissions were painted for Verona and mentioned by Guercino's biographer Malvasia, as well as being listed in the artist's *Libro dei Conti* (account book). The first possible early provenance for the Bob Jones fragment is the collection of Pier Luigi Pecana of Verona, as part of the picture depicting the "Holy Virgin, the Christ Child and St. Anthony of Padua," finished in 1658. Alternatively, it could be from the altarpiece "for the Capuchins of Verona with St. Anthony of Padua," commissioned by an Emanuele Emanuelli in 1662-63.[2] A photograph taken in Julius Weitzner's gallery and studio about 1972 of the Bob Jones *St. Anthony* in a stripped state confirms Mahon's observation that, having seen it "both before and after restoration," an "area to the left of Saint Anthony's right hand had been cut away (in the top left corner of the canvas) and a newer patch of dark background substituted. Behind St. Anthony's right hand there remained, however, a fragment of red drapery, which clearly indicated that a figure (probably life-size, according to Guercino's normal practice) had existed above. This small fragment, being inexplicable in relation to the picture as it now is, has naturally now been covered over."[3] The photograph reveals not only the drapery, both behind the saint's gesticulating hand and to the right of his head along the present top of the canvas, but the toes of the Virgin in the area immediately to the upper left of Anthony's fingers.[4]

The few other examples of the theme of St. Anthony in earlier works by Guercino include an altarpiece depicting the saint kneeling before the Christ Child, dating to 1649-51 and also painted for Capuchins, but in Persiceto.[5] Around the same time, Guercino produced one of his rare etchings, showing St. Anthony of Padua in half-length, as a single devotional figure. Ironically, the Bob Jones picture in its fragmentary state is just such a single-figure composition as the etching. Ten years later Guercino produced an altarpiece of *St. Anthony and the Christ Child* now at Rimini, a variation on the Persiceto painting, and also in 1659, a half-length devotional picture of the same subject, now in a private collection.[6] All show the saint with fairly similar features and with his attributes of the book and his symbol of purity, the lily.

As discussed above with respect to Denys Calvaert's *St. Francis Adoring the Christ Child* (cat. no. 15), that unusual subject derived in part from the legend of St. Anthony and his vision of the Infant Christ. The Capuchin monks were responsible for the extension of Franciscan imagery with an emphasis on the mystical and ecstatic. St. Anthony, a thirteenth-century Franciscan monk himself, together with St. Francis with whom he had become in a sense interchangeable, was the favored subject for Capuchin commissions. This provides the attractive possibility that the altarpiece of which the present picture is a fragment was the 1662-63 commission for the Capuchin church in Verona, rather than that done for Signor Pecana completed in 1658. The theme of St. Francis and the Christ Child is also treated in Guercino's graphic oeuvre.[7]

1. Letter to Dr. Arthur K. Solomon, Cambridge, Massachusetts, 28 May 1972, on file at the Art Gallery, Bob Jones University. In a later letter published in Pepper 1984a, p. 318, Mahon expanded upon his earlier thoughts, noting both the Pecana and the Emanuelli commissions; he recently reconfirmed his opinion as to its autograph status without reservation in oral communication, 4 March 1993.

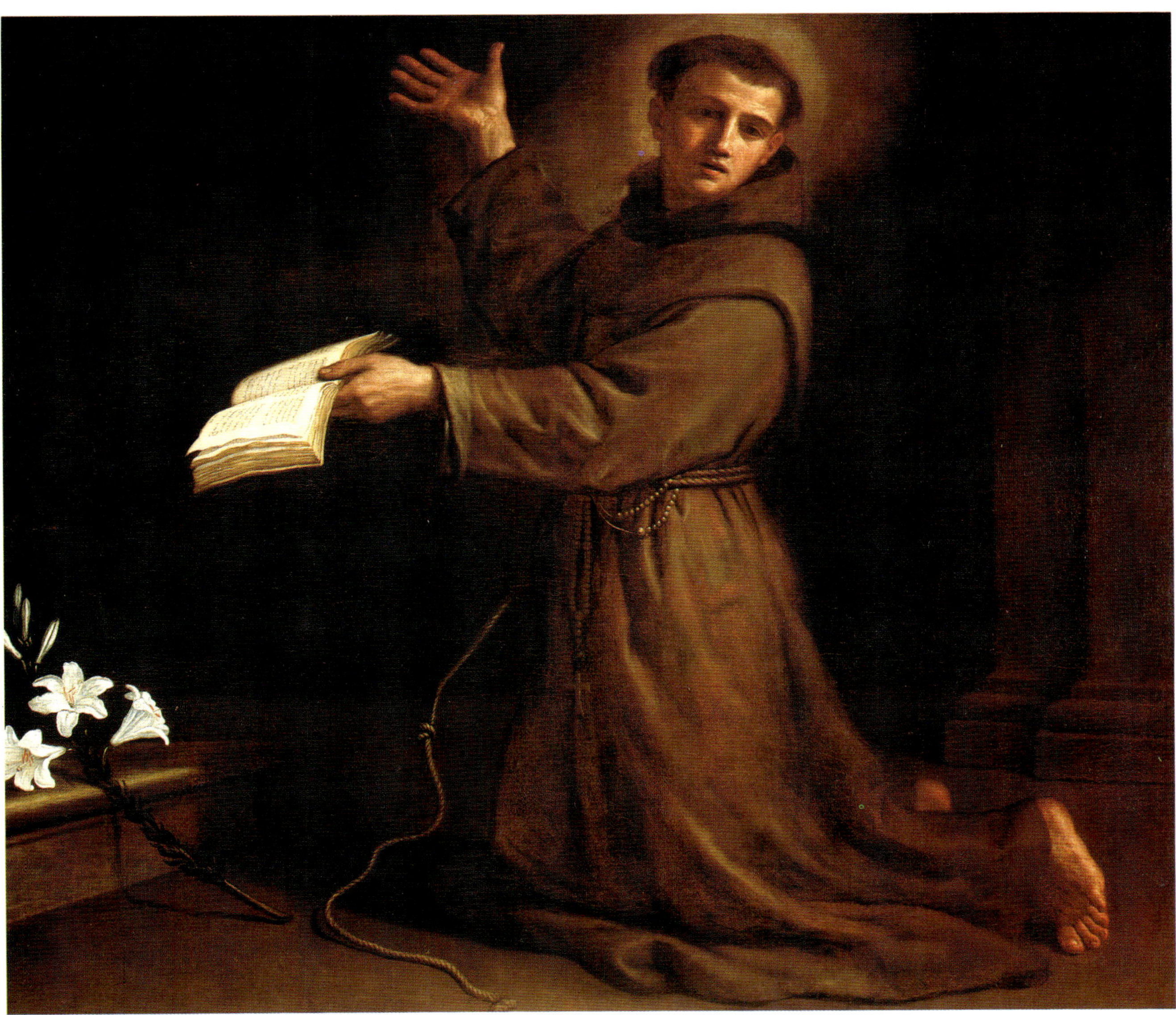

2. See Salerno 1988, p. 391; Stone 1991, p. 322.
3. Letter to Dr. Arthur K. Solomon (see note 1). The photograph is in the files of the Art Gallery, Bob Jones University.
4. The seam—where the original canvas joins the addition that completes the painting's upper left corner—runs from the left edge at a level just below Anthony's chin to his arm, cuts up and out away from his hand so as to encompass it, thus including several toes from the left foot of the Virgin and some drapery; it then turns back in toward the saint's head and up several inches to provide a more comfortable margin between his head and the present edge of the painting. It seems logical that, if indeed the figure of the Virgin (and for that matter the Child) still exists in its own fragment, that students of Guercino should look for a late composition, clearly cut down, in which the Virgin is in three-quarters or half-length, since her presentation must have been modified to account for the missing toes.
5. See Bologna 1991, pp. 338-40.
6. See Stone 1991, pp. 325 and 328, respectively.
7. See Blume 1991, pp. 52-58.

- 2 1 -

JUSEPE DE RIBERA
CALLED LO SPAGNOLETTO

Játiva 1591-1652 Naples

Ecce Homo, 1638

Oil on canvas

30 x 25 inches

Signed and dated:

Jusepe de Ribera español/,F, 1638

PROVENANCE: E. and A. Silberman Galleries, New York, 1952

EXHIBITIONS: New York 1955, no. 20; Indianapolis 1963, no. 64; Fort Worth 1982, no. 28; Raleigh 1984, no. 35; Austin 1990

REFERENCES: Greenville 1954, p. 126; Gaya Nuño 1958, no. 2346; Kerrigan 1960, p. 355; Havens 1961, p. 112; Greenville 1962, p. 346; Wethey 1963, p. 208; Pérez Sánchez and Spinosa 1978, no. 123; Naples 1992, p. 229

Ribera's arresting, bust-length portrayal is not simply a Christ of Derision—that is, a depiction of Jesus being mocked, crowned with thorns, and given a purple robe and reed scepter as described in the Gospels—but an *Ecce Homo* (Behold, the Man!), since he is presented to the viewer in a direct fashion as an image for contemplation.[1] A recent cleaning has further revealed the artist's exquisite execution and his sensitive interpretation of the humanity of Christ, leaving no doubt as to its autograph status. The existence of a number of versions of this subject—the most important of these are at Helsinki, St. Petersburg, and in the Zeri collection, Mentana—does not preclude the Greenville picture's authenticity, as has been implied on occasion. In fact, it is important to note that the Bob Jones *Ecce Homo* is similar to, but not a replica of the pictures cited above. Those are clearly variants of one another, depicting Christ with his face turned three-quarters to the left and his right hand holding the reed scepter positioned toward the lower left corner. Christ's cloak is depicted with slight differences in each of the three versions; the broad folds in the Helsinki *Ecce Homo* are closest to the Greenville painting in this respect. An important distinction between the Helsinki, Mentana, and St. Petersburg paintings is that in the former two, Christ engages the viewer directly, while in the Hermitage picture he looks upward. This direct gaze is the one aspect that connects the two versions with the Bob Jones painting, which is otherwise quite different: here Christ's head is turned to the right and the hand holding the reed is at the lower right corner of the canvas. This does not suggest a studio copy, but rather Ribera improvising upon a favorite theme at a later date (the others have been dated to the early 1630s).[2]

The *Ecce Homo* in the Real Academia de San Fernando, Madrid, datable to 1618-20, is the earliest antecedent of the four paintings discussed thus far. The Madrid picture, however, shows a half-length figure. Its general disposition, with Christ's head inclined to the left and the manner in which the drapery is worn, aligns it more closely to the three other versions of the *Ecce Homo.* The present picture may be seen as a reduction of a larger composition, the *Christ Mocked and Crowned with Thorns* in the Brera, Milan, which Ribera signed and dated the same year, that is, 1638.[3] In this composition, which shows Christ derided by five of his persecutors, the orientation of the head to the right and the features of the Savior are analogous to those seen in the Bob Jones canvas.

The subject of the *Ecce Homo* in Italian art takes one of three forms: a devotional image, a narrative scene, or a combination of the two. Another Neapolitan work in this exhibition, Francesco de Mura's painting of 1725 (cat. no. 36), provides an example of the second type, in which Christ, accompanied by a Jewish priest and a Roman soldier, is presented to the crowd who shout "Crucify Him! Crucify Him!" (John 19:4-6). The intermediate type of composition shows only the usually half-length figure of Christ and his "presenters" from the larger narrative, sometimes behind fenestration (alluding to the praetorium's balcony).[4] The most distilled image, and thus the most effective in terms of a devotional picture, is exemplified by Ribera's iconic *Ecce Homo* in the Bob Jones collection.[5]

1. For arguments concerning whether this is a Christ of Derision as opposed to a Man of Sorrows or an *Ecce Homo,* see Raleigh 1984, p. 112, and Fort Worth 1982, p. 197.
2. The following is a brief summary of the recent critical opinion on the four versions of the *Ecce Homo:*
   A. Helsinki: Pérez Sánchez and Spinosa 1978, p. 102, by an "imitator of the master" (signature and date not noted); Fort Worth 1982, p. 197, autograph, calls it "noteworthy";

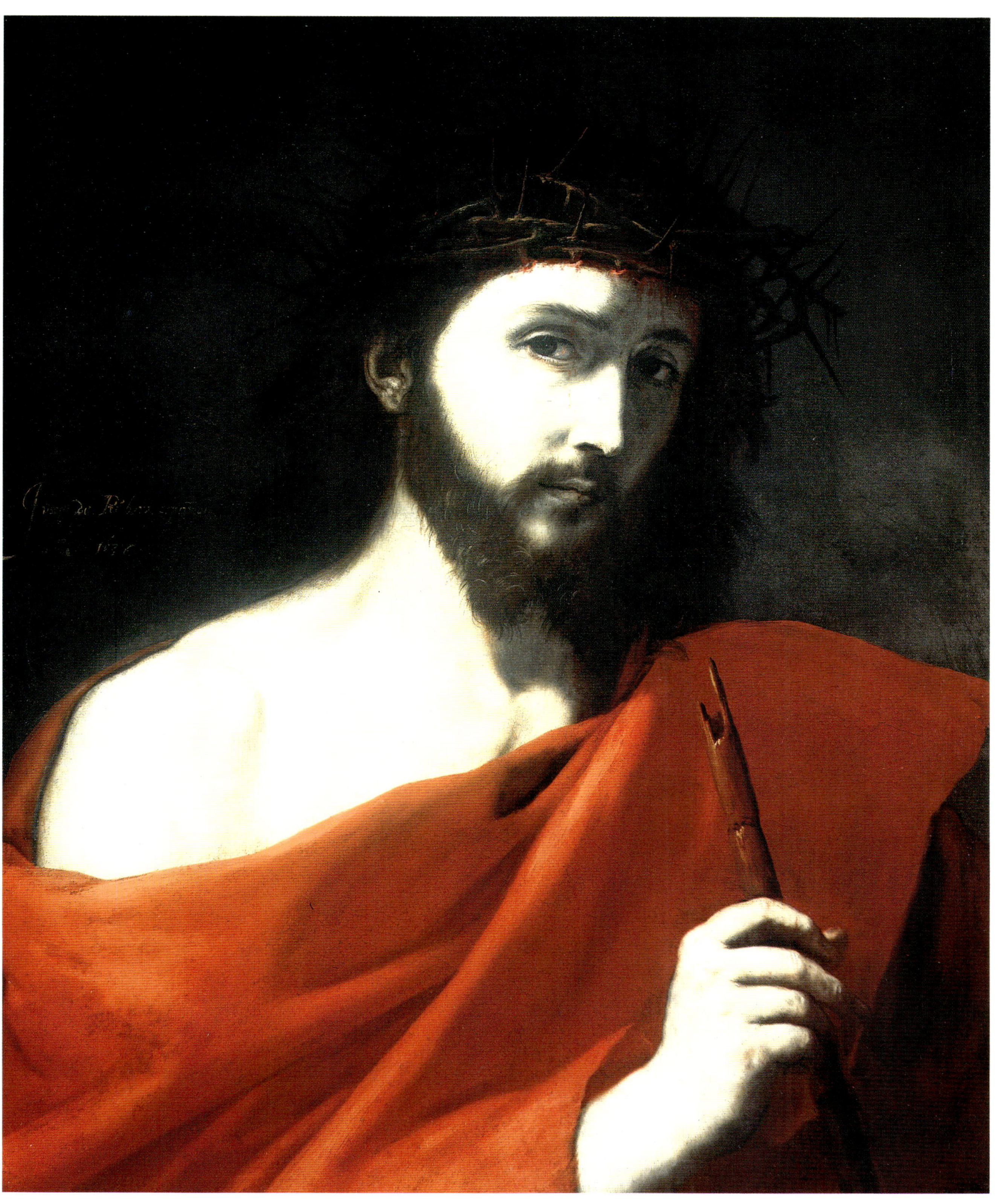

Raleigh 1984, p. 112, autograph, similar to the Greenville picture "in composition and mood"; Naples 1992 (Pérez Sánchez), p. 229, "and there is from 1644 the excellent canvas in the Helsinki Athenaeum, signed and dated that year, little known."

B. St. Petersburg: Pérez Sánchez and Spinosa 1978, p. 102, Spinosa calls it a secure work, but cites Felton's opinion calling it a product of general Riberesque influence; Raleigh 1984, same as A; Naples 1992, p. 229 (Pérez Sánchez), not a secure work of Ribera's, but when in the past it was accepted, dated to around 1632.

C. Mentana: Pérez Sánchez and Spinosa 1978, p. 105, Spinosa notes a signature and date, "Jusepe de Ribera español/ F 1634," and, while qualifying his opinion due to condition, suggests "probably the work of Ribera"; Naples 1992 (Pérez Sánchez), p. 229, closest to the Helsinki picture and "plausibly a work painted in the same period," although, given its condition, "difficult to give a definitive judgment."

D. Greenville: Pérez Sánchez and Spinosa 1978, p. 113, the painting begun by Ribera (especially the hands and face), but finished by a collaborator (Spinosa cites the beard and drapery); Fort Worth 1982, p. 197, "unquestionably the finest" of the several versions; Raleigh 1984, concurs with Fort Worth 1982; Naples 1992 (Pérez Sánchez), p. 229, damaged and "probably carried out in collaboration with workshop assistants."

3. The Brera painting is signed and dated, "Jusepe de Ribera español/F. 1638." Its authenticity and the veracity of its signature and date have been much debated. It is now accepted as autograph despite its poor condition, and was included in the recent Ribera exhibition. Felton has placed the picture in Ribera's early years, 1615-16, between Rome and Naples. Spinosa proposes either an earlier dating, 1613-14, or conversely, one in the late 1620s. See Naples 1992, p. 146, and, for a discussion of its closest replica from Ribera's workshop, now at Hartford, see Cadogan 1991, pp. 309-13.

4. The remarkable *Ecce Homo* by Andrea Mantegna in the Musée Jacquemart-André, Paris, datable to around 1500, provides an earlier example of the same type of devotional image (see New York 1992b, pp. 245-47). Seventeenth-century examples include the Cigoli in the Palazzo Pitti and the Daniele Crespi in the Suida Manning collection, New York, both of which depict Christ in the center between the Jewish priest on the left and the Roman soldier on the right.

5. Sixten Ringbom, in his study on devotional iconography, *Icon to Narrative: The Rise of the Dramatic Close-Up in Fifteenth-Century Devotional Painting,* traces the development of this theme from early icons to full-scale narrative adaptations of the single-figure (bust-length or half-length) compositions (Ringbom 1984, pp. 142-47). Intervening between early icons and worked-up multi-figural scenes were fifteenth-century devotional woodcuts with their simple, strong images (for rare Italian examples, see, for instance, Toronto 1989). However, by the time the narrative variations on these iconic types were firmly established, and certainly by the seventeenth century, this process seems also to have worked in reverse; that is, an artist would select a few elements from a larger composition to suit a devotional purpose. This is clearly the case in the Sassoferrato *Young Christ* (cat. no. 27) or in reductions of earlier successes, such as Ribera's scene of *Christ Mocked* in the Brera, Milan, cited above. Related subjects—variations on the *Ecce Homo* or "Suffering Christ" theme, as Ringbom termed it—include Christ Crowned with Thorns (for example, the several versions by Reni, one in Detroit) or the Veil of Veronica, which presents Christ's face imprinted on a cloth (for example, the Domenico Fetti in Washington), or the variation that includes Veronica holding the veil (for example, the Mattia Preti in Los Angeles).

- 2 2 -

FRANCESCO DE ROSA CALLED PACECCO DE ROSA

Naples 1607-1656 Naples

The Martyrdom of St. Lawrence, 1635-40

Oil on canvas

50½ x 71 inches

PROVENANCE: Julius Weitzner, London, 1963

EXHIBITIONS: London 1982, no. 91

REFERENCES: Pugliese 1983, pp. 124-25; Naples 1984, p. 131; Pepper 1984a, no. 100.1

The depiction of St. Lawrence martyred on the grill was an especially favorite subject with Neapolitan painters. The city's most prominent artist, Jusepe de Ribera, painted a version around 1613, the popularity of which is proven by the numerous copies after it.[1] As has been observed, Pacecco's style while displaying a Bolognese and Roman classicism, was influenced by Ribera's naturalism.[2]

The picture exhibited here can be associated with Ribera's painting, now in the Artemis Trust collection, London. While Ribera employed a vertical format, Pacecco organized his composition similarly within a horizontal one.[3] The man carrying wood for the fire over which Lawrence is grilled and the boy holding the saint's dalmatic occupy identical places at the left; and the saint and his executioner are similarly disposed in the right foreground in both paintings. Deborah Marrow reads the inclusion of the grinning boy as a breach of decorum,[4] but Pepper interprets the contrast between this motif and the brutishness of the executioner as a rhetorical device that allowed for the representation of "moral" types as opposed to "realistic figures."[5] However, seen within the context of Ribera's oeuvre (see, for example, his *Martyrdom of St. Bartholomew* in the Palazzo Pitti [6]), the boy's cruel response appears to emphasize the "street-wise" nature of Pacecco's painting. The harsh reality of the culture in which Ribera and Pacecco lived is reflected in the brutal

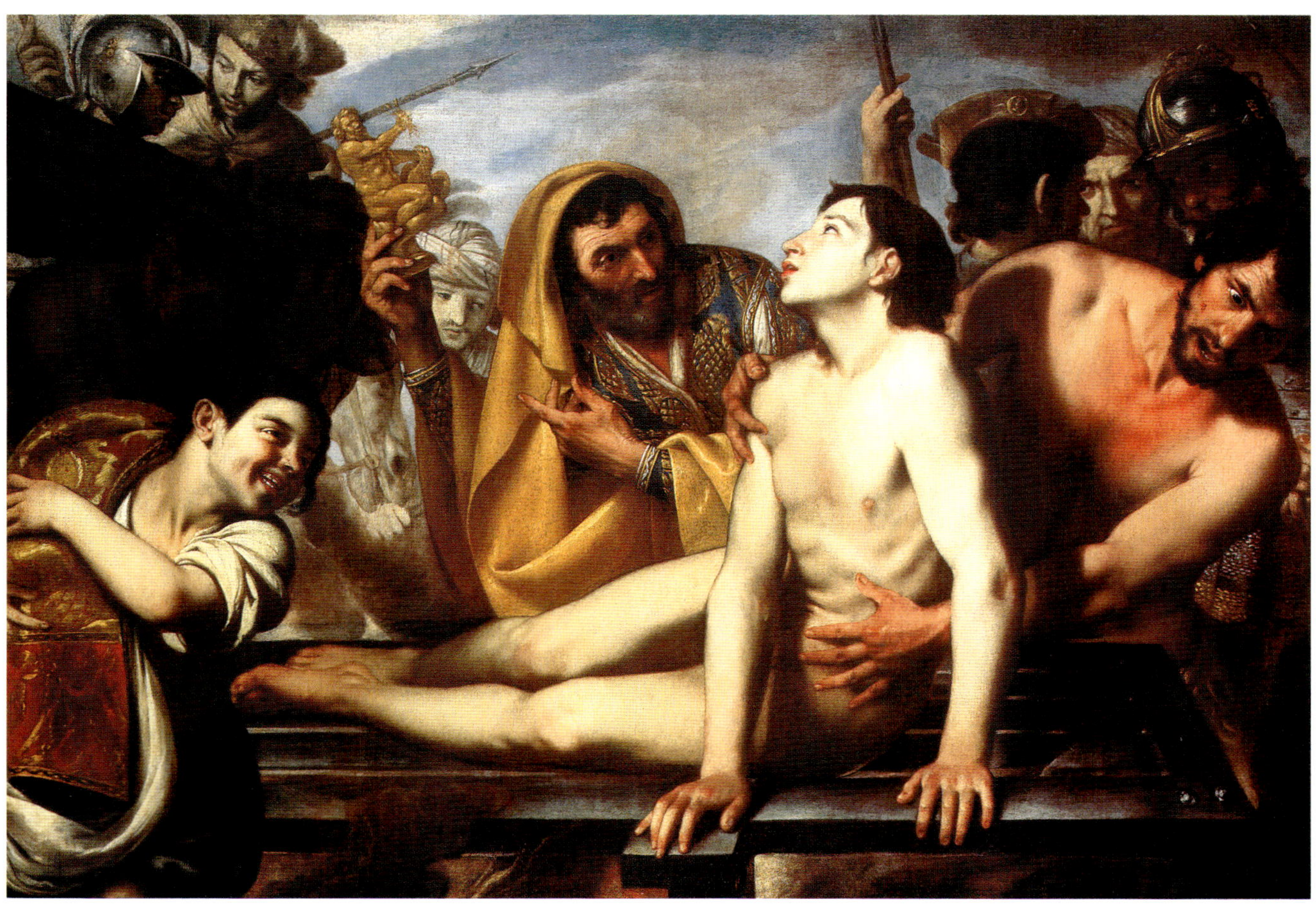

and coarse types that coexist in their paintings alongside figures that exhibit nobler aspects of humanity.[7]

1. Vincenzo Pugliese (1983, pp. 111-12, 125) has connected the Bob Jones *Martyrdom* by Pacecco de Rosa to another canvas of the same subject in the parish church of S. Lorenzo, Lizzanello (Lecce), calling the former picture a replica of several years later. Pugliese notes only slight differences between the two versions, but it is important to point out here that the compositions are reversed. Lilia Rocco retains the attribution of the Lizzanello painting to the "Master of Bovino," citing it as an example of Pacecco's influence in Puglia; she believes the Bob Jones picture to be the original (Naples 1984, p. 131).
2. Naples 1984, p. 130; see also Pugliese 1983, pp. 121-23.
3. See New York 1992b, pp. 58-60, in which a horizontal version of Ribera's *Martyrdom* in the Nelson-Atkins Museum of Art, Kansas City, is discussed by Nicola Spinosa, who regards it as a workshop copy of the Artemis Trust work.
4. Marrow 1978, p. 9.
5. Pepper 1984a, p. 99.
6. Indeed, Pugliese (1983, p. 124) has suggested the ultimate dependence of the Lizzanello *St. Lawrence* on the Pitti *St. Bartholomew* due to Pacecco's knowledge of two pictures that derive from the Ribera and are attributed to Pacecco's brother-in-law and Ribera student, Giovanni Do: one of these is at Grenoble and the other in S. Maria della Neve, Naples.
7. Ribera made drawings of public displays of torture and execution, probably of actual events seen in Naples, such as the punishment of offenders outside the Tribuna della Vicaria, the main judicial tribunal of the city (see, for example, the painting of the Tribuna by Carlo Coppola in the Museo di San Martino, Naples).

~ 23 ~

LUCA GIORDANO CALLED LUCA FA PRESTO

Naples 1634-1705 Naples

Christ Driving the Merchants from the Temple, c. 1660

Oil on canvas

88½ x 120 inches

PROVENANCE: probably Count Horace St. Paul, Ewart Park, Wooler, near Berwick-on-Tweed, England, late 18th century; by descent to Maria St. Paul, wife of George Grey Butler, c. 1900;[1] Tómas Harris, London, 1951

EXHIBITIONS: Raleigh 1984, no. 18; Austin 1990

REFERENCES: Knox 1980, p. 25; Pepper 1984a, no. 59.1; Ferrari and Scavizzi 1992, no. A81 and p. 30

An early work by Luca Giordano, and one of his most important paintings in America, *Christ Driving the Merchants from the Temple* occupies an exceptional place in the artist's oeuvre. The special care lavished on the painting can be seen, for example, in the brilliant passage of the pigeons and their eggs (some broken) at the lower left of the composition or in the veracity of the expression of the moneychanger Christ has seized. The roughly woven canvas is typical for pictures painted in Naples. Due to its immense size, it has been pieced together with three lengths of fabric. The painting retains much of its original surface; Giordano's characteristic heavy impasto and fluid brushwork is visible, for example, in the market woman in the background at right. It has been suggested that the Bob Jones picture was one of four in a suite of Giordano paintings owned in the eighteenth century by Angelo Vecchia and recorded in the Palazzo Vecchia, Vicenza, from 1761 to about 1840.[2] However, the recent identification of the four Vecchia paintings by Oreste Ferrrari and Giuseppe Scavizzi disproves this hypothesis.[3] It has also been proposed that the Greenville picture is the pendant to a painting of similar dimensions, internal scale, and subject matter, the *Christ Among the Doctors* in the Galleria Nazionale d'Arte Antica, Palazzo Corsini, Rome.[4]

The present work was indeed painted around the same time as the Corsini picture; its placement within Giordano's oeuvre is evident from its style and technique, which reveal lessons the artist learned during his first trip to Venice in the early 1650s. Veronese's

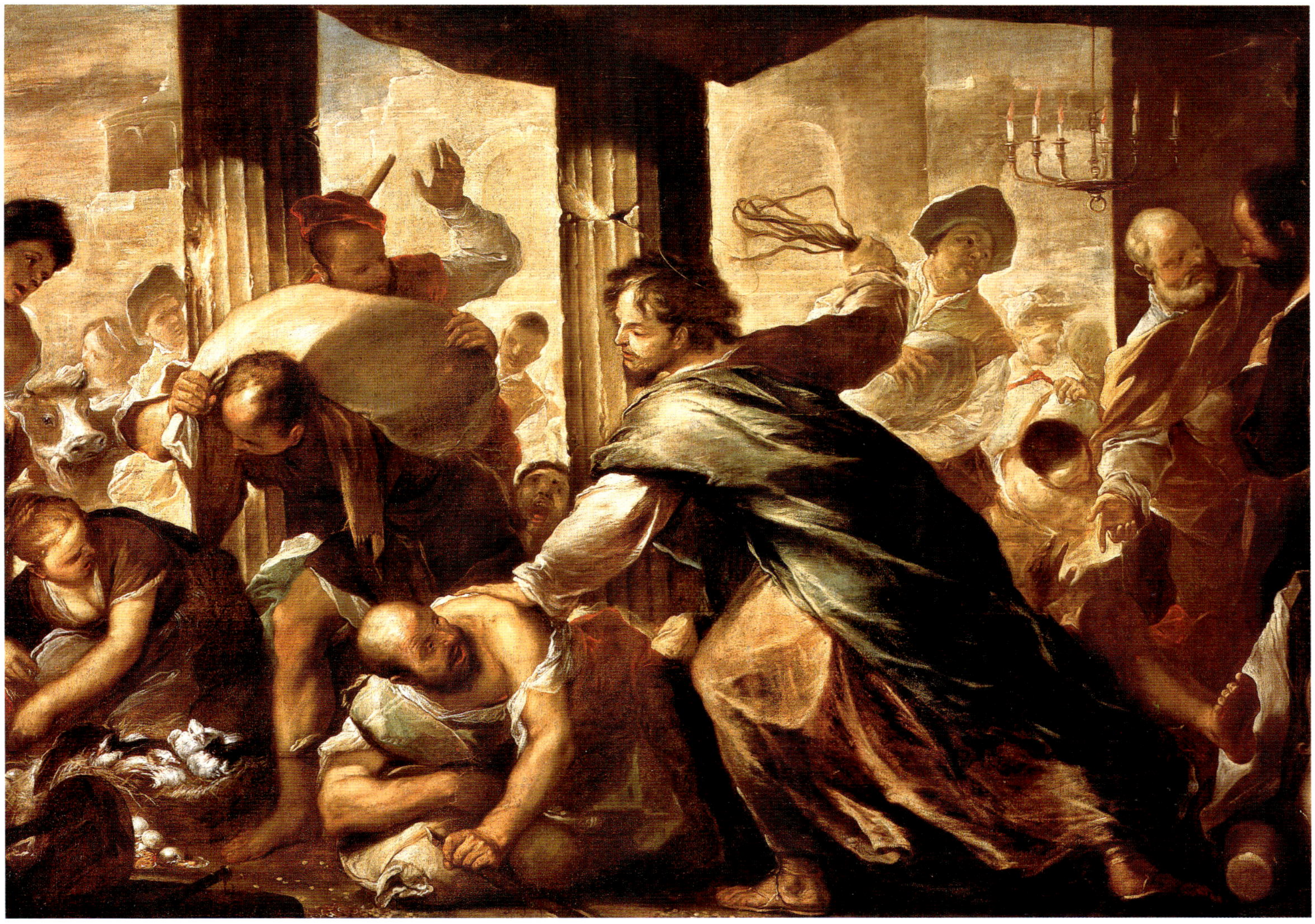

impact on Giordano can be seen in the golden tonality, shot through with light; the grand composition in a monumental setting; and the execution in a "neo-Venetian" style. Also apparent is the influence of other Venetian masters whose works the young artist would have seen in Rome and in the Veneto, particularly compositions by Jacopo Bassano and his studio of this same subject.[5] In addition to these Venetian overtones, Giordano's fascination with the work of his compatriot Mattia Preti may also be gleaned from the *Christ Driving the Merchants from the Temple.* Preti's influence is seen in the facial types and the manner in which the figures are blocked in—like Preti, Giordano created a sense of depth by silhouetting the foreground figures and painting those in the middleground in half-tones (see, for example, Preti's *David Playing the Harp Before Saul* of about 1668, presently on the New York art market, or his *Martyrdom of St. Paul,* of about 1656, in Houston).

1. The traditional provenance, "Butler collection, Woolen Hall, Berwick-on-Tweed," must be a corruption of Wooler, a village ten miles south of Berwick, where the Butlers lived at Ewart Park. The family appears to have moved into town when it seems the military occupied the house during the second World War, a logical point during which the St. Paul-Butler collection (see also Raleigh 1984, pp. 68-70) would have been dispersed. George Knox, written communication, 14 April 1994.
2. The four Giordanos are recorded there for the first time in 1761 and in detail by Francesco Vendramin Mosca in 1779, see Knox 1980, p. 25.
3. Ferrari and Scavizzi (1992, pp. 60, 288-89) have demonstrated that the Palazzo Vecchia canvases are the ones to be found in the Museo Diocesano, Venice

(*Massacre of the Innocents* and *Christ Driving the Merchants from the Temple*) and presently on the New York art market (*Rape of the Sabines* and *Judgment of Solomon*). They have dated the pictures around twelve years later than the Bob Jones canvas. For other examples of our subject in Giordano's oeuvre, see Ferrari and Scavizzi 1992, nos. A192, A348, and fig. 1084.

4. Most recently in Raleigh 1984, p. 68. Ferrari and Scavizzi have refuted this in both editions of their Giordano monograph (1966, I, p. 51, and II, p. 43; and 1992, p. 263).
5. See Fort Worth 1993a, figs. 69 and 78, the versions in a private collection, Bassano, and the National Gallery, London, respectively. Note the same use of a grand architectural setting and the pose of Christ striding across the picture, flail upraised, before a kneeling usurer. A drawing in the Prado that Ferrari and Scavizzi (1992, D205, fig. 1068) date to the late years, in the "style of El Greco," recalls Bassano's influence (seen in the latter's motifs such as the kneeling figure and the cattle).

- 24 -

GIOVANNI BATTISTA BEINASCHI

Fossano 1636-1688 Naples

St. Cecilia and Angel Musicians, c. 1680

Oil on canvas

86½ x 66¼ inches

PROVENANCE: W.P. Wilstach collection, Philadelphia Museum of Art by 1922; Samuel T. Freeman & Co., Philadelphia, 29-30 October 1954, lot 147; Julius Weitzner, New York, 1955; Gift of Mrs. and Mrs. Lawrence Stewart, 1956

EXHIBITIONS: Detroit 1965, no. 30 (as Giacinto Brandi)

REFERENCES: Hibbard and Lewine 1965, p. 371; Mirimonde 1974, p. 115; Pepper 1984a, no. 32.1; Naples 1984, p. 117

This *St. Cecilia,* at the time of its inclusion in the landmark exhibition of Italian Seicento art at Detroit in 1965, was catalogued under its former attribution to Giacinto Brandi, for whom Beinaschi worked decorating S. Carlo al Corso, Rome, in 1677. Within that entry, however, Robert Enggass reassigned it to Beinaschi.[1] In fact, it was Robert L. Manning and the late Bertina Suida Manning who in 1963 initially suggested the new and correct attribution.[2] Enggass dated the Greenville picture to Beinaschi's Roman period, contemporary with his work in S. Carlo al Corso. Recently, Fausta Navarro placed it just after his return to Naples from Rome in 1679, when the artist was decorating the churches of SS. Apostoli in 1680 and the church of the Girolamini in 1681.[3]

This exuberant late Roman Baroque composition depicts the patron saint of music playing the organ, about to be crowned with roses by a putto. A grand concert of angels accompanies her on string and wind instruments. The saint's depiction derives from the tradition established by the Stefano Maderno sculpture, with its inclusion of the flowing veil or turban (see commentary under cat. no. 16). Given the picture's scale and the foreshortening of the angels, which indicate that it was meant to be seen at some height, the Bob Jones *St. Cecilia* was probably intended as an altarpiece.

1. Detroit 1965, pp. 47-48. See also in this catalogue, p. 82, fig. 22.
2. Oral communication, the Mannings, September 1992.
3. Naples 1984, p. 117.

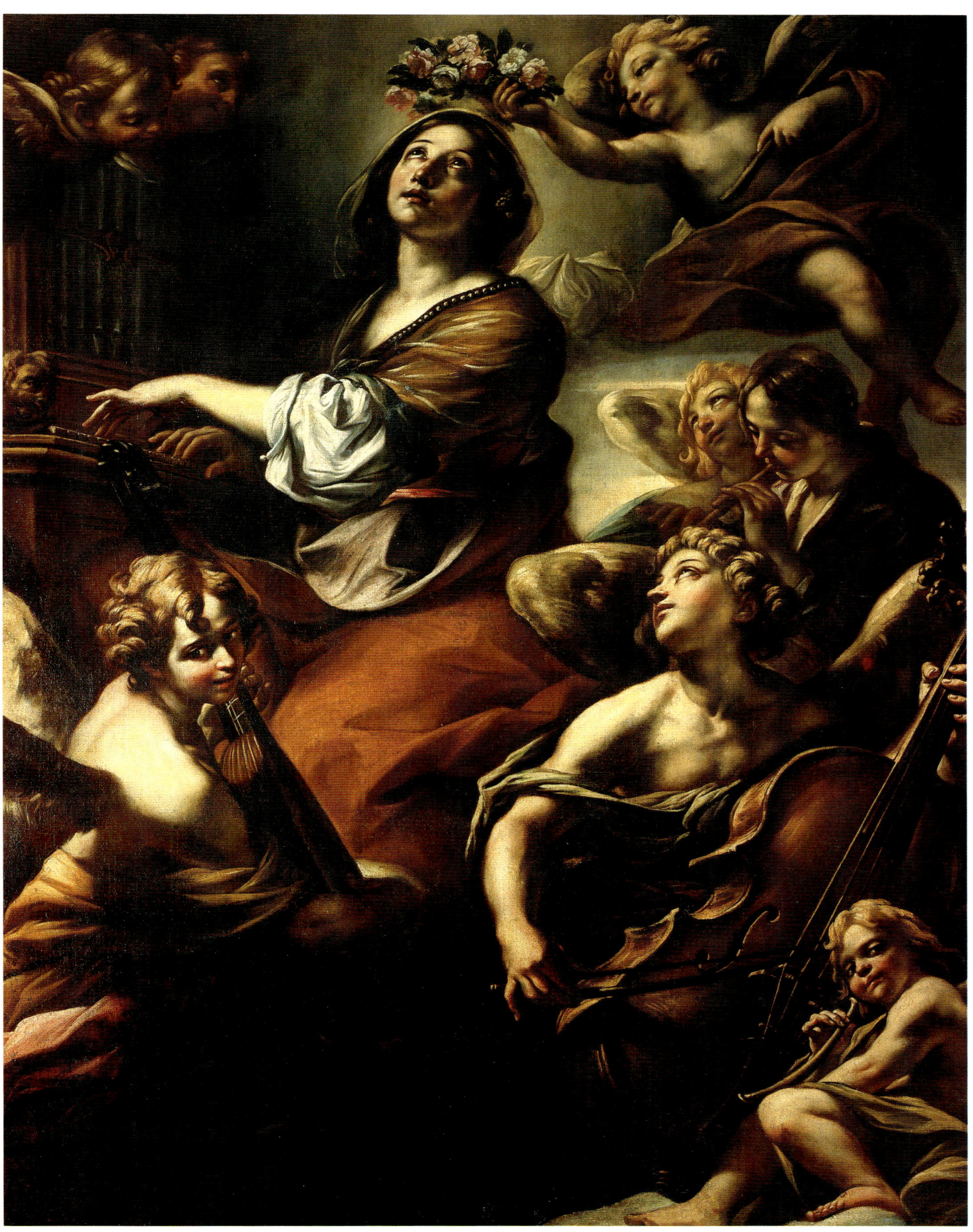

~ 25 ~

MATTIA PRETI CALLED IL CAVALIERE CALABRESE

Taverna 1613-1699 Malta

Christ Seating the Child in the Midst of the Disciples, 1680-85

Oil on canvas

49 x 77 inches

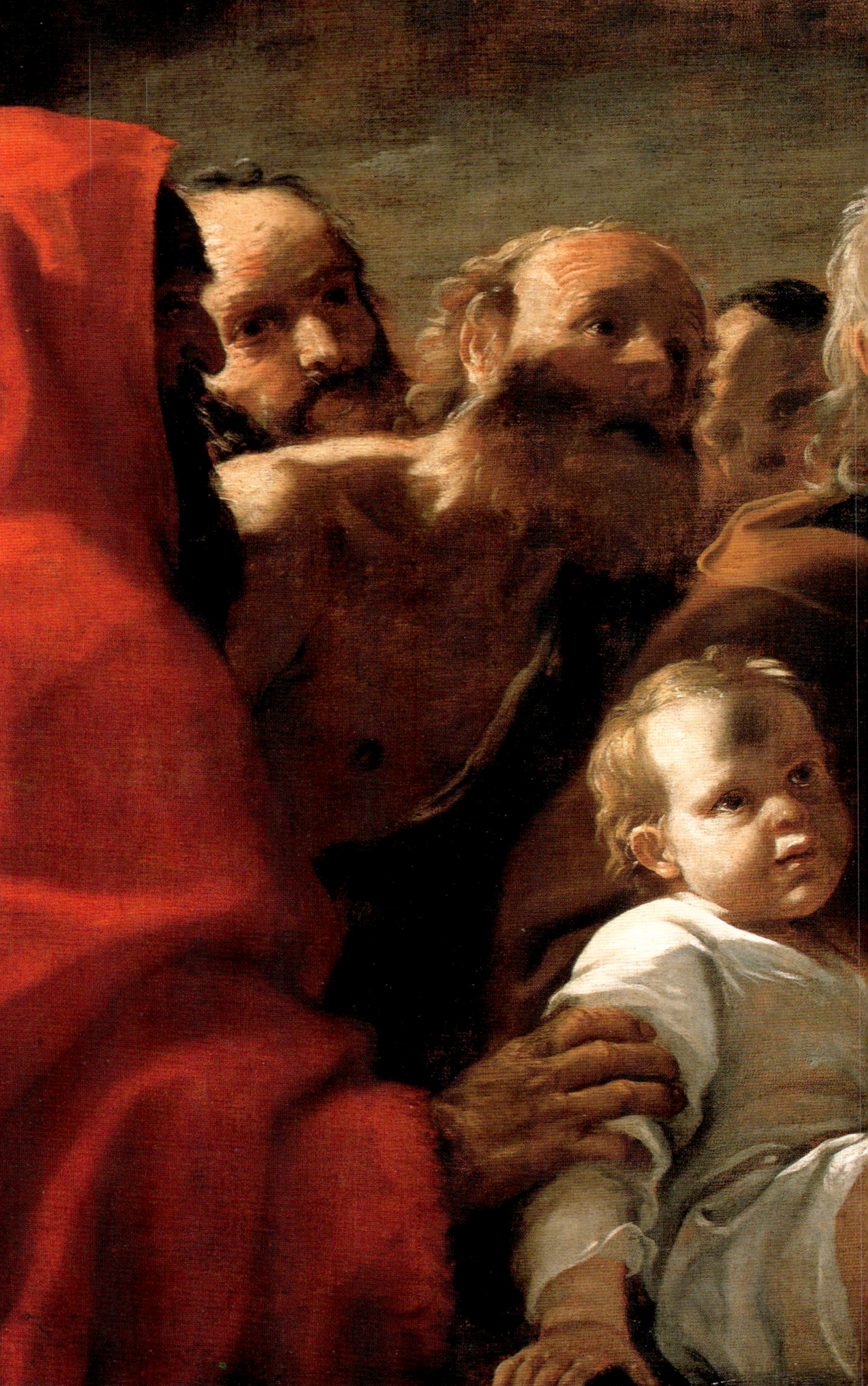

PROVENANCE: Julius Weitzner, New York, 1953

EXHIBITIONS: Oberlin 1952; Sarasota 1961; Raleigh 1984, no. 29; New Haven 1987, no. 6 and pp. 84, 91; Austin 1990

REFERENCES: Pepper 1984a, no. 96.1

Bob Jones, Jr.'s pioneering taste in Neapolitan pictures manifested itself with very early purchases of the Luca Giordano (cat. no. 23) in 1951 and the present picture by Mattia Preti in 1953—the earliest autograph painting by the master to enter an American museum.[1] John Spike dates the work to the years 1680-85, based on comparison with a number of altarpieces that were painted for the artist's birthplace of Taverna in Calabria.[2]

Like his coeval Luca Giordano, Preti came under the spell of Venetian painting, which can be observed in the rich, saturated colors and flickering light effects (as opposed to the harder chiaroscuro of Caravaggio and Ribera) reminiscent of works by the late Titian, Veronese, and especially, the Bassano family. The composition is worked out within the parameters of the narrow horizontal canvas like a classical frieze, which lends weight and grandeur to the biblical figures. The scene shows Christ pointing to a small child, who serves as an illustration to the disciples of the innocence one must possess in order to gain salvation: "Except ye be converted, and become as little children, ye shall not enter into the kingdom of heaven" (Matthew 18: 1-4). George Hersey's reading of the gestures and his differentiation of this particular representation from that of other, similar accounts in the Gospels are doubtless correct: the gesture of Christ's right hand links the child with Christ himself; his left hand leads the viewer's eye upward to the kingdom of God.[3]

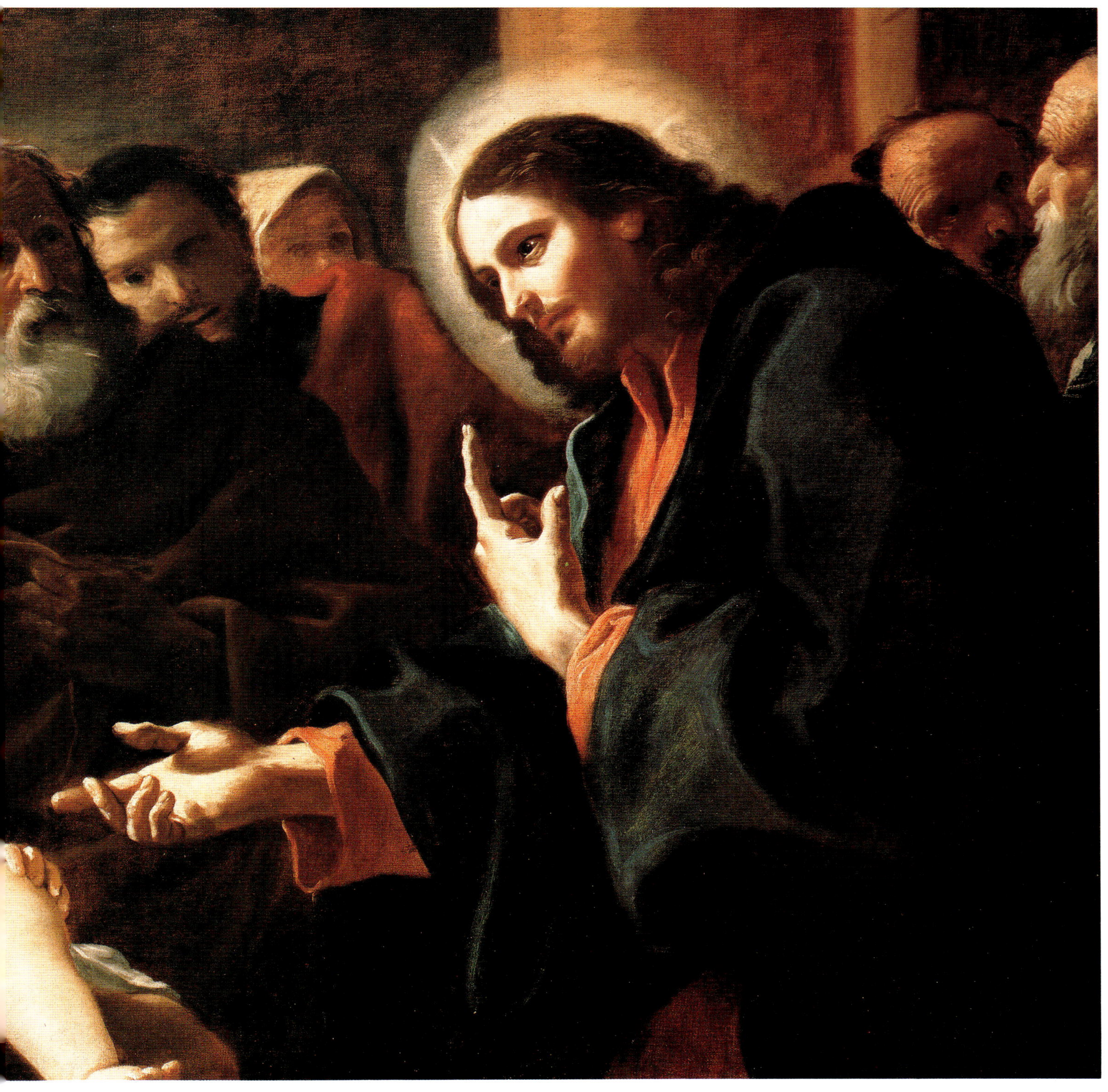

1. Greenville 1954, introduction, New Haven 1987, p. 107. On the history of the American taste for Neapolitan paintings, see Eric M. Zafran's essay at the beginning of this catalogue, and George Hersey, "The Critical Fortunes of Neapolitan Painting: Notes on American Collecting" in New Haven 1987, pp. 69-80.

2. Pepper 1984a, p. 96.

3. New Haven 1987, pp. 107-108.

– 26 –

CARLO MARATTA

Camerano 1625-1713 Rome

The Martyrdom of St. Andrew, c. 1656

Oil on canvas

47½ x 62 inches

PROVENANCE: Cardinal Giuseppe Renato Imperiali, Genoa and Rome; Sir Erasmus Philipps, Picton Castle, England, before 1752 and thence by descent until 1948; David Koetser, New York, 1951

EXHIBITIONS: Charlotte 1959; San Francisco 1964-65; Detroit 1965, no. 54; Gainesville 1982, no. 15; Raleigh 1984, no. 25; Frankfurt 1988, no. D21; Austin 1990

REFERENCES: Hibbard and Lewine 1965, p. 370; Pepper 1984a, no. 72.1

Numerous preparatory drawings for this composition at Düsseldorf[1] attest to the academic nature of Maratta's working process, in which finished works were arrived at through application of an established method. This rigorous approach to art was embodied in the institution of which Maratta was *Principe* (President) for life—the Accademia di San Luca in Rome. Maratta dominated the artistic scene in that city during the late seventeenth century, and the aftereffects of his work—a combination of the classicism of Andrea Sacchi, his teacher, and the High Baroque of Bernini and Cortona—lasted well into the eighteenth century.

The scene depicted is of St. Andrew being led to the site of his martyrdom, where the X-shaped cross upon which he will be executed is standing. According to legend, Andrew requested that he not be crucified on the traditional cross, as he was not worthy of the same cross as Christ. In gratitude for the granting of this request, the saints clasps his hands in thanks, kneeling before the instrument of his death. Maratta based this painting (there are several other variants) on Sacchi's altarpiece of 1633-34 in St. Peter's of the same subject,[2] although the figures in the central group, Andrew and the executioner at the left, have been reversed. Interestingly, a small picture by Sacchi of *St. Andrew,* mentioned in his house after his death in 1661, was recorded in Maratta's collection, listed in a 1712 inventory.[3] While it is tempting to identify this work as the direct inspiration for the Bob Jones canvas, the latter painting has been dated about 1656 by Harris and Schaar based on the compositional sketches at Düsseldorf.[4] Nevertheless, this small painting must have served Maratta later as a reminder of the great debt he owed to his master, a debt seen plainly in the Bob Jones *St. Andrew.*

1. Harris and Schaar 1967, pp. 91-94.
2. See Harris 1977, p. 72.
3. Harris 1977, p. 72: "un quadretto abbozzo del Sacchi. . . quale rappresenta Sant'Andrea condotto al martirio."
4. On the verso of one the sheets (inv. no. FP 8248) is a study for the *Adoration of the Three Kings,* an altarpiece for S. Marco painted in 1656. Harris and Schaar 1967, p. 92.

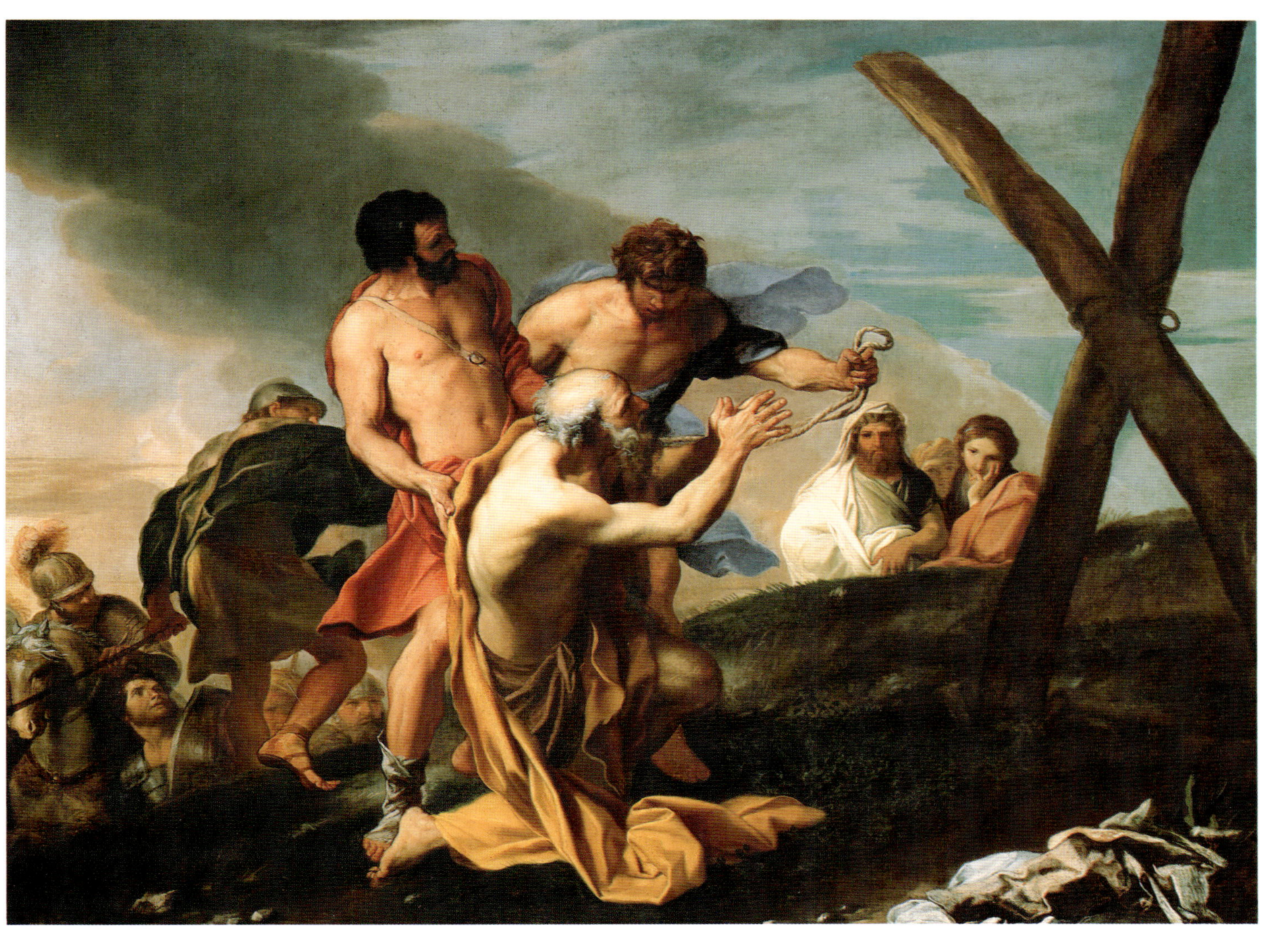

- 27 -

GIOVANNI BATTISTA SALVI CALLED IL SASSOFERRATO

Sassoferrato 1609-1685 Rome

The Young Christ, c. 1650s (?)

Oil on canvas

25½ x 19½ inches

PROVENANCE: Conte Orza, Orvieto, inherited from his wife the Contessa Maria Marticelli; consigned by a Mr. McDonald to Christie's; their sale, 7 February 1857, lot 166, sold to a Mr. Delessen or DeCessen;[1] Julius Weitzner, London, 1968

REFERENCES: Pepper 1984a, no. 108.2

This charming devotional painting underscores a vital aspect of Sassoferrato's oeuvre, that of the *copista*.[2] As has been noted, rather than being mere copies, these works, which continue in the vein of such great masters as Raphael, Federico Barocci, and Guido Reni, take on a life of their own outside the pictures from which they are derived.

The Bob Jones *Young Christ* was once attributed to Francesco Albani, a pupil of Annibale Carracci.[3] A drawing, now recognized to be by Salvi, formerly in the Earl of Plymouth's collection,[4] demonstrates the artist copying from Albani's altarpiece of the *Holy Family and God the Father* of 1628-32 for the Cagnoli chapel, S. Maria di Galliera, Bologna.[5] Sassoferrato lifted the figure of Christ out of Albani's picture for his drawing and squared it for transfer to canvas. The clouds of glory upon which putti play with the instruments of the Passion in the altarpiece now form a large halo or mandorla around the young Christ in Sassoferrato's painting. This innovation effectively eliminates the vacuum created by the isolation of the figure from the earlier composition and simultaneously emphasizes the work's devotional nature. As Francis Russell has written of this and Salvi's large production of similar pictures, "repetition has not drained these images of their devotional validity and they remain among the most telling statements of seventeenth-century pietism."[6]

1. The painting bears on its verso a label with the inscription in a nineteenth-century hand: "Sasso-ferrato p./from the Palazzo Mar-/-ticelli, Orvieto." Burton B. Fredericksen kindly informed me of the above provenance as contained in the Christie's catalogue, with the caveat that Roman export documents of the time do not contain a reference to this picture or others also reputedly from this collection nor to the names of these noble Orvietese.
2. For a general overview of Sassoferrato's work as a copyist, see Sassoferrato 1990, pp. 40-41. See also the excellent article by Francis Russell (1977).
3. Carlo Volpe is responsible for the reattribution to Sassoferrato (Pepper 1984a, p. 106).
4. It was included in a sale of drawings at Christie's, London, 1 July 1986, lot 129. I am grateful to David Steel for this information.
5. Russell 1977, p. 699.
6. Russell 1977, p. 695.

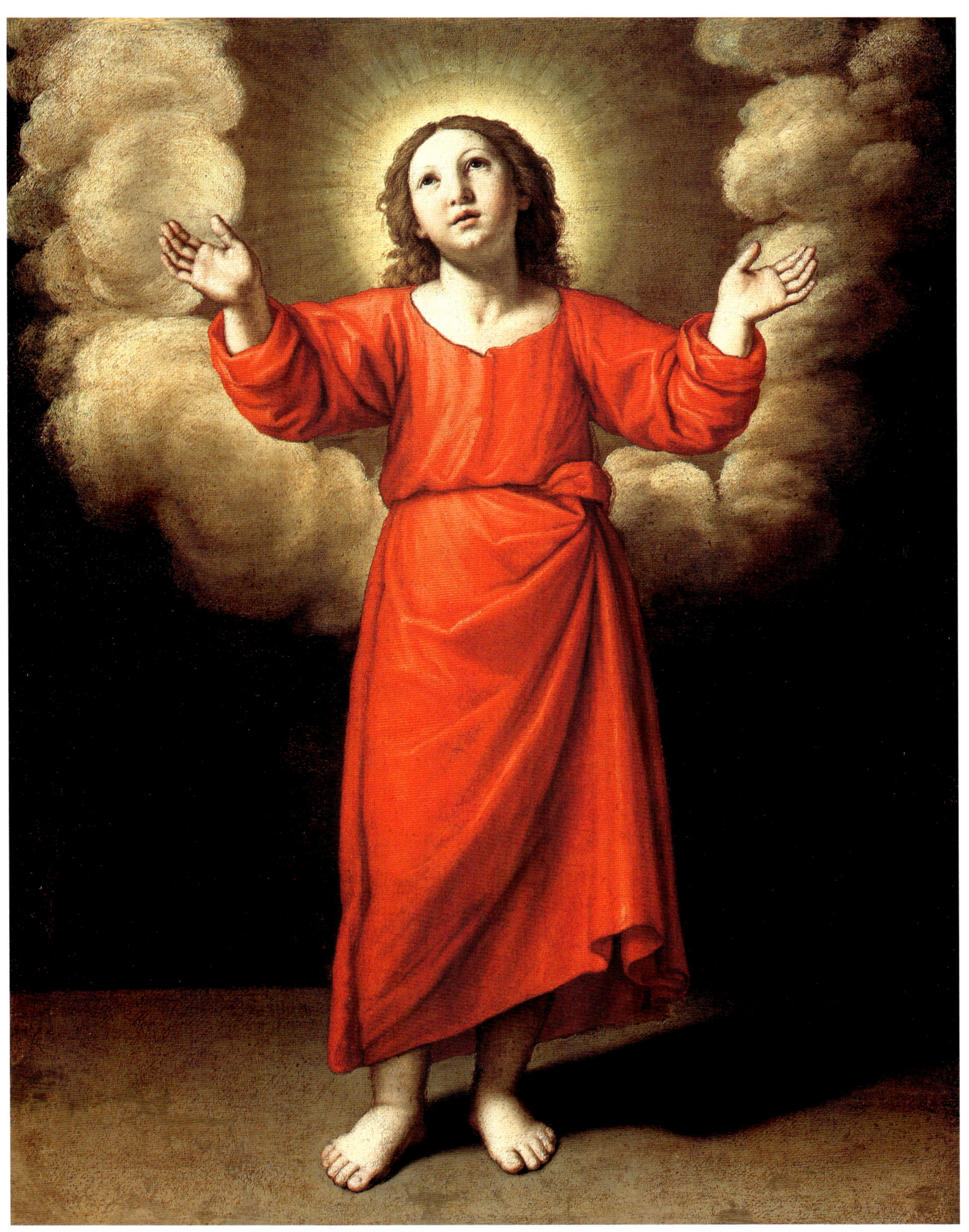

- 28 -

CIRCLE OF MATTEO ROSSELLI

Florence 1578-1651 Florence

Head of the Young Christ, c. 1610-30

Oil on panel

21⅜ x 17 inches

PROVENANCE: Galerie Farow, Paris; Wildenstein, New York; Gift of the Josephine Bay Paul and G. Michael Paul Foundation, 1964

REFERENCES: Pepper 1984a, no. 50.1 (as Jacopo da Empoli); Marabottini 1990, p. 278 (listed among works attributed to Empoli)

This panel has borne the ascription to Jacopo da Empoli since 1966, when his name was proposed by Philip Pouncey.[1] While the attribution to Empoli himself is difficult to sustain, the painting's context in seventeenth-century Florentine art is fairly certain. The *Head of the Young Christ* can be placed somewhere in the overlapping ambient of Empoli and Rosselli. The works of these two have been confused with one another and with those of Filippo Tarchiani (who with Rosselli frequented the studio of Gregorio Pagani).[2] Comparison with two paintings by Empoli—the *Incredulity of St. Thomas* of 1602 in the Museo della Collegiata, Empoli, and the *Calling of St. Matthew* of about 1618-20 in the Museo del Cenacolo di Foligno, Florence—casts some doubt on his responsibility for the Greenville panel. While both offer naturalistic, sensitively rendered images of the Savior like that of the present picture, ultimately, neither persuades—although it has been observed that the *Calling of St. Matthew,* the more similar in feeling to the Greenville *Christ,* is Empoli at his closest to Matteo Rosselli. [3] Alessandro Marabottini, in his monograph on Empoli, laid to rest the traditional attribution of the Bob Jones panel, while noting that the work is definitely Florentine, from the early part of the century. He suggests instead an artist from the circle of Rosselli, "probably a young pupil of Matteo."[4] Turning to Rosselli, there are two works by him that are analogous to the Bob Jones *Christ.* The earliest, of around 1621, is a *Holy Family with St. Anne and St. John the Baptist* (art market, London). The moist eyes and slightly opened mouth of this emotive portrayal of the admittedly younger Christ match the features in the Greenville painting. Also similar is the rendering of the halo. The later work is the *Supper at Emmaus* of 1643 in the Accademia Carrara, Bergamo.[5] While slightly more sentimental in feeling, the figure of Christ is close in physiognomy and pose. Until better evidence surfaces for a more secure attribution, this moving image should be ascribed to Matteo Rosselli or an artist in his circle.

The Bob Jones *Head of the Young Christ* finds its context in the reformist trend of late sixteenth- and early seventeenth-century Florentine art that fostered simple devotional images in which naturalism was employed to bring religious subject matter closer to the viewer's experience. Works similar in representation and function from the third generation of Seicento Florentine painters include Francesco Curradi's *Young Christ* (private collection, Florence) and Carlo Dolci's *Christ Blessing the Bread* (Dresden and another with Lord Methuen, Corsham Court). Elisabetta Sirani's *Bust of Christ* in the Museo de Arte de Ponce, Puerto Rico, is a Bolognese example of this same type of picture. The sheer quantity of these heads speaks to the contemporary demand for compelling and comforting images of Christ. Obviously, there were thematic as well as compositional variations within these devotional pictures, such as are explored here in the paintings of Ribera (cat. no. 21) and Sassoferrato (cat. no. 27).

1. This attribution has been maintained by Pepper (1984a, p. 54). Philip Pouncey had reversed himself from his opinion a year earlier (1965), when he tentatively gave the panel to Matteo Rosselli (opinion on file at the Art Gallery, Bob Jones University). My thanks to Miles Chappell for his expertise in helping me catalogue this work.
2. A prime example of this is a *Supper at Emmaus* in the Los Angeles County Museum of Art. This painting, attributed to Matteo Rosselli up to 1987 (Schaefer 1987, p. 87), has been recently and convincingly assigned to Tarchiani, along with two other versions in Munich and Aberdeenshire, the former also once misattributed to Rosselli (Claudio Pizzorusso in Florence 1987, p. 159). The Los Angeles painting, however, has also been associated with Empoli in the past via a picture in St. Petersburg (Marabottini discusses both; 1990, p. 277).
3. Marabottini 1990, pp. 118, 249-50.
4. Marabottini 1990, p. 278.
5. See Steingräber 1979; for the former, color plate II, p. 388, and for the latter, fig. 13, p. 389.

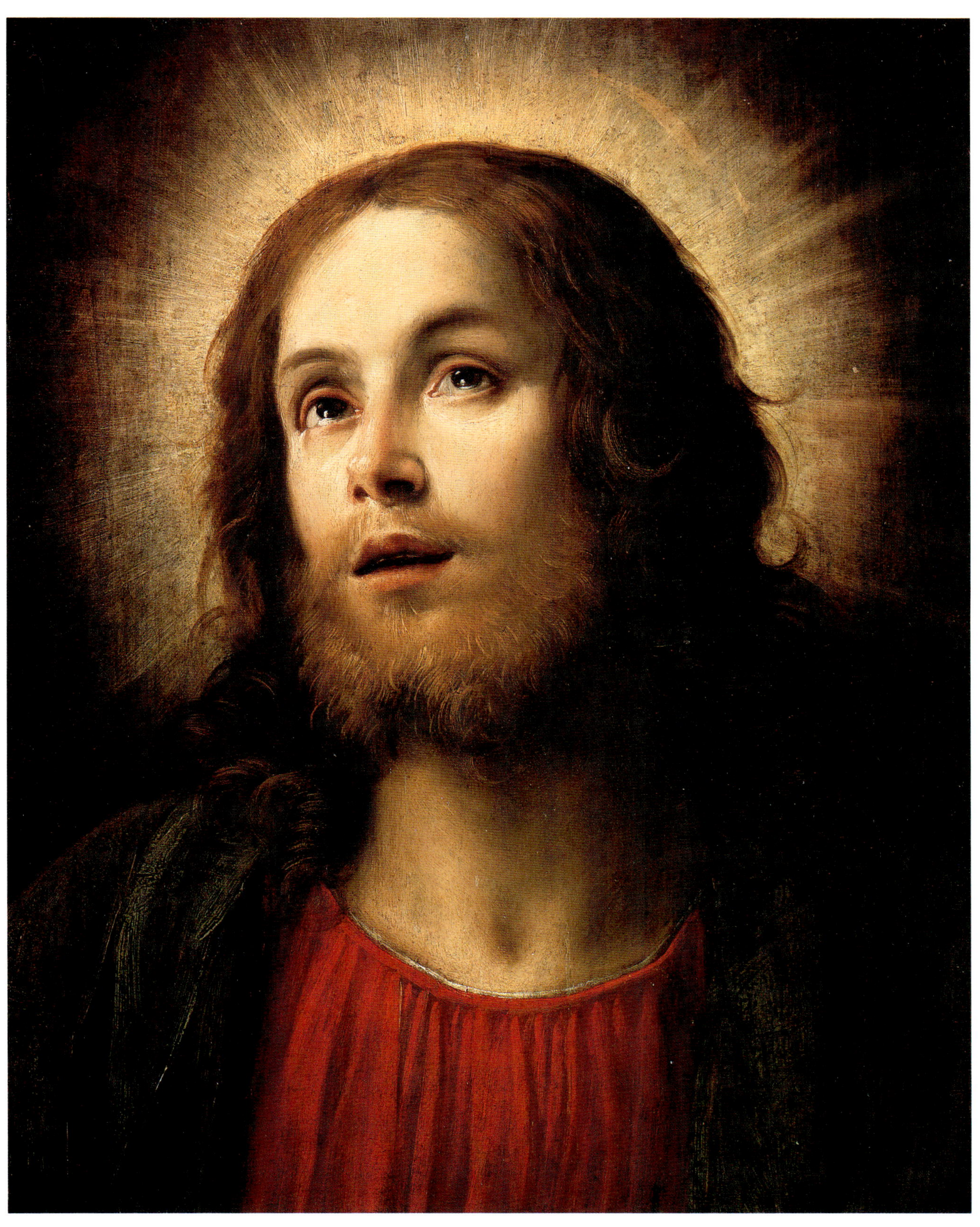

- 29 -

JACOPO VIGNALI

Pratovecchio 1592-1664 Florence

The Triumph of David, c. 1620

Oil on canvas

78⅝ x 92¼ inches

PROVENANCE: traditionally held to be from the Conti family, Florence; Dr. Isaac Lea, England, 1852; Elizabeth Jaudon Lea, Philadelphia, until 1960; Julius Weitzner, London, 1961

EXHIBITIONS: Philadelphia 1926 (as Rosselli); St. Petersburg 1965 (as Rosselli); Detroit 1965, no. 27 (as Rosselli); Hagerstown 1969; New York 1969, no. 26; Austin 1990

REFERENCES: Pepper 1984a, no. 132.2; Chappell 1990, p. 57

Vignali's *Triumph of David* is a fascinating example of Florentine Seicento painting. The two extremes of the school—one, the reformist trend with its interest in naturalism of which Cigoli and Empoli were exponents, and the other, a legacy of the *maniera* of Pontormo, Rosso, Bronzino, and Vasari—are here combined. The soft modeling of the faces reveals the seventeenth-century penchant for naturalism. The costumes reveal, simultaneously, this concern for realistic detail—as seen in the elaborate dress of the woman at the left or the brilliant red leggings and green tunic of David—and the Cinquecento taste for the bizarre and strident. The morbid, gigantic severed head of Goliath and the incongruousness of his oversized sword as contrasted with the slender physique of David are further evidence of this. Ultimately, the inherent mannerism of the composition, with its flat figures and their intricate poses, prevails. Vignali's vivid description of the various figures and their costumes foreshadows the style of his famous pupil, Carlo Dolci (cat. no. 30). There exists, in fact, a sketchbook of drawings "deriving from the circle of Vignali and possibly the work of the young Dolci in the 1630s," which includes a sheet of studies after the Bob Jones Vignali.[1] In this drawing, what appears to be the head of David taken from the present painting is consummately rendered in red chalk, surrounded by various pen and ink sketches.

The Greenville composition was formerly given to Matteo Rosselli, who was, or influenced, the artist responsible for the previous entry, the *Head of the Young Christ*. However, this painting can be given without reservation to Rosselli's student, Jacopo Vignali. [2] Painted scenes from the life of David were common in Seicento Florence—not surprising given the biblical figure's importance as a civic symbol during the fifteenth century, as seen in works by Donatello, Verrocchio, and Michelangelo. Single-figure compositions by Giovanni Biliverti (Dresden), Ottavio Vannini (Uffizi), and Dolci (Boston) show David dressed extravagantly (he wears a leopard skin in all three), as is his resplendent counterpart in the Bob Jones painting. Comparison with an extremely close composition of an analogous subject, Francesco Curradi's *Triumph of Judith* (in which the protagonist has just severed the head of the Assyrian general, Holofernes, seen carried by an attendant) in the Musée des Augustins, Toulouse, demonstrates the affinities between the work of Vignali and Curradi.[3] The procession in Curradi's picture also moves from right to left, where Judith is met by an Israelite priest. In both, the city walls form a backdrop at the left, a small child accompanies the hero or heroine, and the figures are splendidly arrayed.

1. Chappell 1990, pp. 56-57. The drawing is in the collection of the Indiana University Art Museum.
2. The ascription to Rosselli was proposed early by Hermann Voss (Pepper 1984a, p. 131), but in 1961 Roberto Longhi, Gerhard Ewald, and Carlo del Bravo identified the painting as by Vignali (opinions on file at the Art Gallery, Bob Jones University; see also Del Bravo 1961, p. 32).
3. Similarities in style between the paintings of Vignali and Curradi are noted only generally in New York 1969, p. 33.

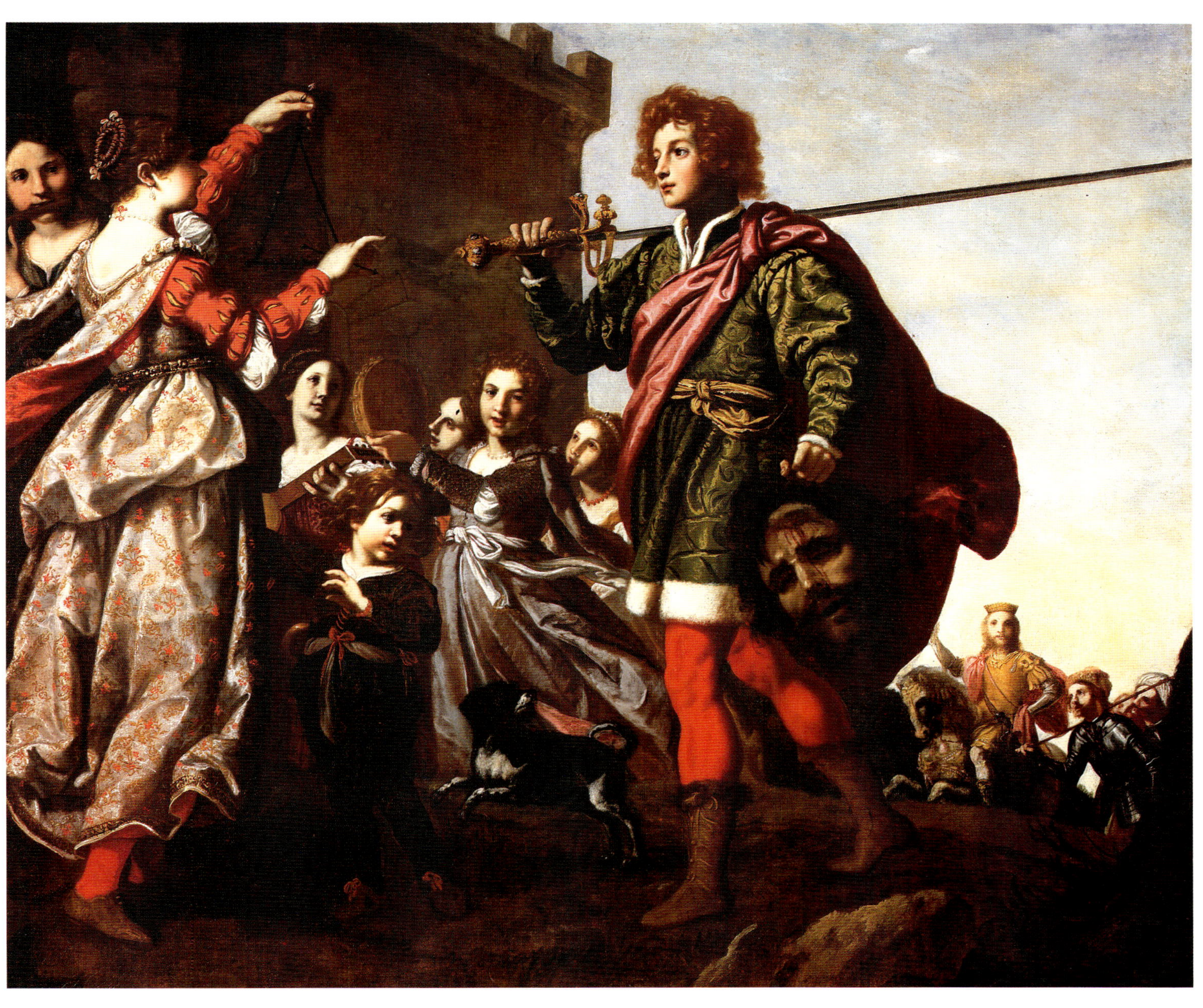

- 30 -

CARLO DOLCI

Florence 1616-1686 Florence

Madonna and Child, c. 1675

Oil on canvas

46½ x 40½ inches[1]

PROVENANCE: Fortier sale, Paris, 1770; Lord Clive; Baroness Darcy de Knayth; Sotheby's, London, 8 July 1964, lot 168A; Julius Weitzner, London, 1965

EXHIBITIONS: Winnipeg 1967; New York 1969, no. 67; Raleigh 1984, no. 11; Montgomery 1988, pp. 18, 27-29; Austin 1990

REFERENCES: Pepper 1984a, no. 49.2

Carlo Dolci, as noted in the previous entry, continued in the vein of his teacher Jacopo Vignali to paint in a realistic manner, with figures and costumes carefully observed. However, Dolci's style became hyperreal, with the artist's almost obsessive, painstaking approach to detail. This style, together with his tendency toward extreme piety, made the artist an ideal vehicle for the production of devotional subjects. The climate at the court of the Grand Duchy of Tuscany, with its bent toward the morbid and the extremely religious, both was reflected in and encouraged the kind of art practiced by Dolci. The Bob Jones University *Madonna and Child* is a superb example of the type of devotional painting that the pious Grand Duchess Vittoria commissioned from Dolci; a number of such works are still in the Palazzo Pitti in Florence.[2] The high quality of the painting and the artist's use of gold leaf in the halos of the Virgin and Child indicate that the picture was destined for a member of the Medici family or some other extremely important patron. This technique recalls the gold-ground panels of the Trecento and Quattrocento and must have appealed to the artist for its evocation of the nontemporal world.

In this graceful composition, the Virgin steadies the Christ Child as he strides forward, his hand raised in benediction. Among the several versions of this subject by Dolci, the best known is that in the Palazzo Pitti.[3] Although this work differs from the Greenville canvas in its familiar Florentine octagonal shape and its lack of the exquisite still life formed by the cushion and the sewing basket, the figures of the Madonna and Child are nearly identical. Filippo Baldinucci, Dolci's friend and biographer, records that two images of "Maria Vergine gloriosissima" were painted in 1675, one for the Grand Duchess Vittoria and the other for the "rich" Florentine gentleman, Filippo Franceschi.[4] If this is in fact a reference to the Pitti *Madonna* (there are no other pictures referred to by Baldinucci painted for Vittoria resembling the description of the Pitti *Madonna*), then dating the Bob Jones version to 1675 is plausible, and, moreover, suggests that it may be the picture painted for Filippo Franceschi. A *tondo* representing the *Madonna and Child with St. John the Baptist* in the Houston Museum of Fine Arts should probably be ascribed to Dolci's workshop. It is clearly yet another, close variation on this subject; there are subtle alterations in the composition, as well as the obvious difference in format and the inclusion of St. John.[5]

The representation of the Madonna and Child extends far back into Italian art. However, just as the development in North Italy of half-length devotional pictures of the Madonna and Child (as seen, for example, in the works of Andrea Mantegna and his brother-in-law Giovanni Bellini) depended on the models of Donatello,[6] Dolci's image ultimately owes its existence to Florentine Quattrocento sculptural reliefs.[7] Moreover, Dolci has infused this painting with a grace and sweetness reminiscent of Raphael's Florentine Madonnas.

1. A strip of canvas approximately ¼ inch wide has been added to the left edge of the picture.
2. The collections there having been formed by the Medici and given to the city by the last of the Medici, Anna Maria Luisa, at her death in 1743.
3. For the painting, see Detroit 1974, no. 122.
4. Baldinucci ed. Ranalli 1681-1728, V, p. 355. Gerhard Ewald accepts G. Masselli's suggestion that this citation refers to the Pitti *Madonna* (Detroit 1974, p. 214), and consequently, its date of 1675. However, the question of identifying and thus dating from Baldinucci's reference the Bob Jones *Madonna* is not so easily resolved; numerous other versions of the Madonna and Child are mentioned by Baldinucci, such as those including flower still lifes painted around 1650 for the Marchese Gerini, Monsignore Albizzi, Duke Salviati, and an unknown patron (Baldinucci ed. Ranalli 1681-1728, V, p. 349). There is the *Madonna dei gigli,* dated 1642, at Montpellier (see Del Bravo 1963, pp. 36, 39, fig. 44b; and Pepper 1984a, p. 53). Finally,

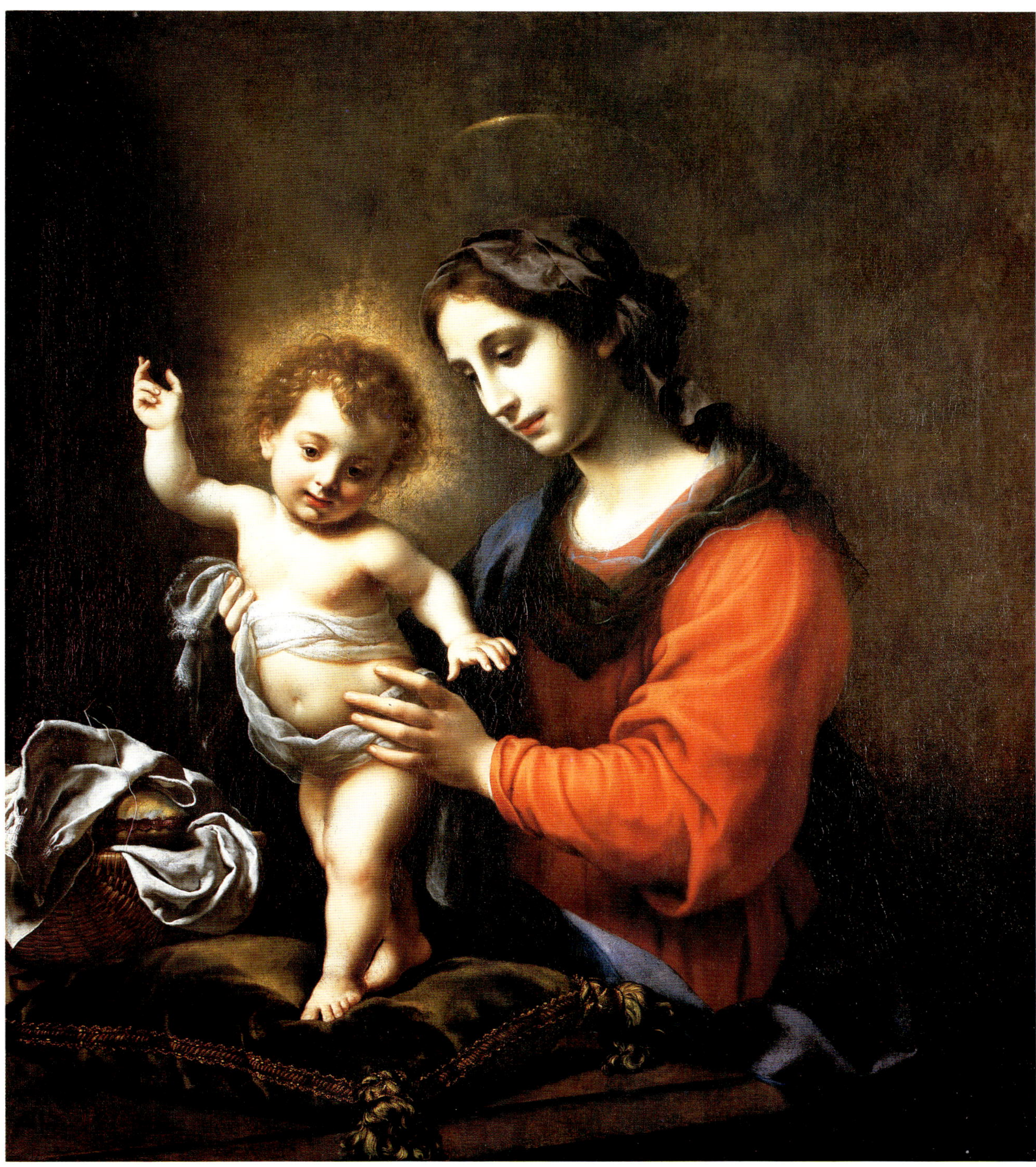

Baldinucci mentions yet another version, "a beautiful Virgin with Child, similar to that done for the Marchese Gerini" and describes the Madonna with a lily and a basket of flowers. This was one of the "entirely finished" works found in Dolci's studio after his death in 1686 (Baldinucci ed. Ranalli 1681-1728, V, p. 362).

5. Gift of Herbert Godwin, inv. no. 46-28. The museum's dating of their picture to about 1636 should be revised in light of its apparent derivative relationship to the other two.
6. See, most recently, Keith Christiansen in New York 1992a, pp. 97-98, 139.
7. Günther Heinz (1960, pp. 233-34) remarks on the tradition in Florence of the influence of sculpture on painting, noting that the *Madonna* in the Palazzo Pitti is a variation on reliefs from Bernardo Rossellino's workshop.

– 31 –

DOMENICO FIASELLA
CALLED IL SARZANA

Sarzana 1589-1669 Genoa

The Flight into Egypt, c. 1615

Oil on canvas

62⅛ x 44½ inches

PROVENANCE: Pope Paul V (?); Durlacher Brothers, New York, 1933; Minneapolis Institute of Arts, 1934; Julius Weitzner, New York, 1958

EXHIBITIONS: Dayton 1962, no. 32

REFERENCES: Pepper 1984a, no. 53.1; Genoa 1990, pp. 18, 96

This important painting from the early career of Domenico Fiasella has suffered from the same neglect that has shadowed the achievements of the Genoese school. Fortunately, several exhibitions and publications have drawn the attention of American scholars and the public to this movement, in large part due to the efforts of Robert Manning and Bertina Suida Manning and Mary Newcome Schleier. The present picture was featured in one of these early, groundbreaking exhibitions, *Genoese Masters: Cambiaso to Magnasco, 1550-1750,* held in Dayton and Sarasota in 1962.[1]

Despite reservations expressed at that time,[2] it is now generally accepted that the Bob Jones *Flight into Egypt* is by Fiasella. In fact, it may well be the painting characterized as one of his most famous by Raffaello Soprani, the seventeenth-century historiographer of Genoese artists. Soprani records its being given to Pope Paul V, who is said to have liked it very much.[3] The artist's work must have been popular in Rome (where Fiasella is known to have been in 1615), for two impressive paintings, comparable in style to the Bob Jones picture and now in the John and Mable Ringling Museum of Art, Sarasota, are documented as having been in the renowned collection of the Marchese Vincenzo Giustiniani, patron of, among others, Caravaggio.[4] The lessons learned by Fiasella in the Eternal City—where he saw, firsthand, works by the Bolognese school and by Ludovico Carracci, as well as those by Caravaggio and his circle—infuse this composition and date it, as Piero Donati has written, "with certainty to the Roman years."[5]

The frieze-like arrangement of the figures of Mary, Joseph, and the Christ Child contributes to the stately quality of the composition, and reflects Fiasella's exposure to the art of ancient Rome as well as the Bolognese artists there reinterpreting it at that moment. Also evident in the Bob Jones painting is the influence of Caravaggio, especially in the *verismo* of the face of Joseph. It should be pointed out that the altarpiece of the *Visitation* in S. Maria Assunta in Fiasella's hometown of Sarzana incorporates the same figure of Joseph as that in the Bob Jones *Flight into Egypt.* The Sarzana painting is datable to after 1616 (when the artist is recorded back in Sarzana), near the *Martyrdom of St. Barbara* of 1622.[6]

1. The importance of this exhibition is noted in Eric M. Zafran's essay in this catalogue (pp. 79-80).
2. See Rosenberg 1963, p. 209, where the author assigns it to the Bolognese school, understandable given those distinct overtones in Fiasella's Roman works.
3. Soprani and Ratti 1768, I, p. 227.
4. See Salerno 1960a, p. 27; Salerno 1960b, nos. 161-62.
5. Genoa 1990, p. 96.
6. Genoa 1990, p. 96. This correspondence was noted earlier in Dayton 1962, no. 32. The *Visitation,* vis-à-vis the Bob Jones picture, contains other Roman reminiscences, particularly as seen in the figures of Mary and Anna, which recall those of Federico Barocci's famous and influential altarpiece in the Chiesa Nuova, in place by 1586.

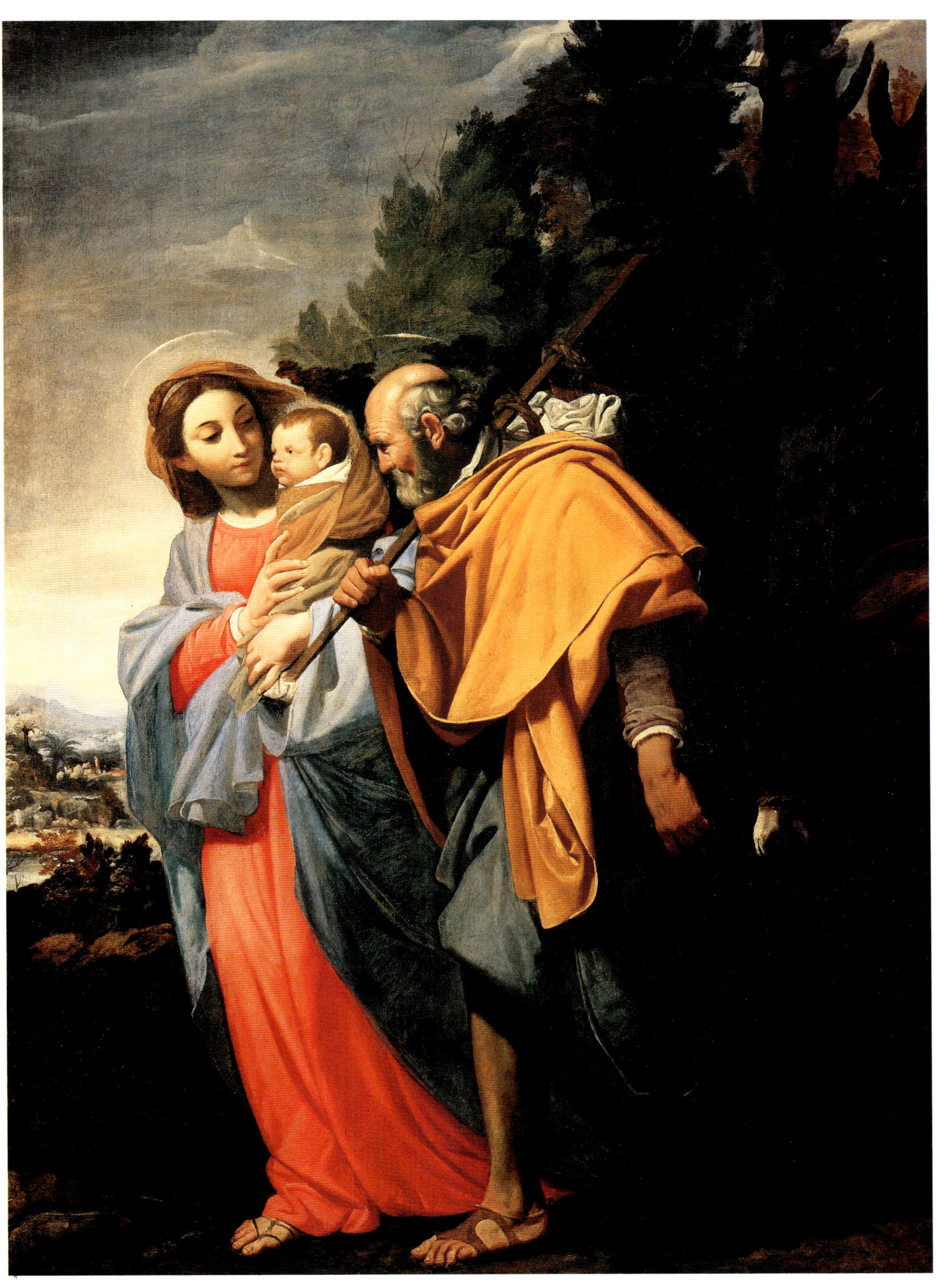

- 32 -

BERNARDO STROZZI

Genoa 1581-1644 Venice

Christ and the Woman of Samaria, c. 1630

Oil on canvas

44½ x 47¾ inches

PROVENANCE: Julius Weitzner, New York, 1956

EXHIBITIONS: Lawrence 1958; Binghamton 1967, no. 26; Hagerstown 1969; Raleigh 1984, no. 41; Austin 1990

REFERENCES: Pepper 1984a, no. 119.1

Scholars have dated the Bob Jones *Christ and the Woman of Samaria* either to Strozzi's last years in Genoa or to his first years in Venice.[1] One of the painting's striking aspects is the evident influence of the Lombard school—as exemplified by Giulio Cesare Procaccini and Giovanni Battista Crespi, called Il Cerano—which favors its execution during the later years in Genoa. The delicate coloration and the profile of Christ recall works by Procaccini, while the dazzling brushwork is reminiscent of Cerano.[2]

The scene is described in John 4:1-30, in which Christ speaks to a sinful woman of the despised people of Samaria. His metaphor alludes to the nearby well: "Whosoever drinketh of this water shall thirst again: But whosoever drinketh of the water that I shall give him shall never thirst; but the water that I shall give him shall be in him a well of water springing up into everlasting life." As with many other Strozzi compositions, several versions exist. The one closest to the Greenville painting is in the Viscount Scarsdale's collection, Kedleston Hall. The two are nearly identical in composition with only slight differences in the brushwork. The present picture is certainly as fine as the Kedleston version; in some passages it excels over that painting and in others areas it is different or less successful. There is a third, in a Dutch collection, that is later in date, reversed in composition, and different in details.[3] A drawing by Strozzi in the Museum of Fine Arts, Budapest, like the Dutch picture, reverses the composition, but it is very close in concept and in many details to the Greenville and Kedleston versions.[4]

1. Luisa Mortari (1966, p. 144) proposes either dating. Milkovich (in Binghamton 1967, p. 64) suggests the late Genoese period. Others scholars date it early in the Venetian period; see London 1979, p. 91; Pepper 1984a, p. 115; and Raleigh 1984, p. 132.
2. For the Genoa-Milan connection, in particular the visits between the two cities by Genoese aristocrats and collectors and the presence of Lombard artists and their works in Genoa, see Maria Clelia Galassi, "I Lombardi e i loro 'amici' genovesi: Pittori e collezionisti fra Genova e Milano, 1610-1630," in Genoa 1992a, pp. 11-20.
3. Mortari 1966, p. 138.
4. Mortari 1966, fig. 473.

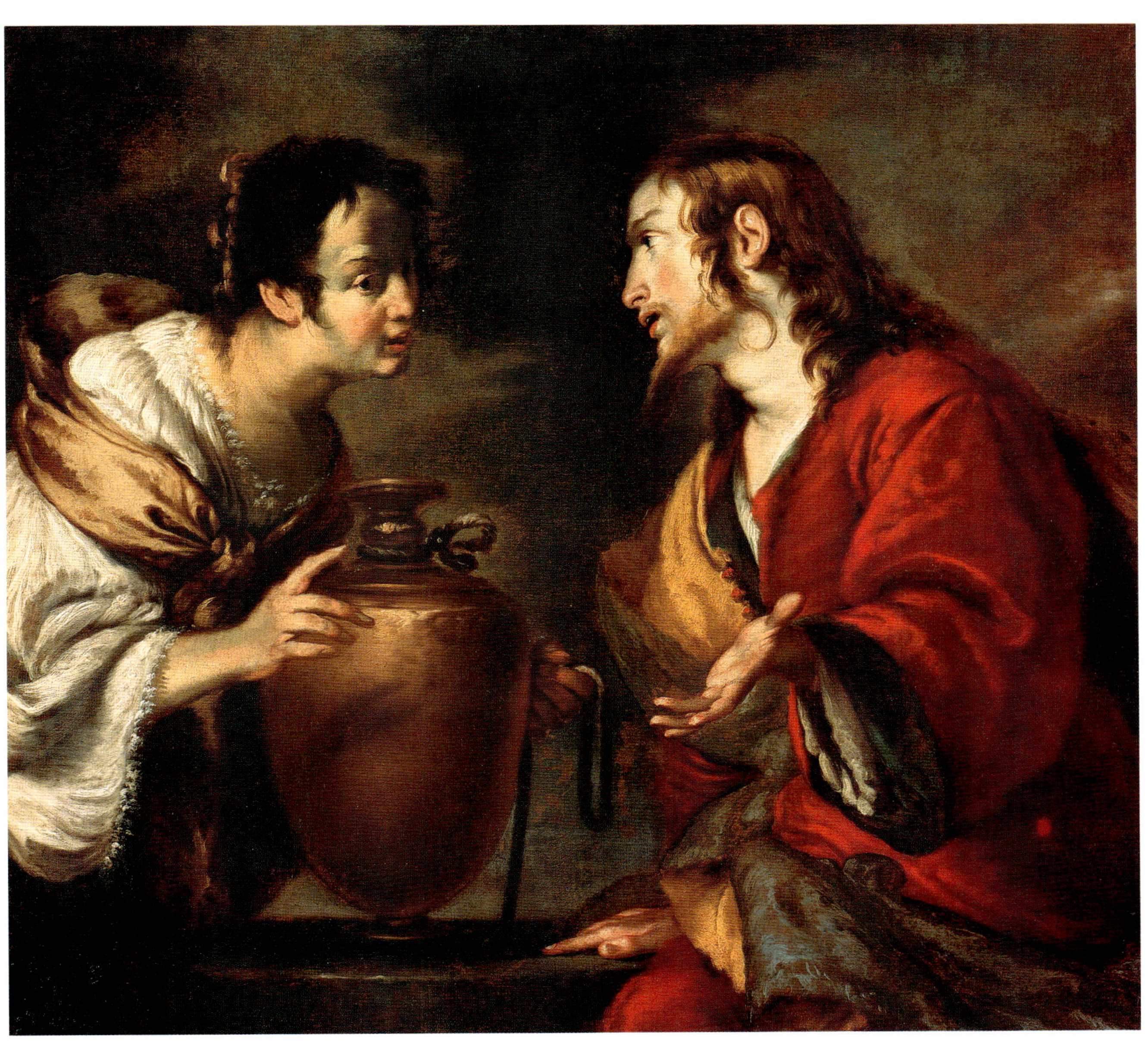

- 33 -

BARTOLOMEO GUIDOBONO CALLED IL PRETE DI SAVONA

Savona 1654-1709 Turin

Rest on the Flight into Egypt, c. 1680

Oil on copper

19⅛ x 15½ inches

PROVENANCE: Gift of Mr. and Mrs. Morris Kaplan, Chicago, 1961

EXHIBITIONS: Raleigh 1984, no. 21; Austin 1990

REFERENCES: Pepper 1984a, no. 64.1; Frankfurt 1992, p. 177

Bartolomeo Guidobono's decorative and highly finished style is perfectly consonant with the medium of oil on copper. The overall impression conveyed by this small-scale work is of great charm and preciousness. It comes as no surprise to learn, then, that Guidobono's early training was with his father, Giovanni Antonio, who was a painter of majolica.[1] Apart from its polished execution, the *Rest on the Flight* has a Correggesque air, no doubt due to the influence of the sixteenth-century artist as filtered through other Genoese painters of the time, Domenico Piola and Gregorio de Ferrari, in addition to Guidobono's own visit to Parma in the 1670s. It was there, in the cupola of the Cathedral, that Bartolomeo would have seen Correggio's angelic company floating in ethereal clouds around the Virgin. Similar angels, delicately modeled in the master's soft *sfumatura,* are found in the Bob Jones composition.[2] An influence closer to home is a painting by Piola in the Church of the Gesù, Genoa, depicting the same subject.[3] The impact on Piola of Correggio's *Rest on the Flight* (or the *Madonna della Scodella*) is obvious despite Piola's rearrangement of elements from Correggio's composition. The variations that are carried over from Piola to Guidobono are telling. In both, palms form a canopy over the Virgin and Child, the latter reaches up for dates proffered by an angel, while putti hover above. The broken idol's head—which simultaneously situates the scene in Egypt, alludes to Antiquity, and refers to an episode during the Flight[4]—occupies the lower left corner in both the Piola and the Bob Jones picture. (For an earlier Genoese treatment of this subject, see the painting by Piola's teacher, Domenico Fiasella, cat. no. 31.)

Guidobono painted yet another version of this theme, now in the Suida Manning collection, New York, which is distinctly different, oval in format, and should be dated later, toward 1685.[5] There are also two drawings by Guidobono of the *Rest on the Flight,* one in the collection of the Art Gallery of the University of Colorado at Boulder, and the other in the Palazzo Rosso, Genoa. Newcome Schleier notes that the Palazzo Rosso sheet is a preliminary sketch for the Greenville painting, since the basic elements in each relate in terms of placement and action.[6]

1. For Guidobono's life, see Newcome Schleier 1981, pp. 25-36.
2. The comparison with Correggio, specifically, his *Madonna della Scodella* (Parma), has been made on several occasions, first in Suida Manning 1972, p. 205.
3. Guidobono worked with Piola, with whom he also shared family ties (Newcome Schleier 1981, p. 25). The Piola *Rest on the Flight into Egypt* is reproduced in Genoa 1992b, p. 64.
4. See Raleigh 1984, p. 78.
5. Newcome Schleier (in Frankfurt 1992, p. 177) proposes a time frame of 1680-85. The Bob Jones copper would certainly appear to date earlier than the version in New York (Newcome herself says as much; see Pepper 1984a, p. 67); indeed, the Suida Manning picture seems to foreshadow the *dix-huitième* (in fact, it was once attributed to Jean-Baptiste Le Prince).
6. Newcome 1976, n.p.

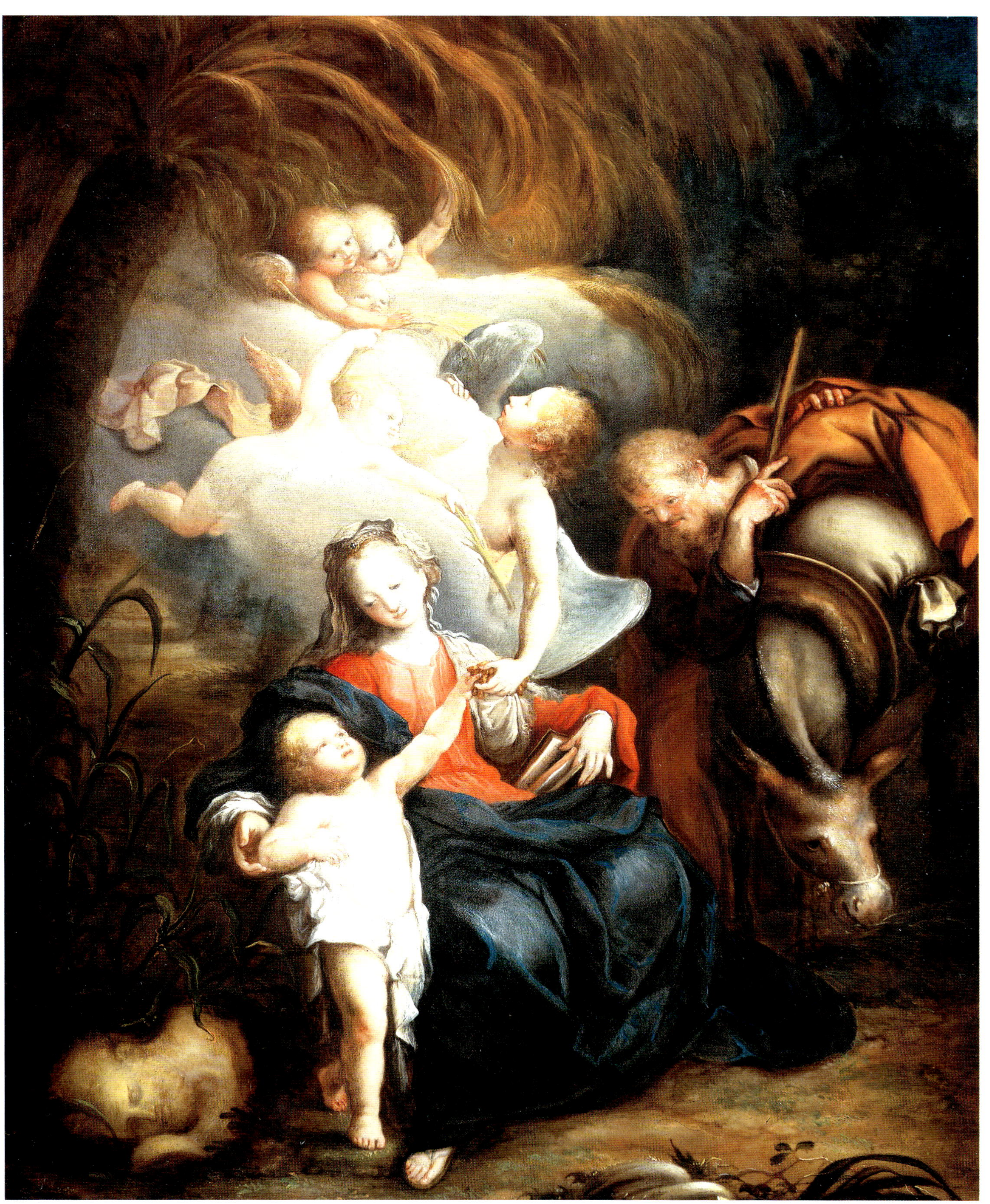

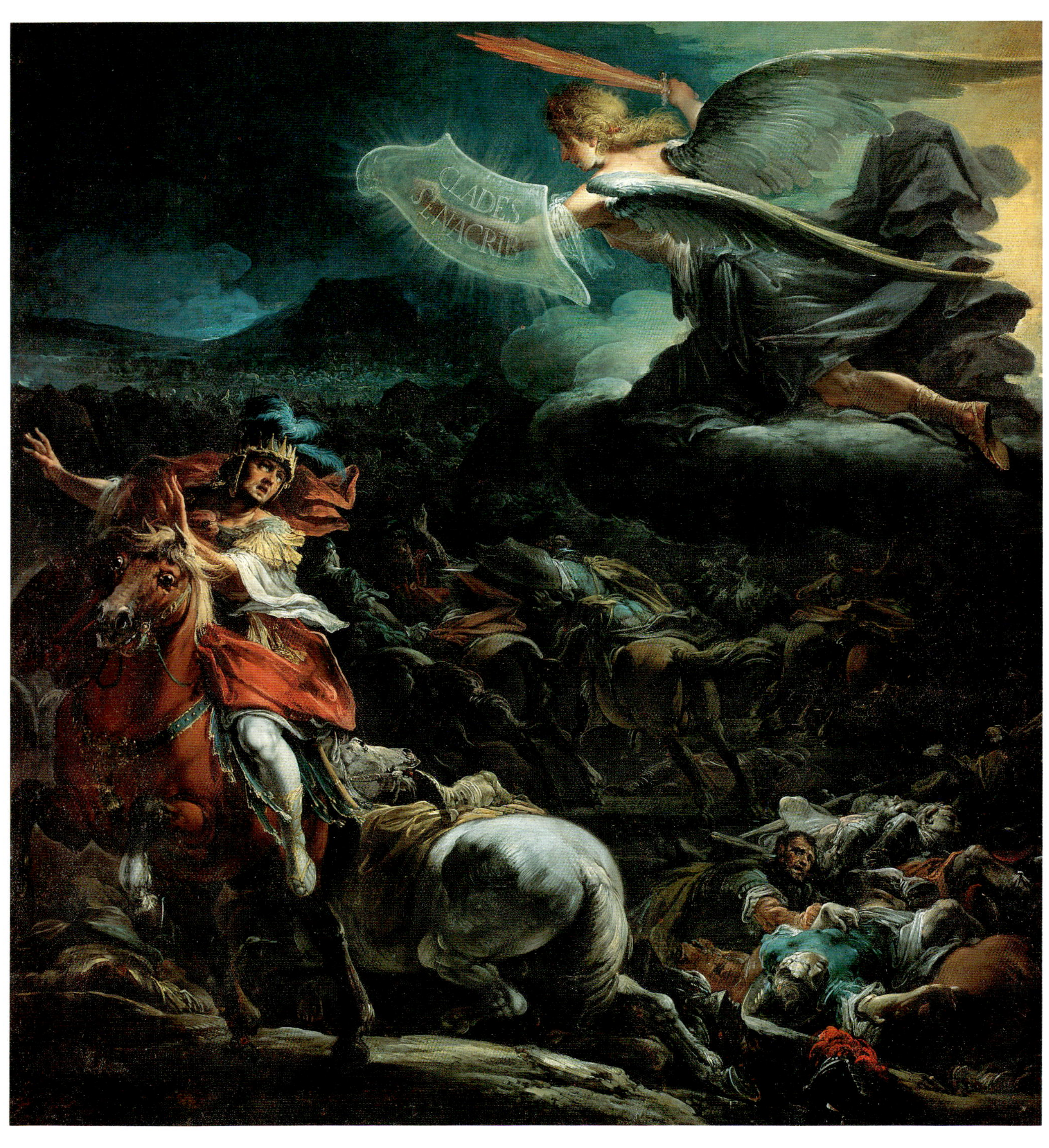
CLADES
SENACRIB

- 3 4 -

ILARIO MERCANTI CALLED SPOLVERINI

Parma 1657-1734 Parma

The Destruction of the Army of Sennacherib, 1690-1700 (?)

Oil on canvas

66 x 63¾ inches

PROVENANCE: brought from Italy by Algernon William Bellingham Greville; sale of his widow, Louisa Fanny, died 1904, sold to J.W. Pickaine;[1] Naval, Army, and Air Force Institutes, Aldershot; Sotheby's, London, 30 April 1947, lot 84, sold to Messrs. Soames;[2] Sotheby's, London, 28 April 1965, lot 105; Julius Weitzner, London, 1965

EXHIBITIONS: Hagerstown 1969

REFERENCES: Pallucchini 1949, p. 164; Liverpool 1977, p. 177; Zava Boccazzi 1979, p. 134; Pepper 1984a, no. 118.1

Spolverini is described by Raffaella Arisi Riccardi in the title of her 1979 monograph as a "pittore di battaglie e cerimonie." This appellation aptly sums up Spolverini's production, which consists primarily of battle scenes and depictions of ceremonial pageantry. The Bob Jones work is remarkable not only for its exceptional quality, but also as an infrequent foray by Spolverini into religious subject matter.

The biblical story, from 2 Kings 18-19, relates how the Assyrian king Sennacherib and his army were poised to invade the kingdom of Judah. However, responding to King Hezekiah's plea to God for assistance, the Angel of the Lord destroys the Assyrian army at night; here, the avenging angel's shield is inscribed in Latin "Clades Senacrib," or "Destruction to Sennacherib." This work is a powerful synthesis of religious painting and the then fashionable battle scene. Stephen Pepper has already noted compositional affinities between the Bob Jones picture and that by Spolverini's teacher Francesco Monti, called Il Brescianino, *The Hebrews Conducted to Safety by Moses and Aaron,* painted before 1695 and now in the Museo Civico, Piacenza.[3] Moreover, Arisi Riccardi has observed that such similarities between works by the two artists in this genre have caused some confusion as to attribution.[4] In addition to the compositional correspondences, both scenes are characterized by flashes of color—predominantly blues and touches of red with dramatic white highlights—and are painted with rapid, staccato brushstrokes.

The present work was one of seven first recorded together at Sotheby's in 1947 (lots 82-88). According to that sale catalogue, Algernon Greville (1815-1887) brought seven paintings back from Italy, which had formerly belonged to "a Cardinal."[5] In addition to the Bob Jones canvas, the group comprised the following: Antonio Balestra's *Death of Abel* (Graves Art Gallery, Sheffield; Fig. 1),[6] a *Raising of Lazarus* either by Balestra or his studio (Walker Art Gallery, Liverpool; Fig. 2),[7] Giambattista Pittoni's *Solomon and the Queen of Sheba* (Walker Art Gallery, Liverpool; Fig. 3),[8] and *Christ and the Woman Taken in Adultery* (Graves Art Gallery, Sheffield; Fig. 4),[9] and two untraced works attributed to G.A. Boni, a *Christ Healing the Blind* and *Christ in the House of Simon.*[10] The relationship of the five extant paintings is not clear, either stylistically, thematically, or compositionally, although they do share identical dimensions. (They are reproduced for the first time together here.) It has been suggested that the theme of this series, if indeed it was a commission by a single patron, is that of justice and mercy, and that the paintings once decorated "the hall of a legal or charitable fraternity or the refectory of an order devoted to the care of prisoners or the infirm."[11] Although the thematic connection between the paintings may be plausible, the proposed function of the group is purely supposition. The Old Testament scenes do appear to deal with the idea of justice—that is, God's condemnation of Cain and divine retribution against the Assyrians—and the New Testament, with Christ's acts of mercy—Christ restoring life to Lazarus, forgiving the adulteress, healing the blind man, and forgiving the sinful woman, who washed his feet with her tears in the house of Simon the Pharisee. The Liverpool *Solomon and the Queen of Sheba,* however, does not fit as easily into either of these categories. While the subject may be loosely construed as treating the theme of justice,[12] if the painting actually depicted Esther before Ahasuerus, it could be interpreted as a scene of both mercy and justice.[13]

The predominance of artists from the Veneto—Balestra and Pittoni with six canvases between them (assuming the two "Boni" were in fact by Pittoni)—would suggest that the hypothetical patron was also from that region. It is possible that Spolverini's battle scene was produced while there, although a Venetian visit cannot be ascribed with certainty to the artist.[14] In any case, a stay in Venice could not have been after 1692, which is when

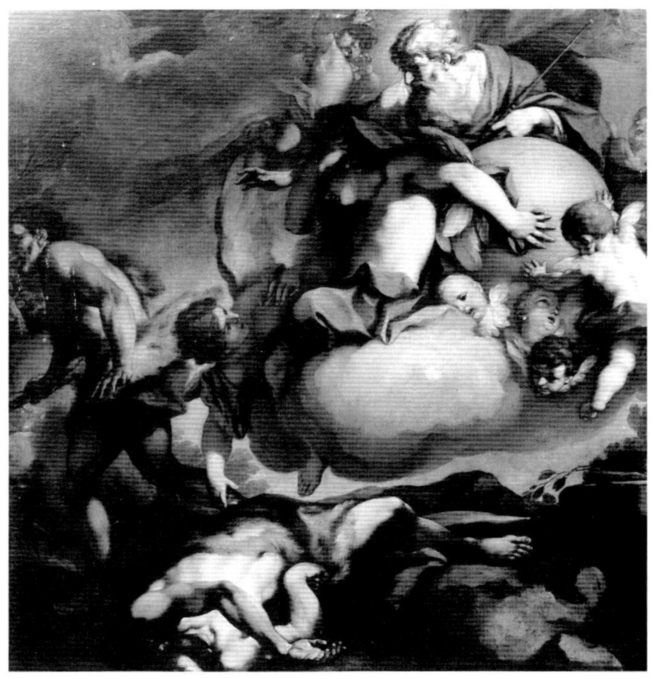

Figure one. Antonio Balestra, *Death of Abel,* Graves Art Gallery, Sheffield. Photograph courtesy of the Sheffield City Art Galleries.

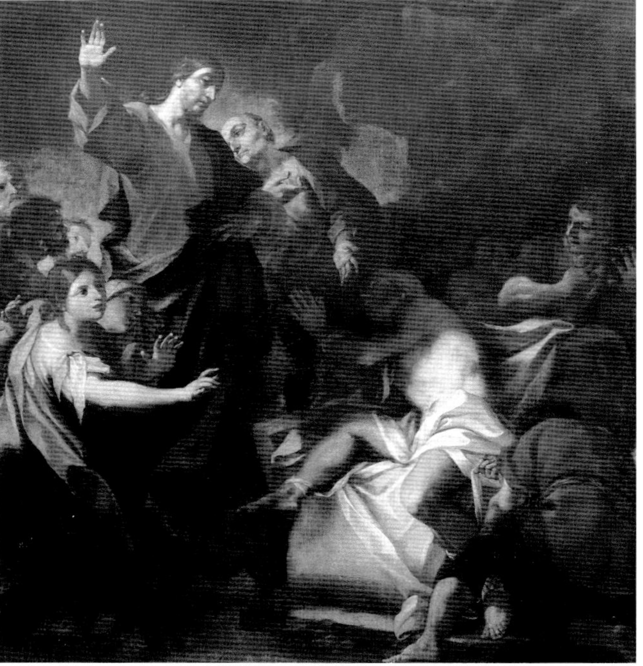

Figure two. Studio of Balestra, *Raising of Lazarus,* Walker Art Gallery, Liverpool. Photograph courtesy of the National Museums and Galleries, Merseyside.

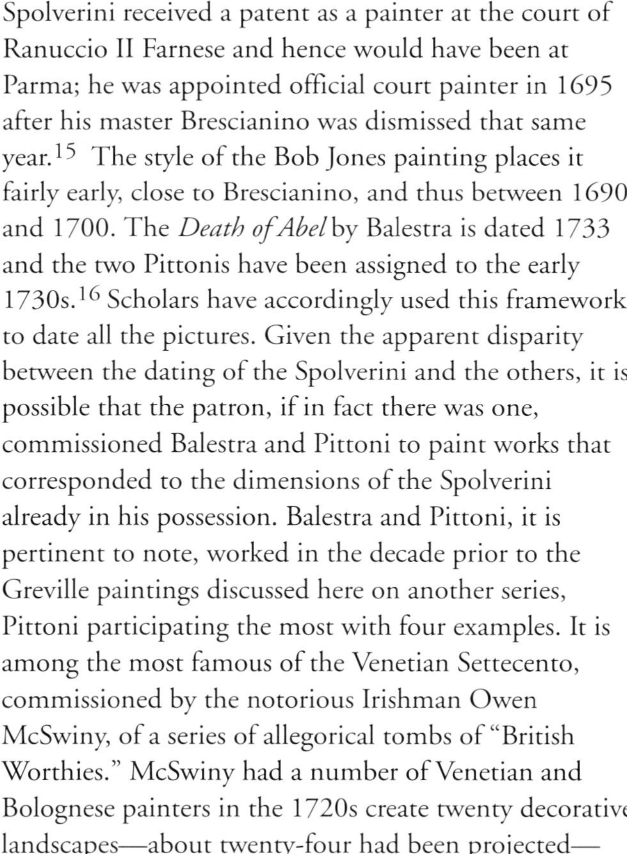

Spolverini received a patent as a painter at the court of Ranuccio II Farnese and hence would have been at Parma; he was appointed official court painter in 1695 after his master Brescianino was dismissed that same year.[15] The style of the Bob Jones painting places it fairly early, close to Brescianino, and thus between 1690 and 1700. The *Death of Abel* by Balestra is dated 1733 and the two Pittonis have been assigned to the early 1730s.[16] Scholars have accordingly used this framework to date all the pictures. Given the apparent disparity between the dating of the Spolverini and the others, it is possible that the patron, if in fact there was one, commissioned Balestra and Pittoni to paint works that corresponded to the dimensions of the Spolverini already in his possession. Balestra and Pittoni, it is pertinent to note, worked in the decade prior to the Greville paintings discussed here on another series, Pittoni participating the most with four examples. It is among the most famous of the Venetian Settecento, commissioned by the notorious Irishman Owen McSwiny, of a series of allegorical tombs of "British Worthies." McSwiny had a number of Venetian and Bolognese painters in the 1720s create twenty decorative landscapes—about twenty-four had been projected—depicting the imaginary funerary monuments of the Duke of Devonshire, Isaac Newton, and Lord Stanhope, among others. Other Venetian artists patronized by McSwiny include Canaletto, Piazzetta, Cimaroli, and the Ricci.[17] Thus, this probable series to which the Spolverini *Destruction of the Army of Sennacherib* at Bob Jones University belongs would not have been an isolated example in eighteenth-century North Italian painting.

1. According to the label found on the verso of another picture in the group of seven works that included the present painting (Balestra's *Death of Abel,* now in the Graves Art Gallery, Sheffield; see below). Presumably this provenance is common to all seven until their dispersal at auction in 1947.
2. According to the records of the Graves Art Gallery, Sheffield.
3. Pepper 1984a, p. 114. For Francesco Monti, see Piacenza 1975.
4. Arisi Riccardi 1979, pp. 10, 22.
5. Sotheby & Co., *Catalogue of Old Master Drawings and Paintings...*, London, 30 April 1947, p. 10. Greville's ownership of the pictures is confirmed by the presence of his monogram "AG" on the stretcher of the Pittoni

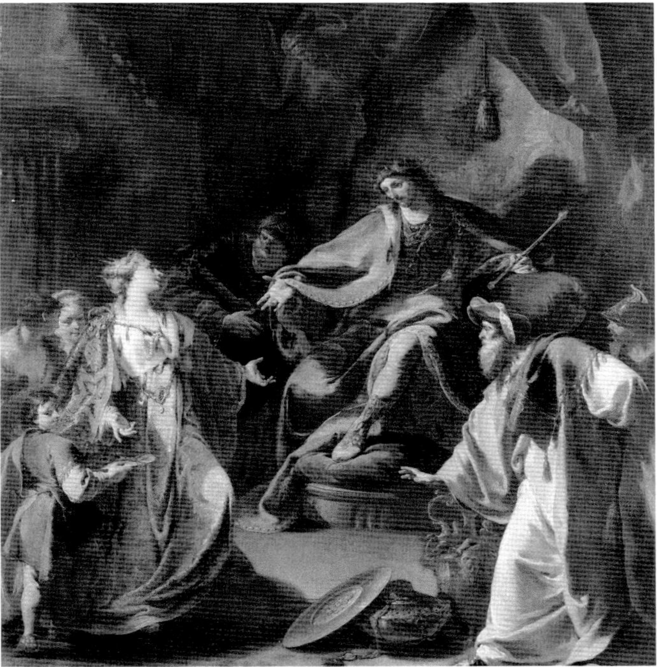

FIGURE THREE. Giambattista Pittoni, *Solomon and the Queen of Sheba,* Walker Art Gallery, Liverpool. Photograph courtesy of the National Museums and Galleries, Merseyside.

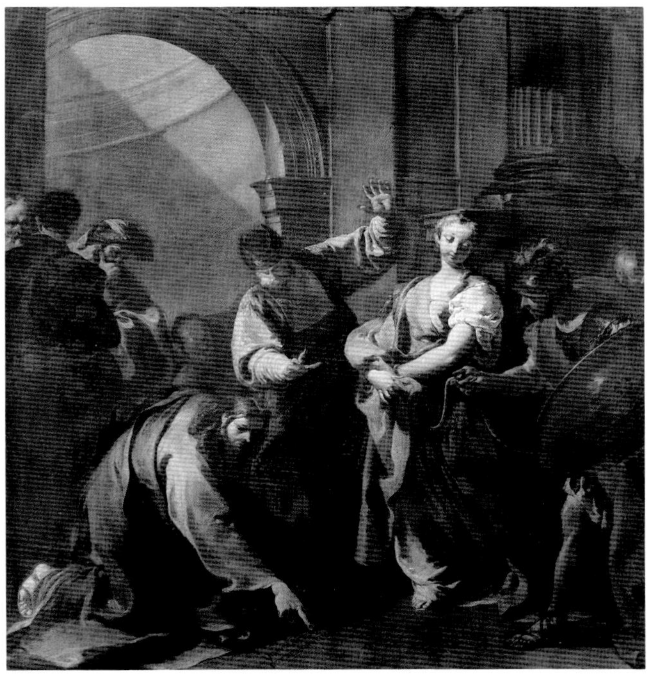

FIGURE FOUR. Giambattista Pittoni, *Christ and the Woman Taken in Adultery,* Graves Art Gallery, Sheffield. Photograph courtesy of the Sheffield City Art Galleries.

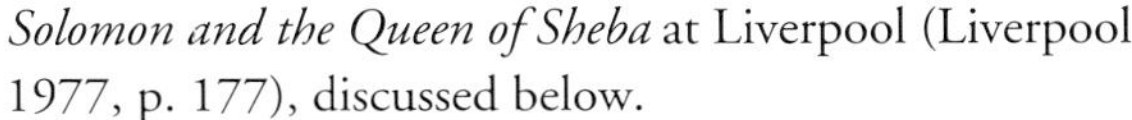

Solomon and the Queen of Sheba at Liverpool (Liverpool 1977, p. 177), discussed below.

6. Sheffield 1966, p. 38; Polazzo 1990, no. 57. Signed and dated, "Ant. Balestra Veronensis fec. 1733."
7. Ascribed to the studio in Liverpool 1963, no. 619. Given to Balestra alone in Liverpool 1977, no. 619. Not included in Polazzo 1990.
8. Liverpool 1977, no. 2798; Zava Boccazzi 1979, no. 82. The painting was misattributed to Sebastiano Ricci at the Sotheby's sale in 1947.
9. Sheffield 1966, p. 40; Zava Boccazzi 1979, no. 183. The painting was misattributed to G.A. Boni in the 1947 Sotheby's sale, but subsequently published as Pittoni by Rodolfo Pallucchini (1949, p. 165), who pointed out its close relationship to a drawing at that time in a Paduan private collection.
10. James Byam Shaw suggested in a letter of 22 September 1951 (on file at the Graves Art Gallery, Sheffield) that the three pictures ascribed to Boni are in fact by Pittoni, which at the very least is borne out in the case of the Sheffield *Christ and the Woman Taken in Adultery.*
11. Liverpool 1963, p. 155.
12. The biblical passage, 1 Kings 10:9, relates Sheba's words to Solomon: "Blessed be the Lord thy God, which delighted in thee, to set thee on the throne of Israel: because the Lord loved Israel for ever, therefore made he thee king, to do judgment and justice."
13. The Book of Esther tells how Esther called uninvited on her husband King Ahasuerus, an act punishable by death. Rather than killing his beloved Queen, he granted her request to spare her people, the Jews, from the persecution of the king's advisor Haman, who was in turn, executed. The Liverpool picture, however, does not follow the traditional representation in which Ahasuerus extends his scepter to Esther.
14. Arisi Riccardi (1979, p. 11) discusses this possibility.
15. Arisi Riccardi 1979, p. 12.
16. Pallucchini 1949, p. 164; Zava Boccazzi 1979, pp. 134, 160 (c. 1730-32).
17. George Knox has kindly brought to my attention yet another series by Sebastiano and Marco Ricci. In this instance, Consul Smith commissioned from them in 1724-26 seven biblical scenes, including Christ and the Adulteress and Christ in the House of Simon, two of the subjects also depicted in the present group. Written communication, 15 January 1994.

- 3 5 -

GIUSEPPE BARTOLOMEO CHIARI

Rome 1654-1727 Rome

The Return from the Flight into Egypt, c. 1712

Oil on canvas

19½ x 26⅛ inches

PROVENANCE: Baron de Breteuil in the 18th century; [1] Julius Weitzner, New York, 1955

EXHIBITIONS: East Lansing 1959; Detroit 1965, no. 120; New York 1965-66; Lexington 1967; Providence 1968, no. 11; Storrs 1973, no. 10; Corpus Christi 1979; Gainesville 1982, no. 7; Raleigh 1984, no. 10; Austin 1990

REFERENCES: Pepper 1984a, no. 44.1; Johns 1988, pp. 11, 13, fig. 3; Johns 1992, pp. 199-200, fig. 112

This painting was once attributed to the last great figure of seventeenth-century Roman painting and Giuseppe Chiari's teacher, Carlo Maratta (cat. no. 26).[2] Bernhard Kerber proposed the dating of about 1712, significantly one year prior to Maratta's death.[3] David Steel has correctly identified the subject of the painting; the scene appears not to represent the rest on the flight into Egypt but the Holy Family's return, when they are greeted by the young St. John the Baptist.[4] There exist several related pictures.[5]

Christopher Johns, in two recent incisive studies,[6] places the picture in the context of the Accademia degli Arcadi—the circle of cognoscenti frequented by Pope Clement XI and Maratta, president of the Roman art academy. Founded in 1691, the group pursued, through their various interests, the concept of a Golden Age in which " 'true erudition' stressed simplicity, sensibility, and naiveté." [7] (This anticipated the predilection for the rustic and the primitive during the Enlightenment of the later eighteenth-century.) Johns proposes that the present picture's emphasis on the landscape, its "diffuse" composition, and general air, denote its participation in this Arcadian circle; he even suggests that one of its members, Cardinal Pietro Ottoboni, may have commissioned it. While this remains interesting conjecture, we can say with certainty—due to its recently discovered provenance—that because of the painting's obvious transitional nature from the more classicizing, late seventeenth-century Roman style to a softer, less formal aesthetic, it appealed to early

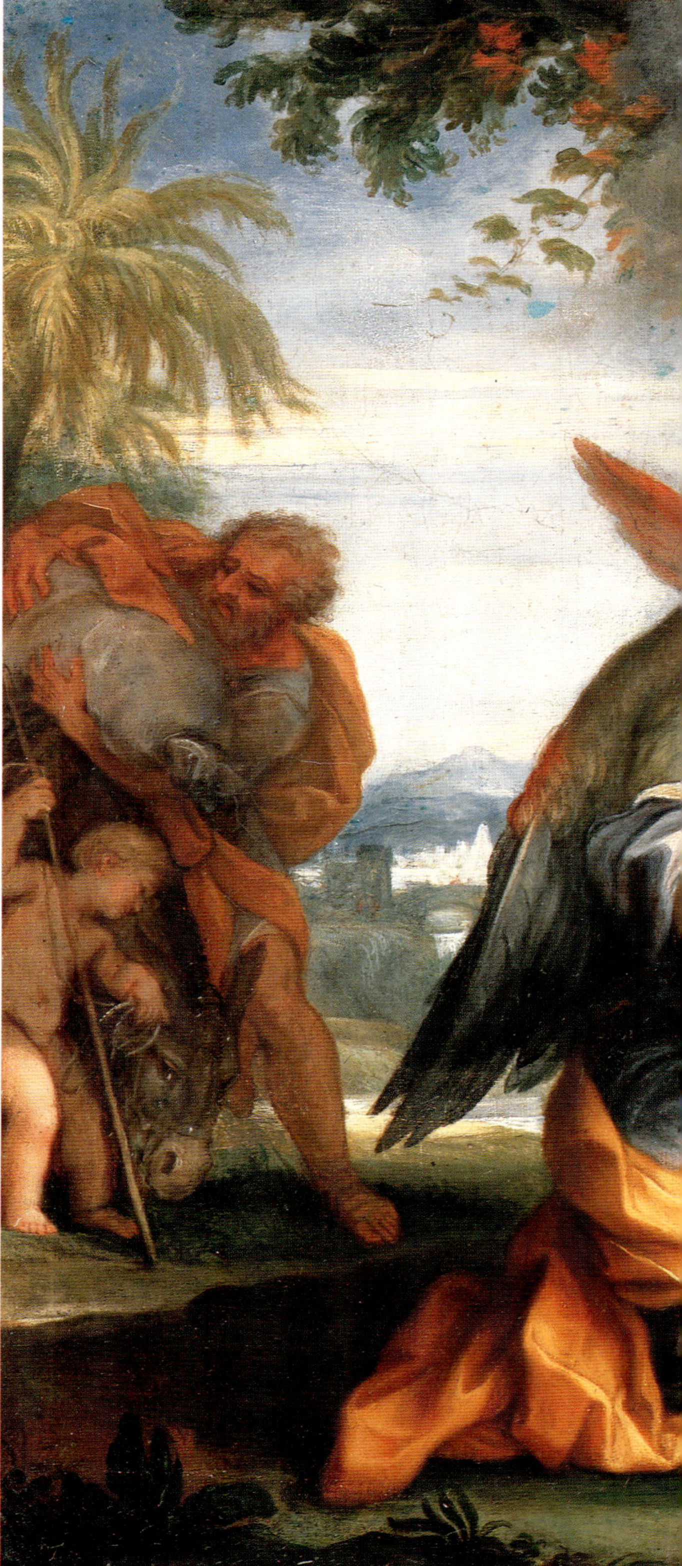

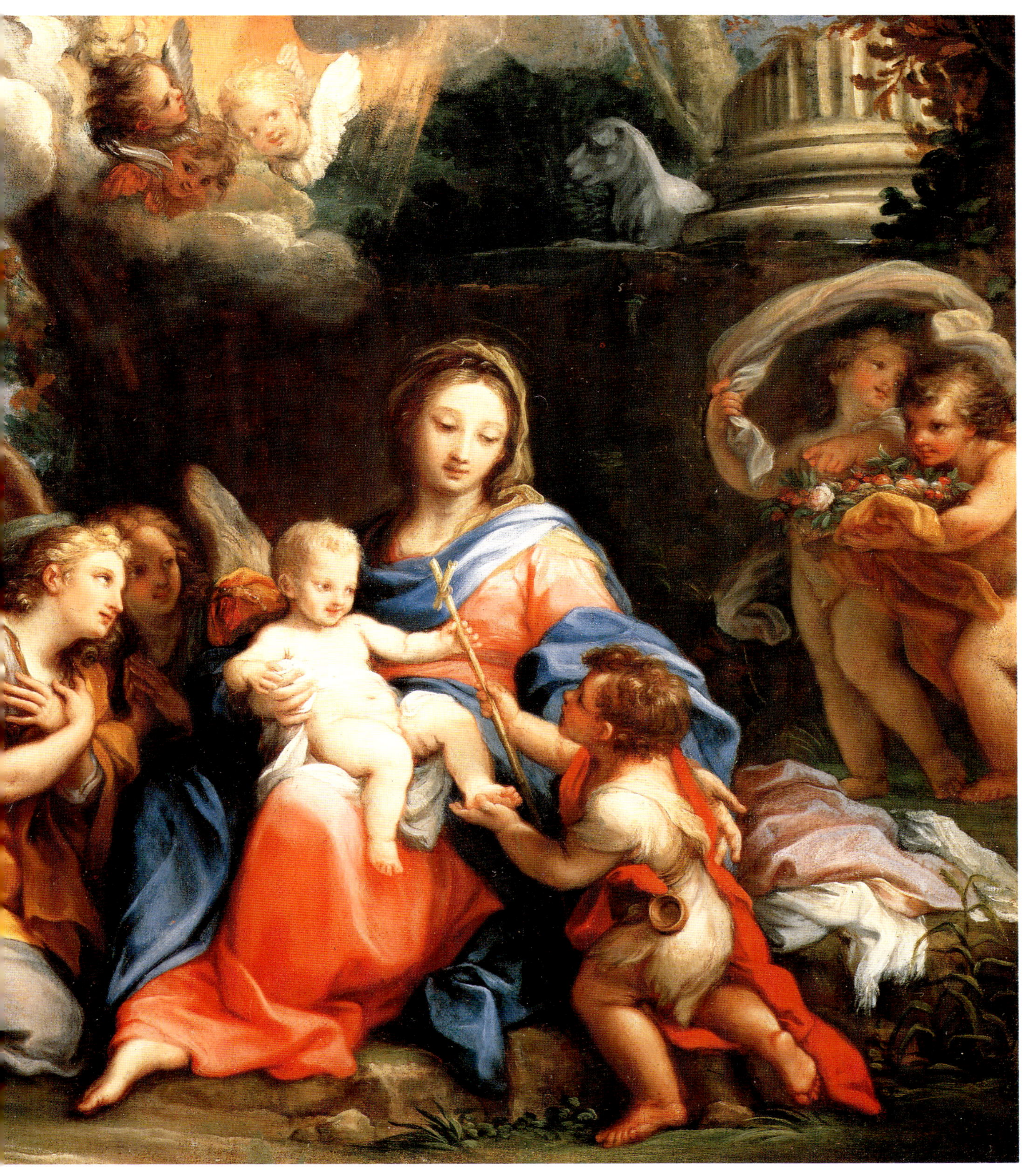

eighteenth-century French taste. In my view and contrary to Johns's appraisal of the picture, the landscape does not dominate the subject, nor is the composition or narrative confusing;[8] indeed, the central group is tightly composed, with flanking figures on either side, and the painting's palette, painterly style, and sweetness reflect a revival of the style of Pietro da Cortona.

1. An inscription in an eighteenth-century hand discovered on the back of the original canvas before a relining in 1979 read, "Du Cabinet de Mons.r le Baron/de Brereüil." Burton Fredericksen has suggested that this was a misspelling of "Baron de Breteuil." Fredericksen further proposes that the collector referred to on the back of the canvas was one of two persons: either Louis-Auguste Le Tonnelier (1733-1807), whose collection of pictures was confiscated around 1794, in the sales of which no record of the present picture can be found; or the earlier Baron de Breteuil, whose residence in the Place Royale was described in 1752 and who, in 1713, is said to have sold a painting by Mola to the Duc d'Orléans. There is no known inventory of this collector.
2. First correctly identified by Federico Zeri (Pepper 1984a, p. 45) and by Anthony Clark (Kerber 1968, p. 82, n. 61).
3. See Kerber 1968, p. 82, in which the author notes that Clark dated it to the 1720s.
4. Raleigh 1984, p. 44. Steel voices doubts raised by the presence of the sphinx and the column, which refer to Egypt. These, however, need not be troubling, since these elements are behind the Virgin and Child. In contrast, in the Guidobono copper (cat. no. 33), which definitely portrays the flight into Egypt, the fallen Egyptian idol is at their feet in front of them.
5. One in the Nelson-Atkins Museum of Art, Kansas City, is attributed to Chiari (inv. no. no. 80-49). Another is also at Bob Jones University, but its quality makes it at best from the circle of Chiari. Both of these pictures differ from the present painting in that they are vertical in format. Kerber (1968, p. 82) also mentions a Chiari *Rest on the Flight* in Copenhagen.
6. See Johns 1988 and Johns 1992.
7. Johns 1988, p. 9.
8. Johns 1988, p. 11; Steel (in Raleigh 1984, p. 44) has clearly explained the narrative found in the Bob Jones picture.

- 36 -

FRANCESCO DE MURA

Naples 1696-1782 Naples

Ecce Homo, 1725-27

Oil on canvas

24½ x 29½ inches

PROVENANCE: John Levy Galleries, New York, 1951

EXHIBITIONS: Raleigh 1984, no. 26; New Haven 1987, no. 33

REFERENCES: Pepper 1984a, no. 81.1;[1] Spinosa 1986, p. 156

This painting was previously attributed to Francesco Solimena, Francesco de Mura's teacher and himself a pupil of Luca Giordano (see cat. no. 23), until Nicola Spinosa identified it as a *bozzetto,* or painted sketch, preparatory for the larger composition in the Collegiata dell'Assunta, Casteldisangro, Isernia (Abruzzi). This latter painting is part of the Collegiata's decoration along with another canvas by De Mura, a *Christ with St. Veronica on the Road to Calvary* and other Neapolitan works, including examples by Paolo de Matteis (also a Solimena pupil) and Domenico Antonio Vaccaro.[2] The large *Ecce Homo* at Casteldisangro contains the same number of figures as the Bob Jones *bozzetto,* but differs in the depiction of the landscape seen through the architecture, as well as the balcony, which is balustraded in the larger work. Christ's pose in the preliminary version at Bob Jones University is more complex as De Mura employed a subtle torsion, with the body of Christ shifted to his left and his head inclined in the opposite direction.

Spinosa, in an essay on sacred art in Naples at the turn of the eighteenth century, discusses the role that Solimena and then De Mura, De Matteis, Vaccaro, and others played in the adaptation of religious subjects to the heroic mode, one normally employed for allegorical paintings. [3] The increasingly rigorous methods and prevailing classicism promoted by art academies across Europe, as well as the replacement of the church as patron, contributed to a blurring of distinctions between the depiction of the sacred and the secular.[4] The Greenville De Mura conveys some sense of this with its impressive, classicizing architectural setting and its emphasis on the elaborately varied poses of the figures. For the iconography of the *Ecce Homo,* see the

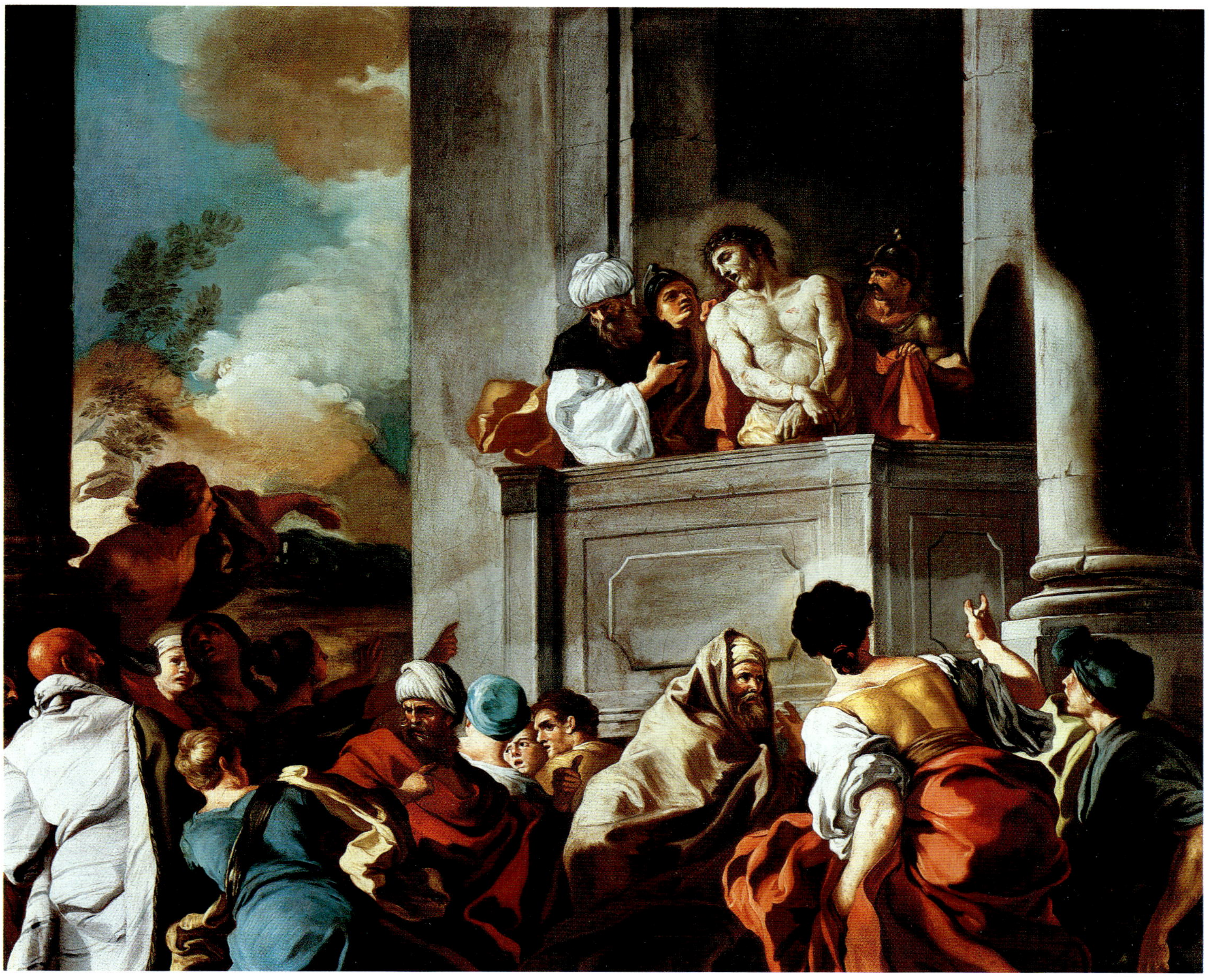

discussion of a Neapolitan painting of the preceding century by Jusepe de Ribera (cat. no. 21).

1. There is no record at the Columbus Museum of Art, Ohio, of the exhibition of a "Solimena" *Ecce Homo* between the years 1949 and 1956, despite the exhibition history provided in Greenville 1954, Pepper 1984a, Raleigh 1984, and New Haven 1987.
2. Naples 1980, p. 102. The inclusion of the preparatory *bozzetto* for the *Christ and St. Veronica* (Molinari Pradelli collection) in that exhibition provided the opportunity to connect the Bob Jones *bozzetto* with the Collegiata program. Spinosa, however, mistakenly cited the present picture as being in the collection at Oberlin.
3. Naples 1980, pp. 11-19.
4. Solimena's *St. Christopher* in the Chiesa di Monteoliveto, Naples, offers an excellent example in which the heroic academic nude is employed in a sacred composition (see Naples 1980, no. 32).

- 37 / 38 -

SEBASTIANO CONCA
CALLED IL CAVALIERE

Gaeta ca. 1680-1764 Naples

Prudence and Fortitude Overcoming Evil and *Justice and Temperance Overcoming Vice, 1738-40*

Oil on canvas

22½ x 28 inches each

PROVENANCE: Central Picture Galleries, New York, 1978

REFERENCES: Pepper 1984a, nos. 46.1, 46.2

Sebastiano Conca—like his fellow Neapolitan Francesco de Mura, who was also a pupil of Solimena—excelled at grand, classicizing compositions. And, in a similar manner as his contemporary in the previous painting, Conca interpreted this quasi-religious subject of the Four Cardinal Virtues, in a heroic, allegorical mode.[1] An internationally renowned painter based in Rome, Conca probably received the commission to decorate the ceiling and walls of the *salone* of the Palazzo Lomellini-Balbi-Lamba-Doria in Genoa in 1738—the ceiling, which depicts the *Allegory of Liguria,* is signed and dated "Fecit Roma A. 1740."[2] Each of the four wall paintings represents a Virtue, and, while one must take into account the disparity of scale and intent, it is clear that these Genoese Virtues are the progenitors of the figures in the Greenville works. The attributes and poses remain constant to a degree between the large-scale decorations and the pair of smaller cabinet pictures. This can be explained by Conca's fidelity to Cesare Ripa's *Iconologia,* first published in Rome in 1593, the essential emblem book for artists in the seventeenth and eighteenth centuries.

In an early edition of Ripa (Padua 1618), woodcut illustrations amplify the author's descriptions. Included there are entries and their corresponding images for the four Virtues: *Fortezza, Giustizia, Prudenza,* and *Temperanza.* Fortitude (see page 190) is represented by a woman clothed in armor who carries on her left arm a shield embossed with a lion attacking a wild boar (the lion symbolizing the soul, and the wild boar, thoughtlessness and rash action). In her right hand, she holds a pole with an oak branch (in the present picture it lies at her feet). Ripa describes Fortitude's clothing as being of a "leonine color," connecting the golden color with the lion pelt worn by Hercules. In fact, Conca painted a tawny gold cloak around Fortitude's shoulders; the association is made even more explicit by the motif of the lion, who appears, not on the shield but alive and crouching next to it. Altogether, Conca's Fortitude presents a suitable image of strength and endurance. The figure of Prudence resembles Ripa's description less than that of Fortitude, but she is shown with two prominent attributes mentioned by him, the mirror and the snake.[3]

In Conca's second pair of Virtues (see page 191), the figure of Justice is a combination of several characterizations by Ripa, one of a woman dressed in white (underneath the green garment is a white tunic) holding a sword and scales of justice, and another of a beautiful virgin with a gold crown.[4] Here, as is usual, Temperance is shown with a silver bridle in one hand (reining in the passions). Her animal attribute in Ripa is the elephant, which is absent from the Bob Jones picture but seen in the Genoese decoration. In the latter are the other elements found accompanying the Bob Jones figure of Temperance, however: the palm held in her hand is borne by an angel in the Palazzo Lamba-Doria canvas, and the motif of the putto pouring water from a vase while another with tongs "tempers" iron has been reduced to a simpler passage in the present painting.[5] Thus, Conca's four large canvases decorating a Genoese palace were effectively scaled down to the format of pendant cabinet pictures, in which two Virtues are paired in each. The painter's combinations are particularly appropriate: prudence should always inform fortitude and justice should be dispensed with temperance.

1. For an example of another pair of Conca cabinet pictures with an allegorical or mythological theme, see London 1987, no. 33. These works share compositional similarities, as well as the same dating, with the Greenville paintings.
2. Schleier 1980b, p. 21; see also Gaeta 1981, p. 268.
3. In Ripa's *Iconologia* (1618), Prudence holds a caduceus, usually a symbol of Mercury. In the Genoa painting, her attributes include a snake held in her hand and a caduceus formed of two serpents coiled around a staff carried aloft by a spirit. In the Bob Jones example, the artist reduced this motif to a single snake entwined around her right arm. A similar simplification is seen in the lack of Prudence's attribute of a deer, described by Ripa and included in the Genoa painting. Erich Schleier deals in detail with the iconography of the Palazzo Lomellini-Balbi-Lamba-Doria decoration and its divergences from and similarities to Ripa (Schleier 1980b, pp. 22-24).
4. The former description by Ripa includes a flame of fire in Justice's left hand, which is how she is depicted in the Palazzo Lamba-Doria painting.
5. This iconographical motif is not found in the Paduan 1618 edition used here, but in that published in the same city in 1611, referred to by Schleier 1980b, p. 23.

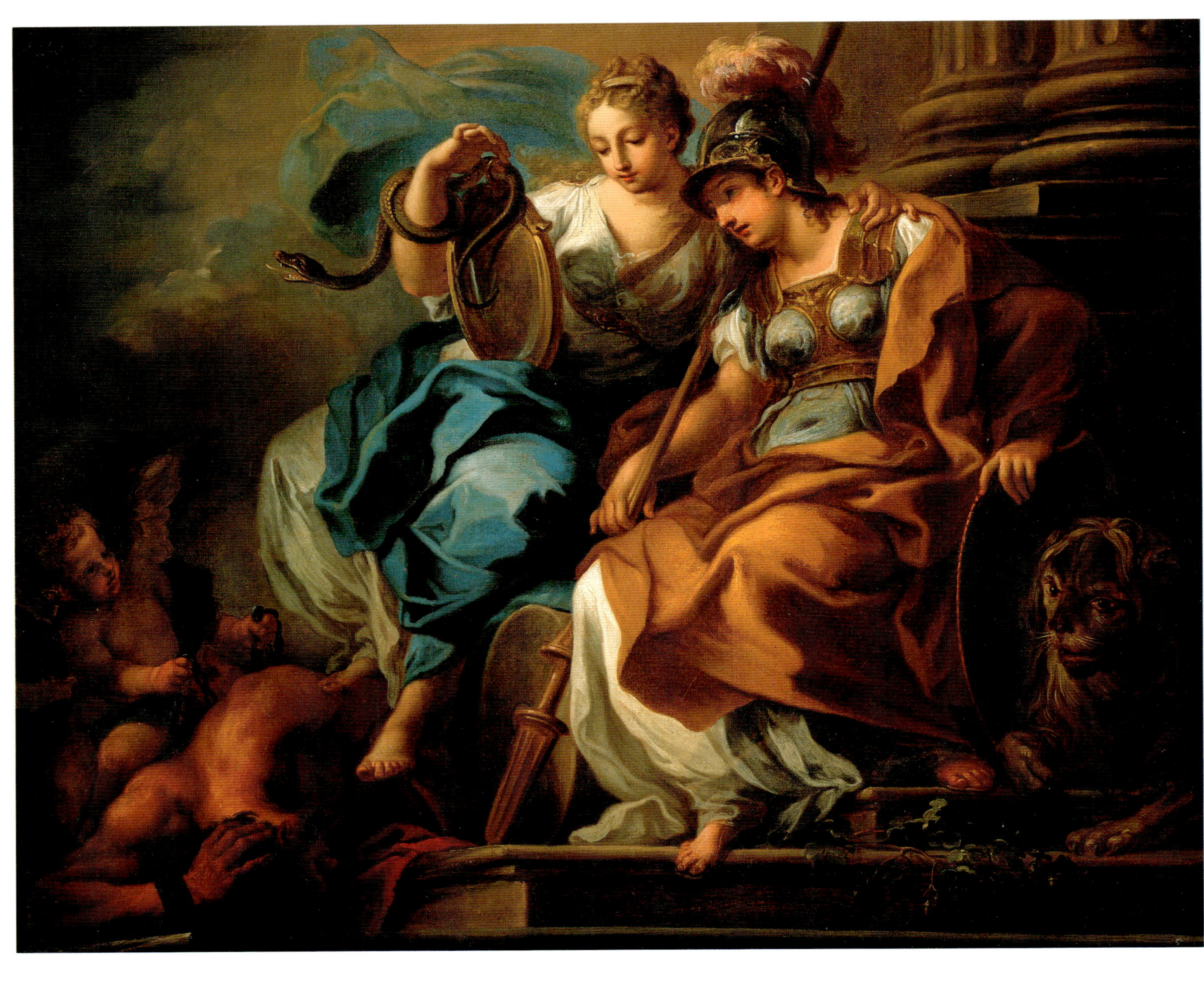

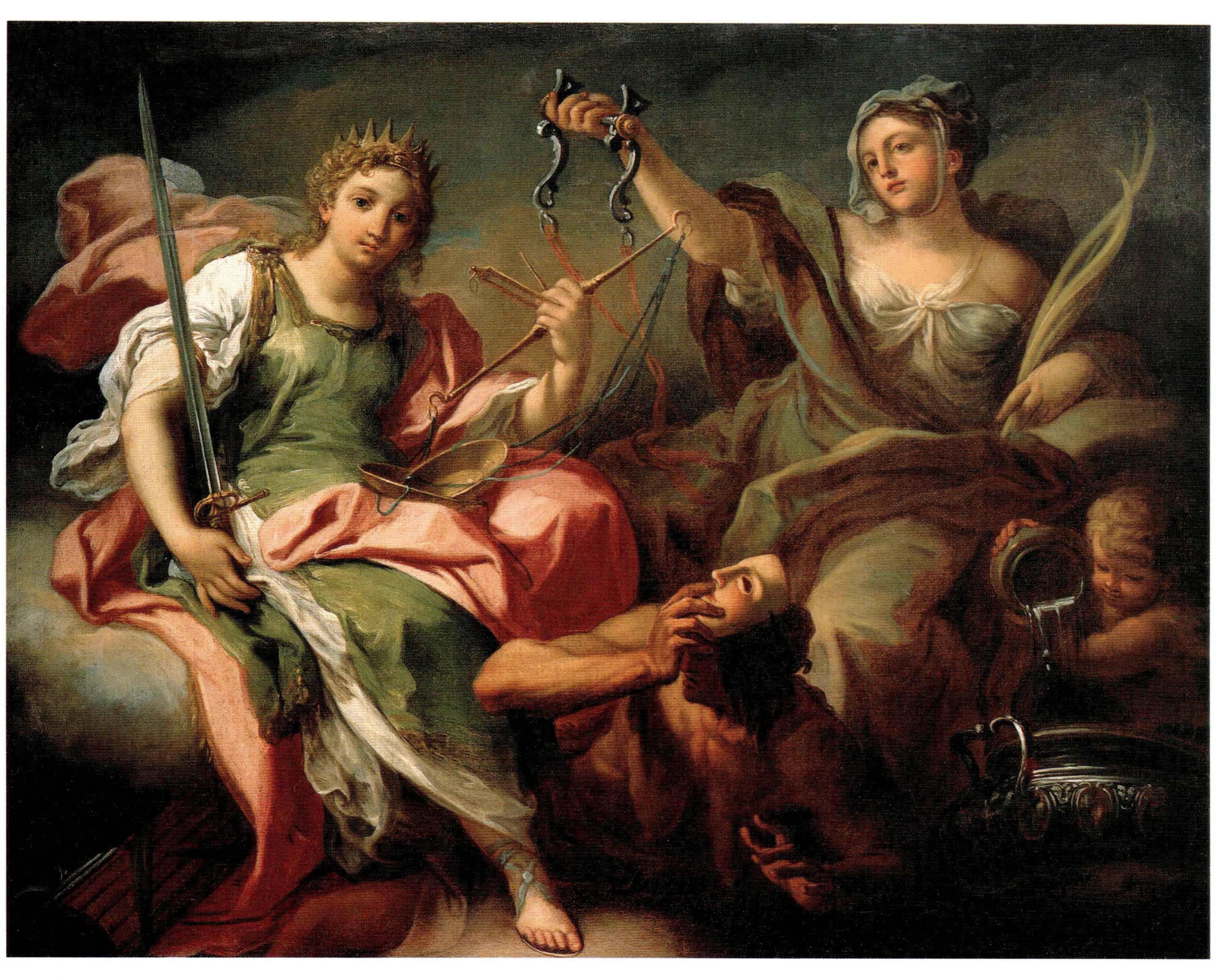

~ 39 ~

POMPEO BATONI

Lucca 1708-1787 Rome

St. James the Greater, c. 1740-43

Oil on canvas

28½ x 23¾ inches

PROVENANCE: Count Cesare Merenda, Forlì, 1740s; thence by descent until c. 1958; Julius Weitzner, London, 1961

EXHIBITIONS: New York 1982, no. 2; Raleigh 1984, no. 3

REFERENCES: Merenda collection house-lists, nos. 77, 158; Pepper 1984a, no. 31.1; Clark and Bowron 1985, no. 78 and p. 27 (with earlier references); Chicago 1986, p. 69; London 1987, p. 19

This *St. James the Greater* is part of a series of half-length portrayals of the Apostles, ostensibly consisting of twelve images, of which today we know only ten. Aside from the present picture, there exist the *St. Andrew* (Art Institute of Chicago) and the *St. Bartholomew* (formerly in the Anthony Clark collection and now in a private collection, Rome); the remaining seven (representing James the Less, John the Evangelist, Matthew, Paul, Peter, Philip, and Thomas), now at Basildon Park, were given by Lord Iliffe to the National Trust in 1979. The painting's early provenance can be traced to Count Cesare Merenda, who in the 1730s had constructed a large picture gallery (housing some 350 paintings) in the Merenda palace at Forlì. [1] The collection's emphasis was on contemporary Roman painting and the count's advisor was Pompeo Batoni, whom he patronized extensively, all in all purchasing some thirty pictures from the artist. Among these were the ten (or twelve) paintings of the Apostles. The extant works retain the "Salvator Rosa" style frames that Merenda had made for them and other pictures by Batoni and in which they were seen in the gallery until its destruction during the Second World War; Merenda's collection was dispersed in the 1950s and 1960s. On the basis of style, Batoni's series can be dated to the first years of the 1740s. [2]

There are several well-known sets of Apostles and Evangelists from the seventeenth century by Jusepe de Ribera and Guido Reni (see under cat. nos. 18-19). Andrea Sacchi and Carlo Maratta are known to have supplied full-length pictures of the Apostles to the Barberini. [3] Northern artists were not immune to the tradition either, for Anthony van Dyck produced a set around 1620. [4] By the eighteenth century, this sort of series was a well-established convention. A particularly beautiful example that directly precedes Batoni's effort is Benedetto Luti's series of heads of the Twelve Apostles, executed in pastel in 1712.[5] The freshness and energy of execution, for which Luti is justifiably known, has been skillfully appropriated by Batoni for his half-length figures. Indeed, apropos of Luti's stylistic influence on Pompeo, Edgar Peters Bowron has observed, "The rich effects of color . . . in the 1740s derive from a variety of antecedents from Federico Barocci . . . to Benedetto Luti, whose *Allegory of the Enthronement of Pope Martin V* in Palazzo Colonna Batoni knew intimately as he painted his own canvases for the same ceiling complex [c. 1737-40], to the recent paintings of Pierre Subleyras, which unquestionably influenced Batoni's palette toward a higher key." [6] One need only compare Domenichino's *St. John the Evangelist* (cat. no. 17) to the present picture to see how Batoni took the earlier, classicizing prototype and invigorated it with the *sensibilité* of the eighteenth century. Comparison of the *St. Matthew* by Guido Reni (cat. no. 18) and Batoni's *St. James the Greater* demonstrates the proximity of the two masters' styles: both portrayals exhibit a delicacy and spontaneity of touch. As Bowron has remarked with respect to the Merenda Apostle series, Batoni was here returning to "Seicento practice and the paintings of Domenichino, Albani, and Guido Reni." [7]

1. For a recent consideration of Count Merenda's collecting and the family picture gallery, see Edgar Peters Bowron's essay, "A Little-Known Settecento Collector in Rome: Count Cesare Merenda," in London 1987, pp. 18-20, and earlier, his entry for the Bob Jones picture in New York 1982, pp. 14, 16.
2. For a summation of the various scholarly opinions, see Clark and Bowron 1985, p. 231.
3. Russell 1980, p. 36. Seven from this series are in the Galleria Nazionale d'Arte Antica, Rome. Print series of the Apostles have also been cited as an example of this tradition by Steel (Raleigh 1984, p. 26).
4. Washington 1990, pp. 130-34.
5. The twelve pastels by Luti were dispersed at Sotheby's, New York, 14 January 1987, lots 120-31. Some of these have resurfaced, the most recent occasion being at Christie's, New York, 11 January 1994, lots 223, 224. At least two have entered museum collections: Sotheby's, lot

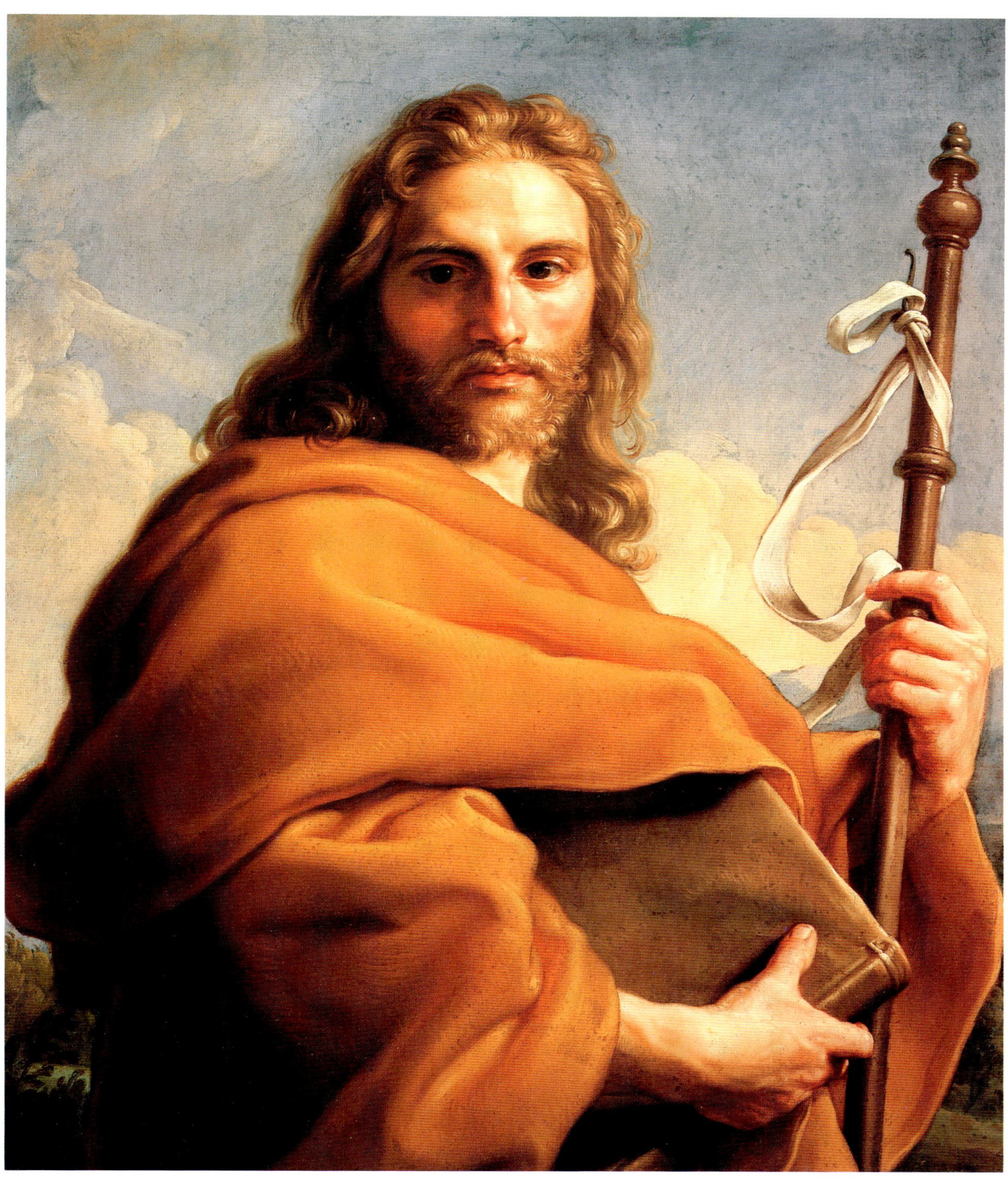

121, is now in the Spencer Museum of Art, University of Kansas, Lawrence; lot 124 was recently purchased by the Philbrook Museum of Art, Tulsa. While the Luti figures have no identifying attributes, it seems possible to work backward from the Batoni series to identify the earlier works. For example, there is an uncanny physical resemblance between the figure in the Spencer Luti drawing and that in the Bob Jones *St. James the Greater,* which figure has in fact been identified as the same saint (file in the Spencer Museum of Art). The same is true for the *St. Thomas* at Basildon and the Luti drawing, Sotheby's, lot 125. The sheet acquired by the Philbrook Museum must depict St. John the Evangelist as the figure fits the iconographical type of the sweet-faced young man as seen, for instance, in Domenichino's rendition (cat. no. 17).

6. Clark and Bowron 1985, p. 27.
7. Clark and Bowron 1985, p. 27.

- 40 -

GIOVANNI BATTISTA TIEPOLO

Venice 1696-1770 Madrid

A Philosopher Holding a Book, 1753-57

Oil on canvas

23¾ x 19½ inches

PROVENANCE: G. Gurschner, Vienna; R. Kuhe, New York, 1919; Gladys Adler; Christie's, London, 1 April 1966, lot 34; Julius Weitzner, London, 1966

EXHIBITIONS: Birmingham 1978, no. 93 (as Domenico Tiepolo); Raleigh 1984, no. 42

REFERENCES: Rizzi 1971, p. 352; Ottawa 1976, p. 116; Pepper 1984a, no. 121.1

Giambattista's older son, Domenico, produced in the winter of 1757-58 the first of two groups of etchings entitled *Raccolta di Teste* (*Collection of Heads*), comprising thirty prints.[1] He based twenty of them on paintings and drawings by his father. The original paintings are of uniform size (24 x 20 inches) and depict bust-length portrayals of old men, wearing elaborate headdresses and usually holding a book. Several series of paintings done after Giambattista's pictures and Giandomenico's prints also exist.[2] The three series by Giambattista's youngest son, Lorenzo, are the result of a studious process, as he, and for that matter, his brother Domenico, relied on their father's art for inspiration. Lorenzo's series indicate the presence of Giambattista's philosopher paintings in the Tiepolo family studio for a lengthy period, which calls into question the nature of Giambattista's original commission. George Knox has noted that the philosopher series was highly unusual for Tiepolo both in terms of format (small and regularized) and concept. He surmises that "the commission must have come from a close friend, a labor of love in fact, or the patron must have been exceptionally powerful."[3]

Because of the confusion surrounding these images until Knox's study of them, the Greenville *Philosopher Holding a Book* was initially attributed to Domenico, presumably on the basis of his well-known etching. [4] In 1978 Knox correctly identified it as one of the original philosopher paintings by Giambattista. [5] He has dated Giambattista's entire group to after the family's move to Würzburg to paint the Residenz frescoes in December 1750; a *terminus ante quem* is provided by the date of 1757 inscribed on one of Domenico's *Raccolta di Teste* etchings.

The subject in this painting by Tiepolo has been previously identified as a Jewish priest or prophet. The painting and the series of which it is a part fit better, however, within the tradition of the representation of the philosophers of Antiquity. This is reflected in their fanciful costumes, classicizing accoutrements (note, for example, the cameo clasp of the old man's cloak in the Bob Jones painting), and the ubiquitous book. The identification of these figures as ancient philosophers is further reinforced by the inscriptions found on two paintings, one by Domenico of *Diogenes* (Testa I.17D; formerly Tacoma Art Museum, Washington) and the other by Lorenzo of *Pythagoras* (Testa I.29E; private collection, Friuli), both of which Knox dates to after 1762, the Tiepolo's Spanish period.[6] By way of contrast, Giambattista's conception of an Old Testament prophet may be seen in the frescoes found in the Sala Rossa of the Palazzo Arcivescovile, Udine, painted in 1732-33. There, the prophets Isaiah, Ezekiel, Daniel, and Jonah are represented, clearly identified by their attributes.[7] The figure in the Greenville painting and his counterparts in the series (and the subsequent copies after Giambattista's originals), bear no iconographical relation to the Udine prophets. In fact, the Greenville *Philosopher* and the entire group relate better in figural type to the images found in G.B. Castiglione's series of etchings, the *Large and Small Turbanned Heads*.[8] These depict young and old male heads adorned with exotic headdresses. That the same motif is found in the Tiepolo philosopher series can be explained by the fact that the Near Eastern headdress denoted, not only exoticism, but the Ancient World before Christ, as well. It is this very connection that makes it possible to confuse this ancient philosopher with a Jewish prophet, as Knox appears to imply.[9]

Acceptance of the subject's identification as a Greek philosopher need not imperil the painting's inclusion in the Bob Jones Collection of Religious Art. In fact, like the sibyls portrayed by Domenichino and Guercino,[10] the Greek philosophers were seen to presage Christ's coming, particularly in light of the fashion for Neo-Platonism during the Renaissance. One need only look to Raphael's Stanza della Segnatura for the prominent disposition of Plato and Aristotle in the

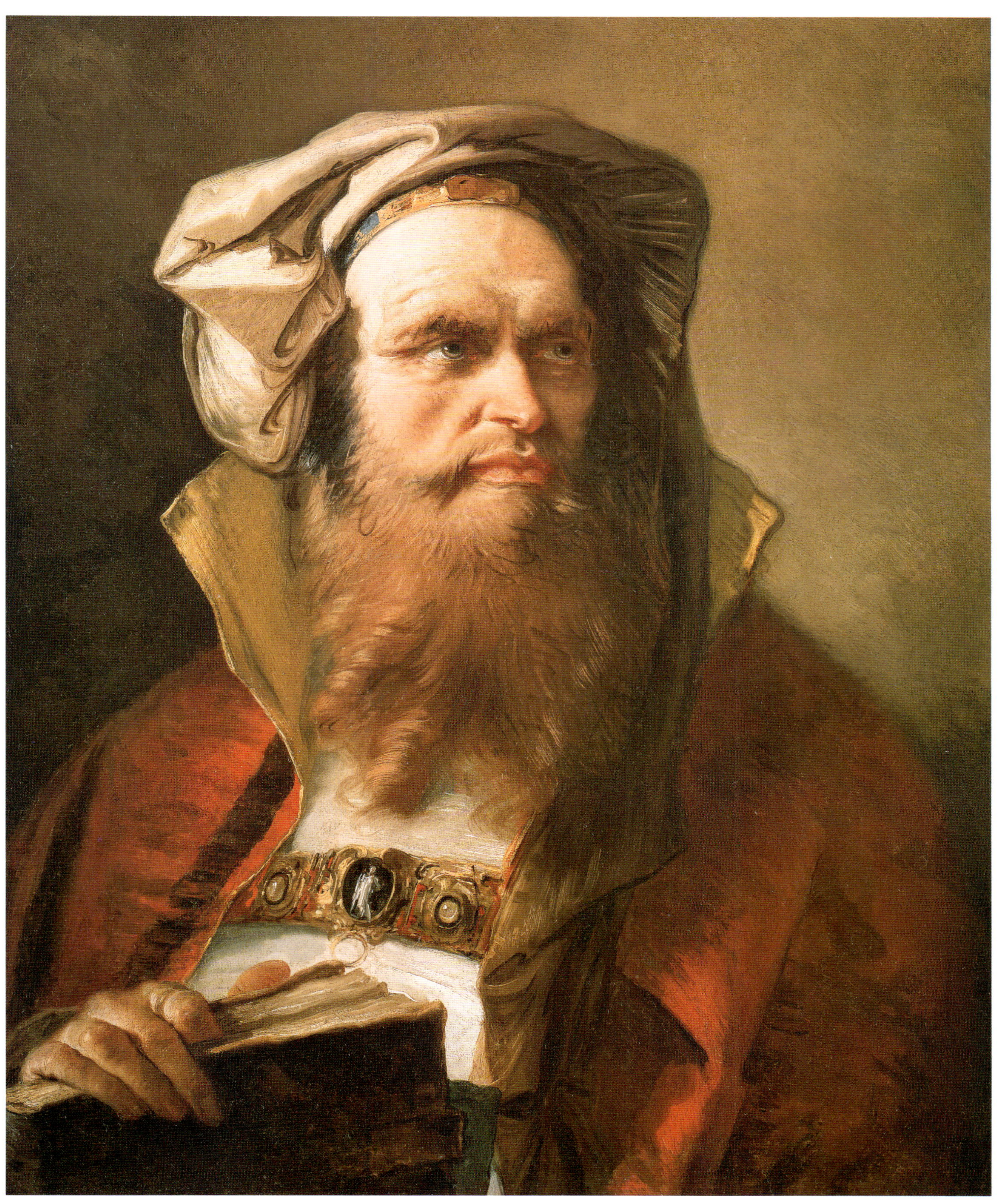

School of Athens, which parallels the Church Fathers' theological debate surrounding the Eucharist depicted just opposite in the *Disputà.*[11]

Knox ventures a tentative identification of the philosopher portrayed in the present painting as Xenophon, the fifth-century B.C. student and historiographer of Socrates, who was said to have been an "extremely good-looking man."[12] Knox has also published a preparatory chalk drawing for the hand of the Bob Jones *Philosopher Holding a Book,* which is in the Museo Correr, Venice.[13] The tradition of a gallery of philosophers in the seventeenth century is represented by, for instance, Jusepe de Ribera's commission for the Prince of Liechtenstein in 1637 [14] or Don Antonio Ruffa of Messina's commissions of a portrait of *Aristotle* from Rembrandt (Metropolitan Museum of Art, New York), its pendant of *Plato* from Guercino, and later additions of Preti's *Dionysius of Syracuse,* and another Rembrandt, *Alexander the Great* (Glasgow Art Gallery).[15]

1. The following summary is derived from Knox 1975.
2. Knox designates the father's paintings as Set A; the copies by Lorenzo, Sets B & C; those by Domenico based on his own prints after Giambattista, Set D; and a final series of philosophers by Lorenzo, Set E.
3. Knox 1975, p. 148.
4. The *Raccolta di Teste,* Testa I.7.
5. In his review, Knox 1978, p. 189.
6. Knox 1975, pp. 148, 151. These works by Domenico and Lorenzo are from Sets D and E, see note 2 above. The *Diogenes* by Giandomenico has been in the Tacoma Art Museum since around 1981 and was recently deaccessioned and offered for sale at Butterfield & Butterfield, San Francisco, 18 May 1994, lot 2751. My thanks to Alan Fausel for this information.
7. For an iconographical discussion of these paintings, see Jordan 1985.
8. Knox has noted this parallel, but only with respect to the etching style of Giandomenico in his prints after his father's paintings (see Knox 1970, introduction).
9. Knox 1970, introduction.
10. See discussion under cat. no. 16.
11. It is interesting to note here that Knox has suggested that a picture from one of the several philosopher series, an example painted by Lorenzo now in the Baltimore Museum of Art, represents Aristotle; see Knox in Rosenthal 1981, p. 314.
12. Knox (1975, p. 152) qualifies his identification of the subject of the series as philosophers: "the attributes of the various 'philosophers,' if so they be, in Set A are never sufficient to make a clear identification possible...Testa I.7A [the Bob Jones picture] could be Xenophon...." The quotation about Xenophon's good looks comes from Diogenes Laertius, cited in Knox 1975, p. 152.
13. It is part of the Quaderno Gatteri. Knox 1980, p. 149, D.223.
14. See New York 1992b, pp. 112-19. The series was dispersed in 1957 and the paintings may be found at Los Angeles, Hartford, Tokyo, and elsewhere.
15. The concept of the philosopher series is discussed in Fitz Darby 1962.

Arisi Riccardi 1979
Raffaella Arisi Riccardi, *Il Spolverini: Pittore di battaglie e cerimonie.* Piacenza, 1979.

Askew 1969
Pamela Askew, "The Angelic Consolation of St. Francis of Assisi in Post-Tridentine Italian Painting," *Journal of the Warburg and Courtauld Institutes,* XXXII, 1969, pp. 280-306.

Austin 1990
Masterpieces of Baroque Painting from the Bob Jones University Collection, Huntington Art Gallery, University of Texas, Austin, 1990, no publication.

Baldinucci ed. Ranalli 1681-1728
Filippo Baldinucci, *Notizie de'professori del designo da Cimabue in qua.* 6 vols., Florence, 1681-1728. Ed. F. Ranalli, Florence, 1845-47. Reprint, 1974.

Baltimore 1961
Bacchiacca and his Friends. Exh. cat., Baltimore Museum of Art. Baltimore, 1961.

Barocchi 1964
Paola Barocchi, "Appunti su Francesco Morandini da Poppi," *Mitteilungen des Kunsthistorischen Instituts in Florenz,* VIII, 1964, pp. 117-48.

Bartsch 1818
Adam Bartsch, *Le Peintre-graveur.* 21 vols. Vienna, 1818.

Béguin 1987
Sylvie Béguin, "Paris Bordon en France" in *Paris Bordon e il suo tempo: Atti del convegno internazionale di studi.* Treviso, 1987.

Bianchi and Giunta 1988
Lidia Bianchi and Diega Giunta, *Iconografia di S. Caterina da Siena.* Rome, 1988.

Binghamton 1967
Michael Milkovich, *Bernardo Strozzi: Paintings and Drawings.* Exh. cat., University Art Gallery, State University of New York at Binghamton. Binghamton, 1967.

Birmingham 1978
The Tiepolos: Painters to Princes and Prelates. Exh. cat., Birmingham Museum of Art, and Museum of Fine Arts, Springfield, Massachusetts. Birmingham, Alabama, 1978.

Bissell 1981
Roger Ward Bissell, *Orazio Gentileschi and the Poetic Tradition in Caravaggesque Painting.* London, 1981.

Blume 1991
Andrew Blume, "A 'Vision of St. Francis' by Guercino in the Wadsworth Atheneum," *Master Drawings,* XXI, 1991, pp. 52-58.

Bologna 1971
Ferdinando Bologna, "Il soggiorno napoletano di Girolamo da Cotignola con altre considerazioni sulla pittura emiliana del Cinquecento" in *Studi di storia dell'arte in onore di Valerio Mariani,* Naples, 1971, pp. 147-65.

Bologna 1991
Denis Mahon et al., *Giovanni Francesco Barbieri: Il Guercino.* Exh. cat., Museo Civico Archeologico, Bologna, and the Pinacoteca Civica and the Chiesa del Rosario, Cento. Bologna, 1991.

Broun 1978
Elizabeth Broun, ed., *Handbook of the Collection: Helen Foresman Spencer Museum of Art.* Lawrence, Kansas, 1978.

Budny 1983
Virginia Budny, "The Sequence of Leonardo's Sketches for *The Virgin and Child with Saint Anne and Saint John the Baptist,*" *Art Bulletin,* LXV, 1983, pp. 33-50.

Buffa 1983
Sebastian Buffa, ed., *The Illustrated Bartsch, XXXVIII: Italian Artists of the Sixteenth Century.* New York, 1983.

Cadogan 1991
Jean K. Cadogan, ed., *Wadsworth Atheneum Paintings II: Italy and Spain: Fourteenth through Nineteenth Centuries.* Hartford, Connecticut, 1991.

Canova 1964
Giordana Canova, *Paris Bordon.* Venice, 1964.

Causa 1970
Raffaello Causa, *Opere d'arte nel Pio Monte della Misericordia a Napoli.* Naples, 1970.

Chappell 1990
Miles Chappell, "Drawing in Seventeenth-Century Florence," *Drawing,* XII, 1990, pp. 53-58.

Charlotte 1959
The Mint Museum, Charlotte, North Carolina, 1959, no publication.

Charlotte 1982
Italian Renaissance Paintings From Southern Museums. Exh. cat., The Mint Museum. Charlotte, North Carolina, 1982.

Cherici 1926
Ugo Cherici, *Guida storico-artistica del R. Spedale degli Innocenti di Firenze.* Florence, 1926.

Chicago 1986
Richard Brettell and Steven Starling, *The Art of the Edge: European Frames, 1300-1900.* Exh. cat., Art Institute of Chicago. Chicago, 1986.

Clark and Bowron 1985
Anthony M. Clark and Edgar Peters Bowron, *Pompeo Batoni: A Complete Catalogue of his Works with an Introductory Text.* New York, 1985.

Columbus 1946
The Age of Titian. Exh. cat., Columbus Gallery of Fine Arts. Columbus, Ohio, 1946.

Corpus Christi 1979
Museum of South Texas, Corpus Christi, 1979, no publication.

Corti 1989
Laura Corti, *Vasari: Catalogo completo dei dipinti.* Florence, 1989.

Dayton 1962
Genoese Masters: Cambiaso to Magnasco, 1550-1750. Exh. cat., The Dayton Art Institute and The John and Mable Ringling Museum of Art, Sarasota. Dayton, 1962.

De Grazia and Schleier 1994
Diane De Grazia and Erich Schleier, "Saint Cecilia and an angel: 'the heads by Gentileschi, the rest by Lanfranco'," *Burlington Magazine,* CXXXVI, 1994, pp. 73-78.

De Grazia forthcoming
Diane De Grazia, ed., *The Collection of the National Gallery of Art Systematic Catalogue: Italian Paintings of the Seventeenth and Eighteenth Centuries.* Washington, D.C., forthcoming.

Del Bravo 1961
Carlo del Bravo, "Per Jacopo Vignali," *Paragone,* XII, 1961, pp. 28-42.

Del Bravo 1963
Carlo del Bravo, "Carlo Dolci, devoto del naturale," *Paragone,* XIV, 1963, pp. 32-41.

Detroit 1965
Frederick Cummings, ed., *Art In Italy, 1600-1700.* Exh. cat., The Detroit Institute of Arts. Detroit, 1965.

Detroit 1974
The Twilight of the Medici: Late Baroque Art in Florence, 1670-1743. Exh. cat., The Detroit Institute of Arts. Detroit, 1974.

Dufour 1970
Colette Bozzo Dufour et al., *La pittura a Genova e in Liguria: Dagli inizi al Cinquecento.* Genoa, 1970.

East Lansing 1959
College Collections, Kresge Art Center, Michigan State University, East Lansing, 1959, no publication.

Ferrari and Scavizzi 1966
Oreste Ferrari and Giuseppe Scavazzi, *Luca Giordano.* Naples, 1966.

Ferrari and Scavizzi 1992
Oreste Ferrari and Giuseppe Scavizzi, *Luca Giordano: L'opera completa.* Naples, 1992.

Fitz Darby 1962
Delphine Fitz Darby, "Ribera and the Wise Men," *Art Bulletin,* XLIV, 1962, pp. 279-307.

Florence 1987
Il Seicento fiorentino. Exh. cat., Palazzo Strozzi. Florence, 1987.

Florence 1989
Giovanni Pagliarulo and Riccardo Spinelli, eds., *Pitture senesi del Seicento.* Exh. cat., Pratesi Antiquario. Florence, 1989.

Fort Worth 1982
Craig Felton and William B. Jordan, *Jusepe de Ribera: Lo Spagnoletto, 1591-1652.* Exh. cat., Kimbell Art Museum. Fort Worth, 1982.

Fort Worth 1993a
Beverly Brown and Paola Marini, eds., *Jacopo Bassano, 1510-1592.* Exh. cat., Kimbell Art Museum. Fort Worth, 1993.

Fort Worth 1993b
Beverly Brown et al., *Giambattista Tiepolo: Master of the Oil Sketch.* Exh. cat., Kimbell Art Museum. Fort Worth, 1993.

Frankfurt 1988
Sybille Ebert-Schifferer et al., *Guido Reni und Europa: Ruhm und Nachruhm.* Exh. cat., Schirn Kunsthalle. Frankfurt, 1988.

Frankfurt 1992
Kunst in der Republik Genua, 1528-1815. Exh. cat., Schirn Kunsthalle. Frankfurt, 1992.

Fredericksen and Zeri 1972
Burton B. Fredericksen and Federico Zeri, *Census of Pre-Nineteenth-Century Italian Paintings in North American Public Collections.* Cambridge, Massachusetts, 1972.

Friedmann 1980
Herbert Friedmann, *A Bestiary for Saint Jerome.* Washington, D.C., 1980.

Gaeta 1981
Sebastiano Conca (1680-1764). Exh. cat., Palazzo De Vio. Gaeta, 1981.

Gainesville 1982
Jean K. and Robert H. Westin, *Transformations of the Roman Baroque.* Exh. cat., University Gallery, University of Florida. Gainesville, Florida, 1982.

Gaya Nuño 1958
Juan Antonio Gaya Nuño, *La pintura española fuera de España.* Madrid, 1958.

Genoa 1990
Piero Donati, ed., *Domenico Fiasella.* Exh. cat., Palazzo Reale. Genoa, 1990.

Genoa 1992a
Clario di Fabio, ed., *Procaccini, Cerano, Morazzone: Dipinti lombardi del primo Seicento dalle civiche collezione genovesi.* Exh. cat., Palazzo Bianco. Genoa, 1992.

Genoa 1992b
Ezia Gavazza and Giovanni Rotundi Terminiello, *Genova nell'età barocca.* Exh. cat., Palazzo Spinola and Palazzo Reale. Genoa, 1992.

Giusti Maccari 1987
Patrizia Giusti Maccari, *Pietro Paolini, pittore lucchese, 1603-1681.* Lucca, 1987.

Greenville 1954
The Bob Jones University Collection of Religious Paintings. Greenville, South Carolina, 1954.

Greenville 1962
The Bob Jones University Collection of Religious Paintings. Volume I: Italian and French Paintings. Volume II: Flemish, Dutch, German, and Spanish Paintings. Greenville, South Carolina, 1962.

Gregori 1988
Mina Gregori, *Pittura a Pavia dal romanico al Settecento.* Milan, 1988.

Guglielmi 1954
Carla Guglielmi, "Intorno all'opera pittorica di Giovanni Baglione," *Bollettino d'arte,* 4, 1954, pp. 311-26.

Hagerstown 1969
Masterpieces of Religious Art, Washington County Museum of Fine Art, Hagerstown, Maryland, 1969, no publication.

Harris and Schaar 1967
Ann Sutherland Harris and Eckhard Schaar, *Kataloge des Kunstmuseums Düsseldorf: Handzeichnungen Band 1: Die Handzeichnungen von Andrea Sacchi und Carlo Maratta.* Düsseldorf, 1967.

Harris 1977
Ann Sutherland Harris, *Andrea Sacchi: Complete Edition of the Paintings with a Critical Catalogue.* Princeton, 1977.

Havens 1961
Murray Havens, "Collection of Religious Art at Bob Jones University," *Art Journal,* XXI, 1961-62, p. 112.

Heinemann 1959
Fritz Heinemann, *Giovanni Bellini e i Belliniani.* Venice, 1959.

Heinz 1960
Günther Heinz, "Carlo Dolci: Studien zur religiosen Malerei im 17. Jahrhundert," *Jahrbuch der Kunsthistorischen Sammlungen in Wien,* LVI, 1960, pp. 197-234.

Held 1984
Julius S. Held, *Paintings and Sculpture of the European and American Schools.* Museo de Arte de Ponce. Ponce, Puerto Rico, 1984.

Hibbard and Lewine 1965
Howard Hibbard and Milton Lewine, "Seicento at Detroit," *Burlington Magazine,* CVII, 1965, pp. 370-72.

Hills 1983
Paul Hills, "Piety and Patronage in Cinquecento Venice: Tintoretto and the Scuole del Sacramento," *Art History,* VI, 1983, pp. 30-43.

Von Holst 1974
Christian von Holst, *Francesco Granacci.* Munich, 1974.

Indianapolis 1963
David Carter and Wilbur Peat, *El Greco to Goya: A Loan Exhibition of Spanish Painting of the 17th and 18th Centuries.* Exh. cat., Herron Museum of Art, Indianapolis, and Museum of Art, Rhode Island School of Design, Providence. Indianapolis, 1963.

Johns 1988
Christopher M.S. Johns, "Papal Patronage and Cultural Bureaucracy in Eighteenth-Century Rome: Clement XI and the Accademia di San Luca," *Eighteenth-Century Studies,* 22, 1988, pp. 1-23.

Johns 1992
Christopher M.S. Johns, *Papal Art and Cultural Politics: Rome in the Age of Clement XI.* Cambridge, 1992.

Jordan 1985
Sandra Johnson Jordan, "The Iconography of the Sala Rossa Frescoes by Tiepolo," *Arte veneta,* XXXIX, 1985, pp. 170-73.

Kerber 1968
Bernhard Kerber, "Giuseppe Chiari," *Art Bulletin,* XL, 1968, pp. 75-86.

Kerrigan 1960
Anthony Kerrigan, "Sobre las razzias en el arte europeo," *Goya,* 36, 1960, pp. 352-67.

Knox 1970
George Knox, *Domenico Tiepolo: Raccolta di teste, 1770-1970.* Udine, 1970.

Knox 1975
George Knox, "'Philosopher Portraits' by Giambattista, Domenico, and Lorenzo Tiepolo," *Burlington Magazine,* CXVII, 1975, pp. 147-55.

Knox 1978
George Knox, "Tiepolo Paintings at Birmingham, Alabama," *Burlington Magazine,* CXX, 1978, p. 189.

Knox 1980
George Knox, *Giambattista and Domenico Tiepolo: A Study and Catalogue Raisonné of the Chalk Drawings.* Oxford, 1980.

Lawrence 1958
Masterworks from University and College Collections, University of Kansas Museum of Art, Lawrence, 1958, no publication.

Lexington 1967
Masterpieces from University Collections, University of Kentucky Art Gallery, Lexington, 1967, no publication.

Lightbown 1978
Ronald Lightbown, *Sandro Botticelli.* Berkeley, 1978.

Little Rock 1959
The Face of Christ in Art. Exh. cat., Museum of Fine Arts. Little Rock, Arkansas, 1959.

Liverpool 1963
Walker Art Gallery, *Foreign Catalogue: Paintings, Drawings, Watercolours...* . Liverpool, 1963.

Liverpool 1977
Walker Art Gallery, *Foreign Catalogue: Paintings, Drawings, Watercolours...* . Liverpool, 1977.

London 1798
The Orléans Collection, Pall Mall, London, 1798.

London 1851
Exhibition of Pictures by Italian, Spanish, Flemish, Dutch, French, and English Masters. Exh. cat., British Institution. London, 1851.

London 1938
17th-Century Art in Europe. Exh. cat., Royal Academy of Arts. London, 1938.

London 1979
Homan Potterton, *Venetian Seventeenth-Century Painting.* Exh. cat., National Gallery. London, 1979.

London 1982
Clovis Whitfield and Jane Martineau, eds., *Painting in Naples 1606-1705: From Caravaggio to Giordano.* Exh. cat., Royal Academy of Arts, London, and National Gallery of Art, Washington, D.C. London, 1982.

London 1987
The Settecento: Italian Rococo and Early Neo-Classical Paintings, 1700-1800. Exh. cat., Matthiesen Fine Art Ltd. London, 1987.

Longhi 1967
Roberto Longhi, *Saggi e ricerche, 1925-1928.* Florence, 1967.

Los Angeles 1949
Leonardo da Vinci: Loan Exhibition. Exh. cat., Los Angeles County Museum of Art. Los Angeles, 1949.

Los Angeles 1988
Guido Reni, 1575-1642. Exh. cat., Los Angeles County Museum of Art, and Kimbell Art Museum, Fort Worth. Los Angeles, 1988.

Macandrew 1980
Hugh Macandrew, *Ashmolean Museum Oxford: Catalogue of the Collection of Drawings, Volume III: Italian Schools: Supplement.* Oxford, 1980.

Malvasia trans. Enggass 1678
Carlo Cesare Malvasia, *Felsina pittrice, vite de'pittori bolognesi.* Bologna, 1678. *The Life of Guido Reni translated and with an introduction by Catherine and Robert Enggass.* University Park, Pennsylvania, 1980.

Manchester 1857
Art Treasures of the United Kingdom. Exh. cat., Manchester, 1857.

Marabottini 1990
Alessandro Marabottini, *Jacopo di Chimenti da Empoli.* Rome, 1990.

Marrow 1978
Deborah Marrow, "A *Massacre of the Innocents* and the Neapolitan Baroque," *Philadelphia Museum of Art Bulletin,* 4, 1978, pp. 3-11.

Memphis 1963-64
The Nativity, Brooks Memorial Art Gallery, Memphis, 1963-64, no publication.

Mirimonde 1974
Albert P. Mirimonde, *Sainte-Cécile: Métamorphoses d'un thème musical.* Geneva, 1974.

Montgomery 1988
The Grand Tour: The Tradition of Patronage in Southern Museums. Exh. cat., Montgomery Museum of Fine Arts. Montgomery, 1988.

Montreal 1965
Images of the Saints. Exh. cat., Montreal Museum of Fine Arts. Montreal, 1965.

Mortari 1966
Luisa Mortari, *Bernardo Strozzi.* Rome, 1966.

Mullaly 1974
Terence Mullaly, review of "Cinquant'anni di pittura veronese, 1580-1630," *Burlington Magazine,* CXVI, 1974, pp. 692-99.

Naples 1980
Nicola Spinosa, *Pittura sacra a Napoli nel '700.* Exh. cat., Palazzo Reale. Naples, 1980.

Naples 1984
Fausta Navacco, ed., *Civiltà del Seicento a Napoli.* Exh. cat., Museo di Capodimonte. Naples, 1984.

Naples 1992
Alfonso Pérez Sánchez et al., *Jusepe de Ribera, 1591-1652 .* Exh. cat., Castel Sant'Elmo. Naples, 1992.

New Haven 1987
A Taste For Angels: Neapolitan Painting in North America, 1650-1750. Exh. cat., Yale University Art Gallery, The John and Mable Ringling Museum of Art, Sarasota, and the Nelson-Atkins Museum of Art, Kansas City. New Haven, 1987.

New York 1955
An Exhibition of Paintings for the Benefit of the Research Fund of Art and Archaeology, The Spanish Institute. Exh. cat., E. and A. Silberman Galleries. New York, 1955.

New York 1965-66
The Christmas Story in Art, IBM Gallery, New York, 1965-66, no publication.

New York 1967
The Italian Heritage. Exh. cat., Wildenstein & Co., Inc. New York, 1967.

New York 1969
Joan Nissman and Howard Hibbard, *Florentine Baroque Art from American Collections.* Exh. cat., The Metropolitan Museum of Art. New York, 1969.

New York 1982
Edgar Peters Bowron, *Pompeo Batoni, 1708-1787.* Exh. cat., P. & D. Colnaghi. New York, 1982.

New York 1985
The Age of Caravaggio. Exh. cat., The Metropolitan Museum of Art. New York, 1985.

New York 1990
Important Old Master Paintings: Within the Image. Exh. cat., Piero Corsini Gallery. New York, 1990.

New York 1991
Frank Dabell, *Piero Corsini: Venetian Paintings: From Titian to El Greco.* Exh. cat., Piero Corsini Gallery. New York, 1991.

New York 1992a
Jane Martineau, ed., *Andrea Mantegna.* Exh. cat., Royal Academy of Arts, London, and The Metropolitan Museum of Art. New York, 1992.

New York 1992b
Alfonso Pérez Sánchez et al., *Ribera.* Exh. cat., The Metropolitan Museum of Art. New York, 1992.

Newcome 1976
Mary Newcome, "Two Drawings by Bartolomeo Guidobono," *University Art Gallery, State University of New York, Binghamton, Bulletin II,* 1976.

Newcome Schleier 1981
Mary Newcome Schleier, "Notes on Guidobono," *Antichità viva,* X, 1981, pp. 25-36.

Nicolson 1979
Benedict Nicolson, *The International Caravaggesque Movement.* Oxford, 1979.

Nicolson and Vertova 1989
Benedict Nicolson and Luisa Vertova, *Caravaggism in Europe.* Turin, 1989.

Notre Dame 1970
The Age Of Vasari. Exh. cat., Art Gallery, University of Notre Dame, and University Art Gallery, State University of New York at Binghamton. Notre Dame, Indiana 1970.

Oberlin 1939
Allen Memorial Art Museum, Oberlin College, Ohio, 1939, no publication.

Oberlin 1952
Italian Paintings of the Seventeenth Century, Allen Memorial Art Museum, Oberlin College, Ohio, 1952, no publication.

Ottawa 1976
George Knox, *Etchings by the Tiepolos: Domenico Tiepolo's Collection of the Family Etchings from an Album in the Cooper-Hewitt Museum of Design, Smithsonian Institution, New York.* Exh. cat., National Gallery of Canada. Ottawa, 1976

Pallucchini 1949
Rodolfo Pallucchini, "Dipinti del Pittoni ritrovati," *Arte veneta,* III, 1949, pp. 164-66.

Pallucchini and Rossi 1982
Rodolfo Pallucchini and Paola Rossi, *Tintoretto: Le opere sacre e profane.* 2 vols. Milan, 1982.

Pepper 1984a
D. Stephen Pepper, *Bob Jones University Collection of Religious Art: Italian Paintings.* Greenville, South Carolina, 1984.

Pepper 1984b
D. Stephen Pepper, *Guidi Reni: A Complete Catalog of his Works with an Introductory Text.* New York, 1984.

Pepper 1988
D. Stephen Pepper, *Guido Reni: L'opera completa.* Novara, 1988.

Pérez Sánchez and Spinosa 1978
Alfonso E. Pérez Sánchez and Nicola Spinosa. *L'opera completa del Ribera.* Milan, 1978.

Philadelphia 1926
Pennsylvania Museum, Philadelphia, 1926, no publication.

Piacenza 1975
Raffaella Arisi, *Il Brescianino delle battaglie.* Exh. cat., Museo Civico. Piacenza, 1975.

Polazzo 1990
Marco Polazzo, *Antonia Balestra, pittore veronese del Settecento.* Verona, 1990.

Pope-Hennessy 1948
John Pope-Hennessy, *The Drawings of Domenichino in the Collection of His Majesty the King at Windsor Castle.* London, 1948.

Providence 1938
Cornerstones for a College Art Collection, Museum of Art, Rhode Island School of Design, Providence, 1938, no publication.

Providence 1968
Stephen E. Ostrow, *Baroque Painting: Italy and her Influence.* Exh. cat., American Federation of the Arts: Museum of Art, Rhode Island School of Design. Providence, 1968.

Pugliese 1983
Vincenzo Pugliese, "Pacecco de Rosa e il Maestro di Bovino," *Napoli nobilissima,* XXII, 1983, pp. 111-38.

Raleigh 1984
David H. Steel, Jr., *Baroque Paintings from the Bob Jones University Collection.* Exh. cat., North Carolina Museum of Art, Raleigh, and P. & D. Colnaghi, New York. Raleigh, 1984.

Rearick 1987
W. R. Rearick, "The Drawings of Paris Bordon" in *Paris Bordon e il suo tempo: Atti del convegno internazionale di studi.* Treviso, 1987.

Rice 1985
Eugene F. Rice, Jr., *Saint Jerome in the Renaissance.* Baltimore, 1985.

Riedl 1963
Peter Riedl, "Zu einigen Toskanischen Bozzetti," *Pantheon,* 21, 1963, pp. 14-19.

Ringbom 1984
Sixten Ringbom, *Icon to Narrative: The Rise of the Dramatic Close-up in Fifteenth-Century Devotional Painting.* Second edition. Doornspijk, 1984.

Ripa ed. Buscardi 1618
Cesare Ripa, *Iconologia.* Padua, 1618. *Iconologia: Edizione practica.* Ed. Piero Buscardi. Turin, 1987.

Rizzi 1971
Aldo Rizzi, *The Etchings of the Tiepolos.* London, 1971.

Robertson 1954
Giles Robertson, *Vincenzo Catena.* Edinburgh, 1954.

Rome 1982
L'immagine di San Francesco nella Controriforma. Exh. cat., Istituto nazionale per la grafica. Rome, 1982.

Rosand 1981
David and Ellen Rosand, " 'Barbara di Santas Sofia' and 'Il Prete Genovese': On the Identity of a Portrait by Bernardo Strozzi," *Art Bulletin,* LXIII, 1981, pp. 249-58.

Rosenberg 1963
Pierre Rosenberg, "Genoese Paintings in American Museums," *Burlington Magazine,* CV, 1963, p. 209.

Rosenthal 1981
Gertrude Rosenthal, ed., *Italian Paintings XIV-XVIIIth Centuries: From the Collection of The Baltimore Museum of Art.* Baltimore, 1981.

Russell 1977
Francis Russell, "Sassoferrato and his Sources: A Study of Seicento Allegiance," *Burlington Magazine,* CXIX, 1977, pp. 694-700.

Russell 1980
Francis Russell,"Batoni at Basildon," *National Trust Studies,* 1980, pp. 35-42.

Salerno 1960a
Luigi Salerno, "The Picture Gallery of Vincenzo Giustiniani, I: Introduction," *Burlington Magazine,* CII, 1960, pp. 21-27.

Salerno 1960b
Luigi Salerno, "The Picture Gallery of Vincenzo Giustiniani, II: The Inventory, Part I," *Burlington Magazine,* CII, 1960, pp. 93-104.

Salerno 1965
Luigi Salerno, *Palazzo Rondinini.* Rome, 1965.

Salerno 1988
Luigi Salerno, *I dipinti del Guercino.* Rome, 1988.

San Francisco 1964-65
Man: Glory, Jest, and Riddle, M.H. de Young Museum, San Francisco, 1964-65, no publication.

Sarasota 1961
Baroque Painters of Naples, The John and Mable Ringling Museum of Art, Sarasota, 1961, no publication.

Sassoferrato 1990
Giovan Battista Salvi, Il Sassoferrato. Exh. cat., San Francesco. Sassoferrato, 1990.

Schaefer 1987
Scott Schaefer et al., *European Painting and Sculpture in the Los Angeles County Museum of Art: An Illustrated Summary Catalogue.* Los Angeles, 1987.

Schleier 1980a
Erich Schleier, "Due opere 'toscane' del Lanfranco," *Paragone,* XXX, 1980, pp. 22-38.

Schleier 1980b
Erich Schleier, "Una decorazione poco nota di Sebastiano Conca a Genova," *Antichità viva,* XIX, 1980, pp. 20-26.

Scrase 1991
David Scrase, "A Drawing by Francesco Menzocchi acquired by the Fitzwilliam Museum," *Burlington Magazine,* CXXXIII, 1991, pp. 773-76.

Sedini 1989
Domenico Sedini, *Marco d'Oggiono: Tradizione e rinnovamento in Lombardia tra Quattrocento e Cinquecento.* Milan, 1989.

Sgarbi 1984
Vittorio Sgarbi, "La Mostra di Paris Bordon a Treviso," *Arte veneta,* XXXVIII, 1984, pp. 253-55.

Sheffield 1966
Sheffield City Art Galleries, *Provisional Catalogue of Foreign School Paintings.* Sheffield, 1966.

Siena 1978
Pietro Torriti et al., *Rutilio Manetti, 1571-1639.* Exh. cat., Palazzo Pubblico. Siena, 1978.

Smith O'Neil 1985
Maryvelma Smith O'Neil, "Stefano Maderno's 'Saint Cecilia': A Seventeenth-Century Roman Sculpture Remeasured," *Antologia di belle arti* 25-26, 1985, pp. 9-21.

Soprani and Ratti 1768
Raffaello Soprani and Carlo Ratti, *Vite de'pittori, scultori, ed architetti genovesi.* 2 vols. Genoa, 1768. Reprint, Bologna, 1969-70.

Spear 1968
Richard E. Spear, "Preparatory Drawings by Domenichino," *Master Drawings,* VI, 1968, pp. 110-31.

Spear 1979
Richard E. Spear, "Further Preparatory Drawings by Domenichino," *Master Drawings,* XVII, 1979, pp. 245-60.

Spear 1982
Richard E. Spear, *Domenichino.* London, 1982.

Spear 1989a
Richard E. Spear, "Domenichino Addenda," *Burlington Magazine,* CXXXI, 1989, pp. 5-16.

Spear 1989b
Richard E. Spear, "Re-viewing the 'Divine' Guido," *Burlington Magazine,* CXXXI, 1989, pp. 367-372.

Spinosa 1986
Nicola Spinosa, *Pittura napoletana del Settecento dal Barocco al Rococò* Naples, 1986.

Steingräber 1979
Erich Steingräber, " 'Christus in Emmaus' von Matteo Rosselli: Eine Neuerwerbung fur die Bayerischen Staatsgemäldesammlungen," *Pantheon,* 37, 1979, pp. 383-90.

St. Petersburg 1965
Museum of Fine Arts, St. Petersburg, Florida, 1965, no publication.

Stone 1991
David M. Stone, *Il Guercino: Catalogo completo dei dipinti.* Florence, 1991.

Storrs 1973
The Academy of Europe: Rome in the 18th Century. Exh. cat., William Benton Museum of Art, University of Connecticut. Storrs, 1973.

Suida 1943
William E. Suida, "Addenda to Titian's Religious Oeuvre," *Gazette des Beaux-Arts,* VI, 1943, pp. 355-62.

Suida Manning 1972
Bertina Suida Manning and Robert L. Manning, "Notes on Genoese Paintings" in *Studi di storia dell'arte in onore di Antonio Morassi.* Venice, 1972.

Toronto 1989
Fifteenth-Century Italian Woodcuts from Biblioteca Classense in Ravenna. Exh. cat., Fisher Rare Book Library, Toronto, and The Pierpont Morgan Library, New York. Ravenna, 1989.

Treviso 1984
Paris Bordon. Exh. cat., Palazzo dei Trecento. Treviso, 1984.

Venturi 1924
Adolfo Venturi, *L'arte a San Girolamo.* Milan, 1924.

Verona 1974
Liscisco Magagnato, *Cinquant'anni di pittura veronese, 1580-1630.* Exh. cat., Palazzo della Gran Guardia. Verona, 1974.

Washington 1984
Diane De Grazia, *Correggio and his Legacy: Sixteenth-Century Emilian Drawings.* Exh. cat., National Gallery of Art. Washington, D.C., 1984.

Washington 1986
The Age of Correggio and the Carracci: Emilian Painting of the Sixteenth and Seventeenth Centuries. Exh. cat., National Gallery of Art and The Metropolitan Museum of Art, New York. Washington, D.C., 1986

Washington 1990
Arthur K. Wheelock, Jr. et al., *Anthony van Dyck.* Exh. cat., National Gallery of Art. Washington, D.C., 1990.

Wethey 1963
Harold E. Wethey, "Spanish Painting at Indianapolis and Providence," *Burlington Magazine,* CV, 1963, pp. 206-208.

Wethey 1969
Harold E. Wethey, *The Paintings of Titian: Volume I: The Religious Paintings.* London, 1969.

Winnipeg 1967
Winnipeg Art Gallery, Winnipeg, Canada, 1967, no publication.

Zava Boccazzi 1979
Franca Zava Boccazzi, *Pittoni.* Venice, 1979.

Zeri 1976
Federico Zeri, *Italian Paintings in the Walters Art Gallery.* Baltimore, 1976.

INDEX OF ARTISTS

Richard P. Townsend has been the Ruth G. Hardman Curator of European and American Art at the Philbrook Museum of Art, Tulsa, Oklahoma, since 1991. His many contributions to catalogues and publications include articles in *Master Drawings* and *Apollo.* Townsend received his undergraduate degree from Virginia Commonwealth University, Richmond, and a graduate degree from the Institute of Fine Arts, New York University.

Eric M. Zafran is presently the acting Mrs. Russell W. Baker Curator of European Paintings at the Museum of Fine Arts, Boston, having earlier served as curator at a number of distinguished institutions: the Walters Art Gallery, Baltimore, the High Museum of Art, Atlanta, and the Chrysler Museum, Norfolk, Virginia. He has organized several exhibitions devoted to French and Italian paintings and drawings of the 17th through the 19th centuries and has authored numerous catalogues and articles in such journals as *The Art Bulletin, The Journal of the Warburg and Courtauld Institutes,* and *Apollo.* Zafran received his BA from Brandeis University and his PhD from the Institute of Fine Arts, New York University.